THE EARLY MODERN OTTC

An innovative reinterpretation of the middle years of the Ottoman Empire, from the conquest of Constantinople in 1453 to the establishment of the Tanzimat in 1839. This period saw the evolution of the Empire from the height of its powers to – as the traditional view has it – an empire in decline, unable to modernize in the face of globalization and European ascendancy. The contributors challenge this view, demonstrating how the Ottomans came to be modern on their own terms. They explore the Ottomans as politicians and diplomats, military reformers, artists and historians. They also map out and redefine the material worlds which they inhabited – the courthouse, the cemetery, the Turkish garden. This book, which represents a turning-point in the intellectual history of the Ottoman Empire, promises to become a key text for students, scholars and anyone interested in the Ottoman world.

VIRGINIA H. AKSAN is Associate Professor of History at McMaster University, Ontario. Her publications include *An Ottoman Statesman in War and Peace: Ahmed Resmi Efendi, 1700–1783* (1995) and *Ottoman Wars 1700–1870: An Empire Besieged* (2007).

DANIEL GOFFMAN is Professor of History at DePaul University and author of *Britain in the Ottoman Empire* (1998), *Izmir and the Levantine World* (1990), *The Ottoman Empire and Early Modern Europe* (2002) and *The Ottoman City Between East and West: Aleppo, Izmir, and Istanbul* (1999).

THE EARLY MODERN OTTOMANS

OTTOMANS

Remapping the Empire

EDITED BY

VIRGINIA H. AKSAN

AND

DANIEL GOFFMAN

CAMBRIDGE
UNIVERSITY PRESS

CAMBRIDGE UNIVERSITY PRESS
Cambridge, New York, Melbourne, Madrid, Cape Town, Singapore, São Paulo, Delhi

Cambridge University Press
The Edinburgh Building, Cambridge CB2 8RU, UK

Published in the United States of America by Cambridge University Press, New York

www.cambridge.org
Information on this title: www.cambridge.org/9780521520850

First published 2007
Reprinted 2009

Printed in the United Kingdom at the University Press, Cambridge

A catalogue record for this publication is available from the British Library

ISBN 978-0-521-81764-6 hardback
ISBN 978-0-521-52085-0 paperback

Contents

Illustrations

MAP

PLATES

vii

Notes on contributors

GÁBOR ÁGOSTON is Associate Professor at the History Department of Georgetown University. He is the author of *Guns for the Sultan: Military Power and the Weapons Industry in the Ottoman Empire*, and more than fifty scholarly articles and book chapters on Ottoman, European, and Hungarian history.

VIRGINIA H. AKSAN is Associate Professor in the Department of History at McMaster University, Hamilton, Ontario, Canada. She is the author of *An Ottoman Statesman in War and Peace: Ahmed Resmi Efendi 1700–1783*, and *Ottoman Wars 1700–1870: An Empire Besieged*.

PALMIRA BRUMMETT is Professor of History and Distinguished Professor in the Humanities at the University of Tennessee. She is the author of *Ottoman Seapower and Levantine Diplomacy in the Age of Discovery* and *Image and Imperialism in the Ottoman Revolutionary Press, 1908–1911*. Her current projects are focused on early modern mapping of Ottoman space and on the rhetorics and imagery of travel literature.

EDHEM ELDEM is Professor of History at Boğaziçi University, Istanbul. His publications include *French Trade in Istanbul in the Eighteenth Century; A History of the Ottoman Bank, The Ottoman City Between East and West: Aleppo, Izmir and Istanbul* (with Daniel Goffman and Bruce Masters); and *Death in Istanbul: Death and its Rituals in Ottoman-Islamic Culture*.

DAN GOFFMAN is Professor of History at DePaul University and author of *Britons in the Ottoman Empire; Izmir and the Levantine World, The Ottoman Empire and Early Modern Europe*, and with Edhem Eldem and Bruce Masters, *The Ottoman City Between East and West*.

MOLLY GREENE is Professor at Princeton University, with a joint appointment in the Department of History and the Program in

Hellenic Studies. She is the author of *A Shared World: Christians and Muslims in the Early Modern Mediterranean*, and is currently working on a project on the relationship between Greek commerce and Catholic piracy in the seventeenth century.

SHIRINE HAMADEH is Assistant Professor at the Department of Art History at Rice University. Her upcoming book is titled *The City's Pleasures: Istanbul in the Eighteenth Century*.

DOUGLAS A. HOWARD is Professor and Chair of the History Department at Calvin College. He is the author of *The History of Turkey*, and is currently working on a translation and study of Ayn Ali's *Kavanin-i Al-i Osman*.

DINA KHOURY is Associate Professor of History and International Affairs at George Washington University. She is the author of *State and Provincial Society in the Ottoman Empire: Mosul 1540–1834*, and articles on state–provincial relations, urban rebellions, and the intellectual history of Ottoman Iraq; more recently she has begun a project on war and memory in modern Iraq.

LESLIE PEIRCE is Silver Professor of History and Middle East Studies at New York University. She is the author of *The Imperial Harem: Women and Sovereignty in the Ottoman Empire* and *Morality Tales: Law and Gender in the Ottoman Court of Aintab*. She is currently working on a cultural history of the premodern Ottoman Empire.

NAJWA AL-QATTAN is Associate Professor of Middle Eastern History at Loyola Marymount University in Los Angeles. She is currently editing a book entitled *The Ottoman Empire and the Great War: History and Memory* and working on a book project, *Archiving Justice at the Ottoman Muslim Court*.

BAKI TEZCAN is Assistant Professor of History and Religious Studies at the University of California, Davis. He is co-editor of *Identity and Identity Formation in the Ottoman World: A Volume of Essays in Honor of Norman Itzkowitz*, and is completing his book, *The Second Empire: The Transformation of the Ottoman Polity in the Early Modern period*.

Acknowledgments

In January 2006, Dan Goffman, my colleague, friend, and co-editor on this project, suffered a major stroke. Just prior to that, he had emailed me the full draft of all the contributions included here, along with the Introduction, which he had just finished crafting. It has been my pleasure to see them through into print, as a tribute to the vision which Dan had for a volume which would explore lesser-known aspects of the Ottoman universe in the premodern world. Dan's expertise has always been the Ottomans and Europe in the fifteenth and sixteenth centuries. Mine begins in the grey zone after 1700 and before 1850. It was this crossover which allowed us to conceive of a volume which would explore the "early modern" in the Ottoman context.

My first instinct upon assuming sole editorial responsibility for this project was to send the full text to the other ten contributors of the volume, so that they could see the ways in which we had clustered the topics. In return, I received a number of revised and far more polished versions of the pieces: a response, I suggest, to the news of a colleague's illness, but also a measure of engagement with the aims of the project and its participants. Highly idiosyncratic, these essays represent the work of both "junior" and "senior" Middle East and Ottoman historians pushing their well-known work in new directions. I have deliberately tried not to impose too much of a straitjacket on the individual texts, with some editorial exceptions such as a uniform bibliography and footnote style, and a limited set of standard transliterations. As with any such collection, it will be picked over by instructors for classroom texts and graduate examination bibliographies, but can just as well stand alone as a reader reflecting the terrain of Ottoman studies in its era. I owe a debt of thanks to Carolyn Goffman, Marigold Acland, our anonymous reader, and all the contributors. I know they join me in wishing Dan well.

A note on transliteration and the use of foreign words

Words like waqf (in lieu of the Turkish vakıf), shari'a, hadith, Quran, ulema and kadi (instead of qadi) are assumed here to have become part of regular English parlance. For languages such as Arabic and Persian, we have tried to keep the use of foreign words to a minimum, but modern Turkish spelling has been preferred when used, with the first occurrence of a word in each essay followed by its English equivalent or vice versa. For the rest, we have followed the transliteration scheme of the *International Journal of Middle East Studies*.

Introduction: Situating the early modern Ottoman world

Virginia H. Aksan and Daniel Goffman

Historical periodization is always problematic. In part, the difficulty exists because deciding when and why eras begin and end always privileges a particular period or civilization over others. A historian of Renaissance Italy, for example, may refer to the Dark Age that preceded this "rebirth" in order to emphasize the period's marvels of artistic and intellectual rediscovery and innovation. A historian of medieval Italy might object, however, because the periodization appears to belittle the world that he or she knows to be rich and fascinating. In other words, such a demarcation frequently demeans what came before. Periodization can also denigrate contemporaneous civilizations. A historian of the age of European expansion or imperialism, for example, may offer a picture of colonial America, Asia, or Africa that elides those continents' own histories and internal rhythms. Implicit in any such terms of periodization, in other words, are often suspect assessments about what preceded, what followed, and what characterized a particular time and place.

Furthermore, at least in the case of European expansion, historians have imposed the periodization of one place onto others. Such transfers are usually appropriated from Europe, and constitute a component of what is often referred to as a "Eurocentric" view of the world. The idea of the medieval, for example, originated in European historiography. It has, however, been routinely applied elsewhere. To envision a medieval Japan or a medieval Middle East is to begin our examination of those largely self-contained societies by looking for elements of European civilization within them, rather than examining them in their own terms and granting them their own periodizations and histories. Transplanting a word like "feudal" from Europe to the Middle Eastern or Japanese milieus is even more problematic, because the term describes not only a period but also a social and political structure that formed in a particular place and time. Whether such designations help us understand the distinctive worlds of Japan and

I

the Middle East, or merely subsume the rich histories of these largely autonomous peoples under the more recently ascendant civilization of western Europe, remains an open question.

Similar issues of periodization vex Ottoman historiography. In this regard, the title of this book, *The Early Modern Ottomans: Remapping the Empire*, is representative. The period we are examining begins in about 1453, with the Ottoman conquest of the Byzantine Empire – when the Ottoman state began consciously to envision itself as a world-conquering empire – and ends in about 1839, with the establishment of the Tanzimat – when the Ottomans began consciously and deliberately to emulate the West. Historians typically refer to this era as the "early modern" or "premodern," designations that not only derive from western European historiography, but also are teleological in the sense that they privilege a concept and an era that we call the modern. In other words, this terminology may suggest that the principal reason to study the period between 1453 and 1839 is to examine the roots and development of the modern, western-inspired world. These are valid and fascinating reasons to study the Ottomans, but the scholar using such terminology runs the risk of condemning the period's intrinsic substance to a secondary position.

The idea of the modern is itself a western one. While it is a complicated concept, it is generally associated with the rise of the nation-state (as opposed to other ways to organize societies such as empires and city-states) and with the rise of individualism (as opposed to communal or other forms of identity). Both the nation-state and individualism, in turn, are associated with the West, as is the related concept of imperialism, and studies of the early modern or premodern Ottoman world often try to answer such questions as when and how "nations" (the Greek, the Armenian, the Bulgarian, the Turk, the Arab) emerged out of the Ottoman polity, whether and when an Ottoman sense of the individual materialized, and, most commonly, how much the Ottoman Empire was like other European states and societies, and the ways in which it differed from (read: was inferior to) them.

In various ways, the essays in *The Early Modern Ottomans* contribute to such discussions, as some of its contributors search for indications of a movement toward the "modern" in various aspects of the Ottoman Empire and others look for similarities (and differences) between it and the states and societies with which it shared Europe and the Mediterranean Sea. We include here explorations of traces of the individual in the cemeteries of Ottoman cities, in the possessions and economic activities of women in small Anatolian cities, and in the gardens of the Ottoman capital. We have evidence of Ottoman linkages with the European and Mediterranean worlds in the construction of physical and mental boundaries, the creation of new diplomacies, and the legitimization of rule; and we have indications of the creation of a new group consciousness in Ottoman society in the descriptions of Ottoman writers. The interest communities began to take in preserving a local sense of the past, the broad appeal to political ideology through the popularization of scholarly discourse, and the construction of a new conscripted army are also part of the Ottoman movement toward the "modern."

As Edhem Eldem demonstrates, the deceased themselves can reveal an aspect of the Ottoman drift from the premodern toward this more modern vision of society. During the period 1700–1850, for example, one can see in inscriptions preserved on Ottoman gravestones in Istanbul and other urban centers conscious attempts on the part of individuals to claim distinctive personalities. One of the most dramatic of such indications was the association of the deceased with a prominent family member (whether that person be an uncle or a more distant relative) rather than with a relatively obscure father. Such inscriptions were a conscious effort to preserve the memory and individuality of the deceased through association with a visible and historically relevant individual rather than through a more humble parent.

In the early modern Ottoman Empire, as Leslie Peirce and Shirine Hamadeh show, the living as well as the dead, the female as well as the male, began to assert their individuality. In the private sphere, of course, women had long displayed their wealth and personalities. They even found ways to make themselves known (if not to display themselves openly) in the public arena, through servants and endowments (waqfs) and other forms of charity, by gathering in courtyards, through gossip, and by other means. In fact, the very ability of a woman to screen herself from the outside world connoted wealth and prestige. Thus, the less visible a woman was, the more wealth and power she was likely to possess.

Before the eighteenth century, however, Ottoman Muslim women worked to maintain their privacy whether they were wealthy or poor, urban or rural. In that century, not only did the private/public division begin to break down, at least in Istanbul and other major Ottoman cities, but also both men and women started to search for ways to distinguish themselves through their attire and their public personas. They found one outlet for this newfound individuality in the public gardens that characterized eighteenth-century urban life. Whereas in the seventeenth century the coffeehouse had defined sociable public space, in the eighteenth century imperial gardens and other spaces, newly opened to the public, joined, and to an extent replaced such establishments. In the new enthusiasm for safe leisure activities, the urban middle classes, especially women, began to frequent public gardens and fountains, to display themselves in finery there, and thereby to become increasingly visible in the public sphere.

As the definition of the public sphere shifted in Istanbul and other urban centers, so the Ottoman concept of community underwent strain, especially in provinces distant from the capital city. For example, Dina Khoury discusses how the period from the 1770s to the 1820s saw the emergence of a politico-theology in Arabia – Wahhabism – that not only challenged the theological underpinnings of Ottoman society, but also came to mount a considerable political threat. Wahhabism's association with a powerful family, the Sauds, provided this ideology with a political and very public dimension, and protagonists of this faith simultaneously argued for the exclusion of many Sunni Muslims from the Islamic community even as they sought to export their ideology to other Ottoman Arab lands. Aksan, Hamadeh and Eldem explore that same era as an incubator for tranformation in a changing global context.

Such episodes presaged the passage from early modern to modern. First of all, the rhetoric of exclusion in this and other doctrines represented a modernist challenge to the Ottoman polity as well as to other traditional Islamic states and societies, whose political and social systems not only assumed the inclusion of all Sunni Muslims, but also of non-Muslim "People of the Book." Those who belong to nation-states do not often define themselves as did the Wahhabis; nevertheless, a similar process of exclusion certainly plays a vital role in selecting who are allowed to become citizens and who are barred. In other words, the Wahhabis and others opened the door to expanded categories of exclusionary identities in the Islamic world. Furthermore, the Wahhabis' rhetorical appeal to the "masses" not only demanded a popularization and simplification of their message, but it also forced Ottoman theologians to respond in kind. The consequence was a popularization of theology that would help engender a multitude of political ideologies, both religious and secular.

Both transformations in Ottoman gardens and the Wahhabi revolt occurred during the period of global imperialism, a time when the economic, political, and cultural reach of the British, the French, and other European states was beginning to stretch across the globe. The articles in this volume make clear that, during this time, the Ottomans understood and participated in such innovations, as well as the military and political strategies and engagements that made them possible. For example, Virginia Aksan shows how the very meaning of rebellion changed in the early modern Ottoman world, from one that typically was little more than a confrontation between competing foci of authority, such as viziers and sultan, or janissaries and ulema, to one that, by the end of the eighteenth century, more resembled civil war. Such transforming tension forced a more modern "public" – such as that seen in gardens and in theological disputes – into the political sphere, most dramatically seen in the sharing-of-power agreement that provincial notables forced upon the sultan in 1808 and in largely futile attempts to construct a modern, conscription-based military.

Gardens, fountains, coffeehouses, and other public spaces were common in major cities throughout eighteenth-century Europe, as were their habitués; the popularization of religion and politics also occurred in other parts of the European subcontinent; and governments in Britain, France, Prussia, and elsewhere were also collaborating with various elites and building conscription armies. Although all these trends are components of modernity and find their complements elsewhere in Europe, they represent only three of the many ways in which the early modern Ottoman polity resembled other European states and societies. The Ottoman Empire certainly differed from other European states – most dramatically in its roots in central Asia, in its Altaic and Uralic language, and in its Islamic heritage. Nevertheless, as this volume confirms, the early modern Ottoman world and the rest of Europe also shared much – such as the Mediterranean Sea, a seaborne and land-based commercial network, peoples who moved back and forth across the continent, and similar visions of their roles in the world.

As Palmira Brummett convincingly argues, early modern mapmakers, both western European and Ottoman, manifestly expose characteristics of this shared world. Their maps also chart a world that diverges markedly from our own. On these maps, boundaries are often distorted, space is reorganized, and historical times and civilizations are conflated or severed in ways that to us seem illogical or fantastic. It would be a mistake to dismiss the makers of such maps as careless or uninformed, however. Rather, the maps that they produced often precisely indicate state policy, provide manifest justifications for governments and societies, and impart insight into the precise *mentalité* of the period. For example, the conflation of the worlds of ancient Greece and Rome or biblical Palestine and the contemporary world on the same map might provide a justification for state policy or an attempt to legitimize the existence of a particular state, Ottoman as well as Venetian or French. Meanwhile, the mutability of borders common to maps produced throughout the Eurasian world did not always indicate uncertainty, but were in fact a type of polemic, either against another polity or as a manifestation of the desire or intention to expand. Such patterns (and the accounts of travelers exhibit similar patterns) may today seem an alien way of thinking, but they manifested a shared zeitgeist for the entire early modern Christian and Islamic Eurasian world.

In short, maps often served to legitimize the Ottoman and other European states, justify their policies, or suggest ways for them to expand or claim territory. Such guiding principles, as well as the manner in which strategy was formed and acted upon, displayed another kind of similarity between these states. Gábor Ágoston and Molly Greene convincingly demonstrate how, on both the land and the sea, in the sixteenth century the Ottomans joined the Habsburgs in developing a "Grand Strategy." Under the sultan Süleyman (r. 1520–66) and the emperor Charles V (1530–56), the implementation of such a strategy made the two Mediterranean empires appear to mirror each other and served to draw the Ottomans into the world of European politics and ideology. This perspective shows how pragmatic the Ottomans were, makes us see that the empire behaved in ways similar to other states, and leads us to look for rational decision-making in the Ottoman world.

It is a common misconception that the Ottomans were fanatical, both in their religious beliefs and in the sense that they based decisions upon ideology rather than expediency. Ágoston suggests that, in fact, this empire gathered intelligence just as effectively and judiciously as did other European states as it sought to make prudent and rational choices. Domestically, it did so through the use of janissaries, *çavuşes* (messengers, heralds), the archiving of materials, and the survey of lands; internationally, it relied upon client states (such as Dubrovnik and even Venice and France), frontier beys and other administrators, ambassadors in Istanbul and consuls in other Ottoman cities, and espionage networks. Other European states likewise had such mechanisms to collect information. In addition, however, the distinctive structure of Ottoman society gave the state an advantage over its western European rivals. Unlike those more homogeneous societies, which kept the religiously dissimilar either at the fringes of society or completely outside of it, the Ottomans could advantageously utilize the commercial and cultural diasporas of the various communities that were integral to their domains for political and economic purposes. The large communities of Armenians, Greeks, Jews, and others resident in the empire enjoyed strong connections with family members and compatriots living in various European cities. The Ottomans relied upon these communities not only for the import and export of commodities; they also benefited from their military, political, and technological intelligence.

Diplomatic envoys constitute the front line of any government's communications with another state. Consequently, diplomacy both generates intelligence and is particularly dependent upon the accurate intelligence of others. The early modern Ottomans were no exception. As Daniel

Goffman argues, contrary to popular perceptions, not only were they fully engaged in early modern European diplomacy, they participated in the invention of those systems. Borders and frontiers in the Ottoman eastern Mediterranean were porous, shadowy, and uncertain. As Molly Greene demonstrates, when a merchant (or a naval or piratical) vessel sailed across those seas and even anchored in the many ports that dotted their shoreline, its captain could never be certain about which state would claim what right over him, his passengers, and his cargo. In addition, the rapid Ottoman expansion into southeastern Europe and the eastern Mediterranean in the fifteenth and sixteenth centuries made relationships between states and peoples even more ambiguous (an ambiguity that maps and travelers' accounts fully reflect). It was in this environment that the Ottomans and other European states developed new rights and obligations in their dealings with each other, such as the establishment of permanent ambassadorships and consulships, extraterritoriality, and the so-called capitulatory regime. In other words, Ottoman civilization was not the static and enervated entity often portrayed in western narratives, sluggishly reacting to vigorous European states and societies. The Ottomans not only participated in the early modern European world; they also helped to construct it. The early modern Ottoman Empire was so aggressive and innovative, in fact, that it was often other European states that seemed listless and fixed.

Such explorations into the roots of modernity in the early modern Ottoman world and attempts to compare the Ottoman state and society with other contemporaneous ones certainly are instructive and fruitful. Nevertheless, the historian's job is not only to use the past to explain the present; it is also to comprehend a particular time and place on its own terms. In other words, it is not enough simply to reach back into the Ottoman past in order to draw out antecedents and precedents to the modern, the imperial, the nation, or the individual. Indeed, doing so distorts the time and place being studied by overemphasizing certain aspects of that world and dismissing others. English–Ottoman relations constitute a notable example of the consequence of such skewed examinations. The English sense of superiority, baldly displayed in the imperialism of the second British Empire, often is ahistorically imposed upon early modern Anglo-Ottoman relations. In fact, the English were very much the supplicants. Vanished elements of Ottoman civilization may seem insignificant to us today, the mere debris of history. Without them, however, the period and place lose their sense of historical distinctiveness.

The authors of the chapters in this volume are sensitive to such issues, and address them in a variety of ways. First, each possesses a profound familiarity with the sources (principally Ottoman) upon which they base their narratives and arguments. Such an anchor is essential to make sense of that history. Nevertheless, it is too often lacking in historical (and literary) scholarship. The fact that Italians, Englishmen, Frenchmen, and other Europeans visited, studied, and wrote about the Ottoman Empire has both enriched the field and handicapped it. Such sources are enlightening because historians and literary scholars have mined them for rich insight into European perspectives on the East. They are restrictive, however, because these same investigators have often written their accounts exclusively from such sources, which has led to exterior historiography and criticism, that is, work that examines the Ottoman world only through the eyes of often rather ignorant and even hostile foreigners. Consequently, stereotypes, uncalled-for censure, and a distorted understanding of Ottoman civilization have too often slipped into such scholarship. The authors in this volume sometimes use these same western-based sources; but in every case they weigh them against others generated by the Ottomans themselves. In other words, they are fully engaged with the early modern Ottoman world, and are able to view the empire from within as well as without.

Second, these authors understand that the early modern Ottoman state and society possessed their own independent narrative, which consisted of much more than a search for modernity, a comparison with other European countries, or a competition with the "West." These essays demonstrate how fully early modern Ottoman civilization in its own way marked its borders, both on the land and on the sea. It used particular rhetorical constructs and chose certain words to describe its relations with its many peoples and the world around it, including its negotiations with other states and civilizations. Reforms in Ottoman political, military, and monetary structures were not mere responses to outside threats; they had their own internal logic and rhythms. The ways in which Ottomans imagined themselves and organized their society – most clearly reflected in their writings – were distinctive and developed in fascinating ways. The Ottoman legal system, for instance, while certainly based in Islamic law, took on its own characteristics and distinguished itself from the systems of other Islamic states.

Both Palmira Brummett's and Gábor Ágoston's texts quickly reveal how wrong it is to associate the Ottoman Empire exclusively with either western or Islamic methods of marking borders. The Ottomans portrayed themselves and designated their borders in a number of different ways, some of which were their own inventions. The sultan's long title, as a case in point, was intended not only to intimidate; it also helped define Ottoman margins as well as those areas in which the state desired to be unbounded. Similarly,

Ottoman attitudes toward the sea (and especially the Mediterranean) were neither fixed nor unrestrained; rather, they were variegated, and dependent upon routes, methods of naval warfare, and ideology.

Several of these essays provide an important service in their careful examination of various fundamental Ottoman terms and expressions. Investigating the too often ignored cultural specificity of language helps to problematize the meanings of "subject" and "foreigner" in the Ottoman world. These investigations also suggest that incautious translations into English can lead to analyses that fundamentally distort Ottoman institutions and transformations. Dragomans (those who were responsible for translating and easing communication between Ottoman and foreign statesmen and merchants) seem to have realized far more thoroughly than many present-day scholars that contemporaneous French or English understandings of Ottoman terms are misleading; any attempt to extract the Ottoman language from its culture must be undertaken with great care in order to avoid considerable confusion and misinterpretation.

Our uneven grasp of the Ottoman language is a critical component of our incomplete awareness of the internal dynamics of Ottoman civilization. Sometimes misapprehensions appear in our readings of Ottoman texts, such as the "advice to kings" (*nasihatname*) literature. Historians have interpreted these influential writings, largely produced in late sixteenth- and seventeenth-century Istanbul, as direct appeals to the sultan, as comments on the rise and fall of civilizations, and as accurate observations of Ottoman decline. They have usually accepted them pretty much at face value, with little attempt to deconstruct them or situate them in the civilization and the milieu that produced them. Douglas Howard's close examination of these sources, however, reveals that their audiences and their agendas were diverse and that they constituted a literary genre that was anything but transparent. Their authors presented a complicated and deliberately deceptive literary style; the genre developed as direct contact with the sultan became difficult and the written word became more important in communications with him; and its audience more and more became not the sultan but the state bureaucracy that represented him. Writers in the genre assumed a "prophetic" voice as they sought sovereign authenticity and a definition of what the Ottoman state was and should become.

The *nasihatnames*, then, did not exist in a vacuum: Ottoman politics and society shaped their form, substance, and audience. Such is the case with other Ottoman writings as well. For example, beginning in the mid sixteenth century the early modern Ottoman government solicited, sponsored, and endorsed official histories of the Ottoman state and dynasty, and historians have often accepted such writings as authoritative accounts of Ottoman history. Baki Tezcan's essay demonstrates that, in fact, such histories projected a particular agenda that not all Ottomans (and at times not even the sultan) embraced. In fact, it seems that in the late sixteenth and seventeenth centuries most members of the Ottoman elite ignored the sultan's official histories, specifically because many Ottoman elites did not share the dynast's particular view of Ottoman history. It was not until the late seventeenth century, when other prominent families began to wrest control of Ottoman policy away from the imperial family, that the official historiography not only became widely disseminated, but also began to attain exclusive control over the Ottomans' imaginings of their own past. The articles in this book help us avoid misreadings of these and other Ottoman writings, and consequent misconstructions of the Ottoman state and society.

Both the *nasihatname*s and Ottoman histories constituted *conscious* presentations of Ottoman life, institutions, and history. This empire, though, generated a body of writings that had other purposes, such as cadastral surveys meant to count people, land, and wealth; religious polemics meant to convince the reader of one or another set of beliefs; imperial rescripts meant to act on the government's policy; and Islamic court records meant to reflect the judgments of municipal judges (kadis). Historians have made use of such records, to be sure. Nevertheless, we have spent no more time exploring what they meant to the Ottomans than we have spent investigating why Ottomans wrote *nasihatname*s and why they commissioned histories of the dynasty.

The records of Ottoman legal courts constitute one of our most important sources on that world. Such courts had long been an important feature of Islamic states. Nevertheless, as Najwa Al-Qattan insists, it is a mistake to imagine that the Ottomans blindly accepted the legal system of their predecessors. In at least three fundamental ways, they adapted it to the specific needs of their empire. First, they turned kadis into servants of the state, which simultaneously removed them from many local influences and helped regularize Islamic law within the realm. Second, they "territorialized" shari'a law: that is, the state narrowed it in the sense that the law now focused exclusively on Ottoman territories even as the state expanded it to include non-Muslims as well as Muslims. This innovation created a legal (and, in the sense that individuals could there openly communicate across gendered and religious lines, even a public) space in which religious affiliation became less relevant. Third, such courts began preserving the judgments of kadis, which both enhanced the authority of that official and provided a historical memory within a particular court; in other words, a kadi now could refer to his predecessors in a particular place in constructing his own decisions.

Understanding the language, social structure, political institutions, and imagination of a civilization helps us make sense of that entity. Indeed, without such engagement, we are likely to misinterpret that world. We might bestow upon it unwarranted praise. More likely for those of us positioned on the temporal and geographical outside, we will perceive ignorance, immorality, corruption, or other malfeasances in the actions of individuals within it, whose behavior might in fact be forthright or admirable. Such misunderstandings can not only affect our appreciation of such a civilization, it can also undermine our grasp of its relationships with other worlds. The widespread belief that the Ottoman state was ignorant of Europe, for example, is more a consequence of our own ignorance of the Ottomans than of an Ottoman unawareness of Europe.

The Ottoman Empire has meant many things to many people. For some, it signifies the East, especially in stark opposition to the West. For others, it evokes wars between monotheistic faiths. It can symbolize a religious refuge – for Jews, Protestants, Catholics, Sunni Muslims – as well as a place of intense intolerance against Christians, Armenians, Greeks, or Shiite Muslims. It has evoked fear for some in those areas of Europe and the Middle East into which it expanded, and has been perceived as a liberator for others. For some today it represents a utopian society which we should strive to reconstruct; for others, it was a brutal regime that repressed "natural" nation-states across the region.

We should view this astonishing diversity of opinions about the Ottomans not as a confusing obstacle, but as a way of accessing the rare richness of the world being observed. The multiple views also emphasize how historically relevant this empire was (and remains) to so many people. In other words, however diverse and doubtful their recollections may be, most people living in the Middle East and Europe today believe that the Ottomans left a legacy that shapes them still. Furthermore, although each of the above opinions may possess an element of truth about the Ottoman Empire, they are all incomplete, distorted in some way, and based on a very particular reading of Ottoman history. Or they may reflect no reading at all, but rather constitute nothing more than a fantastic hagiography that one group or other wishes to impose upon that state. This volume helps us find our way through the morass of dubious constructs. While its authors examine different aspects of the Ottoman world, they share a deep commitment to understanding that empire on its own terms.

The authors in this volume are certainly aware of the value in seeking in the Ottoman past traces of such modern phenomena as individuality, imperialism, and the nation-state. Indeed, they find in the Ottoman world between 1453 and 1839 many of the very same manifestations of the early modern and modern world found elsewhere. Several of the pieces do suggest a number of ways to problematize and complicate our understanding of the Ottoman Empire. First, they present a lively and aggressive sixteenth- through seventeenth-century Ottoman world, one that saw the development of new legal and diplomatic institutions, new grand political strategies, and new writing genres. Such innovations distinguish what we may call the early modern. Second, the articles make clear that something dramatic happened, especially in the public sphere, in the eighteenth and early nineteenth centuries. Aksan, Eldem, Hamadeh and Khoury argue, for example, for a significant moment of cross-cultural influence in the period 1750–1850. In the popularization of politics, in the creation of public gardens, in transformed and more complicated tombstone inscriptions, in the rise of new understandings of historical time, and in new types of military discipline, novel social clusters were participating in Ottoman society in distinctive ways, and contributing to the transformation of the empire in a changing global context.

PART I

Mapping the Ottoman world

Imagining the early modern Ottoman space, from world history to Piri Reis

Palmira Brummett

Where did the Ottoman Empire begin and end?[1] Where in North Africa does one draw the line between "Turks" and "Moors"? What does one call the geographic zone in which the Ottomans ruled? We encounter these questions each time we are asked to map the empire or to characterize it for a student audience. But boundaries are a function of exigency and ambition. In early modern empires boundaries were measured in terms of the territories from which taxes and armies could be levied. They expressed the visions, imperatives, and anxieties of sovereigns, diplomats, traders, ship captains, and imperial mapmakers, among others.[2] They were drawn to project imperial ideologies as well as to reflect territories actually possessed. And boundaries were as often not drawn, their very ambiguity advancing the interests of empire and the processes of cross-cultural encounter. This essay undertakes three tasks. First, it addresses some of the paradoxes produced in the course of the attempt to impose modern constructs of bounded geographic and political space on the rhetorics and "realities" of the early modern Afro-Eurasian world. Then it examines constructions of Ottoman space in early modern sources (for example, maps, travelers' accounts, and diplomatic reports) to suggest the ways in which Europeans imagined and calculated the limits of Ottoman military, economic, and religious space. Finally, it compares those visual and rhetorical mappings of Ottoman space and power to Ottoman self-representations.

---

[1] The idea for this paper began with a Middle East Studies Association panel in 1994 entitled "Agendas for Early Modern Middle Eastern History." My paper, "Understanding Space: Regions and Empires," contained a set of proposals for reconfiguring the Ottomans in the historiographic imagination.

[2] The applicability of the term "early modern," to non-western space is, of course, contested. I would argue, however, that the designation is not only familiar and identifiable (as long as we specify our timeframe) but that it has framed a tradition of scholarship to which we are attached. We may wish to violate that tradition but we can also reenvision and reinterpret the period to see if its logics transcend particular civilizations.

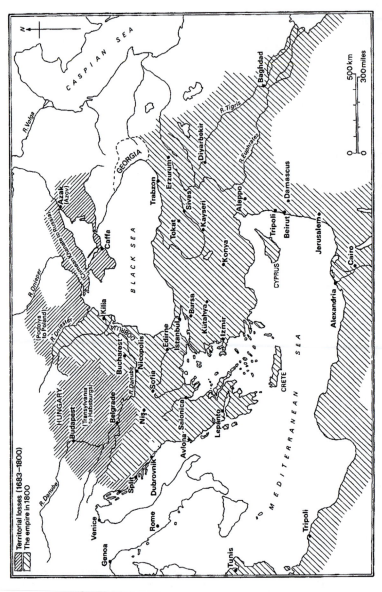

Map 1 The Ottoman Empire, *c.* 1683–1800. Adapted from Halil İnalcık with Donald Quataert (eds.), *An Economic and Social History of the Ottoman Empire, 1300–1914* (Cambridge: Cambridge University Press, 1994). p. xxxvii.

Territorial losses (1683–1800)

The empire in 1800

CASPIAN SEA

R. Volga

R. Dnieper

R. Dniester

Podolya
(to Poland)

Kilia

Azak
(Azov)

Caffa

BLACK SEA

GEORGIA

Trabzon

Erzurum

Diyarbekir

R. Tigris

Baghdad

R. Euphrates

Sivas

Tokat

Kayseri

Aleppo

Tripoli

Beirut

Damascus

Jerusalem

Cairo

CYPRUS

Konya

Bursa

Kütahya

İzmir

Edirne

Istanbul

Nicopolis

Bucharest

R. Danube

Sofia

Niš

Belgrade

HUNGARY

Transylvania
(to Habsburgs)

Budapest

R. Danube

Split

Dubrovnik

Avlona

Salonica

Lepanto

CRETE

MEDITERRANEAN SEA

Alexandria

Tripoli

Tunis

Venice

Rome

Genoa

500 km

300 miles

I propose that, rather than tracing a clear evolution from the unbounded, Ptolemaic maps of the early sixteenth century to the scientific, nation-state-preoccupied maps of the eighteenth century, early modern European mappings of Ottoman space tended to interweave layers of historical time and memory. At times, Ottoman sovereignty was ignored or envisioned as temporary; in other instances, Ottomans were represented as cohabiting with classical Greeks, Romans, or church fathers. Cleopatra could occupy the same space as Barbarossa. Maps of Ottoman space were intimately connected to the concerns and rhetorics of the day, as expressed in diplomatic accounts, histories, travel narratives, literature, plays, and compendia of knowledge. These sources conjured up historic and literary imagery to portray "the Turks" and their territories, not so much as they were, in any precise scientific or geographic sense, but as they might be imagined to meet the needs and interests of statesmen, armchair travelers, educated consumers and collectors of maps, or the literate and semi-literate public. For these readers of maps, Ottoman space was war space, sacred space, and classical space. As for Ottoman self-representation, it too privileged war space, sacred space, and the projection of imperial ambitions. Its notions of "the classics" were, however, rather different than those of "Christian" Europe.

MODELS OF TIME AND SPACE

Questions of imagining time are more or less inextricable from those of imagining space. Within the parameters set by this volume, 1450–1850, scholars diverge markedly on defining a chronology for the Ottomans. Donald Quataert has employed the notion of the "long eighteenth century (1683–1798)," roughly to divide the era of Ottoman successes (1300–1683) from that of "defeats and territorial withdrawals," which culminated in the "long nineteenth century (1798–1922)."[3] The editors of our own text suggest that the latter part of the early modern era, roughly 1750–1850, is a period of dramatic transformation for the empire. Traditional models of

---

[3] Donald Quataert, *The Ottoman Empire, 1700–1922* (Cambridge: Cambridge University Press, 2000), pp. 37, 54. Others group the latter years of the empire with the emergence of the republic. See, for example, Stanford Shaw (and Ezel Kural Shaw for vol. II), *History of the Ottoman Empire and Modern Turkey*, 2 vols. (Cambridge: Cambridge University Press, 2000 and 1997, reprints of 1976 and 1977 editions). Volume I, *The Rise and Decline of the Ottoman Empire*, covers 1280–1808, while volume II, *The Rise of Modern Turkey*, covers the years 1808–1975, beginning with the coming to power of the reformer Mahmud II. This periodization suggests the projection of the nation of Turkey back into the early nineteenth century. I personally prefer to think of a "long" early modern period lasting roughly from the thirteenth to the early nineteenth century.

Ottoman historiography craft a classical age, lasting roughly from 1300 to 1600, or divide the evolution of empire into the periods before and after the death of Sultan Süleyman (ruled 1520–66).[4] For our purposes, however, periodization is pertinent not so much for defining the stages in the political and economic evolution of the empire, but for examining stages in the evolution of ways in which the empire was (and is) mapped. Such a focus on how space is imagined in images and texts over time helps us surmount the obstacles imposed by conventional chronological (and spatial) divisions employed for "Europe" or the "Middle East."[5]

A student of mine, newly enrolled in a class on the Ottomans, wrote that he signed up for the class because "The Ottomans are the black hole of history." He was unaware of the eloquence of that characterization. The Ottomans, in our historical imagination, are often very much a black hole: a powerful, compelling entity, the inner workings of which may seem dark and unfathomable. We employ certain labels to name their domain: "the Porte," a projection of governmental power from the imperial center in Istanbul; "the Ottoman Empire," a designation that suggests conquered lands, borders, provinces, taxes, and measurable space; "Anatolia, Rumelia, and the Arab Provinces," a set of dividers that suggest region, time of conquest, the language of Ottoman administration, and the specializations of scholars working on their own particular parts of the empire. But all of these designations of space and power seem to fit the early modern empire rather badly. They suggest a set of overly neat partitions not reflective of the large, multiethnic empires, unruly client states, and wide frontier zones of this era.

Other characterizations are more specific and more ideological; they link early modern rhetorics to those of modern texts: the empire as a block

[4] See Halil İnalcık, *The Ottoman Empire: The Classical Age 1300–1600* (London: Weidenfeld and Nicolson, 1973); Metin Kunt and Christine Woodhead (eds.), *Süleyman the Magnificent and his Age: The Ottoman Empire in the Early Modern World* (London: Longman, 1995); Halil İnalcık and Cemal Kafadar (eds.), *Süleyman the Second and his Time* (Istanbul: Isis Press, 1993); Colin Imber, *The Ottoman Empire 1300–1650: The Structure of Power* (London: Palgrave, 2002); and Caroline Finkel, *Osman's Dream: The History of the Ottoman Empire* (New York: Basic Books, 2006).
[5] That is, what Walter Andrews has called the "important heuristic shorthand that enables us to talk economically about places or stretches of time in relation to characteristics that seem to dominate them in certain places for certain people." Walter Andrews, personal communication to D-Otto list, December 11, 2000. Andrews briefly discusses here the problems of periodization and the awkward imposition of terms like "the Renaissance" or "the early modern period" on Ottoman time and space. He notes: "the problem with this shorthand is that its terms begin to take on a life of their own. It becomes very difficult to talk outside the boundaries they set and the expectations they presume." I use the term "Europe" here purposefully, as the familiar though obfuscatory convention. On the conceptualization of Europe, see the eloquent and idiosyncratic introduction to Norman Davies, *Europe: A History* (New York: HarperCollins, 1996), pp. 1–46

between Europe and Asia, an obstacle to be surmounted in the context of the spice trade; an alien, heretical entity that controlled the Holy City of Christendom; the occupier of "classical" space where Greece, Rome, and Byzantium (the antecedents of western civilization) once flourished and ruled. The Ottoman Empire is also cast as a vast emporium of the assembled goods of the Afro-Eurasian world, the early modern "slave state" par excellence, and a wealthy, prodigiously consuming palace culture where eunuchs, pashas, and harem women were enmeshed in the politics of notables. There "the Terrible Turks" emerge as a formidable military power which disassociated chunks of territory from "Europe" and threatened to take even more. As the early modern era flows into the modern, there are other characterizations: the exotic, erotic, dirty, chaotic, classical, mesmerizing "East" immortalized by Orientalist painters and by European travelers like Florence Nightingale and Lady Wortley Montagu; the multicultural empire working to reform itself into a modern state system; or the emasculated military power put in its place by an ascendant Russia.[6]

Transcending religion and region – Hodgson, Lewis and Wigen, Abu-Lughod

In the last half-century, various attempts have been made to situate the Ottomans in world history and to disarticulate the notion that the sixteenth- through the eighteenth-century Eurasian world was composed of isolated blocks (Ottoman and Safavid), secure and content in their foreignness and sense of superiority. By modern geographic criteria, the Ottoman Empire is certainly not a "region." It transcends and violates those criteria. Nonetheless, the Ottoman Empire is often treated as a region, which, at some point in the early twentieth century, was attached to Iran and became the "Middle East." Even the "Middle East," however, makes a very awkward world region. Some scholars have focused on the cultural exchanges and shared economic and political interests that linked "East and West," or "Europe and the Ottomans." But those dichotomous, pseudo-spatial designations are themselves problematic. The Ottoman Empire was, after all, an integral part of Europe. Moreover, the exchanges and continuities affecting Ottoman embeddedness in African and Asian (rather than

---

[6] Contemporary historiography has challenged some of these representations while leaving others intact. The empire is now the focus of intense revisionist scholarship. While historians explore court records and revisit well-worn chronicles to explore Ottoman social practice and redefine the nature of power relations, English departments have rediscovered "the Turk" with a vengeance and launched a movement to reassess the literary and artistic ramifications of cross-cultural exchange.

European) space continue to receive little attention, or else that embedding is reduced to the simple cultural construct of "Islam." For some scholars religion is the most significant factor when calculating the division of world space; for others it is the primary determinant for divisions based on civilization or culture.[7] The borders of Islam, however, and the borders of the Ottomans were never coincident.

The problem of situating the Ottomans in early modern world history is illustrated in contemporary world regional models. Lewis and Wigen, for example, in their influential and contested *Myth of Continents*, propose a world-regions division of the global space, which retains enduring cultural affinities as a primary organizing principle. In their words: "like civiliza-tions, world regions are large sociospatial groupings delimited largely on the grounds of shared history and culture; unlike civilizations, they do not presuppose a literate 'high' culture."[8] Lewis and Wigen have devised twelve world regions, and the Ottomans fit, roughly, into the "Southwest Asia and North Africa" region. The authors' dividing lines, however, would cut the Ottomans off from their territories north and west of the Black Sea and from central and eastern Europe (which are assigned to yet two other world regions). The "enduring cultural affinity" for the space the Ottomans occupied is, apparently, Islam. Such divisions of the world space are of necessity rough, and Lewis and Wigen's model is useful. One could easily argue, however, that in the early modern Ottoman Empire cultural affin-ities were stronger between Anatolia and Rumelia (the Balkan provinces) than they were between Anatolia and the provinces of North Africa. If, instead of Islam, ethno-linguistic affinities or association with enduring political units were given primacy of place as cultural delimiters, then a different world regional model might emerge.[9]

Cultural affinities are also a critical focus of Marshall Hodgson's *Venture of Islam*, which, however, preserves "civilization" based on elite culture as a primary measure of space and society. Perhaps Hodgson's regional desig-nation, "Afro-Eurasian Oikoumene," comes closest to reflecting the nature

---

[7] For example, Samuel Huntington, *The Clash of Civilizations and the Remaking of World Order* (New York: Simon and Schuster, 1997); Bernard Lewis, The *Muslim Discovery of Europe* (New York: Norton, 1982; reprint with a new introduction, 2001), and other works by the same author; and numerous school texts.

[8] Martin Lewis and Karen Wigen, *The Myth of Continents: A Critique of Metageography* (Berkeley, CA: University of California Press, 1997), p. 157. The model of "enduring cultural regions," and the paradigm of world regions are delineated primarily on pp. 141–2, 157, 186–8.

[9] This is true even if one employs Lewis and Wigen's notion, ibid., p. 188, of "giving primacy to the spatial contours of assemblages of ideas, practices, and social institutions that give human commun-ities their distinction and coherence."

of the Ottoman Empire because it suggests the ways in which thought, literature, art, and commerce transcend continental boundaries.[10] Hodgson's model was constructed for the purpose of comparing cultures; it is derived without using "state" or "empire" as necessary or even logical starting points; and it insistently violates the political and religious boundaries which many scholars have tended to take for granted. Islam, of course, is a critical cultural indicator for Hodgson, as it is for Lewis and Wigen; but Hodgson was also interested in the tensions among Islam, society, state, and the military. His "Islam" was not monolithic; it was one element in his examination of imperial limits and the dynamic relations of the "central" government, frontier areas, and vassal kingdoms.[11]

If one looks at world-history mapping of the Ottomans in recent years, one sees patterns that are similar to those found in regional schema. William McNeill's *A World History* (1999, fourth edition), is instructive. McNeill's text contains a set of maps for the early modern period, which mark Ottoman space as predominantly religious space and as something bordering on and relevant to European history. His series of maps representing Ottoman space begins with "Moslem Domination of Orthodox Christendom 1453." Then follow the "Expansion of Medieval Europe to *c.* 1492" and "Reformation and Counter Reformation," for both of which the "Ottoman Empire" is tangential. In the text's section on "The Dominance of the West," one finds the following maps: "Empires of Asia *c.* 1600–1700," "Europe 1648–1789,"and "Russia in 1795," all of which include Ottoman territory. Finally, the section on "Global Cosmopolitanism" includes the Ottomans in the following maps: "Europe under Napoleon 1799–1812," and "The realm of Islam since 1850," in which latter map Ottoman territory is already divided into twentieth-century nations such as "Turkey," "Israel," and "Iraq."[12] McNeill's text is a Europe-centered text, and what is notable

---

[10] Marshall Hodgson, *The Venture of Islam: Conscience and History in a World Civilization*, vol. II: *The Expansion of Islam in the Middle Periods* (Chicago: University of Chicago Press, 1974), pp. 330–4, 570–4. Hodgson's language is useful. He speaks of the influence of "regional lettered traditions" (p. 332) and the degree to which a culture "impressed the imaginations" (p. 333) of diverse peoples. He critiques the historiographic inclination to pick one "mainstream" or cultural center at a time in measuring world history. He describes "Islamdom" as a "potent social block" (p. 570) while contextualizing it in terms of China and the European Renaissance. Because "Islam" is a primary category of division for Hodgson, his paradigm, like those of many contemporary analysts, masks divisions not based on "civilization"; still, even Hodgson's lumping categories tend to be marvelously nuanced.

[11] Hodgson, *The Venture of Islam*, vol. III: *The Gunpowder Empire and Modern Times* (Chicago: University of Chicago Press, 1974), pp. 113–15.

[12] William McNeill, *A World History* (Oxford: Oxford University Press, 1999), pp. 252, 258, 322, 339, 362, 387, 430.

here is his construction of Ottoman space in terms of its relatedness to the history of Europe.

Hodgson's maps in *The Venture of Islam* look very different from McNeill's maps. Hodgson's periodization includes what he calls the "Impact of the Great Western Transmutation," and the nineteenth-century era of "European World Hegemony." But his text focuses on the comparative cultures of the Afro-Eurasian Oikumene and his maps are centered in Asia. Hodgson's mapping of the Ottoman place in the early modern era includes: "The Safavi empire, 1500–1722," a map that highlights ruling groups, silk production, shrines, and campaigns; "The Ottoman Empire, 1512–1718," a map of the whole Mediterranean region that highlights frontiers and vassal states; "The Islamic lands before nineteenth-century European expansion," which emphasizes "Muslim lands lost"; and "The central Mediterranean through India, mid nineteenth century," which depicts "Muslim territories" lost to British, French, Portuguese, Russian, and Dutch rule.[13] In Hodgson's maps, religion is also key, and Europe is included but not central. Dynamic relations of power and the nature of territorial rule are emphasized. Territory belongs to kingdoms like the Ottoman Empire, but also to peoples, like Afghans, Uzbeks, and Kurds.

In a different world-history context, in *The World System*, Gills and Frank have employed an emphasis on long-term economic cycles and capital accumulation as a primary frame for interpreting the Ottoman Empire and other polities. They posit a world system that has existed for five thousand years.[14] In this model, the Ottomans are one of a series of competing hegemons expanding in the sixteenth century into politically weak areas but stopped by "competition with the rising West," at Vienna in 1529 and Lepanto in 1571.[15] Gills and Gunder Frank are not particularly concerned with borders and territory except insofar as they reveal the nature of economic activity; hence their model is limited in its ability to

---

[13] Hodgson, *The Venture of Islam*, vol. III, pp. 36, 115, 143, 234. Even now, thirty years after Hodgson's text was published, it is difficult to find maps for classroom use that include both the region of the Mediterranean and all of South Asia.

[14] Barry Gills and Andre Gunder Frank, "World System Cycles, Crises, and Hegemonic Shifts, 1700 B.C. to 1700 A.D.," in B. Gills and A. Gunder Frank (eds.), *The World System* (London: Routledge, 1996), pp. 143–99, see pp. 144–8. Frank is continually refining his theoretical approach to world systems but has retained the general outlines presented here. For his latest description of the Ottomans, see Andre Gunder Frank, *ReOrient: Global Economy in the Asian Age* (Berkeley, CA: University of California Press, 1998), pp. 78–82.

[15] Gills and Frank, "World System Cycles," pp. 183–4. Their analysis does not so much recraft the Ottoman role in world systems theory as it critiques the historiographic privileging of Europe.

advance our discussion of mapping. Still, they use a language of possession that assumes sovereignty and hence territorial divisions.

Another "world systems" model, Janet Abu-Lughod's classic study *Before European Hegemony*, shifts the focus from regions to routes; it privileges neither long economic cycles nor divisions based on cultural affinities. Abu-Lughod's emphasis on exchange and entrepots does not result either in discrete blocks of space or in a center and its peripheries. Rather, as a reflection of production, consumption, and movement, her emphasis on exchange results in a model based on nodes and circuits.[16] Abu-Lughod's influential work focuses on the period 1250–1350. But its premises are easily translatable into the early modern world of the Ottomans. Thus, for example, one could modify and augment the eight circuits of trade that Abu Lughod identifies in the thirteenth century, and map the Ottomans onto a seventeenth-century vision of world circuits of trade and the city nodes from which they emanate. This classification of world space does not require either states or empires. Thus, "the Ottomans" would not be a single entity. Rather, Ottoman cities and subjects would participate in a series of circuits extending within and beyond the territory over which the sultan could enforce some form of Ottoman sovereignty.

Abu-Lughod's model releases us from the necessity of a regional paradigm, and it focuses our attention on movement in space and continuities across political boundaries, two qualities found in early modern maps. Yet it suffers from a failure to take political, military, and cultural factors into account. All of those factors were operational in the early modern Eurasian conceptions of space. While, like Abu-Lughod's model, they routinely highlighted cities and circuits, early modern maps also included visions of sovereign space, sacred space, military action, and boundaries based on physical features, fortresses and "peoples."

DESIGNATING, SITUATING, AND MEASURING THE OTTOMANS – MAPS, TRAVELERS AND ENVOYS

Mapping the Ottomans thus requires that we divert our attention from the regional paradigm and pay attention to the ways in which territory,

---

[16] Janet Abu-Lughod, *Before European Hegemony: The World System A.D. 1250–1350* (Oxford: Oxford University Press, 1989), pp. 32–5. "But over and above these regional subsystems there is an over-arching world system that works through world cities whose 'transactions' are increasing with one another" (p. 32). Abu-Lughod wished to de-center Europe in the thirteenth-century world order. If the Ottomans were inserted into her thirteenth-century "world" map, they would fit into five of the eight circuits of trade.

peoples, identity, exchange, sovereignty, and borders were imagined in the early modern era. It also necessitates dispensing with the notion that those imaginings can be neatly divided spatially along a definitive border between the Ottoman Empire and Europe. I use these quasi-geographic terms because they are both familiar and conventional, but they were not the terms employed, for example, in sixteenth-century maps. Ottoman land borders were imagined, in early modern Europe, to be broad, porous, and impermanent. As we shall see, there were border-marking enterprises in the early modern era aimed at ascertaining exactly what was and was not Ottoman land. But those enterprises did not mark Ottomans off from "Europe." They marked territory into administrative units (from which taxes, troops, and provisions could be or might be levied). Territory was also divided on the bases of ideology, the allegiance of notables, the extent of governments' protective reach, material culture, the circulation of goods, ethnolinguistic affinity, access to security and food, clan and patronage ties, religio-judicial districting, and local patterns of migration and pilgrimage. The "edge" of Europe in early modern imagery ranged from Austria to some point east of Constantinople.

Early modern mappings

Polities, tribes, cities, individuals, even creatures, mark what is theirs, or what they are willing to defend as theirs. Early modern entities such as the Ottoman Empire are no exception. The Ottomans' designation for a border was *had* (pl. *hudud*), from the Arabic, which included many of the same variations of meaning as our English terms "border" (MF, outer part, edge) and "boundary" (fr. ML, *bodina*; something that limits or restrains). *Had* was similar to the Italian *confine*, which suggested limit, borderland, margin, or edge. Treaties could be called *hududname* and border zones *serhad* (a frontier area, march, or garrisoned area).[17] These

---

[17] Very little of the extensive literature on borders and boundary lands focuses on the Ottomans. Jeremy Black, *Maps and Politics* (Chicago: University of Chicago Press, 1997), pp. 121–5, comments on maps as "part of the process by which frontier differences are defined," and discusses treaties as bilateral mapping endeavors. He points out that, "Mapping frontiers is about mechanisms as well as consent." But the mapping of frontiers that we examine here does not really require a treaty or a direct interaction of two "sides"; rather it suggests world-view, visions of space, and the projection of sovereign power. The "mapping cultures," as Black (p. 121) calls them, in this case have a long history of artistic interchange. For an enlightening discussion of the notion of *serhad* in the context of Ottoman-European frontiers in the seventeenth and eighteenth centuries, see Rossitsa Gradeva, "War and Peace along the Danube: Vidin at the End of the Seventeenth Century," in Kate Fleet (ed.), *The Ottomans and the Sea*, special issue of *Oriente Moderno* 20 (81) n.s./1 (2001): 149–75, esp. 160.

designations tended to be little used in the sixteenth-century Ottoman maps that survive. They were, however, employed by boundary commissions empowered to set physical and documentary markers on where Ottoman space ended and the space of its neighbors or rivals began.

The borders between Ottoman and Venetian territory, for example, were much disputed. In 1479–80, the Venetian *provveditore* (commissioner) Bartolomeo Minio reported that an agent of the Ottoman Porte had arrived in Nauplion (NE Peloponnesus) to assign boundaries to the area. Minio's dispatches mention that both the Ottoman *emin* (deputy) and the local notables drew up their own maps of the disputed territories.[18] The sultan's *emin* used documents, the testimony of "elderly witnesses," and tax records to help determine the "proper" boundaries. Then his commission marked off territory based on physical and social features such as coasts, mountains, wells, fortresses, and monasteries. Territory was described primarily in terms of castles and the agricultural lands attached to them.[19]

Very similar markers of territory and bases for claiming possession are found in later accounts. In 1540–1 the Ottoman government proposed to mark certain boundaries between its territory and that of Poland and Lithuania. The demarcation was apparently never carried out.[20] But the demarcation proposal had been prompted by treaty negotiations, complaints about raiding, and Ottoman attempts to make concrete their battle gains and sovereign claims. In 1681 a joint commission of Ottomans and

---

[18] This is important information since there are very few Ottoman maps of any kind extant for this era and Minio's dispatch suggests that it may have been common practice for such border maps to be drawn.

[19] Diana Gilliland Wright and John Melville-Jones, "Bartolomeo Minio: Dispacci 1479–1483 from Nauplion," dispatches of February 10, 1479 and August 14, 1480, pp. 4–14, "Stato da Mar," http://nauplion.net/statomar.html; forthcoming as *The Greek Correspondence of Bartolomeo Minio*, vol. I: *Dispacci from Nauplion*. See Maria Pia Pedani, *Dalla frontiera al confine*, Quaderni di Studi Arabi, Studi e Testi, vol. V (Rome: Herder, 2002). See also Tibor Halasi-Kun, "Ottoman Toponymic Data and Medieval Boundaries in Southeastern Hungary," in János Bak and Béla Király (eds.), *From Hunyadi to Rákoczi, War and Society in Late Medieval and Early Modern Hungary*, Eastern European Monographs, no. CIV (New York: Brooklyn College Press, 1982), pp. 243–50, on the Ottoman retention of "boundaries of established local administration" (p. 245). On a smaller scale, Ottomans employed title deeds called *sınırname* (line or border documents) to define the limits of property.

[20] See Gilles Veinstein, "L'occupation ottomane d'Očakov et le problème de la frontière lituano-tatare 1538–1544," in *Passé turco-tatar, présent soviétique: études offertes à Alexandre Bennigsen* (Louvain: Éditions Peeters, 1986), pp. 123–55, esp. 137–41. Veinstein calls this the first such episode of proposed demarcation. See also Mykhailo Hrushevsky, *History of the Ukraine-Rus*, vol. VII: *The Cossack Age to 1625*, trans. Bohdan Struminski (Edmonton: Canadian Institute of Ukrainian Studies Press, 1999), pp. 7–16, on traditions of border demarcations. Hrushevsky, p. 10, notes that "ancient demarcations" of village and fortress territory as well as "accounts of old people," were used by the representatives of sovereign powers to assess the location of borders.

representatives of the Polish–Lithuanian Commonwealth delineated a set
of borders using natural and built features like those mentioned in Minio's
account.[21] Mounds were employed to indicate borders where natural
features did not make them evident.

Despite the use of such physical markers to divide territory and fix the
limits of sovereign privilege, there is no simple line around the Ottoman
Empire that divides it from "Europe" or "Christendom." Instead there are,
as the border commission noted, cities, fortresses, rivers, and littorals, and
the memory of where past divisions had been made. Lines suggest defen-
sible territory; they presume states, that is, entities which feel the pressure
of the border-marking imperative.[22] But in the early modern era conceptual divisions of space were not primarily linear and did not lend themselves to precise territorial demarcation.

Certainly European publics, mapmakers, and artists imagined spaces
that were "Christian" or "Turkish." But the zones where one merged into
the other were broad and confusing. German woodcuts of the era often
group the Turks and Latin Christians together as sharing the same "side."
The forces of the Reformation battle Turks and Catholic clergy alike as
infidels and violators in a space that all share, caught not between one
earthly state and another, but between heaven and hell.[23] Political territory,
or sovereign space, is not what is primary in these images. Rather, space is
counted in souls and in the human terrain over which preachers can exert

---

[21] Dariusz Kolodziejczyk, *The Ottoman Survey Register of Podolia (ca. 1681): Defter-i Mufassal-i Eyalet-i Kamaniçe* (Cambridge, MA: Harvard Ukrainian Research Institute, 2003), introduction. I am not aware of such border markers on the Ottoman-Safavid frontier where fortresses and the allegiance of beys were the primary measure of territorial sovereignty, but that does not mean they did not exist. In 1699 the Habsburgs established a border commission, including the infamous Count Marsigli, which mapped out part of the Ottoman-Habsburg frontier. See John Stoye, *Marsigli's Europe 1680–1730: The Life and Times of Luigi Ferdinando Marsigli, Soldier and Virtuoso* (New Haven, CT: Yale University Press, 1994), pp. 164–215.

[22] For some interesting thoughts on the evolving and historical delineation of nations and borders, see Thongchai Winichakul, *Siam Mapped: A History of the Geo-Body of a Nation* (Honolulu: University of Hawaii Press, 1994); and Gopal Balakrishnan (ed.), *Mapping the Nation* (London: Verso, 1996). See also Daniel Power, "Frontiers: Terms, Concepts and the Historians of Medieval and Early Modern Europe," pp. 1–12, and Naomi Standen, "Nine Case Studies of Premodern Frontiers," pp. 13–31, both in Daniel Power and Naomi Standen (eds.), *Frontiers in Question: Eurasian Borderlands 700–1700* (New York: St. Martin's Press, 1999). For a discussion of the crafting of divisions of cultural, military, and political space in another geographic context, see Thomas Barfield, *The Perilous Frontier: Nomadic Empires and China* (Oxford: Blackwell, 1989), a work which since its publication has formed a core of contention in the discussion of frontiers.

[23] For example, Walter Strauss, *The German Single-Leaf Woodcut 1550–1600*, vol. I: A–J (New York: Abaris Books, 1975), pp. 289, 305, 308. See also Kenneth Setton, "Lutheranism and the Turkish Peril," *Balkan Studies* 3 (1962): 133–68; Nancy Bisaha, *Creating East and West: Renaissance Humanists and the Ottoman Turks* (Philadelphia: University of Pennsylvania Press, 2004); and Matthew Dimmock, *New Turkes: Dramatizing Islam and the Ottomans in Early Modern England* (Aldershot: Ashgate, 2005).

Figure 1.1 Matthias Gerung, "Die Türken verfolgen die Christen," *c.* 1548.
Kunstsammlungen der Veste Coburg no. I.349.13. This woodcut shows the Turks
persecuting Christians in the foreground and the pope, accompanied by demons, pursuing
the poor, in the midground. Courtesy of the Kunstsammlungen der Veste Coburg.

spiritual and fiscal authority. Such "maps" of fidelity and infidelity envision no clear line between the "Ottoman Empire" and "Europe" (Fig 1.1).
Indeed, they may imagine Ottoman space simply as historically Christian space
in need of redemption. Such was particularly the case with the "Holy Land"
(Terra Sancta), Jerusalem and its environs, which was firmly in Ottoman

hands from 1516 to 1918. This territory, often depicted as the center of the world in medieval European maps, could be mapped simultaneously as the "Holy Land," and as Ottoman sovereign space.

In narrative accounts, Kritovoulos, the Greek-Ottoman chronicler of Mehmed II's 1453 conquest of Constantinople, embodies the dilemmas of mapping the Ottoman Empire and Europe into two distinct regions. Kritovoulos was a Greek who became a subordinate of the sultan, the Ottoman governor of the isle of Imbros in the Aegean, and the author of an Ottoman history written in Greek. He was thus emblematic of the blurred boundaries between Christian Europe and the Muslim empire, which included both land and sea frontiers. Kritovoulos employs "classical" or Ptolemaic designations for regions, seas, and peoples; he compares the fall of Constantinople to the conquests of Troy and Babylon, and he describes the sultan as claiming sovereignty over the "continents of Europe and Asia." His descriptions focus on cities, castles, armies, and peoples that the Ottomans conquer.[24] Borders are designated in terms of rivers, littorals, and some vague notion of where one people ends and another begins.

Ottomans on the map

Narrative and cartographic conventions changed significantly from 1450 to 1850, but the terms by which Kritovoulos imagined Ottoman space remained remarkably enduring in maps and literature.[25] The object of the sixteenth-century mapmaker's art was not a terrain of demarcated nations or even kingdoms; it was a terrain of peoples, historical memories, sacred sites, travel exigencies, and armies on the march. Maps were histories, meant to facilitate travel (including pilgrimage) and the imagining of travel. They were conquest plans and celebrations of conquest. They were versions of reality not necessarily meant to be taken literally. Maps employed Ptolemy's world divisions, invoked the territorial designations (and heroes) of classical Greece and Rome, and emphasized cities, fortresses, and ports as markers of space. The same was true of contemporary

---

[24] Kritovoulos, *History of Mehmed the Conqueror*, trans. Charles T. Riggs (Westport, CT: Greenwood Press, 1970 reprint of 1954 edition), pp. 24–5. See also pp. 17, 32, 79–81, 187.

[25] On cartographic conventions, see J. B. Harley and David Woodward (eds.), *The History of Cartography*, vol. I: *Geography in Prehistoric, Ancient, and Medieval Europe and the Mediterranean*, and vol. II, book 1: *Geography in the Traditional Islamic and South Asian Societies* (Chicago: University of Chicago Press, 1987–92), hereafter *HOC*.

travel narratives.[26] Only gradually (and in patches) did Ottoman sovereignty and demarcated states emerge on the early modern map.

Gastaldi

The Venetian mapmaker Giacomo Gastaldi stands as a model of sixteenth-century conceptions of Ottoman space. In 1548 Gastaldi completed a new edition of Ptolemy, which included a set of modern maps of Asia.[27] His work was widely circulated and imitated by cartographic workshops in the surrounding territories. Gastaldi added to the classical "first part of Asia," which included Ottoman territory, new maps for Anatolia, Muscovy, Syria and the Terra Sancta, Persia, and Arabia Felix.[28] These maps do not mark borders. They are comprised mostly of what J. B. Harley called "socially empty space," that is territory devoid of people and of socio-cultural indicators.[29] Peoples are occasionally designated as occupying or moving through space: for example, the label "Kingdoms of the Tartars," with accompanying tent icons. But such designations are infrequent. For the most part, the viewer of these maps sees only physical features, regions, areas, and cities (Fig. 1.2). Occasionally, there is some reference to the exigencies of travel or to pilgrimage sites. Thus, for example, on Gastaldi's map of Egypt and Arabia, in the lands around Mecca, one notes two separate captions: "Here, Muhammad is buried" and "This is a place full of serpents and assassins" (Fig. 1.3).[30] Such captions

---

[26] See, for a popular example, Nicolas de Nicolay, *The Nauigations into Turkie: London 1585* (Amsterdam: Da Capo Press, 1968; reprint of London 1585 edition), pp. 44–5 for the descriptions of Gallipoli and Istanbul. Joan-Pau Rubiés, *Travel and Ethnology in the Renaissance: South India through European Eyes 1250–1625* (Cambridge: Cambridge University Press, 2000), pp. 99–100, emphasizes the continuity between ancient Greek and Renaissance geographical categories in his important study of European travel accounts of South Asia. While I do not find that my typology of narratives and images of Ottoman space exactly matches that which Rubiés proposes (for example, pp. 80–5), his study provides a very important model and comparative point of departure. See also, for classifications of modes of travel narratives, John Michael Archer, *Old Worlds: Egypt, Southwest Asia, India, and Russia in Early Modern English Writing* (Stanford, CA: Stanford University Press, 2001), pp. 2–3, 12–14, who posits historiographic and observational modes adapted from Bernard Cohn and William Sherman, "Stirrings and Searchings (1500–1720)," in Peter Hulme and Tim Youngs (eds.), *The Cambridge Companion to Travel Writing* (Cambridge: Cambridge University Press, 2002), pp. 17–36.

[27] Robert W. Karrow, *Mapmakers of the Sixteenth Century and their Maps* (Chicago: Newberry Library, by Speculum Press, 1993), pp. 220–1. Gastaldi included the twenty-six maps of the Ptolemy canon plus thirty-four modern maps.

[28] See, for example, Newberry Library, Novacco 4F 374, "Prima Parte dell'Asia," and Novacco 4F 377, "Natolia."

[29] J. B. Harley, *The New Nature of Maps* (Baltimore, MD: Johns Hopkins University Press, 2001), p. 61.

[30] Newberry Library, Novacco 4F 406.

Figure 1.2   Giacomo Gastaldi, Egypt and Arabia, 1560 Newberry Library. Novacco 4F 406. Courtesy of the Newberry Library, Chicago.

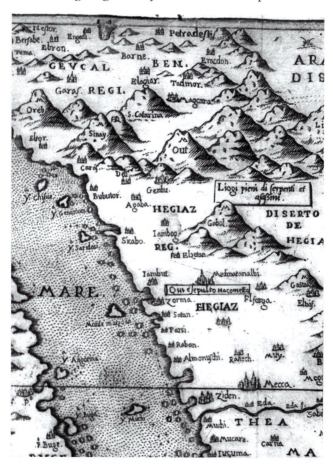

Figure 1.3 Giacomo Gastaldi, Provinces of Egypt and Arabia (inset), 1560. Newberry Library Novacco 4F 406. Note the two small boxed legends in the Hijaz along the west coast of Arabia. These are aimed at travelers or, more likely, armchair travelers. The larger legend box notes "place full of serpents and assassins"; the smaller, north of Mecca, points out "Here, Muhammad is buried." Courtesy of the Newberry Library, Chicago.

were primarily indicators of points of interest, but they may also have been directed at travelers.[31]

Travel and commerce, though not emphasized in the body of Gastaldi's maps, sometimes play a significant role in the legends, thus revealing both

---

[31] Newberry Library, Novacco 4F 385. The main legend on Gastaldi's map of the "second part of Asia," the territory from Syria to India, describes the lands included in terms of rivers, seas, provinces, and sometimes reigns.

the nature of the audience and the referential contexts of the maps themselves. The legend on Gastaldi's map of the "second part of Asia," for
example, describes territory in terms of rivers, seas, provinces, and, occasionally, reigns. Gastaldi notes that his map shows:

all the "steps" of the ships that go and come with the spices of the city of Calicut,
and at the same time, all the places on land that have been named up to the present,
where go and come the caravans of their khan, and Dalacca, the country of Prester
John, and also [those of] Aden and Hormuz and the Basra castle on the river.[32]

Territory is thus represented as inextricably linked to points of interest,
religious imagination, and commerce. Here one sees the preoccupation
with city nodes and the circuits of trade found in the world-systems scheme
of Abu-Lughod; here one also finds things not included in Abu-Lughod's
model: sacred space (usually in the form of religious edifices) and military
campaigns. Gastaldi's maps make no mention of the Ottoman Empire;
there is no projection of Ottoman sovereignty. Rather, the Ottomans are
suggested only by allusion, iconographically, when Gastaldi places cres-
cents on the sails of galleys in the Black and Mediterranean seas.

City views
Beyond Gastaldi's regional maps with their socially empty space, sixteenth-
century European workshops issued two other pertinent (sometimes overlapping) categories of map: city views and visions of the Ottoman military.
Such maps cover much smaller swathes of territory and, unlike the regional
maps of Gastaldi and his imitators, they specifically name and depict the
Ottomans. But they are not concerned with drawing borders, they often do
not specify territorial contexts, and they frequently collapse time to place
classical events in the same space as contemporary ones.

   Sixteenth-century Italian mapmakers produced city views in great abun-
dance. Some showed cities floating in undesignated time and collapsed
space. Others might be considered as news maps: dated pictorial images of
contemporary events of specific interest to the map-consuming public.
While certain views of cities set in Ottoman territory repeated the tendency
found in regional maps to omit reference to the Ottomans entirely, others
identified cities as the stage on which land- and sea-based struggles between
the Ottomans and their rivals were fought out. These news maps proposed
to present to the public a "true image" of Ottoman advances or of the

---

[32] Ibid. Prester John was the mythic Christian king believed from medieval times to be located in
various places from Central Asia to Ethiopia.

battles of "Christians" against "Turks." Ports and fortresses, in particular, were depicted as contested space.

The vision of the fortified port as territorial divider is exemplified by a map showing an attack on the Gulf of Artha on the western coast of Greece (Fig. 1.4).[33] This dramatic and historically contextualized image depicts a land-based besieging army and a vigorous sea battle, with cannons roaring and naked men leaping from a burning ship into the sea. The frontier here is a broad one, comprising the hinterland of the fortress and the surrounding seascape, including the gulf and its islands.[34] This image, presumably a representation of the Battle of Prevesa in October 1538, serves as both news map and history lesson. Its legend informs the reader that this is the place where "at present one finds the navies of Barbarossa [the Ottoman commander] and of the Christians."[35] But the legend also invokes the historical imagination, situating this same contested space in more remote time: "[this is the place] ... called the Gulf of Artha; in ancient times it was called Ambracio da Ambra, the actual city of Pyrrhus, near the promontory of Actium where the memorable victory of Augustus over Marc Antony and Cleopatra took place." Contemporary "Turks" and "Christians" along with figures and fleets from classical Roman history thus share the same mapped space, which embodies a rich history of contention for land, power, and prestige. The mapmaker expects his audience to be familiar with these names and events; they shift the two-dimensional physical map into a three-dimensional mental image crafted out of rich layers of event, memory, and violence.

Enduring and evolving features of early modern mapping of Ottoman terrain

Toward the end of the sixteenth century European maps began increasingly to depict borders in ways that earlier maps had not; *confini* (borders)

[33] Newberry Library, Novacco 2F 22. The Gulf of Arta, or Ambracian Gulf, located in the Ionian Sea.
[34] For two interesting approaches to the question of the ways in which Ottoman-European sea-based frontiers were envisioned and acted out, see Victor Ostapchuk, "The Human Landscape of the Ottoman Black Sea in the Face of the Cossack Naval Raids," pp. 23–95; and Elizabeth Zachariadou, "Monks and Sailors under the Ottoman Sultans," pp. 139–47, both in Fleet, *The Ottomans and the Sea*.
[35] Newberry Library, Novacco 2F 22, no date. For a map and discussion of the Battle of Prevesa, see John Guilmartin, *Gunpowder and Galleys: Changing Technology and Mediterranean Warfare at Sea in the Sixteenth Century* (Cambridge: Cambridge University Press, 1974), pp. 42–56. For a news map image of the Ottoman army at Szigetvar, see Antonio Lafreri, [Szigetvar], Rome, 1566, Newberry Library, Novacco 2F 48. A similar engraving, Newberry Library, Novacco 4F 105, *c.* 1570, by Paolo Forlani, is entitled "The Marvelous Order of the Grand Turkish Army"; see David Woodward, *The Maps and Prints of Paolo Forlani: A Descriptive Bibliography* (Chicago: Newberry Library, 1990), illustration no. 93.

Figure 1.4 Anonymous, Sea Battle in the Gulf of Artha, no date. Newberry Library Novacco 2F 22. The map presumably depicts the 1538 battle of Prevesa in which the Ottoman commander Khairüddin Barbarossa took on a Christian coalition led by Andrea Doria. The legend notes that this is the place in Greece where "at present one finds the navy of Barbarossa and that of the Christians." But it also situates the map in the historic imagination of its readers, indicating that it is the place which "in ancient times was called Ambracio da Ambra, the actual city of Pyrrhus, near the promontory of Actium where the memorable victory of Augustus over Marc Antony and Cleopatra took place." Courtesy of the Newberry Library, Chicago.

were more likely to be marked with dotted or colored lines. Seventeenth-century mapping typically employed regional outlines and the labeling of sovereign space. The designations "Turkey in Europe" and "Turkey in Asia" were increasingly used to label the two parts (as Europeans perceived them) of Ottoman space.[36] These labels preserved the notion of a clear, continental division of space while admitting the existence and persistence of a Turkish presence. By the eighteenth century, the state had become the standard by which lands were divided and demarcated. Nonetheless, the practices of employing classical geographic terminology, of failing to name the Ottoman sovereign entity, and of drawing socially empty space endured alongside the more "modern" or "scientific" marking of territory. The "Tabula Nova Geographica Natolia et Asiae Minoris," for example, composed "most accurately" by Giacomo Cantelli around 1698 and reproduced in Belgium, combines the colored regional (or provincial) borders of "Turquie en Europe" with the socially empty space and geographic markers of Gastaldi's maps.[37] Its regions preserve classical names (Lydia, Phrygia, Bithynia); and there is no reference in image or text to the Ottomans.

"Turks," however, did increasingly appear on early modern maps. Allain Manesson-Mallet's borderless map of Anatolia, *c.* 1683, labels the land to the northwest of the Black Sea as "Europe" in large letters and the land to the northwest of "Constantinople" as "Turquie en Europe" (Fig. 1.5). A troop of seven mounted and rather unthreatening Ottomans (identifiable by their turbans and horsetails (*tuğ*) along with a bristling array of banners and cannon surround the map's large legend, marked simply "Natolie."[38] The cartouche of Jacob Sandrart's detailed 1660 map of Eurasia pairs high-hatted armed janissaries, carrying saber and musket, with Europeans in eclectic garb bearing a shield with a large cross. The Black Sea is labeled not only "Mare Maggiore" and "Pontus Euxinus" (among other names), but

---

[36] North Africa was a separate category. These designations survived until the empire was dismembered in World War I. They are reflected in the classification scheme of the extensive map collection of King George III (1760–1820) now preserved in the British Library's King's Topographical Collection.

[37] Walker Collection, University of Melbourne, Maps MX 410a 1511–1774, no. 130; Giacomo Cantelli (1643–95). The recycling of old map plates was one reason for continuity in mapping conventions, but the persistence of old representational forms and names was the result of intellectual and cultural as well as technical concerns.

[38] Walker Collection, Maps MX 410a 1511–1774, no. 54, Allain Manesson-Mallet (1630–?). "Turks" in the cartouches of European maps are frequently threatening and associated with the accoutrements of war; but they may also be mild-looking and associated with the accoutrements of commerce.

Figure 1.5 Allain Manesson-Mallet, Natolie, *c.* 1683. Walker Maps MX 410a,
1511–1774, no. 54. Image courtesy of the University of Melbourne Library Map Collection,
reproduced with permission.

also "Turcis Caradenis."[39] By including the Turkish name, the mapmaker suggests territorial identity and possession.

Other seventeenth-century maps purposefully outlined and labeled the "empire of the Turk." "A Mapp of The Estates of the Turkish Empire in Asia and Europe, Designed by Mon.sr Sanson Geographer to the French King, and Rendered into English and Illustrated with Figures by Richard Blome, Anno 1669" precisely identifies the Ottomans with sovereign and state power.[40] Despite borders drawn around regions, however, the western boundaries of the Turkish "Estates" are far from clear. Conversely, to the east, a dotted line seems to divide Ottoman turf from that of another sovereign entity, "The Empire of Persia." A map with similar Eurasian parameters (cutting through Italy to the west and Persia to the east), "L'Empire des Turcs en Europe, en Asie, et en Afrique, avec quelques Principales Routes qu'y tiennent les Caravanes," by Pierre Duval, dated 1677, also clearly attests to Ottoman sovereignty.[41] Its legend includes a prominent crescent (symbol for the Ottomans) at the top and the face of a turbaned man at the bottom (Fig. 1.6). Its iconography and text thus proclaim, as did the sultan himself, a Turkish empire that stretched across three continents.

Still, the equivocal cartographic message on the nature and scope of Ottoman sovereignty persisted into the eighteenth century, as seen in a map (*c.* 1729) of "Turquie en Europe" from the workshop of Pieter Van der Aa at Leiden.[42] The labels here include the more "modern" regional designations, such as "Servie," "Bulgarie," "Caramanie," and also incorporate some Turkish names like "Kara Hissart" (sic).[43] Yet the map mimics Gastaldi's socially empty space, marked with cities, fortresses, monasteries, and natural features (although the regions are bounded by unobtrusive dotted lines). The legend is distinctive. It is set in a rectangle against an image of a port city (presumably a rather fanciful Istanbul) with ships in the harbor and buildings and minarets on shore. The entire device, with its smiling janissary musketeer on one side and Ottoman and European merchants on the other, suggests that "Turquie

---

[39] Walker Collection, Maps MX 410a 1511–1774, no. 104, Jacob Sandrart (1630–1708). This multiple labeling is common in many maps of the period.

[40] Walker Collection, Maps MX 410a 1511–1774, no. 12, Richard Blome (d. 1705). On the Sanson family in French mapmaking, see R. V. Tooley, *Maps and Map-Makers* (New York: Crown Publishers, 1982, reprint of 1970 rev. edn), pp. 40–1.

[41] Walker Collection, Maps MX 410a 1511–1774, no. 33, Pierre Duval (1619–82).

[42] See Ariel Salzmann, *Tocqueville in the Ottoman Empire: Rival Paths to the Modern State* (Leiden: Brill, 2004), pp. 31–74, for a large, anonymous Ottoman map, dated 1727–8, of Eurasia which merges the qualities of the sixteenth-century unbounded maps with those of later, more demarcated maps.

[43] Walker Collection, Maps MX 410a, 1511–1774, no. 4, Pieter van der Aa (1659–1733), *c.* 1729.

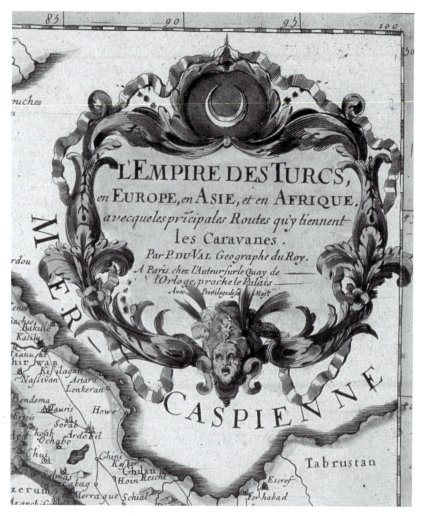

Figure 1.6 Pierre Duval, "Empire des Turcs en Europe, en Asie, et en Afrique," 1677.
Walker Maps MX 410a, 1511–1774, no. 33. Image courtesy of the University of Melbourne
Library Map Collection, reproduced with permission.

en Europe" is a prosperous, commercial space. The reader is advised that this
map is based on "new observations by the members of the Royal Academy of
Sciences." Thus we have an eighteenth-century map that represents itself as
both modern and scientific (Fig. 1.7). It depicts Ottomans but mentions them
in its text only by regional allusion. The empire's lands are a source of profit,
marked by provinces, rivers, and mountains, but not by sovereign states.

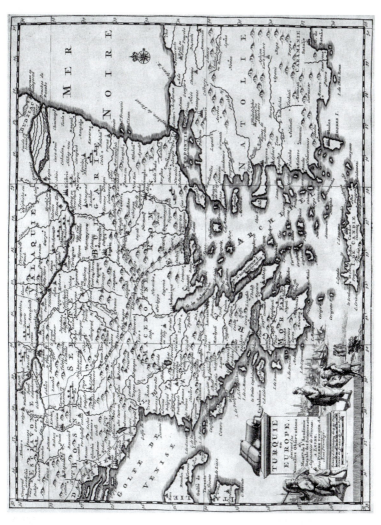

Figures 1.7 Pieter van der Aa, "Turquie en Europe," *c. 1729*. Walker Maps MX 410a, 1511–1774, no. 4. Image courtesy of the University of Melbourne Library Map Collection, reproduced with permission.

Travelers and envoys

Maps were the counterparts of narratives, particularly travel narratives. In many cases, the legends of maps cited travelers as authorities for the crafting of physical and social space. Though mapmakers increasingly applied scientific principles of measurement throughout the period under discussion, the "eyewitness" account remained a critical element in early modern mapping. Europeans journeying to the Ottoman Empire mapped its space in language directed at their sovereigns, their associates, or a broader literate audience. Some aimed to provide military intelligence, others principally to entertain. Their observations were more or less precise, some crafted primarily from a combination of history, imagination, and expectation. Trade or diplomacy ordinarily motivated sixteenth-century travelers, while eighteenth-century travelers might visit the sultan's lands for purposes of education, pilgrimage, or adventure. Their tales suggest the varying modes by which Ottoman territory could be envisioned.[44]

In 1591 the Republic of Venice sent Lorenzo Bernardo as a special envoy to Istanbul, where he had previously served as bailo (consul). Bernardo, in his *Relazioni* of 1592, asked this rhetorical question about the Ottoman Empire:

Who is he ... whose ingenuity is so acute and tongue so quick that in a single argument he can eloquently explain the precepts of such an empire ... that like a lightning bolt has acquired, almost transfixed, so many kingdoms, so many provinces, that now it rules 8,000 miles of the circuit of the world, three thousand five-hundred and more in length, from the furthest limits [*confini*] of Hungary to the city of Tabriz, and beyond that from the furthest limits of Tartary, and from Tana to the ends [*termini*] of the kingdom of Aden on the southern Ocean sea [*mar Oceano meridionale*], such that now it finds itself in possession of more than forty kingdoms ... and rules a grand part of the three [continents] of the world, that is Asia, Africa, and Europe.[45]

---

[44] See Stéphane Yerasimos, *Les voyageurs dans l'Empire ottoman (XIVe–XVIe siècles): bibliographie, itinéraires et inventaire des lieux habités* (Ankara: Imprimerie de la Société Turque d'Histoire, 1991), which contains an elaborate list of travel accounts along with routes of travel. Also interesting are: Gerald Maclean (ed.), *Re-Orienting the Renaissance: Cultural Exchanges with the East* (Houndmills: Palgrave Macmillan, 2005); and Matthew Birchwood and Matthew Dimmock (eds.), *Cultural Encounters Between East and West: 1453–1699* (Newcastle upon Tyne: Cambridge Scholars Press, 2005).

[45] Eugenio Alberi (ed.), *Relazioni degli ambasciatori veneti al Senato*, series 3, vol. II (Florence: Tipografia all'Insegna di Clio, 1844), p. 324. All translations, unless otherwise noted, are mine. On Venetian and European mapping of the Ottomans see Bronwen Wilson, *The World in Venice: Print, the City, and Early Modern Identity* (Toronto: University of Toronto Press, 2005), pp. 133–84; and Jerry Brotton, *Trading Territories: Mapping the Early Modern World* (London: Reaktion Books, 1997), pp. 87–118.

Bernardo thus neatly expressed for his contemporaries the dilemma with which we are now faced. What words were there to articulate the territorial scope of the Ottoman conquests? The envoy chose a vision for the Venetian government that shaped the Ottoman Empire in terms of miles, kingdoms, provinces, cities, seas, continents, and the projection of power (made manifest, like lightning, in the form of military and political expansion). That power ended either at the sea (the *termini*) of Aden, at the furthest limits (*confini*) of land that Hungary or Tartary could defend, or, more ambiguously, at Tabriz, a city point in a large and contested frontier between the Ottomans and Safavids.

Another sixteenth-century Venetian bailo, Marino Cavalli, writing in 1560, had described the length and breadth of the Ottoman kingdom in the same terms, but included a different dimension, that of peoples, their faiths, and their level of contentment with Ottoman rule:

[In this empire of the sultan] more than two thirds of the country is inhabited by Christian Greeks, Bulgars, Slavs, and Albanians in Europe, and Armenians in Asia, all discontented with the Turks because of extortion, rape, violence, and unjust administration . . .

Their neighbors [*vicini*], who are Arabs, Persians, Georgians, Mingrellians, Circassians, Russians, Moldavians, Hungarians, Germans and Your Serenity [Venice], are likewise discontented with the Turks because, in truth, this their neighbor who shares a border with them [*confinare*] is always attacking, always robbing, and making excuses as it is wont to do.[46]

Marino Cavalli's account is a bit unusual when compared to other Venetian *relazioni*, not because of its emphasis on discontent with Ottoman rule but because of the way it divides Ottoman space. For Cavalli, there is Christian–Ottoman space; Muslim–Ottoman space; neighbors (*vicini*), both Christian and Muslim but designated by ethnicity; and those who share borders (*confinanti*). "Neighbors" do not necessarily share borders, and borders cross religious and ethnic lines. In this narrative, the critical factors for mapping the Ottomans are sovereignty, religion, ethnicity, and whether or not borders are sources of conflict. The envoy draws lines of sympathy between Venetians and Persians because they share a bad neighbor, "the Turks."

In an itinerary appended to his report, Cavalli also documented the over-land route between Dolcigno on the Adriatic coast and "Costantinopoli,"

---

[46] Alberi, *Relazioni*, series 3, vol. I, p. 277. Cavalli also distinguishes among the Arab peoples under Ottoman rule. Most he calls "Moors," but he seems to reserve the term "Arab" for the desert dwellers or Bedouin, some of whom are distinguished further as bandit groups.

noting miles, the principal cities of Macedonia and Greece, a few pleasant or prosperous locales (*buona terra*), the locations of mineral baths, and the places where horses could be changed or shoed.[47] Such issues of logistics and the nature of travel in Ottoman space are addressed in more detail by other European travelers, such as Ogier Ghiselin de Busbecq, Habsburg ambassador to the Ottoman Porte, who remained in the empire from 1554 to 1562, becoming well acquainted with Ottoman affairs. Busbecq journeyed overland to Istanbul, commenting on mountain passes, stopping places, cities, fortresses, and the safety of boat travel down the Danube. His narrative highlighted both "classical" history and local culture. He might comment on why the Muslims saved papers with God's name written upon them, or describe the women's dress in Bulgaria, its "clumsy and ridiculous embroidery," and its "towering head-dresses ... of extraordinary shape."[48] But at each stage of his journey the envoy also called up classical imagery to describe Ottoman space. Thus he compared the carriage of the Bulgarian women in their headdresses to that of Clytemnestra and Hecuba, and he subjected Roman and Byzantine ruins to extensive commentary.[49]

When Busbecq reached Belgrade he described it in terms of Roman antiquities and the power of Ottoman armies unleashed when European rulers did not exert sufficient energy and organization to restrain them. Territory he divided into those lands that the Ottomans had seized and those that they might seize. Belgrade was a dividing line, the first place where Busbecq found merchants offering "ancient (Roman) coins."[50] The availability of such coins was a marker of Ottoman space, which, in turn, Busbecq wryly characterizes as barred to foreigners except those who are willing to disburse money freely:

In fact, a man who intends to go among the Turks must be prepared, as soon as he has crossed the frontier, to open his purse and never close it till he leaves the country ... Money acts as a charm to sooth their otherwise intractable minds. Were it not for this expedient, their country would be as inaccessible to foreigners as those lands which are supposed to be condemned to perpetual solitude by excessive heat or cold.[51]

In the lands beyond the frontier, money becomes a substitute for familiarity. Busbecq's ethnocentric rhetoric reveals cultural categories of marking

---

[47] Ibid., pp. 297–8.
[48] Ogier Ghiselin de Busbecq, *The Turkish Letters of Ogier Ghiselin de Busbecq: Imperial Ambassador at Constantinople 1554–1562*, trans. Edward Forster (Oxford: Clarendon Press, 1968), pp. 21–2, 26. For a travel narrative preoccupied with descriptions of women and their dress, see De Nicolay, *Nauigations*, pp. 51–68, 119.
[49] Busbecq, *Turkish Letters*, p. 22.   [50] Ibid., pp. 14–15.   [51] Ibid., p. 25.

space. Lands are accessible or inaccessible; and it is not Ottoman armies but lack of resources that keep travelers out of the lands ruled by "Turks."

Towards the end of the early modern era another traveler also documented one of the overland routes to Istanbul. John Morritt was an Englishman who journeyed from Vienna to Istanbul in 1794. Eloquent and enthusiastic, he was representative of a certain type of affluent, educated English traveler who crafted the Ottoman Empire in letters written to his family.[52] Morritt described the boundaries between the Ottoman Empire and Vienna in terms similar to those employed by Cavalli, though in much more detail. He too wanted to convey what being in Ottoman territory meant for the traveler; he repeated many of the tropes of sixteenth-century narratives, including complaints about bedding and the obligatory description of women's dress. Writing ("from a small inn between Temesvar and Hermanstadt") Morritt told his family:

> Their language here changes from Hungarian to Wallach . . . Farther on they talk Greek and Turkish, so between Vienna and Constantinople the language changes six times, viz.: German, Sclavonian, Hungarian, Wallach, Greek and Turkish, which I do not suppose happens in so short a space in any other part of the world. Transylvania is certainly a fine, and might be a fertile province, but being a frontier, one exposed to the Turks, is not cultivated as it might be, and the Turks have hardly any commerce with them.[53]

Although Morritt, unlike Cavalli, had little conception of Ottoman commercial affairs, his language reveals the ways in which he counted territory. Space is marked by mountains, states (like Austria), cities, languages, religions, and peoples (like "Turks"). Frontiers are those spaces where agricultural activity is impeded by "exposure" to threatening people.

Later in the narrative Morritt wrote of the empire in terms of dominion over specific provinces, avenues of travel, and cultural conventions:

> You will see by your map that very soon afterwards we left Transylvania, and entered the Turkish dominions. Wallachia, which is the first province belonging to the Porte, is under the immediate government of the Prince of Wallachia, and is entirely Christian, no Turk, by the treaty of alliance, being allowed the exercise of his religion or to bring his wives . . . Our road to Bucharest was through the towns

[52] The editor of his missives tells us that Morritt was "a good scholar, well-read in Greek and Latin literature." When he returned from his travels he "settled down as an influential country squire and admirable landlord in Yorkshire." John B. S. Morritt, *The Letters of John B. S. Morritt of Rokeby, Descriptive of Journeys in Europe and Asia Minor in the Years 1794–1796*, ed. G. E. Marindin (London: John Murray, 1914), pp. v–vi.

[53] Ibid., pp. 52, 58–9.

of Arjis and Pitesti, which you will perhaps see marked on your map, though they are neither of them larger than Bowes [in England]. On leaving Transylvania we bid adieu to our beds, tables and chairs, the Wallachians, who are Greek Christians, as well as the Turks, never sitting on a raised seat, and always sleeping on carpets in their clothes.[54]

The adventuresome Englishman assumes his correspondents have maps readily to hand and will consult them as they read his letters. This element of his narrative seems to be a characteristic of the eighteenth century. In terms of the political division of space, Morritt designates Wallachia as "belonging" to the Ottoman government. Yet its treaty rights protect its status as an entirely Christian place. "Turks" apparently reside there, but their Turkishness is muted by the absence of wives and the provisions against the practice of Islam. For Morritt, a Turk is, by definition, a Muslim. But Islam provides no conclusive regional boundary. When it comes to cultural affinities (the delineators employed by Lewis and Wigen to draw the lines separating world regions), we see that Morritt emphasizes the shared culture of Wallachia and Turkey, of Greek Christians and Turks.

Where the "Orient" begins and ends is also a question in Morritt's letters. As he proceeds towards Istanbul he crafts the journey, much like sixteenth-century travelers, in terms of how many days' ride it is between one city and another. But he also deals with space in terms of oriental imaginings and tourist logistics.

Since we left Hermanstadt we have been traveling in a Greek country, and the whole scene is so new, so extraordinary that we are afraid we are dreaming out of the "Arabian Nights Entertainments." On arriving here we were fortunate enough to find the couriers for Constantinople just setting off, and have agreed with them to take us. We ride the whole way, and are accompanied by two janissaries, who have the care of us. We pay them here for everything (a great price, to be sure) but they procure us eating, homes and everything we want the whole way without our taking any trouble or having an interpreter. We hope to be at Constantinople in about nine days; in a carriage it is about fifteen, and very bad road. There is, we are told, no danger, as merchandise and other things go every day.[55]

The interesting elements in this narrative are the transition to Ottoman space and the location of the "Orient." The "Greek country" becomes

[54] Ibid., p. 62.
[55] Ibid., p. 60. The *Arabian Nights Entertainments* were first translated from Arabic into French in twelve volumes by Antoine Galland, beginning in 1704 and shortly afterwards translated into English; they then circulated widely in Europe. See *Arabian Nights Entertainments*, ed. Robert Mack (Oxford: Oxford University Press, 1995).

part of the Arabian Nights. This is an eloquent example, among many in early modern narratives and images, of the difficulty involved in placing, or even locating, a discrete East or West. Morritt couples pragmatism with fantasy as he discusses his travel arrangements. The space between Bucharest and Istanbul is not so much Christian or Muslim, European or Ottoman; rather it is characterized as safe and commercial.[56] Travelers with enough money need not be conversant with the languages of the lands through which they are traveling in order to be quite comfortable.

Morritt was also attached to classical designations, though not obsessively so. He often added names from Greek history and mythology to the contemporary names of places he passed through, but these were always additions rather than replacements. For example: "The next day we arrived in the plain on the banks of a broad torrent now called the Maritza . . . this river which is now almost an unknown stream, was the Hebrus, so famous for the unfortunate story of Orpheus."[57] Morritt's primary frame of comparison for his correspondents was the contemporary England of their experience. Although he expected them to be familiar with classical designations, and he traveled in Anatolia expressly to see ancient sites, the classical frame did not dominate his narrative. Indeed, in that regard, Morritt's narrative is much like eighteenth-century maps. It presumed a literate, map-using public with a historical memory. "Classical" times, literature, figures, and deeds lurk in the background, but they are no longer the primary frame of reference; nor are they the primary mode for denoting Ottoman space.

The early modern period produced a vast array of travel accounts depicting the Ottoman realm. As suggested here, these accounts vary according to the knowledge, task, and personality of the authors, literary conventions, and the demands of audiences both formal and informal. Nonetheless, we can see that the logistics of travel and war, and the

---

[56] Morritt, *Letters*, p. 64, does suggest the boundary of Christendom is Sistova: "On entering Bulgaria at Sistova, we bid adieu to Christianity." Morritt was traveling during the reign of Selim III (1789–1807), who had signed a peace treaty with Austria in 1792 at Sistova. In 1774 the treaty of Küçük Kaynarca had fixed relations between Ottomans and Russians. Many maps of the era were generated to depict the newly crafted boundaries between the Ottoman, Russian, and Habsburg empires. See Virginia Aksan, *An Ottoman Statesman in War and Peace: Ahmed Resmi Efendi 1700–1783* (Leiden: Brill, 1995), pp. 201–3. See also Norman Itzkowitz and Max Mote (ed. and trans.), *Mubadele: An Ottoman-Russian Exchange of Ambassadors* (Chicago: University of Chicago Press, 1970).

[57] Morritt, *Letters*, p. 65. When he takes a trip from Istanbul to the Asian side he notes that the place they visited was called "Giant Mountain" locally, but "it is marked in the ancient maps" as the "Bed of Hercules."

symbols of "classical" history, constituted powerful frames through
which Ottoman space was articulated. Narrators might be fearful of the
Ottomans, ignorant of them, or little concerned with the current occupants of "the first part of Asia." But they were all preoccupied with safety,
the temporal and physical demands of travel, and familiarizing the
Ottoman lands in comparison to their own domestic and imaginary
landscapes. Religion at times played a prominent role and at times did
not. Travel accounts were sometimes socially overflowing rather than
socially empty. They detailed individuals, government officials, housing,
family relations, costume, food, wonders, crimes, modes of transport,
shrines, illnesses, lusts, pleasure, and despair. While their icons for
marking space paralleled those found in contemporary maps, the difference was in the details.

HOW THE OTTOMANS SITUATED, DESIGNATED, AND MEASURED THEMSELVES: SOVEREIGNS, MAPS, ENVOYS AND TRAVELERS

We possess from the Ottomans a greatly unexplored mass of archival
material, a set of narrative sources that have not been fully exploited,
various rhetorical pronouncements of sovereignty, and numerous legal
and diplomatic delineations of the scope of territory and power. We also
have intriguing visualizations of space as expressed in architecture, miniatures, and the decorative arts.[58] The supply of Ottoman maps for the
period in question, however, is limited, particularly for the sixteenth
century. That means that we cannot match Ottoman cartographic self-
representation with cartographic representation of Ottoman space deriving
from societies outside the empire.[59] While we know that the sultans
patronized the production of maps, the size, nature, and expectations of

---

[58] For Ottoman architectural self-mapping, see Gülru Necipoğlu, *Architecture, Ceremonial, and Power: The Topkapı Palace in the Fifteenth and Sixteenth Centuries* (Cambridge, MA: MIT Press, 1991); and Zeyneb Çelik, *Displaying the Orient: The Architecture of Islam at Nineteenth-Century World Fairs* (Berkeley, CA: University of California Press, 1992).

[59] *HOC*, vol. II, book 1, is the best up-to-date treatment of Ottoman cartography. See also Thomas D. Goodrich, *The Ottoman Turks and the New World: A Study of Tarih-i Hind-i Garbi and Sixteenth Century Ottoman Americana* (Wiesbaden: Otto Harrassowitz, 1990); Franz Taeschner, "Ottoman Geographers," in the article "Djughrāfiyā," in *Encyclopaedia of Islam* (EI2), 2nd edn, vol. II, pp. 587–90; Ekmelledin İhsanoğlu, *Osmanlı Coğrafya Literatürü (History of Ottoman Geographical Literature During the Ottoman Period)*, 2 vols. (Istanbul: İslâm Tarih, Sanat, ve Kültür Araştırma Merkezi, 2000); and Gottfried Hagen, *Ein osmanischer Geograph bei der Arbeit, Entstehung und Gedankenwelt von Katib Celebis Gihannüma*, Studien zur Sprache, Geschichte und Kultur der Türkvölker (Berlin: Klaus Schwarz Verlag, 2003).

audiences for early modern Ottoman maps are mostly undocumented. Evliya Çelebi (1611–84) briefly notes the presence of eight ateliers of map-makers in seventeenth-century Istanbul, but he neither names the shops nor gives details of their patrons and production.[60] Much has yet to be revealed. What I propose to present here is a selection of Ottoman articulations of space, to suggest the ways in which the Ottomans imagined themselves and their spatial contexts and to ponder the ways in which that self-mapping does and does not correspond to ways in which historians and early modern European contemporaries have mapped the Ottomans.[61]

Narratives of power

The sultan measured his domains in terms of lands, seas, reputation, and submission. He was the "Lord of the two seas and two continents" and the "Refuge of the World" (*alempenah*), both titles designating space, but more than that designating expansive power and authority. Ottoman rhetorics are reflected in a letter sent to King Louis XIV of France announcing the accession of Süleyman III in 1687. This letter describes the sultan as master of the world (*cihandar*), ruler of the well-protected lands, a lord whose name is read in the *hutbe* (Friday prayer sermon) in the Holy Places and in all the mosques of the believers, and inscribed on the coins issued by numerous mints. The sultan's domain is characterized as having administrative units and officers of varying rank, but the boundedness of his territories is not a critical factor in this projection of sovereign power. Rather, the crucial factors are that his name is known and enunciated in civic and sacred space and his commands obeyed.[62]

Administratively, the empire of the "world-refuge" had two "halves," Rumeli and Anadolu; various big appendages (like Egypt); and provinces (*sancak*s) and sub-provinces from which taxes were levied and provisions mobilized, and to which appointments (of military and legal officials)

[60] Svat Soucek, "Islamic Charting in the Mediterranean," pp. 265–79, in *HOC*, vol. II, book 1, p. 284 (citing Dankoff), on "*esnaf-ı haritaciyan*."
[61] See Ahmet T. Karamustafa, "Introduction to Ottoman Cartography," and "Military, Administrative, and Scholarly Maps and Plans"; and J. M. Rogers, "Itineraries and Town Views in Ottoman Histories," all in *HOC*, vol. II, book 1, pp. 206–8, 209–27, 228–55. Karamustafa argues that Ottoman geographic literature relied primarily on Arabic and, to a lesser extent, Persian classical sources from the mid fifteenth to the mid seventeenth centuries, after which the influences were primarily European (p. 218). Rogers argues that the sixteenth century was a time of experimentation in style and technique using primarily Persian and European influences with a significant rise in European influence by the early seventeenth century (pp. 228–9).
[62] Faik Reşit Unat, *Osmanlı Sefirleri ve Sefaretnameleri*, Türk Tarih Kurumu Yayınları, vol. VII, no. 8a (Ankara: Türk Tarih Kurumu Basımevi, 1987), pp. 28–9.

were made.[63] Land frontiers were measured in terms of fortresses held, transport routes protected, villages incorporated, and local lords persuaded or forced to submit.[64] Sea frontiers were counted in terms of islands, ports, and coasts that could be more or less defended by small Ottoman fleets. The sultan's sovereignty, however, did not end at the seacoast. It was construed as extending not only across the seas (to North Africa, for example) but onto the seas as well, borne by ships and by the power of the written word. That claim is embodied in an imperial order, dated October 1799 to the *beylerbeyi* (governor-general; provincial governor) of Tunis, which reaffirms the conditions of the treaty between the Ottoman Porte and the French court, and threatens the *beylerbeyi* with considerably more than loss of affection if he continues to turn a blind eye to attacks on French shipping emanating from his territory.[65] Sailing ships at sea, like fortresses on land, became markers of "territory" and of boundaries. The fortresses stayed put, marking bounded space at littorals or in broad landed frontiers; the ships circulated through seascapes claimed by various potentates, carrying the goods and personnel of their "nations" along with them. In this regard, the ships were like envoys or travelers; they embodied their "nations" even when they moved through contested terrain or established themselves temporarily in the lands of sovereigns not their own.[66]

Ottoman chronicles divided the land and seascapes of the world, constructing regions and the peoples who occupied them according to "nation" (for example, *Macar*/Hungarian, and *Macaristan*/the land of the Hungarians) or religion (*ehl-i İslam*/the people of Islam and *dar-ı küffar*/land of the unbelievers). The Ottoman admiral, Sidi Ali Reis, in his

[63] See Halil İnalcık, "Ottoman Methods of Conquest," *Studia Islamica* 2 (1954): 104–29. In Kritovoulos, *History of Mehmed*, p. 17, Mehmed says, "I rule over both Asia and Europe." Also, on the constitution of *sancaks*, see Caroline Finkel, *The Administration of Warfare: The Ottoman Military Campaigns in Hungary, 1593–1606* (Vienna: VWGÖ, 1988), p. 8 and passim. For the language used in counting the administrative space of Rumeli in 1530, see M. Tayyib Gökbilgin, *XV–XVI. Asırlarda Edirne ve Paşa Livası: Vakıflar, Mülkler, Mukataalar* (Istanbul: Üçler Basımevi, 1952), pp. 7–12, and passim.

[64] The Ottomans employed many of the strategies of frontier management suggested in Barfield, *The Perilous Frontier*, pp. 70, 104–5, in his discussion of the relations between the Hsiung-nu and China: extortion relationships, holding territory, raids, supporting frontier rebels, and gift giving. They did not tend to develop "new intermediate states" analogous to Manchuria, but they did to some extent combine Ottoman administrators with local chiefs to craft new governmental units.

[65] A translation of this document is in Daniel Panzac, "L'Adriatique incertaine: capitaines autrichiens, corsaires barbaresques et sultans ottomans vers 1800," *Turcica* 29 (1997): 71–91, see 89–90.

[66] The divisions between the domestic and the foreign are illustrated in many early modern Ottoman and European documents. For one discussion late in our period see Enver Ziya Karal, *Selim III'ün Hat-tı Hümayunları, Nizam-ı Cedit 1789–1807*, T. T. K. Yayınları VII, series no. 14 (Ankara: T. T. K. Basımevi, 1946), pp. 163–202, on the activities of envoys as articulated in Ottoman imperial decrees during the reform period of Selim III (1789–1807).

dramatic saga of a voyage to India, claimed that the sovereign sway of Süleyman II (r. 1520–66) reached all the way to the Indian Ocean littoral, where South Asian Muslims longed to join Süleyman in casting out the Portuguese foe.[67] The chronicle of Kemalpaşazade (d. 1534) describes the exploits of Sultan Süleyman, the "majestic sultan of sea and land, issuer of edicts for the seven climes, whose awe inspiring voice penetrates the six corners of the world and commands the attention of all mankind."[68] Regions in Kemalpaşazade's history of the Ottomans may be circumscribed by rivers, ethnicity, or faith, but he tends not to write of them in terms of "boundaries." One crosses a river and moves into the territory of the Rus, or the Franks, or the "damned infidels." But borders are fuzzy unless marked by specific physical features, and frontiers are wide.[69] In many cases the "border" is that movable space in which enemy armies (or navies) meet in combat.

The Ottomans, like some Europeans, also imagined for themselves a "classical" past, including biblical times, the reign of Alexander, Turkic steppe antecedents, and the life of the Prophet Muhammad. When Mustafa Ali, then Ottoman commander of the port of Jiddah, wrote his description of Cairo in 1599, he introduced it with allusions to Joseph and the pharaohs, and to the Prophet Muhammad's description of the Nile. He called Sultan Mehmed III (1595–1603) the "Solomon-like, Alexander-ranking Monarch who ... is the successful king of the horizons, the fortunate world-ruler of absolute power, the namesake of His Highness the Prophet."[70] Ottoman claims were, thus, not restricted to the caliphate or to Muslim antecedents; they ranged across wide spaces and the multitude of famous monarchs who inhabited the mythologies of the Afro-Eurasian world (Ardeshir, Solomon, Alexander, and Caesar); they were embedded in official documents, legal registers, poems, miniatures, narratives, monuments, and maps.

---

[67] Sidi Ali Reis, *Mir'at ül-Memalik* (Istanbul: İkdam Matbaası, 1313/1987), pp. 22, 27, 94. See also Viorel Panaite, *The Ottoman Law of War and Peace: The Ottoman Empire and Tribute Payers* (Boulder, CO: East European Monographs, New York: Columbia University Press, 2000), for an interesting study of the dimensions and language of Ottoman relations with Balkan states and lords.

[68] See Kemalpaşazade, *Tevarih-i Al-i Osman, X. Defter*, ed. Şefaettin Severcan (Ankara: T. T. K. Basımevi, 1996), pp. 48–53, 86–7, 218–20, for the geography of Ottoman narrative. This famous author (d. 1534) is also known as Ibn-i Kemal.

[69] The term "serhad" is used (e.g. Kemalpaşazade, *Tevarih-i Al-i Osman*, p. 86) in poetic imagery about the Ottoman army "piercing the dikes of the frontier," like a raging torrent. But the boundary here is both physical, territorial (on either side of a river), and conceptual (that movable space at which one army meets another).

[70] Andreas Tietze (trans. and ed.), *Mustafā 'Ālī's Description of Cairo of 1599*, Österreichische Akademie der Wissenschaften Philosophisch-Historische Klasse Denkschriften, Band 120, Forschungen zur Islamischen Philologie und Kulturgeschichte, Band 5 (Vienna: Österreichische Akademie der Wissenschaften, 1975), pp. 25–8.

Ottoman maps

The world map of Piri Reis (*c.* 1470–1554), or at least the segments of it that remain, and his *Kitab-i Bahriye*, "Book of the Sea," are certainly the best-known Ottoman maps. Historians and cartographers have analyzed the Ottoman captain's education, intersections with Columbus, interest in the "New World," desire to please his monarch, and acquaintance with sixteenth-century world maps and portolan charts.[71] But the cartographic context of Piri Reis and the consumption, use, audience, and intent of his works remain the subject of considerable speculation.[72] What can be said in the context of this article is that Piri Reis' *Kitab-i Bahriye* is a set of maps embedded in text that suggests travel guide, celebration of sovereignty, and work of art. Like other atlases of its time it focuses on ports, fortresses, and physical features; its images are not preoccupied with boundaries other than those between navigable and unnavigable space; and it is neither purely representational nor purely practical (Fig. 1.8).

While the discussion of Piri Reis' elaborate charts has centered around their utility for navigation and their depiction of the Americas, the work of another sixteenth-century Ottoman mapmaker, Matrakçı Nasuh (d. 1564), who has received relatively little attention outside the cartographic sphere, is perhaps more revealing. Analysts do not agree on whether Matrakçı was himself a master artist, but he was clearly responsible for the production of a set of campaign accounts illuminated by beautiful and elaborate maps.[73] Like Piri Reis, Matrakçı produced his works as presentation copies for the

[71] On Piri Reis, see Svat Soucek, "Islamic Charting in the Mediterranean," pp. 265–79, in *HOC*, vol. II, book 1; Cengiz Orhonlu, "Hint Kaptanlığı ve Piri Reis," *Belleten* 34 (1970): 234–54; Svat Soucek, *Piri Reis and Turkish Mapmaking after Columbus*, 2 vols. (London: Nour Foundation and Oxford University Press, 1996); and Tom Goodrich, "Supplemental Maps in the Kitab-ı Bahriye of Piri Reis," *Archivum Ottomanicum* 13 (1993–4): 117–41.

[72] Tom Goodrich (personal communication) argues that Piri Reis directly links his text to his images, thus suggesting that the maps were intended to be used as portolans. Maps were, of course, also devised for their artistic, rhetorical, prestige, and entertainment values. See also, concerning early modern Ottoman geographical works, Gottfried Hagen, "Some Considerations on the Study of Ottoman Geographical Writings," *Archivum Ottomanicum* 18 (2000): 183–93.

[73] Most of his manuscripts remain unpublished. On Matrakçı Nasuh, see Halil Sahillioğlu, "Dördüncü Muradın Bağdat Seferi Menzilnamesi," *Belgeler* 2/3–4 (1965): 1–36; Nasûh ül-Silâhî Matrakçı, *Beyān-ı Menāzil-i Sefer-i 'Irākeyn*, ed. H. G. Yurdaydın (Ankara: Türk Tarih Kurumu Basımevi, 1976); Rogers, "Itineraries," pp. 234–45, in *HOC*, vol. II, book 1; Hedda Reindl, "Zu einigen Miniaturen und Karten aus Handschriften Matraqčı Nasuh's," *Islamkundliche Abhandlungen, Beiträge zur Kenntnis Südosteuropas und des Nahen Orients* 16 (1974): 146–71; and Kathryn Ebel, "City Views, Imperial Visions: Cartography and the Visual Culture of Urban Space in the Ottoman Empire, 1453–1603," PhD thesis, University of Texas, 2002.

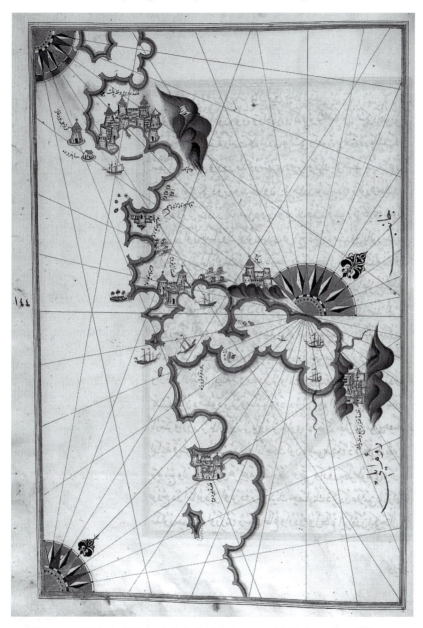

Figure 1.8 Piri Reis, [Kitab-ı Bahriye] Adriatic coast with Dubrovnik and Kotor, no date (possibly a later seventeenth- or eighteenth-century version). Walters Art Museum, no. W. 658, ff. 150 recto. Courtesy of the Walters Art Museum, Baltimore.

sultan, documenting the places he had seen, celebrating conquest, and cultivating patronage.

Matrakçı commissioned the manuscript of *Beyan-ı Menazil-i Sefer-i Irakeyn* ("The Description of the Stages of Sultan Süleyman Khan's Campaign in the Two Iraqs") to commemorate a sultanic campaign in which he himself participated.[74] Explaining the nature of his mapping project, Matrakçı wrote that he was describing:

the captured fortresses, provinces, towns, and places and countries situated between them, caravanserais built for rest; worn out fortresses, ruined places, well-known mountains, difficult straits, renowned rivers, and barren lands, tulips in their meadows, the names, pictures and true realities of the places whose roses were covered with pearls in rose-gardens, and in which places each of these is found over the whole world[,] and new delight taken by frequenting these places and by benefiting from the advantage of each[;] [all these things] were explained one by one in writing and with illustrations in a well ordered, well-arranged, gilded and detailed way.[75]

Like contemporary European mapmakers, Matrakçı focused on fortresses as definitive markers of space, presented his images as representative of "true realities," and envisioned his itinerary in the context of a "world" of seven climes. He measured distance in stages (*menazil*) and in the time it took to march from one stage to another.[76] The idea of *menazil* denotes the stages of a campaign or any journey, marked by cities, towns, rivers to cross, mountain passes, caravansaries, meadows in which to camp, and sacred spaces (religious edifices like tombs, shrines, and sufi lodges) (Fig. 1.9).

Throughout his journey Matrakçı lists the locations of tombs, including the shrines of Imam Husayn in Iraq and other prominent religious figures. His text and images act as a guide of sorts for pilgrims while at the same time legitimizing the sultan who has possessed and redeemed these sacred sites. Interestingly, Matrakçı's maps show no sign of battle or conflict; there

---

[74] Art historians differ on Matrakçı's level of participation in the production of the maps: see Matrakçı, *Beyān-ı*, pp. 132, 151; and Rogers, "Itineraries," pp. 229–30, 239–40. The two Iraqs are Persian Iraq and Arabian Iraq. Yurdadın notes, p. 153, that the topographical information, dates, and place names in the text of this account are very similar to those found in the earlier work (*Münşeat*) of Feridun Bey (which is itself a compilation of earlier works).

[75] Matrakçı, *Beyān-ı*, pp. 131–2. This, Yurdaydın's translation, employs "whole world" for *akalim seb'a*.

[76] Ibid., pp. 134, 173. Matrakçı's account of the first Persian campaign noted dates of departure for each stage; his account of the second Persian campaign gave distances in miles. For an Italian account of the stages on a similar journey, see Giovanni Tommasso Minadoi da Rovigo, *Historia della guerra fra Turchi et Persiani*, Newberry, Case F 5903.578 (1576), pp. 375–6, on getting to Tabriz.

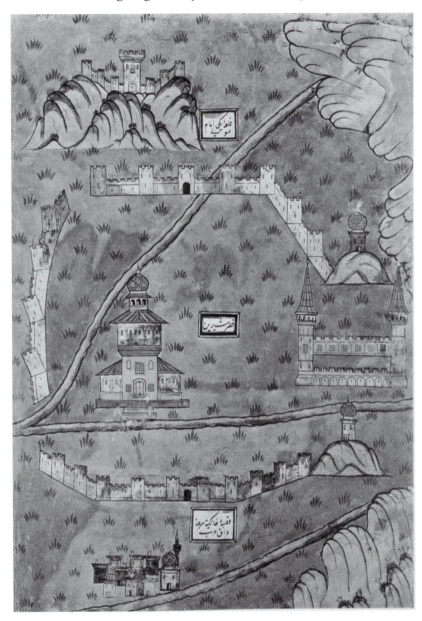

Figure 1.9 Matrakçı Nasuh, "Beyan-ı Menazil-i Sefer-i ʿIrakeyn-i Sultan Süleiman Han." İstanbul Üniversitesi Kütüphanesi, Rare Books Department, MS TY 5964, f.42 verso. This image depicts the fortress, town, and religious structures along the campaign route at the border of "Arab Iraq." Courtesy of T. C., İstanbul Üniversitesi Rektörlüğü Kütüphane ve Dökümantasyon Daire Başkanlığı.

are no human figures, much less roaring cannons or marching troops. One must look to the text for the direct celebration of victory.[77] In Matrakçı's images, boundaries are natural (rivers and mountain passes), not determined by sovereign states. The single reference to a frontier (*serhad*) is that of a regional frontier (between Arabian and Persian Iraq). The Ottomans and Safavids (who ruled Iran) had been engaged in a long series of conflicts over the broad frontier separating their empires; Baghdad had changed hands several times over the course of the early modern era. Yet Matrakçı, despite the claims of his sovereign reflected in his text, does not draw a border between Ottoman and Safavid space. The mental maps of the time seemed not to require such drawing of state boundaries. The narrative did, however, characterize territory as occupied by either enemies (the *kızılbaş* of Shah Tahmasp Safavi in Iran) or supporters of the sultan.[78] That division of space is, of course, reminiscent of various images we have already addressed, whether German woodcuts or Venetian diplomatic reports.

Travel narratives

Ottoman travel accounts possess many similarities to those of contemporary European travelers and envoys. Both emerge out of overlapping contexts of culture, genre, and exigency. Ottoman and European travelers and diplomats were highly conscious of literary precedent. They routinely evoked the descriptions and styles of their travel predecessors.[79] They also expressed the language, cultural preoccupations, knowledge, and ignorance of their day.

Such is the case, for example, in the travel narrative of Yirmisekiz Çelebi Mehmed Efendi, Ottoman ambassador to the French court in 1720–1. Mehmed Efendi sailed on a French ship to Toulon, then made his way to

---

[77] Later images in his manuscripts make more direct references to battle in the context of Süleyman's Mediterranean and Balkan campaigns. See Matrakçı, *Beyān-ı*, p. 130. These later works, however, also suggest travel as an objective. In the *Fethname-i Karabuğdan*, which continues Matrakçı's account of the reign of Süleyman, he notes that "The general aim of Nasuh, known as Matrakçı, who seeks forgiveness of God, being the poorest and the meanest of the soldiers, was that this book should serve as a guide for travelers as well as for those who join in Royal expeditions."

[78] Matrakçı, *Beyān-ı*, *kızılbaş*, pp. 235–8, 250, 265, 272, 275; and references to the religionless enemy (*düşman*) shah, pp. 242, 251.

[79] Rubiés, *Travel and Ethnology*, has addressed some of these questions of genre, style, and tradition in his far-reaching and erudite study of travel narratives on India. He notes (pp. 25–6) the overlap between spatially oriented travel itineraries and temporally oriented historical narratives, but shows the authors' awareness of the different traditions and conventions of the two types. Rubiés also emphasizes the structuring of voyage narratives in terms of a "succession of cities," an organizational framework that is also quite apparent in the visions of Ottoman space.

Paris overland by a circuitous route in order to avoid the ravages of the plague. He measured his travel in miles, days, hours, and in stages from city to city, remarking on natural features, fortifications, palaces, local authorities, safety, food, local customs, and sex.[80] While Mehmed Efendi's travelogue is justly celebrated for its detail, astute observation, and cosmopolitan sensibilities, it nonetheless echoes the measures of space and the concerns of early modern travelers from both sides of the "European" divide.[81]

Diplomats, of course, were not the only Ottoman travelers who recorded their observations of space. Not surprisingly, the modes of marking space found in diplomatic reports mirror those found in other Ottoman narratives – all reflecting the cultural conventions of seeing and telling that characterized their time. The illustrious raconteur Evliya Çelebi, renowned for the detailed, dramatic, and gossipy character of his monumental *Seyahatname*, described his journey through Kosovo in 1660 in much the same terms that Matrakçı charted his own travels through Anatolia, Persia, and Iraq.[82] Fortresses, towns, and shrines frame the territory that Evliya envisions for his readers. Territory is bounded by rivers, travel stations, administrative units, and the notables who belong to those units and owe allegiance to the sultan:

A bowshot from the fortress [of Mitrovica] is the shrine of Mustafa Baba, with a *tekke* [Sufi lodge] inhabited by Bektashi dervishes, where travelers can spend the night. Near this *tekke* is the town of Zveçan, at the utmost frontier [*ahirü'l-hudud*]. This is where the *eyalet* [province] of Bosnia comes to an end. All the notables from the nearby regions of Rumelia gathered at this place in grand procession to wish our master the Paşa a safe journey. They slaughtered animals and distributed

---

[80] Mehmed Efendi, *Le paradis des infidèles: un ambassadeur ottoman en France sous la régence*, ed. Gilles Veinstein (Paris: Librairie François Maspero, 1981), pp. 58–90. The author notes that he must travel to Paris by a circuitous route, "par les frontières" of the province in order to avoid the plague (p. 66). Veinstein employs the earlier French translation from the Ottoman of Julien-Claude Galland.

[81] See also, for another vision of the Ottoman-European divide, Itzkowitz and Mote, *Mubadele*, on the exchange of envoys which took place (July 13, 1775) on a raft in the middle of the Dniester River. The river was the territorial edge, a shared rather than owned space. Yet both Russian and Ottoman accounts depicted the frontier zone as broad and multicultural. For a more recent discussion of eighteenth-century Ottoman embassies to Russia, Vienna, and Berlin, see Aksan, *An Ottoman Statesman*. For an analysis of how a nineteenth-century Ottoman statesman measured European space in terms of its culture and technology, see Carter Findley, "An Ottoman Occidentalist in Europe: Ahmed Midhat Meets Madame Gülnar," *American Historical Review* 103/1 (1998): 15–50.

[82] Evliya was one of the sultan's *kuls*, a member of the military-administrative class and well known for his multi-volume account of his far-flung travels through and beyond the Ottoman realms. See Evliya Çelebi, *Evliya Çelebi in Albania and Adjacent Regions (Kosovo, Montenegro, Ohrid), The Relevant Sections of the Seyahatname*, trans. and ed. Robert Dankoff and Robert Elsie (Leiden: Brill, 2000), pp. 11–23.

the meat to the poor. Our master the Paşa performed two prostrations at the Zveçan mosque and distributed alms.[83]

Evliya's Ottoman space is clearly socially full rather than "socially empty." Where Matrakçı shows the fortresses and shrines, Evliya shows the dervishes who serve the shrines and the people who worship at them. As his journey progresses, the author speaks of hours traveled to mark distance. In each town or city he counted its edifices (houses, mosques, madrasas, bazaars, schools, khans, baths, courts, tombs, and *tekkes*) and provided comments on local custom, culture, and historical background:

In the bazaar [at Prishtina] is the bathhouse of Sultan Mehmed the Conqueror. It has become a pilgrimage site, because a certain saint once performed a forty-day retreat in a cell to the right of the bathhouse and uttered the following prayer, "My Lord, if anyone sick enters this cell, may he find a cure."[84]

The inhabitants of Vushtrria are Rumelians. Most of them do not speak Bosnian but do speak Albanian and Turkish. They wear broadcloth garments and frontier-style red calpacs with low crests of fur and sable. They turn around [?] the fur of their calpacs, and black silken fringes are visible on the edges. They ... wear red trousers with silver buttons and elegant *kubadi* shoes. Such is the fine dress of the Rumelians.[85]

Evliya, for his wealth of detail, is an exceptional source, but his attention to garments, language, and ethnicity call to mind the narratives of our other travelers. Geography was both physical and cultural just as space was both human and sacred.

CONCLUSION

These early modern visions of Ottoman space, projected from within or disseminated from without, suggest some of the distortions in our contemporary models for mapping the Ottomans. The "state" as a sort of default starting point for discussion of space does not coincide with early modern representations.[86] Nor does Lewis and Wigen's definition of a "large socio-spatial grouping delimited largely on the ground of shared history and culture" coincide geographically with the Ottoman entity. That grouping's

---

[83] Ibid., p. 13. When Evliya describes how the *eyalet* is bordered, he mentions towns, fortresses, other *eyalets* and *sancaks*, and Venetian territory.

[84] Ibid., p. 23.   [85] Ibid., p. 17.

[86] The "state" meant something rather different to early modern authors. One need only look, for example, at the Ottoman (and general Middle Eastern) conception of *devlet*, a term that meant state, government, its territory, sovereign power, good fortune, the overturning of rule, and the cycles of change.

definitive cultural element would have to be Islam; but the core Ottoman lands, those with which European societies were principally concerned, were full of zimmis (non-Muslim subjects of a Muslim state) and of ambivalent client governors. Shared culture meant more than religious unanimity. A "geographic" and cultural structure like Hodgson's Afro-Eurasian Oikumene fits more closely because it is, by definition, characterized by the mixing of cultures, its borders are porous, and its essential element is the circulation of ideas and goods.[87] Conversely, if we take Abu-Lughod's trade circuits and city nodes as a paradigm more coincident with early modern representations of space, we still need to fit in pilgrimage and war, two sources of movement and exchange which played prominent roles in early modern Ottoman and European conceptions of space.

Between the sixteenth and the eighteenth centuries, European narrators and mapmakers found the terms to translate parts of Europe and Ptolemy's "first part of Asia" into the sovereign space of the "Great Turk." But they did so while preserving the terms and images of classical myth, history, and Christian memory. Measurements became more precise; landscapes and seascapes were crafted to include more than socially empty space or armadas of "Christians" arrayed against "Turks," such as those drawn to commemorate the Battle of Lepanto in 1571. The Afro-Eurasian Oikumene was bounded and labeled with contemporary empires and states. And yet cities, fortresses, and ports (extracted from their "state" contexts) were still

[87] Albert Hourani, *History of the Arab Peoples* (Cambridge, MA: Harvard University Press, 1991), also uses this idea of the Oikumene to suggest legal and cultural but not economic unity. Two other models for a discussion of divisions and frontiers are those posed by Richard Eaton, *The Rise of Islam and the Bengal Frontier, 1204–1760* (Berkeley, CA: University of California Press, 1993); and Cemal Kafadar, *Between Two Worlds: The Construction of the Ottoman State* (Berkeley, CA: University of California Press, 1995), pp. 151–3. Eaton looks at the diffusion of culture and its intersection with economic and political factors over the long term. He examines, for example (p. 207), associations of popular holy men with the nature of land usage as one mode by which the frontier can be identified. His "frontiers" are demographic and ecological as well as physical and political. Kafadar is concerned with the ways in which the Ottoman polity was constructed, politically and rhetorically, in the fifteenth century. His model looks at "the tension between state building and frontier activities." The Ottoman conquest of Constantinople "spelled the definitive end of the frontier areas (the *ucāt*) as assembly plants of new political enterprises and of the Ottoman polity as a frontier principality." Frontier warriors were "definitively subjugated." In the century after 1453, the state was "codified" and its institutional and cultural parameters set: "The century following the conquest of Constantinople witnessed not only further conquests to expand the empire as territory but also institutional developments that consolidated the empire as state" (p. 153). Thus, in Kafadar's view, the Ottoman state was consolidated just as the period with which we are concerned begins. While I am inclined to emphasize the continuation of these frontier dynamics and the cultural and commercial exchanges which muted the power struggles of lords at the center and in the frontier areas, I think Kafadar's model of the notables' struggle for power provides a useful starting point for a more complex discussion of the Ottoman frontier (if for no other reason than that the parameters of "the state" are clarified).

addressed as the essential markers of distance, space, and identity. Travel was a powerful and primary frame by which space was imagined: to relate the logistics and distances of real travel as carefully as possible, or to draw the reader-viewer into realms through which he or she would never physically pass. Maps collapsed both time and space to accomplish these purposes and there was no incongruity in such acts of collapsing. Contemporary travelers and those long dead walked the map of Ottoman space as authorities for the places and habits of "the Turk." Ottoman maps were also compelled by the travel imperative and by the inclination to project sovereign power beyond the boundaries of the territory that the sultan's armies could possess. Borders, in varying forms, were recognized; but they were subordinated, as they were so often in European maps, to the forces of history, religion, ambition, logistics, and the frailty of political claims when confronted with more formidable physical or cultural realities.

PART II

Limits to empire

2

Negotiating with the Renaissance state: the Ottoman Empire and the new diplomacy

Daniel Goffman

Fifteenth- and sixteenth-century scholarship on the political and diplomatic life of the Italian peninsula has emphasized the striking lack of outside threats. In such a vacuum, the argument goes, Italian states, and especially Florence, Milan, and Venice, were left alone to develop their own innovative diplomatic and political systems and strategies. Powerful empires such as the French, the Ottoman, and the Spanish certainly threatened Italy, but their principal roles, at least until the French invasion of 1494, have been envisioned as little more than a vague and distant rumbling. Instead, our focus has been on internal transformations – especially in the establishment of a "balance of power" between Milan, Venice, Florence, Naples, and the Papal States and an attendant organization of resident embassies in each other's city-states.[1] In other words, historians have concentrated on the Italians themselves when we study the Italian peninsula's politics and diplomacy during the fifteenth century. We have not allowed ourselves to consider the possibility that outsiders played substantive, even essential and constructive roles in the formation of the Renaissance political and diplomatic network.

Envisioning the Ottoman state as little more than a distant outside threat to Italy neglects a vital component in the development of Renaissance diplomacy. Instead, not only were the Ottomans an ever-present menace to the peninsula, but there was also an inventive and productive side to Italian–Ottoman relations, especially in the spheres of commerce and diplomacy. In fact, by examining the experiences of Italian settlements in the Ottoman Empire (as well as Italian experiences in those states that

---

[1] The classic study is Garrett Mattingly, *Renaissance Diplomacy* (Boston: Houghton Mifflin, 1955). More recent works have considerably refined the arguments of Mattingly and others, but have fundamentally followed their lead. See, for example, Daniela Frigo (ed.), *Politics and Diplomacy in Early Modern Italy: The Structure of Diplomatic Practice, 1450–1800*, trans. Adrian Belton (Cambridge: Cambridge University Press, 2000). For an overview, see M. S. Anderson, *The Rise of Modern Diplomacy, 1450–1919* (London: Longman, 1993), pp. 1–40.

preceded the Ottomans in the eastern Mediterranean) we can discover revealing antecedents, precedents, and prototypes for the rise of the system of diplomacy that we generally associate with the West, and more specific- ally with the Italian Renaissance. Some of the chief components of this "new diplomacy" that arose in fifteenth-century Italy and soon spread to the rest of western Europe were the resident embassy, the ideas of reciprocity and extra-territoriality, and a charge to gather intelligence on rival and enemy states. Not only did the looming presence of the Ottoman polity make Italy not nearly the vacuum that diplomatic historians have assumed, but that presence, both threatening and offering opportunities for trade and the circulation of ideas, propelled Italian states, and especially the Genoese and Venetians, into innovations that formed new organizations for trade and, in part as a consequence of commercial experimentation, a framework for the new diplomacy.

Our lack of attention to the Ottoman role in the development of diplomacy during the Italian Renaissance derives from at least two sources. First, historians have focused on the French invasion of 1494, and especially on Milanese diplomatic relations with the French court, both as the culmination of Italian diplomacy and as its failing moment.[2] This orienta- tion has swayed us to concentrate almost exclusively upon the internal and virtually self-directed development of Italian diplomacy, its transalpine export, and its advance into the rising states of France, Spain, and England. Second, a tradition of antagonism against the religious faith and military power of the "terrible Turk" has blinded us to the fact that, during the fourteenth, fifteenth and sixteenth centuries, Italian states cultivated com- mercial, diplomatic, and political relations with first the Turkoman emi- rates of western Anatolia and then the Ottomans (as well as other eastern Mediterranean states) as part of their multifaceted struggle to maintain long-established trading empires and to keep Ottoman armies out of the Italian peninsula.[3] Of all Italian states, the Venetians faced these threats the most directly, both in their commercial colonies in Constantinople and elsewhere, and in the Ottoman armies and navies that pushed up the Dalmatian coast and into Adriatic seas. Nevertheless, other states also felt

[2] On which see especially Vincent Ilardi, "The First Permanent Embassy outside Italy: The Milanese Embassy at the French Court, 1464–1494," in Malcolm R. Thorp and Arthur J. Slavin (eds.), *Politics, Religion, and Diplomacy in Early Modern Europe. Essays in Honor of De Lamar Jensen*, special issue of *Sixteenth Century Journal* 27 (1994): 1–18, and more generally David Abulafia (ed.), *The French Descent into Renaissance Italy, 1494–95: Antecedents and Effects* (Aldershot: Variorum, 1995).

[3] In recent years, historians of the Renaissance world have at least acknowledged, if they have not yet delved deeply into, this relationship. See, for example, Jerry Brotton, *The Renaissance Bazaar: From Silk Road to Michelangelo* (Oxford: Oxford University Press, 2002).

the pressure. It should not be forgotten, for example, that some fourteen years before the French invasion, an Ottoman expeditionary force had landed at the southeast Italian port town of Otranto.

This military threat loomed large in the Italian consciousness; nevertheless, the Genoese and Venetian governments never forgot that their commerce depended less and less upon their navies and more and more upon the maintenance of good relations with the Ottomans. After the Fourth Crusade, each of these states had carved maritime empires out of the moribund Byzantium, and each struggled to maintain their eastern Mediterranean and Black Sea holdings in the face of first Byzantine and Seljuk, then Turkoman, and finally Ottoman advances. The story of the protracted and largely defensive wars in which Genoa and Venice engaged during the fifteenth and sixteenth centuries is well known. Less often acknowledged is that both states (as well as the Florentines and other Italians) persisted in commercial and political relations with the Ottomans (and other Islamic frontier states) throughout the period. Least understood is that these interactions, undertaken by individual merchants, diplomats, and religious men along the middle grounds between the Italian and Ottoman Empires, helped spawn new sorts of diplomacy and statecraft.

I would suggest that one of the chief stimulants toward innovation in Renaissance diplomacy was the urgent need that especially Venice felt to accommodate itself to an Ottoman world in the making. Furthermore, without the distinct organization of the Ottoman polity, such originality would have been impossible. In other words, the structures to which we must turn to make sense of the "new diplomacy" were not only Italian; in addition, the ambiguities, the flexibility, and the porosity of an emerging Ottoman world played a critical role.

The very vocabulary of Ottoman statecraft suggests a world in flux.[4] How would an Ottoman have named a foreigner? Whereas a nineteenth-century diplomat may have used the term *ecnebi* (foreigner), and a nineteenth-century layman may have used *firenk* (a Frank, from Europe) in the fifteenth and sixteenth centuries, there were several other possibilities, including *yabanci* (stranger), *misafir* (guest), *muste'min* (alien, or foreign resident), *gavur* (infidel), and even zimmi. The last of these is a particularly striking case. In Islamic law, the zimmi is a non-Muslim subject in an

---

[4] I owe much to discussion with Edhem Eldem for the observations about terminology that follow, and thank him for the use of his unpublished paper: "The 'Other' in an Ottoman Context: Foreigners and Non-Muslims in Istanbul (Fifteenth to Eighteenth Centuries)."

Islamic state. In early Ottoman usage, however, there was considerable confusion over the question of who constituted such a subject, and at what point a visitor to the empire became a person who was a subject of the empire. Such ambiguity in terminology derived in part from three elements: first, from the fact that the Ottoman Empire had expanded so rapidly and that Ottoman society was subsequently cobbled together from a number of civilizations and traditions;[5] second, from the related fact that Ottoman law constituted an uneasy amalgam between Islamic and sultanic sources;[6] and third from the fact that the Ottoman world consisted of a tapestry of differing cultures, upon which the state superimposed its presence in a variety of ways and always incompletely.[7] The ambiguities that resulted certainly helped force Italian sojourners into a diligence about their identities and their rights as visitors.

This elusiveness in terminology extended to those documents that became the legal basis for first Italian and then northwestern European settlement in the empire. These "capitulations," as they are called in the West, were termed *imtiyazat-i ecnebiye* in the nineteenth-century Ottoman world.[8] In documents of the early modern period, however, the Ottomans did not use this phrase. Instead, they tended to refer to them as *ahidname-i humayun* (or "imperial pledge"), a term of somewhat different and much less exact meaning. In fact, the word was used for a gamut of covenants. For example, in 1454 the charter that Mehmed II granted to the newly appointed patriarch of the Greek Orthodox church was called an *ahidname*, as was the document that the same sultan in 1470 presented to the Genoese rulers on the island of Chios, guaranteeing them continued autonomy in return for a tribute. One and a half centuries later, in the 1620s, the government designated as an *ahidname* a document granting to Ottoman Catholic monks the right to roam across the Balkans to advise, and gather revenue from, Ottoman Catholic subjects.[9] The compilers of such *ahidname*s seem to have drawn upon Islamic, sultanic, and even local legal codes as the situations warranted. There is little indication that in the

---

[5] On which see Cemal Kafadar, *Between Two Worlds: The Construction of the Ottoman State* (Berkeley, CA: University of California Press, 1995).

[6] On which see Colin Imber, *Ebu's-Su'ud: The Islamic Legal Tradition* (Stanford, CA: Stanford University Press, 1997).

[7] Cultural studies is providing new theoretical constructs for our understanding of the relationship between "culture" and "law" in particular, on which see Austin Sarat and Thomas R. Kearns (eds.), *Law in the Domains of Culture* (Ann Arbor, MI: University of Michigan Press, 1998).

[8] Confusions over nomenclature are common. *The Encyclopaedia of Islam*, (EI2) for example, anachronistically inserts the entire history of capitulations under the "İmtiyazat" rubric.

[9] See BOA, Ecnebi Defteri 14/2, p. 62, no. 2.

fifteenth or sixteenth centuries Ottoman officials considered the Italian recipients of such *ahidname*s more privileged, or in a substantively different category, than others.

The Sublime Porte justified and couched the particular *ahidname*s that they granted to Italian visitors in Islamic terms. Thus, the *harbi*, foreign, non-Muslim "enemy," upon taking up residency in Ottoman domains, received an *aman*, or safe conduct, and became a *müste'min*, or foreign inhabitant. Theoretically at least, such residency lasted only so long before such visitors became zimmis and thus liable to the rights and impositions of the non-Muslim Ottoman subject. In other words, the Islamic world-view envisioned Genoese, Venetian, and other merchants, negotiators, and travelers as wayfarers on the road toward absorption into an Islamic state and society. It is clear, then, that a potential rupture existed between the growing sense of extra-territoriality (which, as we will see, ironically owed much to Latin-Ottoman relations) that accompanied the emergence of a more modern state in the West and an Ottoman Empire that remained ideologically wedded to a godly view of the state and its relationships with society and other principalities.

The *ahidname* that the Ottoman government bestowed upon the Dalmatian city-state of Dubrovnik (Ragusa) constituted a close model for those given to Venice and other Italian states. In about 1458, Dubrovnik became an Ottoman tributary state; in return for this tribute, the imperial government conferred almost absolute sovereignty upon this city, and also granted its merchants and representatives considerable autonomy within Ottoman borders. Ragusan settlements soon existed in many cities in the Ottoman Balkans and elsewhere. The presence of these Catholic insiders/ outsiders led to friction with Ottoman subjects and administrators who resented the special privileges written into the agreements. Ottoman collectors of the head tax (*cizye*) upon non-Muslim subjects, for example, doggedly but vainly sought to impose this same levy upon the Dubrovnikan merchants who settled in Ottoman Belgrade after its con- quest in 1521.[10] In the early seventeenth century, using the same argument that Ragusan merchants were members of the "Latin community" (*taife*) and consequently that the government could purchase their goods for one- half their market value, local officials seized from them some buffalo hides for the imperial arsenal. The central government, abiding by the stipula- tions of the *ahidname*, ordered the skins returned.[11] In other ways as well, subjects of Dubrovnik were persistently pressured to conform to normative

---

[10] See, for example, BOA, Ecnebi Defteri 13/1, p. 113, no. 5. [11] Ibid., p. 93, no. 4.

behavior for Ottoman subjects. When they purchased gardens, stores, and houses in Ottoman domains, and collectors and provincial officials sought special taxes from them with the argument that "they are like other subjects," the government referred to their *ahidnames* when they ordered municipal judges to protect the Dubrovnikans from such annoyances.[12] The central authorities did the same when provincial officials sought to register inhabitants of districts outside the city of Dubrovnik for levies for oarsmen and irregular soldiering.[13] In short, over a long period, the leaders of Dubrovnik used the privileges written into their *ahidname* to shield their subjects from integration into Ottoman state and society. In other words, they exploited the particularities of Ottoman laws and procedures to construct a type of extraterritoriality.

Italians emulated Dubrovnik by also using their *ahidnames* to defeat potential absorption into the Islamic world. The documents did so by granting foreigners the right not only to remain in the Ottoman Empire indefinitely, but also to do so in accordance with their own rather than Ottoman law. To those of us accustomed to the rigid boundaries between "us" and "them" that characterized both the early modern western European world and the world of the modern nation-state, this condition may seem radical. The Ottomans, however, did not envision the separate status granted to the Italians as exceptional or as a threat to their body politic. Rather, they imagined these foreigners as members of one of myriad communities (or *taifes*) living within the polity. Just as the state bestowed particular privileges upon religious, economic, and social clusters, so did it grant certain favors to subjects of foreign states; just as the state required from its own subjects certain taxes and imposed upon them various sumptuary conditions in return for these privileges, so did it demand from foreign merchants and envoys a surcharge upon goods traded and certain restrictions in residences and attire. In other words, just as sultanic and customary law supplemented and even overrode Islamic law in Ottoman attempts to integrate various peoples into the state's expanding realm, so did the government strive to accommodate a desirable but legally problematic foreign presence in its domain.

The variety of Ottoman legal and social traditions complicated Italian dealings with the Ottoman government, because the terms of the capitulations embodied a developing disparity between normative Islamic law and the historically concrete. As first Italian – and subsequently French, English, and Dutch – settlements progressed, differing interpretations of

---

[12] Ibid., p. 162, no. 1.   [13] Ibid., p. 164, no. 2.

the rights and obligations of alien sojourners led to frequent clashes between officials and foreigners in Istanbul and elsewhere. The roots of the tension lay in the fact that these alien traders, many of whom spent decades in Ottoman port cities, established their own enclaves (often referred to as "nations" or "factories") and more and more expected to retain capitulatory advantage over their Ottoman rivals. Many Ottoman officials, operating within an Islamic world-view, saw things differently, and continued to seek to convert such habitués into Ottoman subjects.

They attempted to do so in diverse ways. For example, even though the capitulatory agreements more and more often covered not only aliens themselves but also their dependants (such as janissary guards, doormen, and translators), in the early seventeenth century Ottoman administrators who were responsible for administering the community of foreigners at Galata, just across the Golden Horn from Istanbul, persistently ventured to collect the head tax from them as if they were unprotected Ottoman subjects. Also in Galata, janissary watchmen, candle makers, and customs collectors tried to collect taxes on meat and suet bought and butchered for the Venetian community as if it were a non-Muslim subject community. Finally, these same officials repeatedly attempted to categorize as non-Muslim subjects (that is, zimmis) Venetian and French merchants who leased shops in the bazaars of Istanbul.[14] Such behavior certainly threatened the self-rule of these communities of foreigners. Nevertheless, the Ottoman officials were behaving in neither venal nor deviant ways. They intended neither to extort, nor to exclude, nor to convert. Rather, without subverting either religious or civil autonomy, their methods were designed to integrate these long-term sojourners into Ottoman society in accordance with Islamic law.

Discrepancies between *ahidname*s and Islamic and local laws created even more confusion in the Ottoman provinces than in the capital city. In the first decade of the seventeenth century, for example, a certain cavalryman named Ali seized a Venetian merchant, Yakmo, on a Bosnian byroad, dragged him off to his home, slit his throat, tossed his "rotting carcass" into a sack, and buried it in his garden.[15] No one doubted that Ali had committed murder, and the local magistrate had him brought to justice. The difficulty was that a municipal judge in the small Bosnian village, near which Ali had abducted the merchant, ordered Yakmo's goods sold and his money and documents confiscated, in accordance with his reading of

[14] See Ibid., p. 28, no. 6; p. 29, no. 4; p. 35, no. 5; p. 144, no. 3; and p. 54, no. 3.
[15] Ibid., p. 52, no. 3.

Islamic laws governing inheritance but contrary to the Venetian *ahidname*. In two other cases, Ottoman tax collectors on the island of Chios and in the port town of Izmir attempted to collect head taxes from Venetian merchants.[16]

Nor was it only Muslim Ottomans who felt confused by (or perhaps took advantage of) the legal discrepancies between the various legal traditions current in the early modern Ottoman world. Christians and Jews were prominent in the collection of taxes in Ottoman domains, and such agents doggedly sought the head tax and other dues from foreigners. In 1618, for example, the Ottoman government countermanded a command secured by a Jewish collector named al-Kaz ordering that the head tax be taken from Venetian merchants residing on Chios.[17] Such conflicts also intruded into the law courts, such as when in 1613 Christian Ottoman subjects living in Izmir refused to accept foreign legal testimony against them, arguing that such "witnesses must be from the zimmis of this place." The state disagreed, ruling that "all misbelievers are alike" in such matters.[18]

These examples reflect the relative openness of the Ottoman world as well as the inescapable misunderstandings of a frontier zone between civilizations. Some foreigners simply merged into this almost aggressively malleable Ottoman world. Most, however, insisted upon the legal and cultural security that their political and social autonomy afforded, and strove to preserve and even augment collective self-rule. In doing so, they merely emulated the practices of countless other Ottoman communities and associations. Unlike Ottoman subjects, though, the innovations that their activities produced were transferable to their home countries. In short, these sojourners developed methods and procedures that became templates for many of the institutions that we associate with the new diplomacy.

The most celebrated *ahidname*, and the model for those that followed, is the one that Mehmed II granted to the Genoese in Galata in 1453 immediately before his conquest of Constantinople. In a solemn pledge, presented as an imperial decree, Mehmed contracted to leave intact the Genoese community council of Pera, grant the district legal and some political autonomy, exempt its Genoese inhabitants from all extraordinary taxes and forced conversion, and concede its alien residents the freedom to trade and travel in Ottoman domains. In return the Latins relinquished

---

[16] Ibid., p. 70, no. 7 and 16/4, p. 65. This was a chronic problem, on which see also 13/1, p. 120, no. 1; 13/1, p. 150, no. 1; and 16/4, p. 56, no. 1.
[17] Ibid., 13/1, p. 178, no. 2.   [18] Ibid., p. 101.

their weapons, quieted their church bells, allowed their town walls to be pierced at strategic spots, and (in the case of permanent inhabitants but probably not of peripatetic merchants) began paying the head tax that symbolized non-Muslim settlement in an Islamic society.[19]

Such an agreement between an Islamic state and a colony of foreigners was hardly unprecedented.[20] It did, however, allow the Genoese merchants to live in this remote world with some security and according to their own laws and religious practices. Similar contracts between the Ottomans and the Venetians and Florentines soon followed, as these Italian states rushed to safeguard their stakes in the commerce of the eastern Mediterranean and Black seas. Northwestern European states were to follow. France and the Ottoman Empire negotiated – but perhaps never ratified – an *ahidname* in 1535–6 during their anti-Habsburg rapprochement, and by the early seventeenth century both the Dutch and the English had followed suit. Such arrangements served to implant foreign diplomatic and cultural presences in the Ottoman realm. Galata not only became the commercial heart of the empire, but also – with its hauntingly western Italianate architecture, churches, lingua franca, and emissaries – was perceived even before 1453 as a Latin outpost in the Levantine world. Similar quarters were soon installed in other Ottoman cities and by the end of the sixteenth century an array of such sites existed.[21]

It was, then, during the fifteenth century that Italian states began earnestly to heed the kingdom looming to the east. It was also during this period that Italy, fashioning a new diplomacy in the political microcosm that was the fragmented world of Renaissance Italy, is said to have invented the system of representation that after 1494 spread westward and northward across Europe, and whose basic pattern is employed to this day in relations between nation-states. As Garrett Mattingly's still persuasive text on this phenomenon puts it: "the immediate result of the absence of severe outside pressures [during the late fifteenth century] was to set the states of Italy free for their competitive struggle with one another, and so to intensify their awareness of the structure and tensions of their own peninsular system." "These pressures," the author continues, "produced the new style of diplomacy. Primarily it developed as one functional

---

[19] See Halil İnalcık, "Ottoman Galata, 1453–1553," in *Première rencontre internationale sur l'empire ottoman et la Turquie moderne, Institut National des Langues et Civilisations Orientales: Maison des Sciences de l'Homme, 18–22 January 1985* (Istanbul: Isis, 1991), pp. 17–31.

[20] On which, see "Imtiyazat," in EI2.

[21] See Edhem Eldem, Daniel Goffman, and Bruce Masters, *The Ottoman City Between East and West: Aleppo, Izmir, and Istanbul* (Cambridge: Cambridge University Press, 1999).

adaptation of the new type of self-conscious, uninhibited, power-seeking competitive organism." From the cauldron a more secularized and institutionalized diplomacy emerged, soon to be adopted by the great European states (Spain, France, and England) to Italy's north and west. Furthermore, Venice was a principal formulator of this new diplomacy and a key actor in this new drama, for "above the welfare of Italy or Christendom, above any considerations of religion or morality, the rulers of Venice preferred ... the self-preservation and aggrandizement of their own republic."[22]

The Ottoman Empire materializes as no more than a shadowy backdrop in this and most other studies of Renaissance diplomacy. Invariably, the key developments are considered to have occurred as a result of the relations of Italian states with each other and with transalpine European kingdoms. And yet, Venice certainly did experience "dire outside pressures" in exactly this period from the battering the Ottomans inflicted upon the Venetian empire and navy. The pope also experienced enough disquietude to cause him to pack his bags when in 1480 an Ottoman navy landed troops in Italy, which, rumor had it, were preparing to march upon Rome. In the eastern Mediterranean world itself, the Ottoman advance certainly pressured Venice and other Italian states into a dramatic modification of their positions.

These Italian experiences in the Ottoman east were critical in the construction of a new diplomacy. They also helped develop an increasingly subtle and profound understanding of the Ottoman world in Venice and elsewhere in Christian Europe, as resident envoys in Istanbul and others helped to unmask (or at least to temper) myths about the impenetrable Orient and the "terrible Turk," formed during centuries of enmity and warfare. Such perceptions did not evaporate; but concrete and realistic details about Ottoman politics and society evolved to supplement them. In short, despite the lack of Ottoman interest in establishing diplomatic missions in other European capitals (none was organized before the eighteenth century), the requirement that Italian states understand the Ottoman system together with the ability of that society to accommodate Christian settlements and missions determined that the empire would lie at the heart of the new diplomacy. Indeed, the formulating of some of the most essential elements of the modern world's diplomatic system – permanent missions, extra-territoriality, reciprocity, and the gathering of intelligence – drew upon the experiences of the directors of Florentine, Genoese, and Venetian settlements in the Ottoman domain.

[22] Mattingly, *Renaissance Diplomacy*, pp. 61 and 95.

From the very beginning, the Italians felt it essential to protect their merchants in the foreign and fearful places of the Ottoman domains, especially from the dire misfortunes of enslavement and apostasy. The Venetians sought to do so in part by appointing permanent representatives (known variously as consuls, *eminis*, or baili (s. bailo)) whose job was not only to shield their subjects from the perils of life in a foreign and perhaps hostile place, but also to fathom and describe in frequent letters and, upon their return to the Republic in *relazioni*, happenings in the Ottoman polity. Beginning in 1454, such a representative always resided in the Ottoman capital.

These envoys functioned similarly to, and may have been models for, the diplomats that in the 1450s Italians began posting in each other's capitals. One of the principal differences, though, was that whereas the earliest resident ambassadors within the Italian peninsula simply confirmed and maintained alliances, the Ottoman appointees also endeavored to collect information about and predict the actions of an alien and dangerous nemesis. The latter, it seems to me, is a rather closer antecedent than is the Italian case to the objectives, say, of Catholic Spaniard diplomats in Protestant England during the late sixteenth century, or even to "democratic" American diplomats in the communist Soviet Union during the late twentieth century. In each case, one of the emissary's principal tasks was to learn as much as possible about an enemy that was as much ideological as political in order to predict, contain, and counter its policies and actions.

The Ottoman precedent for such activities is nowhere better demonstrated than in the *relazioni* that Venetian consuls routinely delivered before the Senate upon recall from postings in the Ottoman capital. As eloquently expressed by Valensi, the goal of these reports was to contain the Turkish advance and to defend Venetian positions. Thoughts of conquest may have been entertained, but for the future: the Venetians had no illusions as to the difficulty of embarking on a venture that required concerted action on the part of the Christian princes. In the meantime, one needed to know the enemy, to take stock of the situation, to find the stress points and fault lines where the Ottoman system might weaken of its own account or where Venice – with or without the other Christian powers – might intervene.[23] The Venetian aristocracy, from which the bailo almost always came, knew the Ottomans well. Its members suffered no illusions about quickly overthrowing the domain, but instead used their

[23] Lucette Valensi, *The Birth of the Despot: Venice and the Sublime Porte*, trans. Arthur Denner (Ithaca, NY: Cornell University Press, 1993), p. 15.

resident diplomats as would any modern state, to help develop a multi-faceted, flexible, and realistic policy toward a dangerous foe.

Just as reminiscent of modern diplomacy as the long-term residency of envoys in Ottoman lands was their acquisition of a form of communal governance that displayed the form, if not the principle, of extra-territoriality. (It should be remembered, though, that the sultan had no intent to grant extra-territoriality at this time or later, but simply sought to find a place for these foreigners in the fabric of Ottoman society.) The shape of such legal autonomy emerges in the Genoese *ahidname* of 1453, and manifested itself with increasing clarity in subsequent capitulations. This stipulation, by which each group of expatriate people enjoyed the right to be judged according to its own codes, aimed to shield aliens from the supposedly cruel and certainly bewildering system of Ottoman-Islamic justice. It was an idea that was utterly foreign to contemporary Christian Europe, locked as it was in the more and more fictitious concept of a universal Christian body politic. The Ottomans, though, knew and used it as an extension of the system by which they administered their non-Muslim subjects.

In a western European context, the issue of freedom of worship lay at the core of the concept of extra-territoriality. In the century or so after the Protestant Reformation, virtually all of western Europe adopted the hopeful fantasy of *cuius regio eius religio* – the idea that the ruler's religion must also be the religion of her or his subjects. In this climate, the display of heretical worship that most envoys demanded and most states proscribed paralyzed diplomatic relations between Catholic and Protestant states. Only in the seventeenth century did the concept of extra-territoriality help resolve this dilemma. For the Ottomans, though, there never was such an issue. Beginning in the fifteenth century, not only did each ambassador and consul have legal jurisdiction over his "nation," but each legate also had a church or a chapel where he, his staff, and his community could worship freely. Again, I would like to emphasize that this situation resembled but did not constitute extra-territoriality in its modern sense for at least two reasons. First, as a stipulation within an *ahidname*, it represented a privilege granted by the sultan rather than a right. Consequently, at any time the state could legally (if from the point of view of Christian Europeans quite arbitrarily) curtail the license. Second, it was based upon a single strand of Ottoman law. Thus, and especially in settlements outside of Istanbul, officials could and did try to undermine and contravene the privilege, often with the justification of Islamic law. Consequently, foreign residents sometimes found themselves suddenly transformed

into Ottoman subjects, the Venetian bailo sometimes found himself imprisoned, the French ambassador was at times expelled, and chapels were occasionally demolished. Nevertheless, no other European state favored
foreigners with such sweeping autonomy until long after the religious wars
of the sixteenth century had helped shatter the idea of universal law.
Thereafter, of course, the invention became and has remained an axiom of
international diplomacy. Surely in Ottoman accommodation of foreign
settlers we find an antecedent, and perhaps even a precedent, for such
extra-territoriality.

Ironically, the Ottomans resisted implementing their own diplomatic
network longer than any other principal European state; it was not until
the eighteenth century that this government began sending reciprocal
resident embassies to European capitals. The state's reluctance to do so
derived in part from its practice of signing only unilateral documents, such
as the *ahidnames*. Equally important, though, was the reluctance of
Christian European governments to countenance the prospect of a community of Muslims settled in their capitals. Nevertheless, even reciprocity
had some antecedents in the Ottoman world, for the sultan's government
insisted upon entering reciprocal rights for their merchants into each
capitulatory agreement. Consequently, western European states had to
allow settlements of Ottoman subjects (although perhaps because of cultural and society impediments rarely Muslim ones) in their principal cities.

These constructs – so similar in form to resident embassies, extra-
territoriality, and reciprocity – constituted the terms that made possible
the implantation of western European islands into the Ottoman body
politic. They also served as archetypes for the development of a new
diplomacy in the rest of Europe. Those who formed them may have
been Italians; nevertheless, it was undoubtedly the Ottoman manner of
structuring society that made such diplomatic advances possible. Having
chosen to allow Christian and Jewish subjects to live according to their own
laws and traditions, and having developed supple legal and societal devices
in order to permit them to do so, it was not a great step for the state to grant
similar rights to foreign visitors.

The Ottoman port cities in which Genoese, Venetian, and other Latin
merchants lived in the fifteenth and sixteenth centuries constituted middle
grounds between two civilizations. As is often the case in such frontier
worlds, this one proved a cauldron for political and economic innovation.
It was not an encounter between equals, however. The Italians were guests
in a vibrant and expanding society, and it was the Ottoman world that
set the conditions of their settlement. The Italians did, however, have

to adapt themselves to Ottoman society and ideology. This process of accommodation taught first the Genoese and Venetians, and later other western Europeans, much about coexisting with a society of differing faith, language, and culture. These sojourners took home with them the lessons learned in this encounter, and used them to help negotiate the new frontiers of a shattered Christendom.

3

Information, ideology, and limits of imperial policy: Ottoman grand strategy in the context of Ottoman–Habsburg rivalry

Gábor Ágoston

INTRODUCTION

In the burgeoning literature on empires – brought about by the dissolution of the Soviet Union and the emergence of the United States as the only dominant global power – most of the attention has been focused on the "modern" empires, especially on the British Empire, and, following a long period of "imperial denial," also on the "American Empire." While this literature occasionally makes references to premodern empires, including that of the Ottomans, the Ottoman Empire has largely been sidelined in recent discourses, and its history remains an exotic one for the broader public. Many of the old myths of the Orientalist and Eurocentric historiography regarding the supposed conservatism, rigidity, and backwardness of the Ottoman Empire, and Islamic polities in general, still dominate non-specialist historiography. In our post-9/11 politically motivated world, works with Orientalist and western biases flourish, and repeat, time and again, the old facile generalizations emphasized by post-World War I nationalist historiography (especially in the Ottoman successor states), or by Marxist and Weberian social sciences. In these works, the Ottoman Empire and its Muslim rivals – Safavid Persia and Mughal India – are portrayed as failed enterprises, which, as early as the late sixteenth century, were lagging behind the emerging "modern" British, Dutch, and French seaborne empires.[1]

---

[1] See, for example, Arthur Goldschmidt, *A Concise History of the Middle East* (Boulder, CO: Westview, 2002); Bernard Lewis, *The Muslim Discovery of Europe*, 2nd edn (London: Phoenix, 1994) and Bernard Lewis, *What Went Wrong? Western Impact and Middle East Response* (New York: Oxford University Press, 2002). Lewis's generalizations about the unqualified "Islamic world" and "the West," his disregard for chronology, as well as his technique of lumping together pieces of "evidence" that are unrelated and stem from different time periods are often misleading. For a sharp critique of his *What Went Wrong?* see Juan Cole's review at http://www.juancole.com/essays/revlew.htm. For a recent historiographical overview of Orientalism, see Zachary Lockman, *Contending Visions of the Middle East: The History and Politics of Orientalism* (Cambridge: Cambridge University Press, 2004).

Students of the Ottoman Empire have cast serious doubts on the paradigm of "Ottoman decline."[2] Comparative studies of the Ottoman, Habsburg, Russian, and Mughal empires have found notable dynamism in these imperial polities. These works have also shown that examining the Ottoman Empire in a comparative framework can substantially enhance our knowledge of this least understood of premodern empires, while also contributing to the greater appreciation of the Ottomans' imperial rivals.[3] Specialized studies have demonstrated the remarkable flexibility and pragmatism of the Ottomans in such different contexts as provincial administration and frontier management, monetary and economic policy, or warfare and war industry.[4]

By examining elements of Ottoman "grand strategy," in the context of Ottoman–Habsburg imperial rivalry, the present chapter intends to contribute to the emerging comparative literature on the Ottoman Empire. Historians of other empires have applied the concept of grand strategy – a global vision of geopolitics, military, economic, and cultural capabilities of states – to explain the formation, strengths, and weaknesses of their imperial polities. Although the term was unknown to policy-makers of

[2] Cornell Fleischer, "Royal Authority, Dynastic Cyclism, and 'Ibn Khaldunism' in Seventeenth-Century Ottoman Letters," *Journal of Asian and African Studies* 18 (1983): 198–220; Douglas A. Howard, "Ottoman Historiography and the Literature of 'Decline' of the Sixteenth and Seventeenth Centuries," *Journal of Asian History* 22 (1988): 52–77, Douglas A. Howard, "With Gibbon in the Garden: Decline, Death and the Sick Man of Europe," *Fides et Historia* 26 (1994): 22–34; Linda Darling, *Revenue-Raising and Legitimacy: Tax Collection and Finance Administration in the Ottoman Empire 1560–1660* (Leiden: Brill, 1996), pp. 1–21, and Cemal Kafadar, "The Question of Ottoman Decline," *Harvard Middle Eastern and Islamic Review* 4 (1997–8): 30–75.

[3] See, for instance, Palmira Brummett, *Ottoman Seapower and Levantine Diplomacy in the Age of Discovery* (Albany, NY: State University of New York Press, 1994); Virginia Aksan, "Locating the Ottomans among Early Modern Empires," *Journal of Early Modern History* 3 (1999): 103–34; Daniel Goffman, *The Ottoman Empire and Early Modern Europe* (Cambridge: Cambridge University Press, 2002); Dominic Lieven, *Empire: The Russian Empire and its Rivals* (New Haven, CT: Yale University Press, 2002); Molly Greene, *A Shared World: Christians and Muslims in the Early Modern Mediterranean* (Princeton, NJ: Princeton University Press, 2000); Suraiya Faroqhi, *The Ottoman Empire and the World around it* (London: I. B. Tauris, 2004); Sanjay Subrahmanyam, "'A Tale of Three Empires,' Mughals, Ottomans, and Habsburgs in a Comparative Context," *Common Knowledge* 12 (2006): 66–92.

[4] Gábor Ágoston, "A Flexible Empire: Authority and its Limits on the Ottoman Frontiers," *International Journal of Turkish Studies* 9 (2003): 15–31; Şevket Pamuk, *A Monetary History of the Ottoman Empire* (Cambridge: Cambridge University Press, 2000); Şevket Pamuk, "Institutional Change and the Longevity of the Ottoman Empire, 1500–1800," *Journal of Interdisciplinary History* 35 (2004): 225–47; Rhoads Murphey, *Ottoman Warfare, 1500–1700* (London: UCL Press, 1999); Virginia Aksan, "Ottoman War and Warfare, 1453–1812," in Jeremy Black (ed.), *War in the Early Modern World* (London: UCL Press, 1999), pp. 147–75; Gábor Ágoston, "Ottoman Warfare, 1453–1826," in Jeremy Black (ed.), *European Warfare, 1453–1815* (London: St. Martin's Press, 1999), pp. 118–44; Gábor Ágoston, *Guns for the Sultan: Military Power and the Weapons Industry in the Ottoman Empire* (Cambridge: Cambridge University Press, 2005).

past empires, recent scholarship has argued that it is possible to discern and reconstruct such global strategic visions that informed imperial policy and mobilized economic and human resources to achieve policy goals.[5]

The primary purpose of this chapter is to stimulate debate concerning sixteenth-century Ottoman grand strategy (or the lack of it). The following are preliminary results of an ongoing research project that examines Ottoman geopolitics, imperial ideology, economics, and the military in an era of Ottoman–Habsburg and of Ottoman–Russian rivalries.

The main thesis is that the reign of Süleyman I (1520–66) witnessed the formation of what may be called Ottoman grand strategy. This involved the formulation of an imperial ideology and a universalist vision of empire; the collection of information both within and outside the borders of the empire which helped the integration of the Ottomans into European politics and political culture; the elaboration of a foreign policy and propaganda – based partly on knowledge acquired through the channels of Ottoman intelligence-gathering – that furthered the Ottomans' vision of empire; and the mobilization of the empire's human and economic resources and military power in the service of imperial policy. The essay also shows that the application of this grand strategy involved a great deal of pragmatism and flexibility. While ideology and propaganda were important for legitimizing Ottoman power, especially domestically, policy decisions were made after careful analysis of intelligence and policy options, just as in Spain or Austria. In this regard the Ottomans and their Habsburg rivals did not differ much from the "modern" and rational British, Dutch, and French overseas empires.

Many elements of the Süleymanic grand strategy were already present under the Sultan's predecessors. However, changed geopolitics in the early decades of the sixteenth century – most notably the emergence of the Safavids and the Habsburgs as the Ottomans' major rivals – required adjustments in imperial strategy. This essay concentrates on the collection of information and the evolution of Ottoman imperial ideology and policy in the context of Habsburg–Ottoman rivalry. Although the first half of the sixteenth century saw both the Habsburgs and the Ottomans with multiple policy commitments – the Habsburgs were preoccupied with German Protestantism and France, and Safavid Shi'ism hit closer

---

[5] E. N. Luttwak, *The Grand Strategy of the Roman Empire from the First Century to the Third* (Baltimore, MD: Johns Hopkins University, 1976); Geoffrey Parker, *The Grand Strategy of Philip II* (New Haven, CT: Yale University Press, 1998); John P. LeDonne, *The Grand Strategy of the Russian Empire, 1650–1831* (Oxford: Oxford University Press, 2004).

to home for the Ottomans than did the Habsburg advance in the Mediterranean – Habsburg–Ottoman rivalry remained a major theme in international politics. In a recent comparison of Ottoman and Habsburg imperial ideologies and political propaganda – advanced most effectively by Grand Vizier Ibrahim Pasha (1523–36) and Mercurino Arborio de Gattinara, Charles V's Grand Chancellor (1518–30), respectively – I have tried to demonstrate how religion, millenarianism, and competing Habsburg and Ottoman universalist visions of empire were used to strengthen the legitimacy of the two rulers in their own empires and also within the larger Muslim and Christian communities. I have also shown how Habsburg military success against Ottoman Islam (and German Protestantism) as well as Ottoman victories against Habsburg Catholicism (and Safavid Shi'ism) formed an integral part of Habsburg and Ottoman propaganda.[6] While I contend that ideology played a greater role in formulating Ottoman strategy and policy decisions than usually appreciated, I also argue that it was not ideology but a rather pragmatic approach, often in response to the many challenges the early sixteenth-century Ottoman Empire faced, that mattered in the day-to-day conduct of foreign and military affairs. Possessing up-to-date information about Istanbul's rivals was a *sine qua non* of conducting a viable Ottoman foreign policy that also attempted to counter Habsburg aspirations and claims to universal sovereignty.

OTTOMAN INTELLIGENCE AND COMMUNICATIONS

Ottoman information-gathering and decision-making are among the least understood subjects of early modern Ottoman history. Thus it is hardly surprising that sweeping generalizations regarding the Ottomans' supposed lack of knowledge about Europe, their allegedly insufficient understanding of European politics and flawed foreign policy decisions vis-à-vis European affairs continually resurface in the literature. These statements are not only based on anecdotal evidence but also suggest a static view of Ottoman history, as if Ottoman institutions and policy-making techniques had remained unchanged throughout the empire's existence from the early 1300s until the end of World War I.[7] Owing to the nature and

---

[6] Gábor Ágoston, "Ideologie, Propaganda und politischer Pragmatismus: Die Auseinandersetzung der osmanischen und habsburgischen Grossmächte und die mitteleuropäische Konfrontation," in Martina Fuchs, Teréz Oborni and Gábor Újvári (eds.), *Kaiser Ferdinand I. – Ein mitteleuropäischer Herrscher* (Münster: Aschendorff, 2005), pp. 207–33.

[7] See, for example, Lewis, The *Muslim Discovery of Europe*, and Lewis, *What Went Wrong?*

availability of Ottoman source material as well as the lack of research on Ottoman intelligence- and data-gathering, Ottomanist historians cannot dream about the nuanced studies of collection and processing of information we possess, say, regarding the Venetians or the Spanish Habsburgs.[8] However, available evidence suggests that in the sixteenth century, similarly to their rivals, the Ottomans possessed a structured information-gathering network, the main layers of which are not difficult to reconstruct.

Following the example of medieval Muslim states and their Seljuk predecessors in Asia Minor, the Ottomans placed great emphasis on the collection of information both at home and abroad. In the words of Mustafa Ali of Gallipoli, the late sixteenth-century Ottoman bureaucrat and historian:

> If a prospering monarch does not use spies secretly, if the sovereign of the realm does not investigate the conditions of the state and people, if he contents himself with only questioning and believing his ministers, if he only sporadically commands that his *ağas*, who are privy to his secrets, keep him informed, then he forfeits justice for himself, integrity for his ministers, awe and dread for his army, and peace of mind and comfort for his subjects. For whenever leadership and oversight are not paired like twins, and deceiving persons who favor oppression and injustice do not receive the retribution they deserve, then neither do the countries of the world flourish and prosper, nor are the lives and livelihoods of the people blessed with repose in safety and security.[9]

Domestic intelligence was collected, among other ways, through the janissaries, the elite soldiers of the sultan's standing infantry corps, who also acted as military police and played an important role in domestic surveillance. Under the supervision of lower-rank janissary officers, agents were sent out in plain clothes to patrol the markets, bazaars, coffeehouses, and taverns of Istanbul and other major cities, and prepared daily reports for

---

[8] For the Venetian information-gathering service see Paolo Preto, "La guerra segreta: spionaggio, sabotaggio, attendati," in Maddalena Redolfi (ed.), *Venezia e la difesa de Levante da Lepanto a Candia, 1570–1670* (Venice: Arsenale, 1986) pp. 79–85, and Paolo Preto, *I servizi segreti di Venezia* (Milan: Il Saggiatore, 1994). For earlier intelligence-gathering by Venice and other Italian states regarding the Ottomans see Kate Fleet, "Turks, Italians and Intelligence in the Fourteenth and Fifteenth Centuries," in Çiğdem Balım-Harding and Colin Imber (eds.), *The Balance of Truth. Essays in Honour of Professor Geoffrey Lewis* (Istanbul: Isis, 2000), pp. 99–112. An excellent study of Philip II's information and communications services and how the gathered information was processed and utilized is Parker, *The Grand Strategy of Philip II*, ch. 2.

[9] Mustafa Ali, *Meva'idü'n-Nefa'is fi Kava'idi'l-Mecalis. Tables of Delicacies Concerning the Rules of Social Gatherings*, trans. Douglas S. Brookes (Cambridge, MA: Harvard University Press, 2003), p. 25. On Mustafa Ali, see Cornell Fleischer, *Bureaucrat and Intellectual in the Ottoman Empire: The Historian Mustafa Ali (1541–1600)* (Princeton, NJ: Princeton University Press, 1986).

the grand vizier.[10] Central and local Ottoman authorities likewise
employed a large number of informers. The division of labor between
the provincial and district governors (*beylerbeyi*s and *sancakbeyi*s) on the
one hand, and the judges on the other, not only balanced the power of local
Ottoman officials but also acted as a control mechanism in the process of
the collection of information in the provinces. Judging from the numerous
orders issued by the Imperial Council or Divan addressing matters
conveyed to them either by informers or by local Ottoman officials, incoming information from the provinces concerned a great variety of issues that
ranged from adultery and prostitution to misuse of authority by local
officials and garrison soldiers.[11] The range of issues dealt with in the
imperial decrees preserved in the *mühimme* registers (imperial record
books) also suggests a considerable degree of information-based surveillance on the part of the central government and its local agents, a topic that
deserves further study.

It seems that the general "mapping" of the ruler's realms, similar to those
initiated but only partially accomplished by Philip II,[12] was never attempted by the Ottomans. However, the "mapping" of the Ottoman Empire
through regular and surprisingly systematic land/revenue surveys (*tahrir*s)
under Sultan Süleyman I afforded the Istanbul government and its provincial administrators a detailed and collated database regarding the size,
composition, and economic conditions of the population of Ottoman sub-
provinces. Although Ottoman tax registers are perhaps the best studied
documents in Ottoman history,[13] they have not been used to assess the
empire's capabilities regarding data-gathering and processing and to

[10] Robert Mantran, *Istanbul dans la seconde moitié du XVIIe siècle* (Paris: A. Maisonneuve, 1962),
pp. 160–1; Robert Mantran, *XVI–XVII. Yüzyılda İstanbul'da Gündelik Hayat* (Istanbul: n.p.,
1991), p. 80.
[11] Several such cases can be studied on the basis of the Mühimme Defterleri or registers of "important
affairs" preserved in the Başbakanlık Osmanlı Arşivi (BOA) or Prime Minister's Ottoman Archives.
Of the Mühimme Defterleri [= MD] volumes 3, 5, 6, 7, 12, 82, 83, 85, and 113 have been published by
the staff of the Archives. References are to the original volumes, in the case of the published ones to
the facsimile editions. See, for instance, MD 6, p. 567 (regarding a *sipahi* who married a prostitute);
MD 75, p. 227, n. 471 (regarding a wife of a janissary who committed adultery with a Christian
subject); MD 3, p. 304, n. 890 (regarding a false *defterdar*); MD 6, p. 23 (regarding falsification and
misuse of kadi seals); MD 6, pp. 82 and 235 (regarding counterfeiting coins); and MD 10, p. 67
(embezzlement of the former governor of Temeşvar).
[12] For Philip II's mapping of his empire see Parker, *The Grand Strategy of Philip II*, pp. 59–63.
[13] On which see Gyula Káldy-Nagy, "The Administration of the Sanjaq Registrations in Hungary,"
Acta Orientalia Academiae Scientiarum Hungaricae 21 (1968): 181–223; Heath W. Lowry, "The
Ottoman *Tahrir Defterleri* as a Source for Social and Economic History: Pitfalls and Limitations,"
in H. W. Lowry, *Studies in Defterology: Ottoman Society in the Fifteenth and Sixteenth Centuries*
(Istanbul: Isis, 1992), pp. 3–18; Colin Heywood, "Between Historical Myth and Mythohistory: The
Limits of Ottoman History," *Byzantine and Modern Greek Studies* 12 (1998): 315–45, reprinted in

elaborate on the nature of the early modern Ottoman state and its relationship to its inhabitants in the context of information-based surveillance.
Nonetheless, it is safe to say that Ottoman decision-makers had a great
array and variety of data at their disposal: detailed and summary land/
revenue surveys; provincial law codes (*liva kanunnameleri*) that summarized the main regulations regarding taxation and taxes, often registering a
multitude of pre-Ottoman regulations;[14] registers that contained daily
recordings of bestowals of tax benefices (*timar*);[15] a host of financial records
available in the Financial Department;[16] as well as the copies of Imperial
Decrees,[17] and so on. Whenever decision-makers in the Imperial Council
needed such records or had to check the validity of data presented by
petitioners or lower-rank officials, they could get the relevant information
from the pertinent bureaus. Since the most important registers traveled
with the army, information to act upon promptly while on campaign was
available even in wartime.[18] These and similar records afforded the Istanbul
government with "long institutional memories."[19]

In addition to domestic data-gathering and home intelligence, the
Ottoman government also collected information about its neighbors
and adversaries. Such intelligence concerned the enemies' policy decisions
and politics, especially vis-à-vis the Ottomans, as well as their military
and economic strengths and weaknesses. At least four levels of Ottoman
information-gathering may be discerned: (1) central intelligence in Istanbul,

C. Heywood, *Writing Ottoman History: Documents and Interpretations* (Aldershot: Ashgate, 2002); Halil İnalcık and Donald Quataert (eds.), *An Economic and Social History of the Ottoman Empire, 1300–1914* (Cambridge: Cambridge University Press, 1994).
[14] On which see Heath W. Lowry, "The Ottoman Liva Kannunames contained in the Defter-i Hakani," in Lowry, *Studies in Defterology*, pp. 19–46; Ahmed Akgündüz, *Osmanlı Kanunnameleri ve Hukuki Tahlilleri*, 9 vols. (Istanbul: FEY Vakfı, 1990–6).
[15] These registers – called *ruznamçes* and kept in the Ottoman Imperial Registry (Defter-i hakani/ Defterhane) – contained chronological recordings of certificates (*tezkeres*) issued to timariots either by provincial governors or by the central administration, as well as the final diplomas (*berat*) of bestowals, issued by the Imperial Council. See D. A. Howard, "The Historical Development of the Ottoman Imperial Registry (*Defter-i hakani*): Mid-Fifteenth to Mid-Seventeenth Centuries," *Archivum Ottomanicum* 11 (1986[1988]): 213–30.
[16] On which see Darling, *Revenue-Raising and Legitimacy*.
[17] From the latest literature, see Géza Dávid, "The Mühimme Defteri as a Source for Ottoman–Habsburg Rivalry in the Sixteenth Century," *Archivum Ottomanicum* 20 (2002): 167–209.
[18] On the Ottoman Chancery and central bureaucracy, see Josef Matuz, *Das Kanzleiwesen Süleyman des Prächtigen* (Wiesbaden: F. Steiner, 1974); Klaus Röhrborn, *Untersuchungen zur osmanischen Verwaltungsgeschichte* (Berlin: De Gruyter, 1974). Regarding "traveling Ottoman archives" see Feridun Emecen, "Sefere Götürülen Defterlerin defteri," in *Prof. Dr. Bekir Kütükoğlu'na Armağan* (Istanbul: Edebiyat Fakültesi Basımevi, 1991), 241–68.
[19] For the importance of various survey registers for the student of the Ottoman Empire see Halil İnalcık and Şevket Pamuk (eds.), *Osmanlı Devleti'nde Bilgi ve İstatistik* (Ankara: T. C. Başbakanlık Devlet İstatistik Enstitüsü, 2000). I have borrowed the term "long institutional memory" from Parker, *The Grand Strategy of Philip II*.

(2) information-gathering by local Ottoman authorities, especially along the empire's frontiers, (3) intelligence provided by Istanbul's client or vassal states, and (4) espionage and counter-espionage carried out by the Porte's spies and saboteurs in foreign countries.[20]

Intelligence-gathering in Istanbul

While Ottoman information-gathering never quite reached the level of sophistication of the Venetian and Spanish intelligence services, it served Ottoman policy-makers well. Contemporaries were often surprised how well informed the Ottomans were about both major political and military events in Europe and about less important day-to-day policy decisions. News regarding the fire in the Venetian Arsenal in September 1569 and the defeat of the Spanish Armada in 1588 are just two of the most revealing examples in this regard. The Ottomans quickly learned about the 1569 Arsenal fire, purportedly from Joseph Nassí, a member of the influential Jewish Mendes family with numerous agents and vast commercial networks in Europe, who had relocated to Istanbul and become a confidant of several grand viziers.[21] No wonder Süleyman called Nassí "the true mirror, in which he saw all the developments in Christendom and from

[20] For an assessment of the Ottoman information-gathering system, see Gábor Ágoston, "Információszerzés és kémkedés az Oszmán Birodalomban a 15–17. században" [Information-Gathering and Spying in the Ottoman Empire in the Fifteenth to Seventeenth Centuries] in Tivadar Petercsák and Mátyás Berecz (eds.), *Információáramlás a magyar és török végvári rendszerben* (Eger: Heves Megyei Múzeum, 1999), pp. 129–54; Gábor Ágoston, "Birodalom és információ: Konstantinápoly, mint a koraújkori Európa információs központja," [Empire and Information: Constantinople as Center of Information Gathering in Early Modern Europe] in Gábor Hausner and László Veszprémi (eds.), *Perjés Géza Emlékkönyv* (Budapest: Argumentum, 2005), pp. 31–60, an extended English-language version of which will be published in a forthcoming edited volume on the subject. On Ottoman sources of information in general see Faroqhi, *The Ottoman Empire and the World around it*, pp. 179–210.

[21] The Venetians were convinced that the war of 1570–3, which led to the famous Battle of Lepanto in 1571 and ended with the Ottoman conquest of Cyprus, had been "launched against them by the Turks on account of espionage and the evil machinations of Jews." Some even suspected that the agents of Nassí caused the fire to destroy the navy of Istanbul's Mediterranean rival. See Brian Pullan, *The Jews of Europe and the Inquisition of Venice, 1550–1670*, 2nd edn (New York: I. B. Tauris, 1997), p. 179; Benjamin Arbel, "Venezia, gli ebrei e l'attività di Salomone Ashkenasi nella Guerra di Cipro," in Gaetano Cozzi (ed.), *Gli Ebrei e Venezia secoli XIV–XVIII. Atti del Convegno internazionale organizzato dall'Istituto di storia della società e dello stato veneziano della Fondazione Giorgio Cini*, Venice, Isola di San Giorgio Maggiore, June 5–10, 1983 (Milan: Edizione Comunità, 1987), p. 172. For the Venetians' belief in "a Jewish plot" against their republic prior to the war and for a more nuanced assessment regarding Nassí's possible role, see Benjamin Arbel, *Trading Nations: Jews and Venetians in the Early Modern Eastern Mediterranean* (Leiden: Brill, 1995), pp. 55–63. On the family, and especially on its founder, Señora Gracia Mendes (Luna), see Marianna D. Birnbaum, *The Long Journey of Gracia Mendes* (Budapest and New York: Central European University Press, 2003), which also lists earlier works.

which he obtained information about all countries."²² The information regarding the 1569 fire in the Venetian Arsenal and the manipulation of the news proved crucial in launching the war against the Republic of St. Mark. By exaggerating the destruction done by the fire to the Venetian Armada, pro-war politicians succeeded in winning over their opponents.

Our other example is equally telling. In 1588 the English ambassador, eager to share with the grand vizier the news of the great English victory over Spain's "invincible Armada," was surprised to hear that the Ottoman government had already been informed about the outcome of the battle by Don Alvaro Mendes alias Solomon Abenaes (Ibn Yaish), brother-in-law to Queen Elizabeth's physician, who had resided in Constantinople since 1585 and who also assumed Joseph Nassi's influential position in the Ottoman court. The information regarding the destruction of the Spanish Armada was all the more important because the Ragusan representative in Constantinople claimed that the naval engagement ended with Spanish victory, causing obvious anxiety in the Ottoman capital.²³

Besides the Sultan's Jewish subjects, whose role in the collection of information and Ottoman decision-making is often overrated by both contemporaries and later historians, the sultan's government gathered intelligence from European envoys sent to the Porte and from the staff of European embassies in Istanbul. The success of the Ottoman leadership in getting information from European envoys is illustrated by a register of Hungarian fortresses which listed some of the strategically most important Hungarian garrisons, whose conquest, according to the unknown author, was desirable. The fortresses were listed according to their owners, who were the most prominent aristocrats and politicians of Hungary, together with their locations and short comments on their immediate past. The information contained in the report was most likely obtained from the members of the Hungarian embassy sent to the Porte in the fall of 1540, and the list served as a plan of conquest during Süleyman's 1541 Hungarian campaign.²⁴

Despite the unilateral nature of European–Ottoman diplomacy and the lack of Ottoman permanent ambassadors in European capitals until the

²² Salo Wittmayer Baron, *A Social and Religious History of the Jews. Late Middle Ages and Era of European Expansion 1200–1650*, vol. XVIII: *The Ottoman Empire, Persia, Ethiopia, India, and China*, 2nd edn (New York: Columbia University Press, 1983), p. 91.
²³ Ibid., p. 144; Avram Galanti, *Türkler ve Yahudiler* (Istanbul: Gözlem Gazetecilik Basın ve Yayın 1995), p. 138.
²⁴ Pál Fodor, "Ottoman Policy towards Hungary, 1520–1541," *Acta Orientalia Academiae Scientiarum Hungaricae* 45/2–3 (1991): 319–20.

end of the eighteenth century (and practically until the mid 1830s),[25] the Ottomans still managed to use diplomacy and diplomats for collecting information, as the resident ambassadors of competing European governments in Istanbul often shared information concerning their rivals with the Ottomans. For instance, in March and June 1527, the Venetian consul in Constantinople not only regularly informed the grand vizier about the power struggle between the two newly elected Hungarian kings, János Szapolyai (r. 1526–40) and Ferdinand of Habsburg (r. 1526–64) – a direct consequence of Süleyman's victory at Mohács (August 29, 1526) and the death of King Louis of Jagiello of Hungary (r. 1516–26) in the battle – but also urged the Istanbul government to support Szapolyai. Through its bailo, the Venetian government reminded the pashas that Emperor Charles V's power would grow excessively if his younger brother Ferdinand, archduke of Austria and already king of Bohemia, acquired the Hungarian crown (which Ferdinand eventually did on November 3, when he was crowned king of Hungary).[26]

The Ottoman government – which knew that European ambassadors in Istanbul were also engaged in espionage – tried to control the flow of information between Istanbul and the various European capitals. David von Ungnad, Habsburg permanent ambassador in Constantinople between 1573 and 1578, was requested by the Porte "to submit the letters he wished to dispatch to the Emperor for a prior reading." The letters had to be shown to an Ottoman interpreter, a certain "Ali *bey* from Frankfurt" and translated into Turkish. The ambassador was summoned to a hearing, where the letters were read out to him in Turkish. Then the German originals were "stamped in front of his eyes" so that nothing could be added to them. Grand Vizier Sokollu Mehmed pasha assigned a Turkish *sipahi* (cavalryman) to the Habsburg couriers and ordered the men to depart immediately. The grand vizier "also wrote to the Pasha [*beylerbeyi*] of Buda, telling him to strip [the couriers] to their pants and vests, in case they had other letters with them."[27]

---

[25] On Ottoman diplomacy see Daniel Goffman's chapter in the present volume. See also A. Nuri Yurdusev (ed.), *Ottoman Diplomacy: Conventional or Unconventional* (Basingstoke: Macmillan, 2004).

[26] Bárdossy László, *Magyar politika a mohácsi vész után* [Hungarian Politics after the Battle of Mohács] (Budapest: Holnap Kiadó, 1992 [1943]), pp. 62–3.

[27] This is based on Stephan Gerlach's Turkish journal or Constantinopolitan travelogue of a journey made by the imperial ambassador David von Ungnad from 1573 to 1578. To my knowledge there is no modern edition of the original German work, published in Frankfurt in 1674 (*Stephan Gerlachs des aeltern Tage-Buch der von zween glorwürdigsten Römischen Käysern Maximiliano und Rudolpho*

Since European envoys and resident ambassadors in Istanbul did not speak Ottoman Turkish and lacked knowledge of the intricacies of Ottoman diplomacy, they had to rely on interpreters. Language was indeed a major obstacle. Giovanni Maria Malvezzi, the Habsburgs' first resident ambassador in Istanbul, who otherwise proved very successful in acquiring and copying letters written by Ferdinand's enemies to the Porte, complained that Friar Georgious, the leading politician of Szapolyai (and later of his widow and infant son), outwitted him, for "the old fox" sent his letters to the Porte in Ottoman Turkish, which Malvezzi could not read and copy.[28]

Before European embassies, following the Venetian model of *giovani della lingua*, were able to train their own interpreters, European resident ambassadors in Istanbul usually employed Latins and Orthodox Greeks from Galata and Pera. These men, however, were subjects of the sultan and enjoyed no diplomatic immunity. Consequently, the Porte could and did pressure them into revealing information, which made their allegiance to their employers questionable.

European ambassadors not only hired Latin and Greek subjects of the sultan as interpreters, but they, including Malvezzi, often relied upon the Porte's own interpreters. Under Süleyman the Magnificent most of the Porte's interpreters were European renegades, many of them with ties to their Christian relatives living outside the borders of the Ottoman Empire. Yunus Bey was of Greek origin from Modon/Modone, which the Venetians had recently (1500) lost to the Ottomans. Yunus' sister Marietta and his nephew Nicolò Stefani lived in Venetian-controlled Zante, while his brother, Mustafa Agha (d. 1565), was *kapucıbaşı* or chief gatekeeper of Süleyman's court. Ibrahim Bey, alias Strasz/Strozzeni, was

---

beyderseits ... und durch ... David Ungnad ... glücklichst-vollbrachter Gesandtschafft, Frankfurt am Main, 1674). Quotations are from a (partial) Hungarian translation of this work. *Ungnád Dávid konstantinápolyi utazásai* [David von Ungnad's Journeys to Constantinople] (Budapest: Szépirodalmi Könyvkiadó, 1986), p. 174. It is clear from the work that the Habsburg ambassadors found a way to communicate news to Vienna. Letters meant for the eyes of Ottoman officials were written in such a way that "no fault could be found in them. Other letters, however, in which he [Ungnad] reports at length on all his activities and on events, he writes with lemon juice and presses them according to Turkish custom. Thus, not one single character can be seen on the paper. He adds all sorts of silk [into the envelope], as if he were sending a greeting to a sweetheart. The Emperor also wrote with lemon juice between the lines of his letter about things that he thought should not become known to the Pasha" (pp. 173–4).

[28] Pál Török, *I. Ferdinand konstantinápolyi beketárgyalásai* [Ferdinand I's Peace Negotiations in Constantinople] (Budapest: Magyar Tudományós Akadémia, 1930), p. 89. Malvezzi's correspondence is published in *Austro-Turcica. Diplomatische Akten des habsburgischen Gesandtschaftsverkehrs mit der Hohen Pforte im Zeitalter Süleymans des Prächtigen*. Bearbeitet von Srećko M. Džaja unter Mitarbeit von Günter Weis. In Verbindung mit Mathias Bernath herausgegeben von Karl Nehring (Munich: R. Oldenbourg, 1995).

a Polish renegade. Tercüman Mahmud was born as Sebold von Pribach, son of a Viennese Jewish merchant, named Jacob von Pribach, and Mahmud had relatives in Vienna, including his mother. Murad dragoman, alias Balázs Somlyai, was a Hungarian from Nagybánya/Szatmárbánya (Asszonypataka/Rivuli Dominarum, today Baia Mare in Romania), and was captured by the Ottomans in either 1526 or 1529.[29] In order to gain the goodwill (or to evade the malice) of the Porte's dragomans, many of Istanbul's European friends and foes courted these interpreters, offering them annual salaries and presents. Did it mean that the dragomans sold their loyalty to the Europeans and betrayed the sultan? Due to the lack of monographic studies on the Porte's dragomans, it is difficult to answer this question. However, the impression one gets from the, admittedly contradictory, sources is that most of the dragomans cooperated with the European ambassadors with the knowledge of their Ottoman superiors. While some of them copied incoming and outgoing letters for European ambassadors – as did, for instance, Tercüman Mahmud, who copied French and Venetian letters for the Habsburgs – the majority of the dragomans leaked information deliberately in order to get the Porte's message out, to warn Istanbul's enemies and friends, or with the purpose of disinformation.

Due to their knowledge of European languages, to their ties to their Christian relatives, to their intensive correspondence with European resident and ad hoc ambassadors, as well as with European rulers and politicians, the dragomans of the Porte were well positioned to play a crucial role in Ottoman intelligence-gathering and disinformation, not least during their frequent official visits to Europe, as the sultan's envoys.

Equally important was their role in assessing incoming intelligence regarding Habsburg Austria, Venice, Hungary, Transylvania, and Poland, as well

[29] While these dragomans are frequently mentioned in European diplomatic correspondence, references to them are often contradictory, incomplete, and incorrect. Many of the mistakes are repeated in the literature, including Josef Matuz's pioneering introduction to the subject: "Die Pfortendolmetscher zur Herrschaftszeit Süleyman des Prächtigen," *Südost-Forschungen* 34 (1975): 26–60. On Yunus Bey see Maria Pia Pedani, *In nome del gran signore: inviati ottomani a Venezia dalla caduta di Costantinopoli alla guerra di Candia* (Venice: Deputazione Editrice, 1994), pp. 144–53, and Gülru Necipoğlu, *The Age of Sinan: Architectural Culture in the Ottoman Empire* (Princeton, NJ: Princeton University Press, 2005), pp. 484–6; on Ibrahim Bey see Dariusz Kotodziejczyk, *Ottoman-Polish Diplomatic Relations (15th–18th Century). An Annotated Edition of 'Ahdnames and Other Documents* (Leiden: Brill, 2000); on Mahmud and Murad Beył, see Ernst Dieter Petritsch, "Der habsburgisch-osmanische Friedensvertrag des Jahres 1547," *Mitteilungen des Österreichischen Staatsarchivs* 38 (1985): 60–6, and Pál Ács, "Tarjumans Mahmud and Murad: Austrian and Hungarian Renegades as Sultan's Interpreters," in Bodo Guthmüller and Wilhelm Kühlmann (eds.), *Europa und die Türken in der Renaissance* (Tübingen: Niemeyer, 2000), pp. 307–16.

as in providing background information on the history and present state of these countries. We know that several of them purchased and read European works, like Tercüman Mahmud, who in 1573 ordered from Vienna two copies of Abraham Ortelius's (1527–98) *Theatrum Orbis Terrarum* (Theatre of the World), the first true modern atlas, which contained uniform map sheets and supporting text bound together in book format, summarizing the cartographical knowledge of the sixteenth century. Mahmud dragoman was surprisingly up to date, since Ortelius's mapbook was first published in 1570. He had a keen interest in the history of the empire's European rivals, and in the 1540s wrote a chronicle of the Hungarians (*Tarih-i Ungurus*), using now lost medieval Hungarian chronicles in Latin, and perhaps relying on the knowledge of his Hungarian renegade colleague, Murad dragoman.[30]

Intelligence-gathering in the provinces

Apart from intelligence-gathering in Istanbul, one of the main jobs of Ottoman officials in the frontier provinces was to gather information concerning the empire's neighbors, a vital task of which Istanbul frequently reminded them in the imperial decrees. While *beylerbeyi*s and *sancakbeyi*s in the eastern provinces reported on events regarding the Aqqoyunlus, Mamluks, and Safavids,[31] *beylerbeyi*s and *sancakbeyi*s in Hungary sent information to Istanbul regarding Vienna's policy vis-à-vis Transylvania, Poland, and Ottoman Hungary, about Habsburg–Safavid diplomatic relations, Habsburg troop concentrations and strengths, and military campaigns, among other things.[32] Ottoman officials in Hungary collected valuable intelligence from captured soldiers serving in Habsburg Hungary.

---

[30] Österreichische Staatsarchiv, Haus-, Hof- und Staatsarchiv, Turcica Karton 30. Konv. 1. Fol. 29. (January 22, 1574). I am indebted to my colleague and friend, archivist István Fazekas, for this reference. See also Sándor Takáts, "A magyar és török íródeákok" [Hungarian and Turkish Scribes] in Sándor Takáts, *Művelődéstörténeti tanulmányok a 16–17. századból* [Studies on Cultural History of the Sixteenth and Seventeenth Centuries] ed. Kálmán Benda (Budapest: Gondolat Kiadó, 1961), p. 179; György Hazai (ed.), *Nagy Szülejmán udvari emberének magyar krónikája. A Tarih-i Ungurus és kritikája* [The Hungarian Chronicle of Süleyman the Magnificent's Courtier. The Tarih-i Ungurus and its Critique] (Budapest: Akadémiai Kiadó, 1996); see also Ács, "Tarjumans Mahmud and Murad," p. 312.

[31] On which see, for example, J. E. Woods, "Turco-Iranica I: An Ottoman Intelligence Report on late Fifteenth/Ninth Century Iranian Foreign Relations," *Journal of Near Eastern Studies* 38 (1979): 1–9. Jean-Louis Bacqué-Grammont, "Études turco-safavides, XV. Cinq lettres de Hüsrev Paşa, beylerbeyi du Diyar Bekir (1552–1532)," *Journal Asiatique* 279/3–4 (1991): 239–64.

[32] See, for instance, MD 9, p. 107; 10, p. 338, n. 550; 64, p. 121; Halil Sahillioğlu (ed.), *Topkapı Sarayı H.951–952 tarihli ve E-12321 numaralı Mühimme defteri* (Istanbul: İslâm Tarih, Sanat ve Kültür Araştırma Merkezi, 2002), pp. 173–4, no. 215; p. 310, no. 428.

In 1547, for instance, the governor of Buda learned important details regarding Habsburg military preparations, Ferdinand I's whereabouts, and his consultations with his brother, Charles V, from a captured soldier who served in Komárom, the main Habsburg garrison in northwestern Hungary and the center of the Hungarian Danube flotilla. The tongue (*dil*), as these captured men were called in Ottoman documents, also gave a realistic assessment of the strength of Ferdinand's garrison.[33] The information was duly forwarded to Istanbul.

Apart from captured enemy soldiers and agents, *beylerbeyi*s and *sancakbeyi*s also employed their own spies. While *beylerbeyi*s in the eastern provinces employed Turks, Kurds, and Arabs,[34] those in Hungary relied mainly on Hungarians and Slavs. Ottoman spies regularly traveled between Ottoman Hungary and the Habsburg lands. One such spy, called *pribek* in Ottoman and Hungarian documents, confirmed in early 1548 the news extracted from the above-mentioned captured Komárom soldier in late 1547.[35] This shows that the Ottomans tried to get news from more than one source in order to check their authenticity. Ottoman frontier commanders certainly felt that they knew a great deal about the enemy. In 1561, when the *sancakbeyi* of İstolni Belgrad (Székesfehérvár/ Stuhlweissenburg) in Hungary, Hamza Bey, was threatened that a large Habsburg army would be sent against him, he reminded Ferdinand I that the Habsburg king could not possibly have enough soldiers at his disposal for the undertaking. Had Ferdinand I had enough soldiers, Hamza would have been informed:

because I have had a spy living in Vienna for six years, whose wife and child are there, a man who can say mass if he wants, or be a scribe, or a German, a Hungarian, or a good improviser, a soldier, a man with a limp, or someone who walks as steady as you do with a good knowledge of every language.[36]

By relying on their spies and informants, Ottoman authorities along the Habsburg frontier possessed up-to-date information about the state of the

---

[33] "There is a *bey* called Ugnod [= Johannes Ungnad] and there are 1,000 gunmen. The ... castle has thirty-two *şayka*s [= boat] on the Danube and there are thirty men in each *şayka*, which comes to nine hundred and sixty people altogether." Géza Dávid and Pál Fodor, "Ottoman Spy Reports from Hungary," in Ugo Marazzi (ed.), *Turcica et Islamica: studi in memoria di Aldo Gallotta* (Naples: Università degli studi di Napoli L'Orientale, 2003), pp. 121–31, quotation from p. 124.
[34] The *beylerbeyi* of Diyarbakır, Hüsrev Pasha (1522–31), for instance, sent Turkish and Kurdish spies into Azerbaijan to spy on the Safavids. Bacqué-Grammont, "Études turco-safavides."
[35] Dávid and Fodor, "Ottoman Spy Reports," pp. 126–8.
[36] Sándor Takáts, "Kalauzok és kémek a török világban" [Guides and Spies in Ottoman Hungary] in Sándor Takáts, *Rajzok a török világból* [Sketches from Hungary's Turkish Past] 4 vols. (Budapest: A Magyar Tudományos Akadémia Kiadása, 1915–32), vol. II, p. 170.

Hungarian garrisons maintained by Vienna. The success of Üveys Pasha, *beylerbeyi* of Buda (1578–80), can be mentioned in this regard. Shortly after the Habsburg military authorities modernized the Hungarian fortresses around Kanizsa in Transdanubia, Üveys Pasha prepared a detailed and surprisingly accurate map of the region, which indicated all the fortresses and the major river crossings, and sent it to Istanbul.[37]

Intelligence-gathering by Istanbul's vassals

The client or vassal states of the Porte were also expected to provide Istanbul with information about neighboring territories. Ottoman intelligence could rely particularly upon Ragusa (Dubrovnik), Transylvania, and the Romanian principalities of Wallachia and Moldova. On the one hand, Ragusa provided Istanbul with information about the Austrian and Spanish Habsburgs and also about Italy. The city obtained such information from Spanish, Venetian, and French agents residing in or passing through the town, as well as through its own elaborate network of agents and informants (several of whom turned out to be double and even triple agents), as well as through its extensive commercial contacts in Europe and the Ottoman Empire.[38] Transylvania, on the other hand, sent news about Royal Hungary and the Danubian Habsburg Monarchy, informing Istanbul about Vienna's policy decisions regarding Hungary and Transylvania, planned and actual Habsburg troop movements, and the conditions of Hungarian and Habsburg garrisons.[39] While these vassal states, especially Ragusa, often spied on the Ottomans too, and, if their interests dictated it, informed the Habsburgs and Venetians about the Ottomans, the intelligence gathered through these client states was of great value for the Ottomans.

[37] In Istanbul, Üveys Pasha's map was copied and its inscriptions translated into Italian for Joachim von Sinzendorf, Habsburg ambassador to Istanbul (1578–81), who sent it back to Vienna, indicating that the Habsburg ambassadors were also efficient in counter-intelligence. The Italian copy of the original Turkish map is to be found in the Viennese Archives (Österreichische Staatsarchiv, Haus-, Hof- und Staatsarchiv Turcica Karton 43. Konv. 2. Fol. 50) and has been published in facsimile in Géza Pálffy, *Európa védelmében* [In the Defense of Europe] (Pápa: Jókai Mór Városi Könyvtár, 2000), facsimile III.
[38] Nicolas H. Biegman, *The Turco-Ragusan Relationship. According to the Firmans of Murad III (1575–1595) Extant in the State Archives of Dubrovnik* (The Hague: Mouton, 1968); N. H. Biegman, "Ragusan Spying for the Ottoman Empire. Some 16th-Century Documents from the State Archive at Dubrovnik," *Belleten* 27 (1963): 237–55.
[39] See, for instance, MD 7, p. 230, no. 637; 12, p. 339, no. 689; 67, p. 150; 69, p. 107; 71, p. 97; On the Romanian principalities see MD 3, p. 391, no. 1165; ibid., p. 490, n. 1457.

Intelligence-gathering by Istanbul's agents, envoys, and spies in Europe

In addition to spies sent to neighboring countries by Ottoman provincial governors, the central government in Istanbul also employed its own envoys, agents, and spies in Europe in order to collect intelligence. Bayezid II's agents traveled to France and Italy to spy on the sultan's brother, Cem, who had challenged Bayezid's claim to the sultanate and thus was forced to spend his remaining thirteen years in exile in Mamluk Egypt, Rhodes, France, and Rome, where European monarchs and the papacy tried to use him as a pawn in their crusading plans against the Ottomans.[40]

Ottoman envoys under Sultan Süleyman also gathered information during their trips to Venice, Vienna, Hungary, or Poland. In these missions Istanbul often employed its own renegade interpreters who not only spoke the languages of the countries they were sent to, but also had relatives and acquaintances whom they visited or corresponded with. The Greek-born Yunus Bey had visited Venice twice (1519, 1522) before he became chief interpreter in 1525, and at least four times afterwards (1529, 1532–3, 1537, 1542). He was also sent to Vienna (1533) and Hungary (1534). His successor in the office of chief dragoman, the Polish renegade Ibrahim Bey, visited Venice (1553 and 1566), his homeland Poland (1564), as well as Vienna and France (1568). The Viennese-born Mahmud dragoman was sent to Vienna in early 1550, and met his mother and members of his family. He also traveled on official business to Transylvania, Poland, Italy, and France, and died in Prague during his last trip in 1575. When in Vienna in 1550, he gathered important intelligence regarding the negotiations between Ferdinand of Habsburg I and Friar George (Martinuzzi), the leading politician of Transylvania. Mahmud's junior colleague (and perhaps former fellow student in Vienna), the Hungarian renegade Murad, traveled to Hungary in 1551, was captured by Gianbattista Castaldo, and was ransomed – after thirty months in captivity – by Grand Vizier Rüstem Pasha, and made interpreter in 1553. Istanbul dispatched Ferhad dragoman, another Hungarian renegade, to the elected Hungarian king, János Zsigmond (Johann Sigismund, 1554, 1566).[41]

---

[40] V. L. Ménage, "The Mission of an Ottoman Secret Agent in 1486," *Journal of the Royal Asiatic Society* (1965): 112–32; Nicolas Vatin, "Itinéraires d'agents de la Porte en Italie (1483–1495): réflexions sur l'organisation des missions ottomanes et sur la transcription turque des noms de lieux italiens," *Turcica* 19 (1987): 29–50, and Nicholas Vatin, *Sultan Jem. Un prince ottoman dans l'Europe du XVe siècle d'après deux sources contemporaines: Vaki`at-i Sultan Cem, Oeuvres de Guillaume Caoursin* (Ankara : Türk Tarih Kurumu, 1997).

[41] In addition to the literature listed in footnote 29, see also Anton C. Schaendlinger and Claudia Römer, *Die Schreiben Süleymans des Prächtigen an Karl V., Ferdinand I. und Maximilian II.*

The Porte must have valued the expertise and contacts of these renegades and must have trusted them when dispatching them to their former homelands. While several of the renegades offered information to their former countrymen, it happened only rarely that their loyalty was questioned or they were accused of treason. This happened to Hidayet Agha alias Markus Scherer, a Hungarian/Saxon renegade from Szeben (Hermannstadt/Sibiu) in Transylvania. He served as Hungarian and Latin interpreter and secretary under several *beylerbeyi*s of Buda, and later as dragoman of the Porte. He was sent to Vienna to conclude a peace treaty in 1565. However, in the meantime the war party regained control of Istanbul, and upon his return to Istanbul Hidayet Agha was executed for working for the peace between the Habsburgs and the Ottomans.[42]

Apart from official envoys, Istanbul also employed agents and spies in foreign countries, who were especially active in Spain, Venice, and in the Austrian Habsburg lands, as revealed by the reports of the Venetian consul in Istanbul or by the Habsburg resident ambassadors stationed in Istanbul and Venice.[43] Although some of these spies were double agents, others remained loyal to the sultan even at the expense of their lives. "A spy of the Turk . . . who called himself friar Ludovico of Martinengo" was captured in Vienna, thanks to Habsburg counter-intelligence. Although "he began to confess . . . fearing for his life, he took a dagger from one of the guards and he struck himself four times, slitting his throat. Which, by the way, is a great inconvenience since from him we could have known many things," lamented the Habsburg agent.[44]

News and information from the provinces to the Ottoman capital, whether concerned with domestic or foreign affairs, as well as orders from the center to the provinces, were transmitted by an elaborate courier and communications network, the so-called *ulak* or *menzilhane* system. The Ottoman *ulak* (state courier) and *menzilhane* (posting/relay-station)

Transkriptionen und Übersetzungen (Vienna: Verlag der Österreichischen Akademie der Wissenschaften, 1983), p. 27 (on Mahmud); Istanbul, BOA, Mühimme Defterleri 5, p. 443; Nr. 1185 (on Murad and Ferhad).

[42] Takáts, "A magyar és török íródeákok," pp. 182–3.

[43] During the Ottoman–Venetian war of 1570–3, for instance, the Venetian bailo in Istanbul exposed several Ottoman spies operating in Venice. See Preto, "La guerra segreta," pp. 80–1. In May 1581, Joachim von Sinzendorf, resident Habsburg ambassador in Constantinople (1578–81), uncovered an Ottoman spy pretending to be a Swiss merchant. See Robert Anhegger, "Ein angeblicher schweizerischer Agent an der Hohen Pforte im Jahre 1581," *Istanbuller Schriften* 11 (1943): 9. Regarding Ottoman spies operating in Spain, see Miguel Ángel de Bunes Ibarra, "Charles V and the Ottoman War from the Spanish Point of View," *Eurasian Studies*, 1 (2002): 168–9.

[44] "He was a very wise man and a friend of Juan Mida, who has also visited Your Majesty and is a relative of Angulema, and whom I am certain is a spy who pretends to want to serve Your Majesty." Quoted by Ibarra, "Charles V and the Ottoman War," p. 169.

system, like its Roman and Byzantine antecedents, was built on a sophisticated road network, itself inherited from Roman and Byzantine times.
The Ottoman road network had three main routes (left, center, and right
arm/wing), both in Europe and in Asia Minor. Each of the six main routes
had several smaller branches radiating from the capital towards Salonica/
Athens, Edirne/Sofia/Belgrade/Buda and the Crimea in Europe and
towards Erzurum/the Caucasus, Diyarbekir/Mosul/Baghdad/Basra and
Aleppo/Damascus/Cairo (or Mecca) in Asia Minor and the Arab provinces, respectively. Posts established along the road network at intervals of
six to twelve hours' ride (or at distances of between twenty and seventy
kilometers) depending on the terrain, provided the couriers with post
horses and made sure that reports and orders were transported swiftly
and efficiently. While abuses of the system occurred as early as the reign
of Süleyman the Magnificent, the Ottoman communications network
played a crucial role in transmitting intelligence, news, and reports of all
kinds, as well as imperial orders, and is rightly regarded as one of the main
instruments that held the Empire together.[45]

As a result of its information-gathering activities and its road and
communications network, the Ottoman Empire of the sixteenth century
remained an integral part of European politics and information flow. Juan
de Vega, the viceroy of Sicily, stated in 1557 that the Ottomans were as
quick as the Spanish government in receiving information about events in
the Spanish and Italian Mediterranean.[46] A cursory look at the Ottoman
imperial ideology, propaganda, and foreign policy under Süleyman the
Magnificent vis-à-vis the Habsburgs corroborates the above assumption,
and suggests that the masters of the Imperial Council possessed sufficient
information upon which to base their policies.

GEOPOLITICS AND THE CLASH OF IMPERIAL IDEOLOGIES
AND POLICIES

Sixteenth-century Ottoman policy-makers were preoccupied with numerous policy concerns, both internal and external. Of these, the emergence

---

[45] Colin Heywood, "Some Turkish Archival Sources for the History of the Menzilhane Network in
Rumeli during the Eighteenth Century," "The Ottoman Menzilhane and Ulak System in Rumeli in
the Eighteenth Century," and "The Via Egnatia in the Ottoman Period: The Menzilhanes of the Sol
Kol in the Late 17th/Early 18th Century," all reprinted in Heywood, *Writing Ottoman History;* Yusuf
Halaçoğlu, *Osmanlılarda Ulaşım ve Haberleşme (Menziller)* (Ankara: Türk Tarih Kurumu, 2002).
[46] M. J. Rodríguez-Salgado, *The Changing Face of Empire: Charles V, Philip II and Habsburg Authority,
1551–9* (Cambridge: Cambridge University Press, 1988), p. 263.

of two new powerful rivals, the Safavids and the Habsburgs at the beginning of the sixteenth century and in the 1520s, respectively, were probably the most alarming developments for decision-makers in Istanbul. The Safavids challenged Ottoman sovereignty and religious legitimacy in eastern Anatolia and Azerbaijan – particularly among the Türkmen and Kurdish nomadic peoples – whereas the advance of Habsburg rule in the Mediterranean and in Central Europe in the 1520s threatened recently acquired Ottoman positions.

Sultan Selim I (r. 1512–20) devoted most of his energies and his empire's resources to tackle the Safavid problem. Combining sheer military force (Çaldıran, 1514), propaganda, persuasion, and the policy of appeasement and co-optation (especially vis-à-vis Shah Ismail's *kızılbaş* followers among the Türkmen and Kurdish nomads), Selim managed to secure Ottoman rule over most of eastern and southeastern Asia Minor, although Ottoman control in these regions remained shaky. One major consequence of the Ottoman–Safavid confrontation was Selim's victorious campaigns against the Sunni Mamluks of Egypt and Syria and the Ottoman conquest of *bilad al-Sham* – territories extending between the Taurus Mountains and Sinai – and Egypt in 1516–17.

Apart from military commitments on a scale unseen in Ottoman history before, this struggle also required adjustment in Ottoman ideology, legitimation, propaganda, and self-presentation. Ottoman propaganda justified Selim's campaigns against the Safavids by portraying the Shi'ite enemy and its *kızılbaş* allies in eastern Anatolia as "heretics" and even "infidels," whose revolts hindered the Ottomans' struggle against the Christian adversaries of the Empire, the main task of the ghazi (warrior; often warrior for the faith) Sultans according to fifteenth- and sixteenth-century Ottoman chroniclers and authors of advice-for-princes literature. Since the Sunni Mamluks cooperated with the "heretic" Safavids, the war against them was also justifiable. Before the Sultan could turn against the empire's Christian enemies, claimed Ottoman propagandists, these rebel Muslims had to be dealt with.[47]

---

[47] Elke Eberhard, *Osmanische Polemik gegen die Safawiden im 16. Jahrhundert* (Freiburg: Schwarz, 1970); M. C. Şehabeddin Tekindağ, "Selimnameler," *İstanbul Üniversitesi Edebiyat Fakültesi Tarih Enstitüsü Dergisi* 1 (1970): 197–230; Ahmet Uğur, *The Reign of Sultan Selim in the Light of the Selimname Literature* (Berlin: Schwarz, 1985); see also Colin Imber, "Ideals and Legitimation in Early Ottoman History," in Metin Kunt and Christine Woodhead (eds.), *Süleyman the Magnificent and his Age: The Ottoman Empire in the Early Modern World* (London: Longman, 1995), pp. 140–4, 153; Markus Dressler, "Inventing Orthodoxy: Competing Claims for Authority and Legitimacy in the Ottoman-Safavid Conflict," in Hakan T. Karateke and Maurus Reinkowski (eds.), *Legitimizing the Order: The Ottoman Rhetoric of State Power* (Leiden: Brill, 2005), pp. 151–73.

With Sultan Selim's conquests of Syria, Palestine, the Hijaz, and Egypt in 1516–17, the Ottomans became the preeminent Islamic empire. The possession of the Islamic holy cities of Mecca and Medina – together with Jerusalem, the place from which the Prophet was believed to have ascended into Heaven, and Hebron, the burial-place of the patriarch Abraham – gave the Ottoman sultans an unparalleled legitimacy in the Islamic world. Starting with Selim I, Ottoman sultans proudly used the title of "Servant of the Two Sanctuaries" (*Khadim al-Haramayn al-Sharifayn*), that of Mecca and Medina.[48]

The conquest of Egypt also had important consequences for the evolution of Ottoman imperial policy. The defense of the vital lanes of maritime communications between Istanbul and Egypt required the strengthening of the Ottoman navy. It also led to confrontation with the dominant Christian maritime powers of the Mediterranean: the Knights of Rhodes, the Venetians, and the Spanish Habsburgs. Venetian reports explained the large-scale shipbuilding activity in the Istanbul Naval Arsenal in 1518–19 with a planned overall Ottoman assault against Christian Europe, purportedly against Rhodes.[49] More importantly for Ottoman maritime interests, in 1519, threatened by Spanish advance in the western Mediterranean, "the pirate of Algiers" Hayreddin Barbarossa offered his services to Sultan Selim I. By appointing Hayreddin Barbarossa governor of Algiers, Selim extended Ottoman influence as far as Algiers and Tunis.[50] The Ottoman advance was duly registered in the Holy Roman Empire, where the Reichstag accepted one of many submissions regarding the "Turkish threat."[51] However, with the death of Sultan Selim I, the predictable

---

[48] Halil İnalcık, *The Ottoman Empire. The Classical Age, 1300–1600* (London: Weidenfeld and Nicolson, 1973; reprinted New York: Aristide D. Caratzas, 1989, 1995), p. 57; Halil İnalcık, "Selim I," in EI2, vol. IX, p. 129.

[49] Kenneth M. Setton, *The Papacy and the Levant (1204–1571)* vol. III (Philadelphia: American Philosophical Society, 1984), p. 193. Ottoman chronicles also corroborate the news. Apart from the assertions of Hoca Saadeddin (d. 1599) and Gelibolulu Mustafa Ali (d. 1600) (on which see Selahattin Tansel, *Yavuz Sultan Selim* [Ankara: Milli Eğitim Basımevi, 1969], pp. 242–3, footnote 3), Celalzade Mustafa (d. 1567), who was serving in the Divan in 1516 and thus was contemporary to the events, also claimed that the Ottoman navy was preparing to sail against the "infidels." On this see Celia J. Kerslake, "The Selim-name of Celal-zade Mustafa Çelebi as a Historical Source," *Turcica* 9/2–10 (1978): 43.

[50] On Hayreddin Pasha see Aldo Gallotta, "Khayr al-Din Pasha, Barbarossa," in EI2, vol. IV, p. 1155; Svat Soucek, "The Rise of the Barbarossas in North Africa," *Archivum Ottomanicum* 3 (1972): 228–50.

[51] According to Árpád Károlyi and László Bárdossy it was the first such submission accepted at the Reichstag regarding the "Turkish threat." See László Bárdossy, *Magyar politika Mohácsi vész után* (Budapest: Egyetemi Nyomda, 1943), p. 17. However, this must be qualified. Following the fall of Constantinople, at the German imperial assemblies (*Reichstage*) several orations were delivered against the Turks (*Türkenrede* or *Türkenkriegsrede*), and were followed by deliberations and calls

Ottoman–Habsburg confrontation in the Mediterranean was left to his successor, Sultan Süleyman.

A recent study has stressed that Ottoman policy during the early years of Sultan Süleyman was often reactive to internal and external threats to sultanic authority.[52] While Ottoman policy remained multifaceted and indeed often reactive under the new sultan, Süleyman's reign signaled a major shift in Ottoman policy, the main feature of which was the renewal of hostilities with the empire's Christian enemies. Although the reasons for this shift were socio-political, economic, and military, rather than ideological, Istanbul's new policy was also well in line with the evolving Ottoman ideology and propaganda, which portrayed Süleyman in the first three decades of his long reign as "defender of (Sunni) Islam" and "world conqueror."[53] To be sure, neither were new titles. Sultan Selim had also been described as *sahib-kıran*, "Master of the Conjunction" or world conqueror. Sixteenth-century Ottoman sources suggest that, had he continued his conquests (he was stopped by his premature death), Selim "would have become a universal conqueror of the stature of Alexander and Chingiz Khan."[54] However, there was an important difference between Selim and Süleyman. Whereas Ottoman chroniclers seem to have struggled to explain and justify the fact that Sultan Selim had neglected the fight against the "infidel" Christians,[55] Süleyman's image-makers had no such problems, for the latter's many campaigns against the empire's Christian neighbors and the confrontation with the Habsburgs and their allies (a legacy, at least to a certain degree, of his father's conquests in the

---

to arms. On this see Johannes Helmarth, "The German Reichstage and the Crusade," in Norman Housley (ed.), *Crusading in the Fifteenth Century. Message and Impact* (Basingstoke: Macmillan, 2004), pp. 53–69.

[52] Rhoads Murphey, "Süleyman I and the Conquest of Hungary: Ottoman Manifest Destiny or a Delayed Reaction to Charles V's Universalist Vision," *Journal of Early Modern History* 5 (2001): 197–221.

[53] See Imber, "Ideals and Legitimation"; Christine Woodhead, "Perspectives on Süleyman," in Kunt and Woodhead, *Süleyman the Magnificent*, pp. 164–90; Cornell Fleischer, "The Lawgiver as Messiah: The Making of the Imperial Image in the Reign of Süleyman," in Gilles Veinstein (ed.), *Soliman le Magnifique et son temps* (Paris: Documentation Française, 1992), pp. 159–77; Barbara Flemming, "Sahib-kıran und Mahdi: Türkische Endzeiterwartungen im ersten Jahrzehnt der Regierung Süleymans," in György Kara (ed.), *Between the Danube and the Caucasus* (Budapest: Akadémiai Kiadó, 1987), pp. 43–62.

[54] Fleischer, "The Lawgiver as Messiah," p. 162.

[55] It is instructive to remember how some authors of the Selimname literature were at pains to recall (and exaggerate the importance of) Selim's wars against the infidels, that is, the Georgians, which he carried out as sultanic prince and governor of Trabzon. See Tekindağ, "Selimnameler," pp. 204, 215. In an Ottoman chronicle finalized in 1543 the dying Selim laments the fact that he had no chance to fight against the infidels. See Barbara Flemming, "Public Opinion under Sultan Süleyman," in Halil İnalcık and Cemal Kafadar (eds.), *Süleyman the Second and his Time* (Istanbul: Isis, 1993), p. 54.

Mediterranean) provided ample examples to present Süleyman as defender
of Islam.

By the time Süleyman ascended the throne, it had become clear that
Selim's policy vis-à-vis the Safavids was unsustainable. Warfare since 1511
had completely exhausted the eastern provinces of the empire and the
imperial army had arrived at a point of strategic overextension. Distance,
inhospitable climate (early winters and snow), and Shah Ismail's
"scorched-earth" policy caused serious problems for the otherwise well-
organized Ottoman provisioning system, rendering seasonal campaigning
ineffective. The Sultan's Asian troops fought reluctantly against the Shah's
Anatolian *kızılbaş* followers (mainly Türkmen and Kurdish nomads),
often deserted, or allied with the enemy.

According to a Venetian report from March 1519, they had had enough
of the eastern wars and wanted instead to fight against the Hungarians,
whom they considered weaker warriors. By sending exaggerated reports to
Istanbul regarding the wealth of the Hungarian kingdom and the weakness
of its military, the Rumelian troops likewise lobbied for the renewal of
European campaigns, from which they hoped to profit economically.[56]

It seems that the decision regarding Süleyman's 1521 Hungarian campaign, the first major military undertaking that signaled the new course in
Ottoman strategy, was made shortly after the sultan ascended the throne
(September 30, 1520), and that the maltreatment of Süleyman's envoy by
the Hungarian King Louis II of Jagiello was a mere pretext. Preparations
for the campaign must have started in the fall of 1520 and continued during
the winter despite the revolt of the governor of Damascus, Canberdi
Gazali, an Ottoman turned Mamluk. In addition to their strategic significance, the 1521 Hungarian campaign and the conquest of Belgrade, "the key
to Hungary" in contemporaneous Hungarian parlance,[57] as well as the
capture of Rhodes in 1522, established Süleyman's image in Europe as
a formidable adversary and within the Islamic world as a warrior sultan
and "defender of Islam."

Religion remained an important tool of legitimation under Süleyman,
who continued using the title of "Servant of the Two Sanctuaries." By

---

[56] Pál Fodor, "A Bécsbe vezető út. Az oszmán nagyhatalom az 1520-as években" [The Road to Vienna:
The Ottoman Empire in the 1520s], in Pál Fodor, *A szultán és az aranyalma* [The Sultan and the
Golden Apple] (Budapest: Balassi, 2001), p. 370.

[57] On which see Ferenc Szakály, "Nándorfehérvár, 1521: The Beginning of the End of the Medieval
Hungarian Kingdom," in Géza Dávid and Pál Fodor (eds.), *Hungarian-Ottoman Military and
Diplomatic Relations in the Age of Süleyman the Magnificent* (Budapest: Loránd Eötvös University/
Hungarian Academy of Sciences, 1994), pp. 47–76.

organizing the annual pilgrimage to Mecca, protecting the pilgrimage routes, sending the annual aid (*surra*) for the populations of the two Holy Cities, building and restoring mosques and other public buildings in Mecca and Medina, and restoring the Kàba, Süleyman strengthened his legitimacy in the Muslim world.[58] From the 1540s, the sultan also adopted the title of Caliph. In the formulation of his Grand Mufti Ebussuûd Efendi, this was meant to counterbalance the Safavid Shah Tahmaps's assertions regarding sovereignty over Ottoman subjects living in eastern Anatolia and Azerbaijan, as well as Charles V's claims to universal Christian rulership.[59]

One example of the sophisticated propaganda war and clash of imperial ideologies between the Habsburgs and Ottomans is the question of competing titles. Süleyman considered himself the ruler of the four holy cities of Islam, and, along with Mecca and Medina, included Hebron and Jerusalem in his rather lengthy list of official titles.[60] His claim to being the sultan of Jerusalem, however, conflicted with that of Charles V. The emperor not only included Jerusalem among his titles, but was presented by his propagandists as the Christian ruler who would recapture the Holy Land from the "infidels."

Charles inherited both the Spanish and the Austrian/Germanic expectations of the coming of a universal monarch, and was viewed and presented as the "Last World Emperor," under whose reign the Jews and pagans would be converted, and whose sovereignty would be followed by the "millennium," the thousand-year reign of Christ, and by the Last Judgment. As early as 1515, during his state visit to Bruges the then "Prince of Spain" was portrayed as the future re-conqueror of Jerusalem. By 1519–20, Charles was "King of the Romans, elected emperor, always august," also "King of Spain, Sicily, Jerusalem, the Balearic Islands, Hungary, Dalmatia, Croatia and the Indies." In his public address to the ambassadors of the German electors who brought the news of Charles's election as Holy Roman Emperor (1519), Grand Chancellor Gattinara claimed

---

[58] Suraiya Faroqhi, *Pilgrims and Sultans: The Hajj under the Ottomans, 1517–1683* (London: Palgrave, 1994); on the use of the construction of public buildings as a means of legitimization see also Hakan T. Karateke, "Interpreting Monuments: Charitable Buildings, Monuments, and the Construction of Collective Memory in the Ottoman Empire," *Wiener Zeitschrift für die Kunde des Morgenlandes* 91 (2001): 183–99.

[59] Colin Imber, "Süleyman as Caliph of the Muslims: Ebu's-Suʿud's Formulation of Ottoman Dynastic Ideology," in Veinstein, *Soliman le Magnifique*, pp. 179–84.

[60] See, for instance, the *intitulatio* (*unvan*) of Süleyman's letters to the Habsburg rulers Charles V, Ferdinand I, and Maximilian II in Schaendlinger and Römer, *Die Schreiben Süleymans des Prächtigen*, letters 1, 6, 7, 19, 23, 25, and 32.

that Charles's election was divinely inspired and signaled the "restoration of *sacrum Imperium*," and suggested that Charles V would recover the Holy Land. His coronation in Bologna in 1530 presented another opportunity to promote the image of the emperor as a defender of the faith who would defeat the Turks in a new crusade. This was the image of the emperor advocated by his advisors and supporters, and thanks largely to their effective propaganda campaign, it soon became the widespread expectation among Charles's subjects.[61]

Apart from predictions and prophecies, Habsburg propaganda used the emperor's wars against the Ottomans to publicize Charles V's image of "defender of the Catholic faith." Both his propagandists and the emperor himself argued that it was his troops (some 80,000 foot soldiers and 6,000 horses according to Ferdinand)[62] that stopped the sultan from attacking Vienna in 1532.[63] Charles V's greatest victory against Islam, his 1535 Tunis campaign, was presented as a victorious crusade against the enemies of the faith. Painters, poets, and official chroniclers celebrated the victory. The emperor's triumphal march in 1535–6 in Italy and his imperial entries into Palermo, Messina, Naples, Rome, and Florence, organized after similar triumphal entries of the Roman Caesars, presented an unusually prolonged opportunity to propagate the Emperor's image as defender of the faith, "Destroyer of the Turks," and "Tamer of Africa."[64]

[61] Peter Burke, "Presenting and Re-presenting Charles V," in Hugo Soly (ed.), *Charles V 1500–1558 and his Time* (Antwerp: Mercatorfonds, 1999), pp. 411–18, 426–33; John M. Headley, "The Habsburg World Empire and the Revival of Ghibellinism," *Medieval Renaissance Studies* 7 (1975): 93–127, especially 97–8, reprinted in J. M. Headley, *Church, Empire and World. The Quest for Universal Order, 1520–1640* (Aldershot: Ashgate, 1997), article V (with original pagination).
[62] See Ferdinand's letter to his sister, dated October 2, 1532, in Franz Bernhard von Bucholtz, *Geschichte der Regierung Ferdinand des Ersten*, 9 vols. (Vienna: Schaumburg und Compagnie, 1831–8) vol. IV, p. 115, quoted by Bárdossy, *Magyar politika*, p. 344.
[63] See James D. Tracy, *Emperor Charles V, Impresario of War: Campaign Strategy, International Finance, and Domestic Politics* (Cambridge: Cambridge University Press, 2002), pp. 145–6.
[64] Under the emperor's personal command the allied Christian navy captured La Goletta and Tunis and forced Süleyman's admiral, Hayreddin Barbarossa, to abandon his positions in the region. On Charles V's Tunis campaign, and the Habsburg propaganda regarding it, see Wilfried Seipel (ed.), *Der Kreiszug Kaiser Karls V. gegen Tunis Kartons und Tapisserien* (Vienna: Kunsthistorisches Museum, 2000); Alfred Kohler, *Karl V 1500–1558. Eine Biographie* (Munich: Beck, 1999), pp. 106–8; Wim Blockmans, *Emperor Charles V, 1500–1558* (London: Arnold, 2002), pp. 173–4; Burke, "Presenting and Re-presenting Charles V," pp. 433–4. Although Tunis remained in Spanish hands until 1569 (and was taken again in 1573–4), the naval battle at Prevesa in 1538, where the Ottomans were victorious, proved to be more important in the long run. See J. F. Guilmartin Jr., *Gunpowder and Galleys: Changing Technology and Mediterranean Warfare at Sea in the Sixteenth Century* (Cambridge: Cambridge University Press, 1974, reprint London: Conway Marine, 2003), pp. 42–56.

Millenarian prophecies and apocalyptic expectations were also current in the Ottoman Empire in the early sixteenth century.[65] They influenced public opinion and were used by the sultan's image-makers – most effectively by Grand Vizier Ibrahim Pasha and his confidant Lodovico Gritti, the bastard son of the doge of Venice who advised Istanbul on affairs related to Hungary and the Habsburgs – to design and publicize Süleyman's image as *sahib-kıran*, the ruler of a new universal empire. As a result of his influence on and his friendship with the young sultan, Ibrahim Pasha played an unprecedented role in devising Ottoman imperial ideology and policy.[66] The grand vizier viewed in Süleyman the new world conqueror, the successor of Alexander the Great, his and his master's favorite historical hero. It seems that Ibrahim Pasha succeeded where Gattinara failed: his messianic rhetoric and imperial aspirations not only reached the sultan's ears but also influenced his master's mind, whereas Charles V took apocalyptic expectations and his Grand Chancellor's many *consulta*s or memoranda, in which Gattinara sought to prepare his master for the task of universal rulership, with prudent skepticism. Ibrahim mentioned to a Venetian envoy how a book of prophecies, which he and Süleyman had read in their youth, predicted the rise of a man called Ibrahim and his master's becoming the conqueror of the Roman Empire (*l'imperio di Roma*).[67]

Süleyman's European contemporaries also knew about the Sultan's imperial aspirations. In his speech before the Castilian Cortez in late 1527, Gattinara listed all the conquests of the Ottomans in Asia and Europe and reminded his audience that Süleyman was already ruling over a much larger empire than Alexander the Great or the Caesars of Rome. He warned his Castilian listeners that the sultan wanted to build a world empire (*la monarchia de tudo el mundo*).[68] Gattinara did not exaggerate regarding Sultan Süleyman's imperial ambitions. In December 1527, at about the same time as the Grand Chancellor delivered his speech, Second Vizier Mustafa Pasha reminded Hieronim Łaski, the envoy of

---

[65] Fleischer, "The Lawgiver as Messiah."

[66] See Hester Donaldson Jenkins, *Ibrahim Pasha: Grand Vizier of Suleiman the Magnificent* (New York: Columbia University Press, 1911); Ferenc Szakály, *Lodovico Gritti in Hungary 1529–1534: A Historical Insight into the Beginnings of Turco-Habsburgian Rivalry* (Budapest: Akademiai Kiadó, 1995).

[67] Robert Finlay, "Prophecy and Politics in Istanbul: Charles V, Sultan Süleyman, and the Habsburg Embassy of 1533–1534," *Journal of Early Modern History* 2/1 (1998): 22.

[68] John M. Headley, "Germany, the Empire and *Monarchia* in the Thought and Policy of Gattinara," in Heinrich Lutz (ed.), *Das römisch-deutsche Reich im politischen System Karls V* (Munich: Oldenbourg, 1982), p. 22, reprinted in Headley, *Church, Empire and World*, article VI.

King János Szapolyai of Hungary, that Süleyman was second only to the Providence and just as there was only one Sun on the horizon, so was there only one ruler of the world: his master.[69]

THE FAILURE OF UNIVERSALIST VISIONS AND OTTOMAN–HABSBURG STALEMATE IN CENTRAL EUROPE

The Ottoman–Habsburg confrontation in Central Europe is closely related to the events that followed the battle of Mohács, in which Louis II, king of Hungary and Bohemia, was killed. The formation of anti-Habsburg and pro-Habsburg factions under two elected kings, János Szapolyai and Ferdinand of Habsburg, the failure of either party to gain definite victory over the other, and their subsequent dependence on the diplomatic and military assistance of the Ottoman and Holy Roman empires, respectively, led to the inevitable confrontation between the two empires in Central Europe.

The Ottoman threat, real, perceived, or exaggerated, had fostered the establishment of dynastic coalitions in Central Europe from the late fourteenth century onward. Ferdinand learned quickly how to play the "Turkish card" along with another revitalized medieval idea, the bulwark of Christendom (*antemurale Christianitatis*), in order to strengthen his position against Szapolyai. However, the multiple commitments of the Habsburgs (northern Italy, Germany, the Netherlands, the Mediterranean, North Africa, Hungary), as well as the Austrian and Spanish Habsburgs' different priorities led to a stalemate between Ferdinand and János Szapolyai, with each controlling only parts of Hungary. More importantly, the 1532 campaign showed that neither Charles V nor Süleyman wanted to risk a major battle. Occupied with the war against the German Protestant electors and estates of his empire, Charles V instructed his younger brother to avoid confrontation with the sultan and urged Ferdinand to conclude a peace treaty with Süleyman, for "the two of us alone are weak" against the Turks. Ferdinand indeed did everything he could in 1532 to prolong the existing Ottoman–Habsburg

[69] "Nonne scis, quia magnus Dominus noster primus est post divinam Potentiam, et uti unus sol per caelum vagatur, sic tutius mundi Imperator noster Dominus est." Łaski's report on his mission was composed after his journey, presumably in the summer of 1528, and was published by Mátyás (Matthias) Bél, *Adparatus ad Historiam Hungariae, sive collectio Miscellanea ...* (Posonii, 1735), pp. 159–89 and by Eudoxiu de Hurmuzaki, *Documente privitóre la Istoria Românilor I/2, 1451–1575* (Bucharest: C. Göbl, 1891), pp. 38–67. Quotation from p. 42. See also the annotated Hungarian translation by Gábor Barta in Gábor Barta (ed.), *Két tárgyalás Sztambulban* [Two Audiences in Istanbul] (Budapest: Európa Könyvkiadó, 1996) p. 105.

ceasefire, which was about to expire. He was willing to give up Hungary, except for some strategically important fortresses that were vital for the defense of his Austrian hereditary lands, in order to gain a peace treaty from Süleyman and to stop the marching Ottoman army before it reached Vienna, its declared target.[70]

Despite Ottoman rhetoric to the contrary and Süleyman's declaration that he was marching into Hungary in order to meet the emperor's forces at a decisive battle,[71] Ottoman military aims may have been more modest, although not less significant in terms of overall Ottoman strategy. In Gülru Necipoğlu's reading of the relevant sources, the 1532 campaign was a skillfully choreographed imperial procession and a pompous display of Ottoman imperial grandeur, organized by Ibrahim Pasha in order to present his master as world conqueror. It was also Ibrahim Pasha's response to Charles V's coronation celebrations in Bologna in 1530. Süleyman's imperial entries into Nish and Belgrade reminded western observers – many of whom were forced to view the sultan's imperial march from the minarets of the central mosques of those cities – of Emperor Charles V's coronation cavalcade. Süleyman's four-tier parade helmet, which he wore during these triumphal entries and audiences, was commissioned by Ibrahim Pasha from Venice. Mistakenly identified by European diplomats present at those receptions as the sultan's crown, the ceremonial helmet imitated that of the papal tiara and the crown that Charles V had worn during his Bologna coronation. The message was clear: Süleyman was challenging the authority of both the pope and the emperor.[72] Whatever the real goal of the 1532 campaign might have been, the parades orchestrated by Ibrahim Pasha again demonstrate that Ottoman policy-makers not only were well informed about Charles V's imperial ambitions, but they were also familiar with the language and symbols of how such ambitions were displayed in contemporary Europe, and were ready to use the same language of propaganda and symbols of imperial display in order to counter them.

By the early 1540s, however, it had become clear that neither the emperor nor the sultan could establish universal rulership. The confrontation in

[70] Bárdossy, *Magyar politika*, pp. 105–9. See also Ferdinand's instruction to his envoys sent to Süleyman in Bucholtz, *Regierung*, vol. IV, p. 98.

[71] See Süleyman's letter to Ferdinand from the Ottoman camp in Ösek (Eszék/Osijek) dated July 17, 1532, and published in István Bariska (ed.), *Kőszeg ostromának emlékezete* [Remembering the Siege of Kőszeg/Güns] (Budapest: Európa Könyvkiadó, 1982), p. 170.

[72] Gülru Necipoğlu, "Süleyman the Magnificent and the Representation of Power in the Context of Ottoman-Habsburg-Papal Rivalry," in İnalcık and Kafadar *Süleyman the Second*, pp. 163–91.

the Mediterranean and in Hungary ended in stalemate. When the military equilibrium in Hungary was upset by the death of Szapolyai in 1540, the lack of adequate commitments of Habsburg resources in Central Europe led to the tripartite division of Hungary and to the formation of a Muslim–Christian frontier in the middle of the country. In 1541, Ferdinand attempted to extend his rule over the rest of Hungary. By doing so, he threatened Ottoman positions in the region and forced Süleyman, who during Szapolyai's lifetime had maintained his influence through his protégé, to conquer the strategically important central parts of Hungary along with its capital city Buda, which controlled the Danubian waterways into Central Europe. Thus, it was not imperial ideology or the longing for universal rulership, but realpolitik and the defense of Ottoman positions in Central Europe that prompted the conquest of central Hungary in 1541.

CONCLUSION

While early modern polities cannot be compared to the modern "information state," the collection and manipulation of information, both domestic and foreign, as well as information-based surveillance – features that are usually associated with modernity – were methods routinely used by the Ottomans. The examination of Ottoman intelligence-gathering has shown that the Ottomans possessed a structured and well-functioning system through which they collected and assessed information regarding their rivals. Although Ottoman unilateralism in diplomacy, that is, the lack of permanent Ottoman embassies abroad, deprived the Porte of an important means of intelligence – that of the resident ambassador, often labeled as "privileged spy" – other circumstances favored the Ottomans. The empire's awesome military power and successes, its control over major trade routes, its territorial immensity and envied wealth, its relative openness and religious tolerance in an age when most European monarchs desired forced religious homogeneity, as well as the multiethnic nature of the empire's population, made its capital, Istanbul, not only a desirable destination for many Europeans, but also an ideal place where news, information and misinformation, ideas and myths were constantly exchanged. The many ethnic and religious groups living in Istanbul provided a handy pool of people who crossed religious, cultural and linguistic barriers and mediated among ordinary people of different cultures as well as between the Ottomans and their enemies, rivals and allies.

In addition to the empire's Muslim political elite – many of them of Christian (*devşirme*) origin – Jews expelled from Europe, Christian adventurers and renegades, and, later, the Greeks of Istanbul's Phanar district, all played their role in the collection and evaluation of information, as well as in the formulation of Ottoman strategy, foreign policy, and propaganda. Information was crucial in realizing the limits of Ottoman and Habsburg imperial power and it also helped Istanbul to more realistically assess Ottoman policy options vis-à-vis the Habsburgs. Although propaganda and lip service to universal rulership continued to play a role in strengthening the legitimacy of the two competing monarchs, in their confrontation realpolitik and political pragmatism won the day.

4

The Ottomans in the Mediterranean

Molly Greene

INTRODUCTION

The Mediterranean Sea was always an Ottoman frontier, but the nature of that frontier changed over time. For several hundred years (roughly, the mid fourteenth through the end of the sixteenth centuries) the Mediterranean was an offensive frontier as the Ottomans pushed steadily westward from their home territory along the eastern shores of the inland sea. By the end of the sixteenth century the technological and financial costs of further expansion had become so great that the Ottomans fell back to a line that ran somewhere to the east of Malta. From that point onwards the frontier in the Mediterranean was defensive, intended primarily to keep Habsburg power out of the eastern Mediterranean. The hot frontier became, in Hess's words, "the forgotten frontier."

The history of this military frontier is straightforward enough. What is less clear – and has been less systematically considered – is the nature of Ottoman control over its "home" territory of the eastern Mediterranean. What did control mean in a maritime setting? Put differently, what did sovereignty look like when the territory in question was a body of water, dotted with islands, rather than a rolling expanse of hills and valleys covered with villages?

These questions have been considered almost entirely in the negative. Historians have asserted that the Ottomans lost control of the sea in the post-classical era. Yet without a positive argument as to what control looked like in an earlier period, this assertion is hard to evaluate in a meaningful way. In the second part of this chapter, then, we will explore the particular challenges of ruling over literally hundreds of small islands and miles of coastline.

ENTERING THE MEDITERRANEAN WORLD

The central fact of the fourteenth-century eastern Mediterranean was the quickening pace of Byzantine collapse. The struggle to fill the resultant power vacuum in the Aegean as well as in Asia Minor and southeastern Europe was in full swing by the time the Ottomans made their first, faint entry onto the historical stage at the very end of the thirteenth century. On one side were the Islamic states that finally reached the Anatolian coastline about this time. These maritime emirates – of Menteshe, Aydın, Sarukhan, and Karasi – were part of the patchwork of states that had emerged in the wake of the Mongol defeat of the Seljuks. Here, along the shores of Asia Minor, Turkish power ran up against a string of Latin states, a mix of reconfigured Crusader states, and representatives of the commercially powerful republics of Genoa and Venice. These states took territory from each other in a chaotic ebb and flow. The formidable Knights of St. John established themselves on the island of Rhodes in 1309 (with the help of a Genoese corsair) and extended their control to the surrounding Dodecanese islands. Smyrna fell to Umur Pasha of the maritime principality of Aydın in the early 1320s. In 1344 a crusading fleet – with galleys supplied by the pope, Venice, the king of Cyprus, and the Hospitallers – took it back.[1] The Byzantine historian Pachymeres, writing in the early fourteenth century, describes how the Italians moved in as Byzantine power dissolved:

> Seeing that Andronicus II was neglecting the islands of Chios and Mytilene and since their occupation would make their own position untenable, the Italians asked the Basileus either to secure their proper defense himself or to entrust the islands to them so that with the revenues derived from them they could build a fleet to defend them.[2]

A continuous stream of raids and counter-raids across the Muslim/ Christian divide accompanied such official transfers of power. The two procedures combined to turn the Anatolian littoral and the Aegean into a borderland in the fourteenth and fifteenth centuries.

The Ottomans initially had no contact with this world. Their territory, with its origins around the village of Soğut, was inland and they shared a borderland with the Byzantines, not the Italians. But Ottoman expansion soon changed that. At some point in the mid 1330s, Orhan annexed his neighbor to the west, the *beylik* of Karasi, which bordered the Aegean in northwestern Anatolia. Orhan went on to capture Gallipoli (a city that would become the main Ottoman naval base), on the European side of the Dardanelles Straits. By the end of the fourteenth century, the nascent empire controlled the Aegean coastline of Asia Minor.

---

[1] Halil İnalcık, "The Rise of the Turcoman Maritime Principalities in Anatolia, Byzantium and Crusades, *Byzantinische Forschungen* 9 (1985): 197.
[2] Ibid., p. 186.

In this early period, little distinguished the Ottomans as a sea power from their Turkish rivals. They threw themselves into the sea raiding and treaty-making that was so characteristic of the Aegean at this time. The *ghazis* who made up the Ottoman army on land, fighting for God and for booty, now appeared as *azebs* on board Ottoman ships. They had no particular training in seamanship and were drawn from the same volunteers who filled the land armies. For specifically maritime knowledge, the Ottomans relied on both the Christian and the convert population of the eastern Mediterranean, as had earlier Turkish maritime principalities. Native Greeks constituted the professional crews of the first Turkish ships, while others operated independently – but in the service of the various Turkish states – as corsairs. The switch was relatively easy to make; Greek corsairs simply resumed their raids on the Latin-held Aegean islands and mainland Greece, only now they were working for the Turks rather than the Byzantines. Hayreddin Barbarossa, who would rise to become the ruler of Algiers, and later admiral of the Ottoman fleet, was of Greek origin and got his start raiding the southern and western shores of Anatolia on behalf of Korkud, son of Bayezid II.[3]

As long as the Italian states continued to dominate the seas, raiding was preferred over more direct forms of engagement. For example, even though a Spanish visitor described a great arsenal and docks at Gallipoli (the Ottoman naval base) in 1403, the Ottoman fleet stationed there attacked merchant ships and coastal settlements only when they were sure that the Venetian fleet was not in the vicinity.[4]

THE IMPERIAL AGE

The threat of Latin sea power did not come to an end with the conquest of Constantinople. The two most formidable Christian naval powers – the Venetians and the Knights of St. John – remained firmly in place and it would take a series of engagements in the late fifteenth and the sixteenth centuries to extinguish them.

In 1516 and 1517 the Ottomans defeated the Mamluks in Syria and Egypt. Just a few years later, the Knights of St. John surrendered Rhodes to Süleyman and began their retreat to the western Mediterranean. At mid-century Venice lost a whole string of islands in the central Aegean, adding to losses already suffered earlier. Cyprus fell in 1570, leaving only the island

---

[3] Colin Imber, *The Ottoman Empire 1300–1650: The Structure of Power* (London: Palgrave, 2002), p. 47.
[4] İnalcık, "Gelibolu," in EI2, vol. II, p. 984.

of Crete in an otherwise Ottoman sea. Through their naval victories the Ottomans did more than snuff out the last remnants of Latin power. They recreated, and even extended, the old imperial unity of the eastern Mediterranean that had been established by the Romans and maintained by the Byzantines until the Arab conquests of the seventh century wrested the southeastern shores away from Constantinople's control. Now, for the first time since the seventh century, the imperial capital on the shores of the Bosphorus ruled the great Arab cities of Aleppo, Damascus, Cairo, and Jerusalem. One of the most striking signs of this new unity was the resumption of the grain levy from Egypt to Istanbul that the Arabs had abolished with their conquest of Egypt. The grain of the Nile valley became a vital source of food for the capital city. No longer the frontier in the battle against Latin Christendom, the eastern Mediterranean was now an internal lake that linked the European, Anatolian, and Arab provinces of the empire.

THE TURN TO THE WEST

Ottoman victories in the east did not mean the end of the offensive frontier in the Mediterranean. It simply moved to the central Mediterranean as the Ottomans turned their sights towards a different enemy further to the west.

In a remarkable mirroring, the Spanish Habsburg emperors and the Ottoman sultans both consolidated their imperial projects early in the sixteenth century. They then turned their attention to each other, from opposite ends of the inland sea, and fought a series of naval battles to establish sole hegemony over the Mediterranean world. As powers now in possession of extensive resources – both human and material – they were able to construct and man great fleets of galleys. Large-scale galley warfare, rather than the raids and counter-raids of the sea *ghazis*, marked the Christian/Muslim frontier throughout the sixteenth century. And it was the constraints of galley warfare that would eventually determine where the frontier would settle.

The Ottomans first turned their sights to the western Mediterranean through the energy and ambitions of those same corsair captains who had fought on their behalf in the Aegean. As the Ottomans gradually incorporated and stabilized the eastern half of the sea, these pirates/entrepreneurs were drawn far towards the west, where the Spanish defeat of the Muslim kingdom of Granada (1492) had brought the Christian/Muslim frontier to the coasts of southern Spain. When Iberian Muslims sent an appeal for assistance to the Ottoman (and Mamluk) courts in 1487, Bayezid II sent the

corsair Kemal Reis on a reconnaissance mission.[5] Although neither Kemal
nor Bayezid would be able to save Granada, this new frontier offered
opportunities for raiding and other adventurers followed in their wake.
They established themselves along the North African coastline and entered
into alliances with the North African rulers who were threatened by Spain.
By the 1530s these informal relationships had evolved into formal incorporation into the empire. The Spanish resisted the new imperial connection
between the Ottoman capital and northwestern Africa and the two foes
clashed repeatedly throughout the sixteenth century. Full-scale conflict
commenced in the 1530s, by which time Spain had been integrated into
the much larger Habsburg Empire. The clash reflected Ottoman/
Habsburg rivalry on the continent as much as it did the contest between
Christianity and Islam in the Mediterranean.

In 1532 Charles V attacked the Ottoman city of Coron in southern
Greece.[6] The move was intended to divert the Ottoman armies from
their campaign in the Balkans, which was putting pressure on Charles's
Austrian territories. The move did succeed to the extent that Süleyman had
to call off the Balkan expedition, but it also had the effect of galvanizing
him into action in the Mediterranean. The corsair Hayreddin Barbarossa
was summoned from Algiers and put in charge of the Ottoman fleet. In the
summer of 1534 the new Ottoman admiral sailed to Tunis and overthrew
the semi-independent Hafsid dynasty. The Ottomans now controlled one
side of the Sicilian channel, which critically linked the eastern and western
Mediterranean sea. This victory was short-lived, however. Just one year
later Charles I launched a fleet of 400 ships, carrying over 26,000 men, and
retook the city.

A string of Ottoman victories followed the Habsburg recapture of
Tunis. In 1541 the Habsburgs tried to take Algiers, but had to withdraw
with a major loss of men and materiel. The city of Tripoli fell to the
Ottoman armada in 1551 and the Muslim threat grew apace. In the summer
of 1558 the Ottomans slaughtered an entire contingent of Spanish troops
stationed on the Algerian coast and raided the island of Minorca. Truly
alarmed, two years later Philip II (who in 1559 succeeded his father Charles)
sent his galleys once again to the central Mediterranean, where they
suffered a spectacular defeat at the island of Gerba. Busbecq, the ambassador of the Holy Roman Emperor in Istanbul, witnessed the triumphant

[5] Andrew Hess, *The Forgotten Frontier* (Chicago: University of Chicago Press, 1978), p. 60.
[6] Hess describes this battle as the beginning of "the imperial phase of Ibero-African frontier
history," p. 72.

return of the Ottoman fleet. He watched as columns of Christian prisoners were paraded through the streets. The Ottomans were now firmly in control of the central Mediterranean and the Christian world waited with dread as the spring of 1561 turned to summer; they fully expected the Ottoman armada to reappear and attack some portion of the Italian or Spanish coastline. In the event, however, the armada never came and in fact did not reappear for four long summers.[7] The long-expected assault did not come until 1565 when Süleyman finally launched an attack on Malta. Incredibly, the Knights were able to hold off the attackers long enough for disease, heat, and food shortages to do their work. When Don Garcia of Toledo showed up with a relief force of 11,000 in early September, the Ottomans had to abandon the siege; by September 12 "the last Turkish sail had disappeared over the horizon."[8]

The defeat at Malta returned the initiative to the Spanish who did not, however, move right away, due to a decision to concentrate on the deteriorating situation in the Netherlands.[9] It would take the Ottoman conquest of Cyprus (summer of 1570) to bring the Spanish back into the Mediterranean in force. Philip's decision to go to the aid of Venice led directly to the famous battle at Lepanto in 1571, where the allied Christian forces scored a tremendous victory over their Muslim foe.

In all of these battles, the goal of military strategists on both sides was to seize and control as many fortified ports as possible.[10] This goal flowed directly from the limitations of the war galley. While the galley enjoyed great speed and maneuverability, it was relatively fragile – it could not withstand the rough seas of winter – and it was unable to stay at sea for long periods. This stemmed from the fact that storage space on board was very limited; storing more than ten days' worth of food and water on board was impossible. In order to operate effectively, then, the galley could not stray

---

[7] It would have been surprising if the Ottomans had attacked the very next summer, given the difficulties of resource mobilization. Nevertheless, it is not clear why they waited until the summer of 1565. Possibly they were distracted by hostilities in Hungary with the Austrian branch of the Habsburgs. I thank John Guilmartin for these observations (email communication, December 24, 2004).

[8] Fernand Braudel, *The Mediterranean and the Mediterranean World in the Age of Philip II* (New York: Harper and Row: 1972), vol. II, p. 1019.

[9] Hess, *The Forgotten Frontier*, p. 85.

[10] The Ottomans and the Habsburgs were not attempting to establish command of the high seas. Such control would have required both a continuous patrol, in order to keep the sea lanes open for one's own ships and to deny access to the enemy, and the ability to blockade the adversary's ports, thus strangling his trade. Neither of these goals was feasible with the Mediterranean galley. See John Guilmartin, *Gunpowder and Galleys: Changing Technology and Mediterranean Warfare at Sea in the Sixteenth Century* (Cambridge: Cambridge University Press, 1974), ch. 1, passim.

too far or for too long from its own (friendly) ports. When the two imperial fleets engaged each other over the course of the sixteenth century it was typically an assault on a coastal or an insular fortress. With every fortress captured, the victor would increase the range of his war galleys. The Ottomans and the Spaniards fought each other for possession of the best ports in the central and western Mediterranean, ports in which galleys could take refuge and take on supplies before emerging, refreshed, to confront the enemy once again. The Ottoman siege of Malta, for example, was an attempt to secure a raiding base within striking distance of Spanish possessions in the western Mediterranean.

Capturing fortresses became harder and harder over the course of the century. There were several reasons for this. Better fortifications meant that it took longer for cities to be taken. The cities of Modon and Coron in 1500, for example, were taken after brief sieges but the Ottomans had to struggle mightily to take Rhodes in 1522.[11] Besides the strain inherent in longer battles, the increasing length of sieges meant that galleys had less and less time to get to the place of battle, conquer it, and then get back home before winter.[12] The galleys themselves were becoming increasingly cumbersome and expensive to operate. The fierce competition of the sixteenth century required more and more guns on galleys, which in turn forced the development of bigger and stronger ships, a search for more manpower (a perennial Mediterranean problem) and more provisions, at a time when prices were rising.[13] In 1520, ship's biscuit accounted for just under 25 percent of the total cost of operating a galley; by 1590 that figure had risen to between 30 and 50 percent.[14]

It is essential to understand these two aspects of galley warfare – its increasing inability to prevail and its soaring cost – to appreciate why Lepanto was strangely inconsequential. The Ottomans still got Cyprus, despite their defeat, and the Habsburgs did not press their advantage. Lepanto was not followed by yet more spectacular clashes. Rather, a gradual disengagement occurred that, over time, proved to be permanent. By the 1570s each side had reached as far as it could comfortably go and the enormous costs of trying to go further were not worth the incremental

---

[11] Ibid., p. 262. "Unlike the sieges of Modon and Coron less than a quarter of a century before, it was a long drawn-out affair and a costly one for the attacker."

[12] Hess, *The Forgotten Frontier*, p. 85. Galleys set out at the vernal equinox (around March 21) and returned in October or early November.

[13] By the mid seventeenth century the average galley carried 330 men. Imber, *The Ottoman Empire*, ch. 8, "The Fleet."

[14] Guilmartin, *Gunpowder and Galleys*, p. 222.

gains. For the Habsburgs, the victory at Lepanto did not lead to domination of the eastern Mediterranean because it was just too far away from Christian bases to operate the fleet safely.

The Ottomans, too, were no longer willing to undergo the tremendous effort and cost that would have been involved in trying to establish a stronger presence in the western Mediterranean. Already by the middle of the sixteenth century a galley could go no farther than Tunis and still carry the strength needed to mount a protracted siege of a strongly fortified place.[15] Therefore, when Queen Elizabeth attempted to draw the Ottomans into the English confrontation with Spain – she asked that the Ottoman fleet be sent out to confront the Habsburgs – the sultan did not respond.[16]

The military frontier in the Mediterranean, then, came to rest at those outlying ports in the central Mediterranean beyond which the galleys, on both the Christian and the Muslim side, could not comfortably go. The furthest Ottoman outpost was Tunis while for Christendom it was Malta.[17]

It is striking how the location of Ottoman land frontiers in Europe and Anatolia and the naval frontier in the Mediterranean were determined by very similar forces. McCarthy writes that "the army was in practice restricted to one campaign season's march from Istanbul. It is perhaps no accident that the Ottoman borders in Europe and eastern Anatolia were that distance from the capital."[18] He could be describing the Ottoman galleys, leaving the scene of battle and heading home before winter winds began to whip up the waters of the Mediterranean.

INTERNAL FRONTIERS

In 1629 the Venetian governor of Crete relayed the following incident in a report on the general state of the island. On February 14 some local fishermen came to him to say that they had seen a "Turkish" ship off the coast. As he was thinking what to do, the ship came into view. It fired off two cannon shots and then raised white flags, in order to indicate friendly intent. The ship turned out to have been commandeered by the one hundred Russian slaves who were on board. Just a few days later, yet another ship entered the harbor of Candia. Russian slaves had taken control of this one too. In both cases the governor secured the ship and took charge of the Turks on board,

---

[15] Ibid., p. 191.   [16] Braudel, *The Mediterranean and the Mediterranean World*.
[17] Tunis was truly on the frontier. Even though the Ottoman fleet could, theoretically, sail to Tunis, after Lepanto "the Constantinople based galley fleet moldered and never regained more than a fraction of its former strength." Guilmartin, *Gunpowder and Galleys*, p. 263.
[18] Justin McCarthy, *The Ottoman Turks* (London: Longman, 1997), p. 150.

safeguarding their personal effects and other goods which belonged to them. He then wrote to the bailo in Istanbul, to await instructions as to what to do. This was consistent with overall Venetian policy, which sought to demonstrate good faith towards the Ottomans by rescuing and returning Ottoman subjects who had been seized by pirates.[19]

The instructions came down that the Turks, and the ships, should be taken to the island of Milos. The kadi and the local notables had been informed of this and would be waiting to receive them. Upon the advice of Venice, the governor decided against accompanying them to Milos with his own ship. They would be escorted off the coast of Crete and then would continue on their way. The crew of the ships would be exclusively Ottoman subjects, drawn from the Ottoman ships and boats that happened to be in the port at the time. He did send one Venetian captain, who carried letters for Andreas Miliotes, the Venetian consul on Milos. The ship made it to the island without incident, but arguments that broke out subsequently between the islanders and the two Venetians – the consul and the captain – concerning the ships grew so violent that the two temporarily took refuge on a nearby, apparently deserted, island.

The details of this account – the white flags raised, the flurry of letters, the sendoff from Crete, and the Ottoman officials waiting expectantly on Milos – convey the nature of sovereignty, whether Ottoman or otherwise, in the eastern Mediterranean. Crossing the sea meant crossing an endless series of frontiers, ill-defined but nevertheless very real, as one moved in and out of the shadows of state authority.

These multiple frontiers were first and foremost a result of geography. In the eastern Mediterranean one is never very far from land. The greatest expanse of open sea lies between Crete and the Egyptian coastline, a distance of less than 250 miles. Innumerable small islands are scattered across the Aegean Sea, and further south lie the fertile islands of Crete and Cyprus. Therefore, even in this maritime setting, the Ottomans (and the Venetians) had many territorial possessions. In order to benefit from them – to tax the population and its production – and to deny them to others, they had to be made secure. The empire, then, had to be able to defend many miles of coastline as well as numerous small islands with their many ports, inlets, and coves.

The student of the early modern Mediterranean will find no ringing declaration of legal principles concerning the status of the sea, similar to those articulated by Grotius in his *Mare Liberum*, published in 1609 and

---

[19] They hoped that by so doing they could stave off Ottoman attacks on Venetian territories.

intended to address Dutch rights in the East Indies. Nor are we speaking about formal frontiers. Nevertheless, one can discern the location of frontiers in the disputes, agreements, and practices of everyday life. These make it clear that a frontier hovered along every expanse of coastline and encircled every island in the eastern Mediterranean.

Disputes invariably centered around ports and coastlines and took various shapes. One of the most common was the charge of territorial violation. This was the case in the 1638 "Valona incident" which almost led to war between Venice and the Ottoman Empire. In that year Venice entered the port of Valona (on the Adriatic) and seized sixteen galleys belonging to the Algerians and the Tunisians. The sultan was furious; he arrested the Venetian bailo, suspended diplomatic relations, and halted all Venetian trade. Venice defended herself on the basis of her treaties with the sultan, which consistently stated that "no Port or Harbor of his [that is, the sultan's] should be privileged to afford entertainment or protection to any Freebooter or Pirate."[20] The Barbary corsairs were admitted into Ottoman ports, of course, but they had to give various pledges of no harm to the Venetians, otherwise Venice was entitled to pursue them into port.[21] Outside the sultan's ports, however, different rules applied. These same treaties stated that if the Venetians "shall at any time encounter people of Barbary in the Open Sea, it shall be lawful for them to assault, take and destroy them without notice, or exceptions of the Ottoman port."[22]

The Venetians attempted to enforce the same rules with regard to their own ports. If, while bringing a Muslim prize back to the home port, Christian corsairs sought refuge in any Venetian port, then Venice would demand the return of the prize.[23] In the winter of 1582–3, a Spaniard and Knight Hospitaller named Don Diego Brochero de la Paz y Añaya embarked on a corsairing cruise to the Levant.[24] He surprised three Ottoman ships in the vicinity of Crete; they were carrying grain to the island. He seized the ships and diverted the grain to Sicily.

---

[20] Victor Mallia-Milanes, "From Valona to Crete: Veneto-Maltese Relations from the late 1630s to the Outbreak of the Cretan War," in Stanley Fiorini (ed.), *Malta: A Case Study in International Cross Currents* (Malta: Malta University Publishers, 1991), p. 162.

[21] Ibid., p. 72. These are: whenever Barbary pirates enter ports of the Grand Signor, they shall give security that they will not hurt the subjects of Venice. And if they have taken prizes from Venice, they will not be admitted to the said ports. If they have, and are admitted anyway, Venice has the right to pursue them.

[22] Ibid., p. 164.

[23] Victor Mallia-Milanes, *Venice and Hospitaller Malta: Aspects of a Relationship 1530–1798* (Marsa: Publishers Enterprises Group, 1992), p. 34.

[24] Ibid., p. 73.

Where, exactly, had the ships been seized? This was the issue that the two parties quarreled over. Venice claimed that Diego seized the ships along the coast of Crete. The Hospitaller version was different and carefully laid out where each of the ships had been seized, one in the gulf of Thessaloniki (very far indeed from Crete), one near the island of Samos, and the third near Rhodes, over 150 miles off the coast of Crete. The clear implication behind this line of argument was that Venetian sovereignty extended only so far beyond the Cretan, or any Venetian-held, coastline. Once beyond that, infidel ships could legitimately be seized. This is strikingly similar to the Ottoman–Venetian capitulations, in which Venice was permitted to take on the Barbary corsairs as long as the encounter took place on the open sea.

Possession of a port or a coastline conferred not only rights, but responsibilities. Just six years after Valona, pirates once again led to a clash between the Ottomans and Venice. This time it was Christian pirates – the Knights of Malta – and this time the chain of events did lead to war. They seized an Ottoman ship, with a number of high-ranking officials on board, in the vicinity of Crete.[25] When the sultan heard the news, he called in all the western ambassadors in an attempt to extract information from them. But he specifically blamed the Venetian bailo for the fact that the Maltese, apparently, had gone ashore on Crete with their prize.[26] The bailo protested that he knew nothing of the Knights going to Crete but, if they had, they would never have approached the Cretan shore at any place where the Venetians might have used cannon against them.[27] Although the principle at stake was too obvious for either party to state it, it is clear that sovereignty over an island, or a coastline, obliged the sovereign to prevent pirates from landing or even approaching. If the pirates managed to do so nonetheless, then the sovereign – in this case Venice – bore at least some responsibility for their actions.

These incidents, which are just a few of the many that could be cited, all date from the late sixteenth and the seventeenth centuries. This is not coincidental. After the Ottoman loss at Lepanto, levels of piracy began increasing in the eastern Mediterranean. Pirates from Mediterranean Europe – including the Knights of St. John, the Knights of St. Stephen from Pisa, and the fleets of the Spanish viceroys in southern Italy and

---

[25] See Molly Greene, *A Shared World: Christians and Muslims in the Early Modern Mediterranean* (Princeton: Princeton University Press, 2000), p. 14, for a more detailed account of the attack.

[26] Kenneth Setton, *Venice, Austria and the Turks in the Seventeenth Century* (Philadelphia: American Philosophical Society, 1991), p. 114.

[27] As it turned out later, the Maltese had landed on a deserted and unguarded stretch of beach. Ibid., p. 116.

Sicily – swarmed into the eastern Mediterranean. Northern newcomers, the English and the Dutch, soon joined them, although the latter did as much damage to Italian and Spanish shipping as to the Ottomans. The disputes that arose as a result of their depredations – just a few of which I have related above – allow us to reconstruct certain shared, but unspoken, principles that in a more peaceful time would be more difficult to uncover.

In the sixteenth century, for instance, when the Ottoman navy was much more active and western pirates were not active in Ottoman waters, such issues rarely came up in the diplomatic correspondence. It makes sense to assume, however, that the mental organization of space was the same. The frontier lay in that liminal space where the land met the sea.

Beyond the land and the frontier lay the open sea. Unlike the waters near the shore, no one seems to have laid claim to the open sea, or at least the rights and responsibilities of sovereign states on the high seas were unclear. There were probably several reasons for this.

The sensitivity of the shoreline, as opposed to the open sea, must have been related in part to the nature of Mediterranean warfare. Military encounters did not take place on the open sea; they were almost always fought in the shadow of a port, and with the goal, ultimately, of territorial expansion. In other words, even when battles were fought "at sea," as it were, it was still really all about the land.

But the lack of correspondence concerning encounters on the high sea may well signal something much more fundamental, something inherent in the nature of imperial rule. A recent article on empire has argued that "Empires did not cover territory evenly but composed a fabric that was full of holes, stitched together out of pieces, a tangle of strings." The piece continues: "Though empires did lay claim to vast stretches of territory, the nature of these claims was tempered by control that was exercised mainly over narrow bands, or corridors, of territory and over enclaves of various sizes and situations."[28] We can think of the eastern Mediterranean, in other words, much as we think about, for example, the Arabian peninsula. The Ottomans were vigilant in their control over the pilgrimage route that ran down the eastern side of the peninsula, alongside the Red Sea. But they showed no interest in the Arabian interior until the nineteenth century when British incursions began to threaten Ottoman control.[29] Similarly,

[28] L. Benton, "Legal Spaces of Empire: Piracy and the Origins of Ocean Regionalism," *Comparative Studies of Society and History* 47 (2005): 700–24.
[29] Fred Anscombe, *The Ottoman Gulf and the Creation of Kuwayt, Saudi Arabia and Qatar 1871–1914* (New York: Columbia University Press, 1997).

having conquered Egypt at the beginning of the sixteenth century, the Ottomans took care to organize a heavily armed convoy that left once a year from Alexandria, headed for Istanbul. Several large galleys were accompanied by numerous smaller warships as they departed Alexandria, heading for Rhodes. From Rhodes they sailed along the Anatolian coast, stopping at Chios, Samos, and Mytilene before entering the Dardanelles.[30] This convoy continued without interruption until the middle of the seventeenth century, long after Lepanto (1571) which is the conventional date when the Ottomans supposedly lost control of the seas due to the influx of western corsairs. The convoy was often targeted by the Knights of St. John or the Knights of St. Stephen (operating out of Livorno) but they were never able to cause any serious disruption to the ties linking Istanbul to her Egyptian province. It was the almost continuous warfare with the Venetians (1645–69 and 1684–99) that finally destroyed the system. During the course of these wars the Ottomans turned to neutral European shipping – the Dutch, the English, and particularly the French – to maintain the sea routes in the eastern Mediterranean.[31] And although the wars did finally come to an end, the reliance on the Europeans had now become an established fact.

When we think of the eastern Mediterranean, then, we should not think of an uninterrupted expanse of water over which the Ottomans did or did not exercise control. Rather we should picture it as bodies of water are shown in maps which render the water in different colors depending upon the depth of the ocean or of the sea. In our case, different colors would indicate areas of greater or lesser sensitivity. The state lavished attention on the former, while treating the latter with benign neglect.

---

[30] The description is in Daniel Panzac, *La caravane maritime: marins européens et marchands ottomans en Méditerranée (1680–1830)* (Paris: CNRS Éditions, 2004), p. 20.
[31] Ibid., p. 21.

5

Military reform and its limits in a shrinking Ottoman world, 1800–1840

Virginia H. Aksan

The era from 1750 to 1850 is generally acknowledged by western historians to have been the first age of global imperialism, when Britain and France fought for world domination on a number of continents, including the territories of the Ottoman Empire. It is in this period that French and British trade rivalries moved into the Middle East – to the space in between the Atlantic and Indic ocean worlds. Between 1798 and 1840 the French lost out to the British in the contest over control of Middle Eastern markets, as British consuls come to dominate their French counterparts in all the ports of the Arab world. It is thus easy to image a two-tier Ottoman Empire after 1840: the "Turkic" Ottoman world which faced west and north, and the Arab, semi-colonized world, facing south and east, which was drawn into the British trading system of the Indian Ocean. On the northern frontier, the emergence of rival empire Russia as both instigator and collaborator in many of the moments of crisis surrounding the dismemberment of the Ottoman Empire is of most significance in the transformations to be discussed. The Ottomans stood between the rock of British economic imperialism and the hard place of Russian territorial ambitions along the northern frontier.

For Ottoman historians, 1750–1850 is also known as the age of trans-formation, when military defeats and economic crisis forced a radical rearrangement of the Ottoman premise of rule. The challenges to the Ottoman *ancien régime* began around 1730, and resulted in a new order by 1830, still little understood. Even those who could be counted experts have generally evaded the question of how the Ottomans might actually have participated in the transformation of their own society, by avoiding the question altogether. There are, in most accounts, two Ottoman empires: the "Golden Age," which generally ends at 1650 (purists quit with the death of Sultan Süleyman the Magnificent in 1566), and the "Tanzimat Age," normally periodized as 1839–1918, when the centrifugal forces of reform decrees, insolvency, further informal British and French colonialism, and religio-ethnic nationalism tore the empire apart.

We do not yet have an adequate label for the society that emerged in the interim, as it has never been fully explained from within the indigenous Ottoman setting. This article represents some preliminary reflections about the Ottoman transformation, and is influenced by two views of social change. The first, represented by the work of Scholte,[1] argues for a globalizing impulse which has a potential to reorient the "social geography" of regions in profound ways. The other belongs to those who view the arrival of modernity in a colonial (or semi-colonial) setting as the imposition of new forms of order or disciplinary regimes. Influential examples for the latter view include Scott's *Seeing like a State*, and Timothy Mitchell, *Colonising Egypt*,[2] both of which discuss a series of bureaucratic interventions, such as new registration systems, property laws, and other interventions in individual lives, as imposing a new sort of regimen. I do not pretend to be doing other than tweaking the standard explanations for the position of the Ottomans vis-à-vis the superiority of European technologies and modes of thought, *circa* 1800, but I would like to suggest alternative means of mapping the changes.

The Ottomans and the successor states of the Middle East are generally thought to have failed to impose civilian order over militarized regimes, which is demonstrably the case. Yet studies of nation-state emergence often mute the central role played by violence in constructing all modern states, *except* in the Middle East, which is relentlessly castigated for its militarism. Ottoman military history from 1800 to 1840 is approached here from the point of view of two interrelated questions: first, what defensive strategies did the Ottomans take to shore up their vulnerable frontiers? Second, what kinds of disciplinary regimes, such as conscription, were imposed, as part of the social transformation under discussion? There are two assumptions which underlie this excursion. One is that defense, discipline, and order are here assumed to be the primary obligations of rulers of both empires and modern nation-states to their societies. The second presumes a limited successful Ottoman social transformation by 1840 that foreshadows the modern Turkish Republic.

The Ottoman Empire at the end of the reign of Mahmud II (1808–39) had been transformed into a creature we find awkward to describe. What is clear is that the survival of dynasty and empire alike had to depend on a

---

[1] Jan Aart Scholte, "What is Globalization? The Definitional Issue – Again" (Hamilton, Ontario: Institute on Globalization and the Human Condition Working Paper Series, 2003).

[2] Timothy Mitchell, *Colonising Egypt* (Cambridge: Cambridge University Press, 1988), and James C. Scott, *Seeing Like a State* (New Haven, CT: Yale University Press, 1998).

new, modern-style regimental army ethnically and religiously far more proscribed and subscribed than that of pre-1800, a contradictory ideology, and a society which had become somewhat accustomed to new forms of discipline. What were the limits of that transformation?

By 1800, the Ottoman military organization was in complete disarray. Several decades of experimentation with new-style armies had failed to impose any kind of discipline over the unruly janissary organization. The muster rolls of its standing army, and janissary entitlements (*esame*, or pay/ration tickets), had long served as public instruments of exchange, traded on the open market to whoever had the wherewithal to invest. The redistribution of the wealth of the empire through its traditional military system resembled a broad social welfare scheme that proved extremely resilient.

Warfare was unproductive in that setting. At what point Ottoman society became exhausted by continuous war is less of a question than at what point did a majority of the population resist going to war because it was completely unprofitable? The Austro-Ottoman (and Russian) War of 1736–9 is one of the standard choices, when the Habsburg and Ottoman armies reached a stalemate, and neither could force a decisive conclusion to the conflict. Arduous and costly campaigns along the Danube affected both Austria and Turkey, as the two foes remobilized armies year after year with little result. For the Habsburgs, the war proved enough of a disaster to force a total rethinking of military strategy and a gradual stabilization of the Ottoman–Habsburg border. For the Ottomans, the diplomatic triumph of the treaty of 1739, when Belgrade was restored to Ottoman control, misled Istanbul into complacency about the janissary system, and reform was postponed, with disastrous consequences.

The Ottomans did, however, obsess about the northern frontier: rightly so, as the Russians replaced the Habsburgs after 1739 as the chief foe, and threatened the entire northern arc from Belgrade to Kars in the Caucasus after 1768. That concentration of men and resources led to a neglect of relations with the southern tier of the Ottoman Empire, allowing both Kurds and Arabs to drift even further away from imperial oversight. A second development was the growth of a particular kind of warlord governance that challenged the empire's very existence under Mehmed Ali Pasha and his son Ibrahim Pasha of Egypt by 1831. Ottoman sultans relied on regional armies, strengthened precisely by their usefulness against the

Russians, and organized by a series of local magnates (*ayan*) such as Osman Pasvantoglu of Vidin, or Ali Pasha of Jannina, or Alemdar Mustafa Pasha of Ruschuk, to mention just the best-known.

In 1768, the Ottomans had to conjure up an army, and face the challenges of sharing power, or going under, in the first of six Russo-Ottoman wars from then until 1900. Manpower for the 1768–74 war was mobilized largely from among nomadic, multi-religious, and multiethnic warrior bands, a confederative military symbiosis which arose out of the disintegration of the janissary organization across the empire. There is terrific confusion in our sources, and what we make of them as historians, about what these bands of soldiers resembled. This makes an estimation of the real strength of the so-called janissaries practically impossible, but some scant evidence suggests that perhaps as many as 400,000 men were registered in the official muster rolls, of which 10 percent actually might have shown up when mobilized.[3] The alternate manpower, voluntary and for hire, arose sometimes in tandem with so-called janissaries, by association (*beşe* or *yoldaş* – both terms resonating as members, or fellow travelers, in this period) with the traditional corps, or as hired guns for provincial governors, or tax collectors/military contractors (the *mutassarıfs*), who in turn were contracted by the government to report to the battlefield with a specified number of troops. The dynasty was forced to replace a paper army with such troops to shore up the defense on the northern frontier. Repeatedly, from 1768 to 1826, the sultans resorted to the provincial armies to put down rebellions and to face the Russians across the Danube.

By the 1820s, the possibility of complete collapse was even more real, following revolts and ongoing civil war in both Serbia and Greece, as well as some of the worst rebellions in Ottoman history on the streets of Istanbul itself. Still, in 1828 Sultan Mahmud II mustered some 30,000–40,000 recruits and marched them to battle Russian Tsar Nicholas I at the mouth of the Danube – recruits observed as young and raw, but eager. What had Mahmud achieved, and what does that tell us about the limits of social transformation in a premodern empire?

DEFENSES

The northern frontier of the empire stretched from the mouth of the Danube to Ochakov in the Crimea, which had fallen to the Russians in

---

[3] Virginia Aksan, "Mutiny and the Eighteenth Century Ottoman Army," *Turkish Studies Association Bulletin* 22 (1998): 116–25.

1788, and to the eastern Black Sea, especially around Abhiska (Akhaltiske) and Poti, both strategic ports, which were the gateway to the Caucasus, and the strategic fortresses of Kars and Erzurum. For Russians and Ottomans alike the northern frontier was a zone of death. The Ochakov and İsmail garrisons, it will be remembered, were slaughtered by Russian troops in 1788 and 1791 respectively, while Ruschuk town and fortress in Bulgaria was completely demolished in 1810. Military commanders could count on losing a minimum of 25 percent of their armies to wounds, disease, and desertion in the Danubian battlegrounds, as true in 1768–74 as it was in 1828–9. By 1828 Russian troops had been present in (and often in occupation of) most of Moldavia and a good part of Wallachia for close to forty years. Russia had unilaterally annexed the Crimea in 1783, and occupied parts of Georgia as early as 1801, and by the 1829 Treaty of Adrianople Russia had extended its southern boundary to all of Georgia, Dagistan, and Azerbaijan.

Once the Russians occupied Abkhazia and Georgia, south of the Kuban, the two sides engaged in protracted negotiations and renewed hostilities which extended across wars and treaties from 1774 to 1829. The problem of Russian sovereignty over the Caucasus stemmed from the ambiguities of the 1774 Küçük Kaynarca treaty, in ambiguous wording about Kabarda in the Caucasus. Ottoman obstinacy, in spite of resounding defeat, about conceding ports, fortresses and further territory to the Russians, continued through the Crimean War (1853–6).

Russo-Ottoman treaty negotiations are usually represented, like those of the Habsburg–Ottoman 1739 Treaty of Belgrade, as having been successfully concluded only with the intervention of international mediators. To view "Ottoman fate as being decided in European chancelleries,"[4] as did diplomats of the time and most later historians, however, is to lose sight of the astuteness of both the sultan and his grand viziers. For example, Mahmud II convened a general council in early February 1812 which met for three days. The council found the Russian demands for the eastern Black Sea littoral particularly onerous, clearly viewing it as establishing a Russian sovereign presence within striking distance of the heart of the empire. Such a development was completely unacceptable from both a strategic and a religious point of view. The council was fully cognizant of the military and financial woes of the empire, and unwilling to propose a

---

[4] Allan Cunningham, "Stratford Canning and the Treaty of Bucharest," in Edward Ingram (ed.), *Anglo-Ottoman Encounters in the Age of Revolution: Collected Essays*, vol. I (London: Frank Cass, 1993), pp. 144–87.

return to war. Mahmud II remained adamant. His refusal to accept the treaty conditions even at the risk of going back to war was based on the understanding that having access to a port and passage in that area of the Black Sea was just a means for the Russians to supply weapons to the tribes of the Caucasus. In the event, the treaty was never fully enforced, and it took another fitful two years of war, in 1828–9, and the Russian invasion and occupation of Adrianople (Edirne) in 1829, for Mahmud II to give up his stubbornness concerning the preservation of the northern and eastern frontiers.

Defensive strategy after 1828 focused on restoration of the four fortresses at the mouth of the Danube: Varna, Ruschuk, Silistre, and Shumla (since 1768 Ottoman military headquarters in the Balkans). By that time, of course, Bessarabia had also become Russian territory, and the Ottomans were dealing with both the Greek and the Serbian rebellions. Slightly less than two years before Mahmud II's death, he and the young Prussian officer Helmuth von Moltke toured the mouth of the Danube, starting out by ship, and continuing overland on a tour of the four towns mentioned above. The aim of the excursion was mainly to review the reconstruction of the fortifications, but on several occasions that we know of Mahmud II also made public appearances, such as in Silistre in 1837, when he said: "It is our wish to ensure the peace and security of all inhabitants of our God-protected great states, both Muslim and raya. In spite of all difficulties, we are determined to secure the flourishing of the state and the population under our protection."[5] This was theater, perhaps, but it is also the only record of a sultan who had actually walked the frontiers since 1700.

More importantly for our discussion, the fortresses at Ruschuk and Silistre, of which redoubts survive, were laid out according to the most up-to-date European theories of defense (at least according to Moltke), with their gun emplacements facing both the Danube and south, correcting a previous lacuna, and in Silistre, for example, there was a series of seven bastions surrounding the city, this at a time when the government hovered near bankruptcy. Those who are aware of the later history of the empire will remember the ferocity of fighting in this area for the rest of the Ottoman presence in that part of the Balkans, in the Crimean War and again in 1877–8. Bulgarian historians have long viewed the fortresses under discussion as the famous four – the (literally) last-ditch effort of the Ottomans in the Balkans. The decisions and behavior of Mahmud II, in

[5] Viorel Panaite, "The *Re'ayas* of the Tributary-Protected Principalities: The Sixteenth through the Eighteenth Centuries," *International Journal of Turkish Studies* 9 (2003): 79–104.

the maturity of his reign, evince an understanding of that strategic mapping, which included for his part the use of public performance and persuasion. Hence, the external pressures on the frontiers forced a reformation of the empire's social geography, which predicted the territorial dimensions of the late Ottoman state and its successor, the Turkish Republic.

DISCIPLINARY REGIMES

Discipline is assumed to be the primary prerequisite for securing the stability of all modern societies. To comprehend the nature of order and discipline for the period, we need a brief excursion into traditional Ottoman concepts of rebellion (*fitne*), generally represented in the sources as the state of being without order (*nizam*). In our period, the army (and police), that is the janissaries, had become the locus of disorder. Their revolts in Istanbul had often served as a method of restoring the balance of corporate order, with demands usually centered on questions of salary payment, currency debasement, and entitlement, all of which served as a check on the rapaciousness of the sultan. Latterly, however, they protested marching to war at all, especially to the Caucasus and Iran. In one such rebellion in 1703, under Mustafa II (1695–1703), the ulema prepared the official justification for the janissary revolt. In the religious ruling (fatwa), four questions were posed and answered in the public confrontation: the first concerned Mustafa II's neglect of his "trust" in looking after his subjects ("allowing injustice and inequity to reign" while he went hunting and wasting the public treasury); the second legitimated their right as a Muslim community to stand up to an unjust ruler; the third condemned those who sided with an unjust ruler; and the fourth charged Mustafa II "with having compromised his mandate by accepting the peace treaties" and conceding so much territory to the Christian powers.[6]

This manifesto argued that the sultan's chief duty lay in maintaining the balance and stability of the Muslim community, while defending and extending the borders of the territories of Islam. The consistent use of such declarations in manifestos has blinded historians to the reality of dynastic politics, which often operated at odds with such justificatory rhetoric. The sultan was interested in personal and familial survival, but participated in theatricals, "the necessary ceremonial action and illusions

---

[6] Rifa'at Abou-El-Haj, *The 1703 Rebellion and the Structure of Ottoman Politics* (Leiden: Nederlands Instituut voor het Nabije Oosten, 1984), p. 71.

upon which sultanic rule depend[ed]."[7] While we have to accept the story
as filtered through our texts, it is clear that the maintenance of a clear
balance of various corporate orders and a return to order (*nizam*) was a
primary concern. I use it as a latter-day example of the *ancien régime* style
engagement between sultan and corporate elites.

NEW FORMS OF ORDER AND DISCIPLINE

The rebellions around the overthrow of Selim III (1789–1807) and the rise
of Mahmud II resemble a different form of confrontation, more like civil
war than the contest between janissary and sultan of the previous century.
After the fall of Selim III, and his imprisonment in Topkapı Palace, it was
Ruschuk on the Danube that became the center for refugees from reform
circles, who managed to persuade the provincial governor Alemdar
Mustafa, mobilizing troops as war with Russia loomed, of the advantage
of reinstalling Selim III, by force if necessary. Alemdar Mustafa and his
army joined forces with the grand vizier in Edirne, and the combined forces
had restored order to Istanbul by the end of July 1808. Alemdar then
engineered a coup to reinstall Selim III and make himself grand vizier. In
the chaos Selim III was killed, so Mahmud II (1808–39) was elevated to the
sultanate instead.[8] So ended a revolution unprecedented in Ottoman
history, where a provincial army of occupation replaced the ruling sultan,
without (or in spite of) the ruling of the chief mufti (*şeyhülislam*), who had
been removed from office immediately, and without the concurrence of the
janissaries of Istanbul.[9]

In October 1808 the chiefs of many of the great houses of Anatolia, and
some from the Balkans, convened in Istanbul with as many as seventy
thousand soldiers in total, by one contemporary account. In effect the
notables who gathered in 1808 represented the major regional forces
whose territories would make up the rump of the empire by the end of
the nineteenth century. The assembled provincial and urban elites of the
empire, in front of the sultan, and with his acquiescence, signed the Deed
of Agreement, outlining the relationship and obligations between the

---

[7] Stephen Turk Christensen, "'The Heathen Order of Battle,'" in S. T. Christensen (ed.), *Violence and
the Absolutist State: Studies in European and Ottoman History* (Copenhagen: Copenhagen University,
Humanistiske Forskning-center 1990), pp. 75–198.
[8] Ahmed Cevdet, *Tarih*, 1st edn, 12 vols. (Istanbul: n.p., 1858), vol. IV, p. 2203.
[9] A. Juchereau de St. Denys, *Révolutions de Constantinople en 1807 et 1808: précédées d'observations
générales sur l'état actuel de l'Empire Ottoman*, 2 vols. (Paris: Brissot-Thivars, 1819), vol. II, 177;
Stanford J. Shaw, *Between Old and New: The Ottoman Empire under Sultan Selim III 1789–1807*
(Cambridge, MA: Harvard University Press, 1971), pp. 384–407.

sultan and his notables. The document is sometimes called the Ottoman *Magna Carta*, and elsewhere described as the origin of public law in modern Turkey.[10] Of the seven articles, article 1 reaffirmed a pledge from the *ayan* not to oppose or resist the sultan, and to come to his aid should others do so. Article 3 affirmed the commitment to the imperial provincial financial system, essentially confirming the continuation of tax farming (*malikane*). Article 4 asserted the obligations of the grand vizier as absolute representative (*vekalet*) of the sultan, to uphold the laws of the empire (*kanun*), and the obligation of the signatories to the document to stand as his accusers if he violated those laws. Articles 6 and 7 dealt with preventing disorder in the capital city, and protecting the empire's subjects from abuse and oppression, with the *ayan* serving as the watchdogs. It is articles 2 and 5, however, which are the most interesting here. Article 2 committed the signatories to cooperate in providing the state troops (*devlet askeri*) for the benefit of the survival of the empire, and assisting the sultan against foreign and domestic enemies when required. Article 5 regulated the relationships between the *ayan*, the sultan, and the central bureaucracy, on the basis of mutual guarantees. The *ayan* pledged to preserve the authority of the state by maintaining good relations with one another and with the central state authorities, and in return were confirmed in the possession of their lands and the rights of their heirs.[11] The deed was innovative in conceptualizing a sharing of power between the sultan and his noble provincial subjects.

The deed was short-lived, however, because the city erupted in one of the largest rebellions in Istanbul of the entire life of the empire. The ostensible reason for the revolt was that those janissaries who refused to enroll in the new disciplined forces created by Alemdar Mustafa, called *sekban*s, found themselves deprived of their privileges. Not just janissaries, but scores of merchants, civil servants, and other beneficiaries of the janissary payroll, themselves in possession of pay tickets (*esame*), had been deprived of a source of income. Conscription for the *sekban*s began in Istanbul, and four thousand more were added to those billeted at the barracks in Levend Çiftliği and Üsküdar.[12] Alemdar had ambitiously envisioned one hundred *bölük* of 1,600 each, or 160,000 men. The army which supported him against the janissaries, however, probably numbered no more than 25,000.

---

[10] Avigdor Levy, "Military Policy of Sultan Mahmud II, 1808–1839." PhD dissertation, Harvard University, 1968, p. 53.
[11] B. Lewis, "Dustūr," in EI2 (1999 CD edition); Levy, "Military Policy," pp. 54–6.
[12] Levy, "Military Policy," p. 64.

The janissary revolt was a genuine protest against the changes to the system, and the abuses which accompanied them.[13] The coup, or, more accurately, continuing civil war, began among junior officers of the janissary corps, who first attempted to enlist their commander, who was promptly killed when he refused to join them. Alemdar was caught at the Bab-ı Ali, or Sublime Porte – grand vizierial headquarters at the center of the city – where he was killed in an explosion and a fire. The rebels' target remained their own leadership, so ordinary soldiers went unpunished, and much of Alemdar's army vanished into thin air. Still, Grand Admiral (*Kapudan*) Ramiz Pasha elsewhere in the city put up a good fight with the *sekban* troops, and regrouped others. The rebels were initially prevented from storming the Tophane arsenal, where the Levend Çiftlik troops were deployed. Loyal reformed troops in Üsküdar helped to complete the circle of the city, but no one thought to fight their way through to the grand vizier or the sultan. The janissaries demanded concessions from the sultan in traditional fashion, by coercing the ulema to secure the appointment of a new commander and a new grand vizier. Faced with his predecessor's fate, Mahmud II turned to the assembled reformed army for aid. Four or five thousand troops from Üsküdar and Galata were transported to Topkapı Sarayı. The new sultan had made his choice.

The revolt, called the "Alemdar Incident" in Turkish history texts, turned into a general riot, which left six hundred *sekbans*, and perhaps as many as five thousand rebels, dead. The sultan reached an accommodation with the janissary commanders, who were ready to pledge obedience, if the *sekban* corps was dissolved and any of the reformers who escaped were punished. At least one contemporary account, probably an exaggeration, reckoned as many as fifty thousand deaths in the events of November 1808.[14] The old order was permanently broken, even if the new order had also been temporarily stayed.

FURTHER TYPES OF DISCIPLINE

The important element in 1808 was the coalition of provincial forces that offered the sultan the opportunity to recover, and reorganize his empire. It is probably more important in the Ottoman social transformation than the famous final confrontation with the janissaries in 1826, when Mahmud II

[13] Ibid., pp. 62–3.
[14] I have followed Levy's summary of the events here, as he consulted all the contemporary accounts. Ibid., pp. 65–83.

succeeded in quelling the last revolt with some ease, and had the citizenry of Istanbul, tired of the uselessness of the corps, behind him. I also believe one can draw a line from the language of the 1808 Deed of Agreement to the new regulations for the transformed army of 1828, which describe an empire-wide construction of the new military force, based on conscription.

If we concede that between 1730 and 1830 a new system of military organization, resembling far more closely the seventeenth- and early eighteenth-century European coalition forces, had emerged, and that Mahmud II had at his fingertips a new contract with his provincial leaders, responsible for the manning and supplying of his armies, then we have to ask what else in terms of discipline might have occurred to allow the Ottomans to impose other forms of disciplinary regimes, such as replacing the janissaries with a European-style regimental organization.

The most obvious form of discipline would be brute force, of which there is no small measure before and after 1840 in Istanbul and abroad. Mahmud II literally tamed his unruly provincial *ayan* through the instrument of his chief henchman and advisor Halet Efendi – sometimes with brutal suppression – and appointed individuals who would be loyal to him and amenable to the new disciplinary universe. The new army also proved brutal when set against local rebellions, such as those of the Tanzimat age in Kurdish Anatolia and Bosnia.

Another form of pre-transition discipline was unpredictability and serendipity. Kahraman Pasha, an unruly *mutassarıf* in the 1768–74 war, for example, was cut to pieces on the spot for threatening the grand vizier with his sword. The post-mortem verdict was insubordination. This kind of serendipitous, theatrical justice was only a momentary deterrent. Other forms of discipline in all military and imperial environments involve military display and parades, of which the Ottomans were past masters. Mahmud II is applauded by all foreign observers for parading the troops, and for engaging in constant military maneuvers with them, making him resemble Frederick the Great of Prussia and Peter the Great of Russia.

From the military point of view, the most important form of discipline involved the imposition of strict control over troops and commanders. Here there are interesting texts and examples to read. Traditional janissary discipline involved the bastinado (*falaka*); this was internally controlled, regulated by the two *kaziaskers*, or chief army judges, and administered by the hierarchy of commanders. The description of such discipline comes from *the Eyyubi Efendi Kanunname*: the infraction or crime was brought to the attention of the barracks colonel (*çorbacı*); after evening prayers, all the elders and *oda* members were assembled; the accused was brought before them, and verbally castigated by his own commander, the *Odabaşı*; then, depending on the severity of the infraction, he was held face to the ground by two elders, one holding his hands, the other his feet. The severity of the crime determined the number of strokes. If murder was involved, the ceremony stripped the culprit of his *esame*, where a *firman* ordered his execution. Death was by strangulation, and the body was dumped unceremoniously into the Bosphorus.[15] Such janissary discipline proved unenforceable by the mid-eighteenth century, which elsewhere was the century of severest discipline in military terms: the Russian army was notorious for punishing the smallest infraction by forcing the hapless soldier to run the gauntlet, often resulting in the death of the soldier. The British army in India used severe disciplinary measures which by mid-century had proved counter-productive with the native armies – and was the subject of considerable debate about its effectiveness.[16]

In the 1828 Ottoman military reforms, astonishingly, there is page after page of descriptions of discipline, punishments, and categories of crimes, with repeated exhortations that the hierarchies of command be maintained, and that punishment be equitable. In one of the regulations, for example, terms of detention are spelled out; senior officers are to be punished if they raise a hand to their subordinates; junior grade officers are forbidden to mutter or swear at their commanders. Absence at roll call, drills, and firearm practice were all punishable, as well as bad behavior both in and outside the barracks.[17] As I mentioned above, the first use of the troops on the Danube impressed von Moltke and other observers for the docility and enthusiasm of the troops. The actual transformation does not surprise me as much as the rapidity of it.

From where that apparently modern approach to military discipline derives remains a puzzle. Most historians blithely claim that this or that Frenchman taught the sultan everything he needed to know, but Mahmud II was notoriously stingy with foreign advisors and had declined the services of most, except for the young Prussian von Moltke. Mehmed Ali of Egypt astutely refused to send him his experienced officers. The first few commanders of the new Ottoman army came not from abroad or the

---

[15] İ. Hakkı Uzunçarşılı, *Osmanlı Devleti Teşkilatından Kapukulu Ocakları*, 2 vols. (Ankara: Türk Tarih Kurumu, 1944), pp. 622–3.
[16] Douglas Peers, "Sepoys, Soldiers and the Lash: Race, Caste and Army Discipline in India, 1820–50," *Journal of Imperial and Commonwealth History* 23 (1995): 211–47.
[17] *Kanunnâme-yi Asâkir-i Mansure-yi Muhammadiye* (Istanbul: n.p., 1829), pp. 133–41.

provinces, but from within the sultan's court, many of them slaves (*kuls*) from the household of Hüsrev Pasha.[18]

Were such disciplinary reforms effective? Macfarlane, our chief eye-witness of the state of immediate post-janissary Istanbul, observed on numerous occasions that the city had indeed felt the salutary effects of the disciplinary hand of Mahmud II. The most obvious example was that non-Muslims could watch the new troops parade through the city with equanimity, whereas at the beginning of previous campaigns they were often attacked by the janissaries for desecrating the sacred banner, among other supposed offenses.[19]

The intractable problem was the necessity of achieving adequate numbers for the military through a conscription system. Coercion of manpower as cannon fodder is as old as organized armies, and was never a problem for most modernizing states. The Russians transported serfs to the battlefront chained to wagons. The Ottomans resorted to similar methods when necessary. After all, the first janissaries were forced conscripts. It was easy enough to construct a force of twenty thousand men or so from the vagrants and ex-janissaries of Istanbul to create a so-called reformed army. Beyond that, the Ottomans found themselves stymied by the resilience of the voluntary and mercenary military culture which had arisen, and which indeed they can be said to have encouraged, over the previous century. Fiscal problems were an integral part of the problem, but remain outside the scope of the discussion here.[20]

The greater problem was turning independent societies, in our case with proud and fierce warrior traditions, into docile, disciplined soldiers. Here the Ottomans faced a conundrum. On the one hand, internal and external pressures on the capital and on his person drove Mahmud II to restrict enrollment into his new army to born Muslims and "loyal Turkish lads." Rejected were all non-Muslims, converts, Greeks, and Albanians, because they were unreliable or even treasonous. ("Turkish," of course, was an elastic term, which encompassed Caucasian peoples.) On the other hand, Turco-Muslim populations were a minority in the wider Ottoman realms,

[18] Dror Ze'evi, "*Kul* and Getting Cooler: The Dissolution of Elite Collective Identity and the Formation of Official Nationalism in the Ottoman Empire," *Mediterranean Historical Review* 11 (1996): 177–95.
[19] Charles Macfarlane, *Constantinople in 1828: A Residence of Sixteen Months in the Turkish Capital and Provinces*, 2nd edn (London: Saunders and Otley, 1829).
[20] In early 1835, the sultan was spending 2 million *kuruş* a month on the army; by summer 1835, it was 4.5 million, and by early 1839, the amount rose to 18 million *kuruş* a month, when annual revenues have been estimated to have been at somewhere between 300 million and 800 million a year. Three hundred million *kuruş* equaled 3 million pounds sterling at the time. Levy, "Military Policy," pp. 490–500.

and it quickly became apparent that while conscription proved a successful option in Turkic Anatolia, it simply dipped too often and too deeply into one part of the population. Arabs, Kurds, Albanians, even long-loyal Bosnians resisted conscription, Arabs partially because they were drawn into the circle of Mehmed Ali Pasha and Egypt by the 1830s, and Albanians, Kurds, and Bosnians because they understood their privileged independence and warrior traditions were threatened by the new order.[21] Some have argued that old ethnic rivalries – in this case, Balkan versus Caucasus (Circassian, Georgian) military elites (the latter dominating Mahmud II's circle at the time) – contributed to the contempt for the Albanians (*Arnavut*) repeatedly expressed by officers of the new army. A more compelling argument is that the radical reordering of the premises of local rule and military contributions had a profound effect on local economies and traditional relationships.

Christians of all ethnic groups were unreceptive for a variety of reasons. First, they were forced to pay a separate surtax for the army, which by mid-century was converted into the *bedel*, or military service exemption tax. Second, they were bound to be alienated by the name of Mahmud II's new army, which he called the "Victorious Army of Muhammad." Furthermore, in a desperate move to attract more troops in 1828, Mahmud II resorted to declaring a jihad, and a general call to arms (*nefir-i am* of the Muslim community) against Russia, a striking act for the sultan styled an infidel for his reforms. What was different from the days of the janissaries, which after all was a force built on forced conversion of non-Muslim boys? Arguably, under Mahmud II, the discipline of ethnicity and religiosity was fully imposed. Prior to 1826, the janissaries had expanded membership to whoever proved amenable to their rough corporate, coercive regime. The official proclamation eliminating the janissaries makes it explicit that the corps had become polluted with infidels, and that the new force would be purified of such treacherous elements.[22] The new rules for membership in the sultan's army were more restrictive, less tolerant.

Once Mehmed Ali's army had invaded and occupied large parts of Syria in 1831, the issue of conscription became even more pressing. With the Egyptian army under Ibrahim Pasha, son of Mehmed Ali, entrenched in Damascus, Aleppo, and Adana, Mahmud II sought other ways to fill the

---

[21] Hakan Erdem, "Recruitment of 'Victorious Soldiers of Muhammad' in the Arab Provinces, 1826–1828," in Israel Gershoni, Hakan Erdem, and Ursula Woköck (eds.), *Histories of the Modern Middle East: New Directions* (Boulder, CO: Lynne Rienner, 2002), pp. 189–204.

[22] Mehmed Es'ad, *Précis historique de la destruction du corps des janissaires par le sultan Mahmud, en 1826*, trans. A. P. Caussin de Perceval (Paris: F. Didot, 1833).

ranks of the Victorious Army of Muhammad. In 1834, a reserve system, the
Redif (*Asakir-i Redife-i Mansure*, or, Victorious Reserve Soldiers, also
known as *ihtiyat*, yet later *yedek*), was established. The *redif* were recognized
as agriculturalists, who would be called into service as needed. Reservists
could be recruited as such, or were retirees from regular service. Service in
the regular army was five years, later reduced to two, with an additional
seven years in the reserve, making Ottoman military service one of the
shortest of its contemporaries. Reservists were to report annually for training. While the consensus appears to be that this was modeled on Prussia's
Landwehr, I view it as an indigenous institution, which attempted to address
both recruitment difficulties and the pacification of the countryside.[23]

In March 1837 new regulations were issued, and an entire *redif* structure
resulted, patterned on the regular army, to be commanded by nine *müşirs*
(marshals), and located in Bursa, Konya, Ankara, Aydın, Erzurum and
Sivas, Edirne, and subsequently Niş and Şumnu. It should be noted that
those territories occupy some of the spatial geography of the new defensive system described earlier, and, it must be said, that much of the
system remained on paper. The reality of the matter is that, after 1834,
the Ottoman military was engaged in simultaneously quelling significant
centers of revolt and impressing large swathes of the Kurdish, Muslim
population, as it had previously done in Albania. It was mostly Kurdish
redifs who faced the better-organized Egyptian forces at Nizib in 1839,
when for the second time the new army of Mahmud II failed miserably.

New military regulations were instituted in 1843 and 1848. The army,
which was renamed the *Asakir-i Nizamiye-yi Şahane* (or simply *Nizamiye*,
regular army) in 1841, was reorganized in a systematic fashion by the
military law of Rıza Pasha (September 6, 1843), and identified as the Rıza
regulations, as much of the system survived until after the turn of the
century. The new law, actually an elaboration of the *redif* law of 1834,
created a system of five regional armies (*ordus*). A sixth army was added
in 1848 in Iraq (*Bağdat ordusu*), which was responsible for the Arabian
Peninsula. Each of the first five armies was composed of two services:
the *nizamiye* active, and the *redif* reserve, plus auxiliaries (*yardımcı*) and
başıbozuk (irregular cavalry), the last to be called up only in times of war.
Such irregular cavalry could be Cossacks or Tatars from Dobruja, or
Türkmen and Kurds from eastern Anatolia, as well as a myriad of tribes-
men from the Caucasus. This regulation envisioned a training school for

---

[23] Moltke arrived in Istanbul after the promulgation of the *redif*, and may have had some influence in
the later regulations. See Levy, "Military Policy," pp. 573–89.

young recruits at each of the divisional headquarters. Conscription was based upon the drawing of lots of the eligible age group, and projected recruiting 30,000 volunteers and conscripts for an army of 150,000 men.[24]

In subsequent decades, the *nizamiye* became the enforcer of the Tanzimat regulations, most successful in the terrain which had been marked out by Mahmud II and his military reformers: that is, Anatolia, and Bulgaria and Thrace. Still, when most desperate, as in the Caucasus during the Crimean War, the *başıbozuks* were pressed into service by the sultan's commanders, and just as frequently operated independently. They became the symbol of Ottoman barbarism, especially in the Balkans in the 1870s.

Until 1909, the *Nizamiye* remained a Muslim army, constrained by a cultural divide and resistance from non-Muslim populations who made their contribution, after all, through a variety of military taxes. The army was equally unpopular among Muslims, although the wealthy could routinely find ways of being exempted. Insufficient funding and a poorly developed general staff, which was riddled with corruption and cronyism, were endemic problems until the turn of the century: that is, until the Military College could make any headway in terms of the education and training of a junior officer corps.

To achieve universal conscription, most modern states also promoted a sense of universal citizenship. Such a statement of universal conscription and its accompanying justification is assumed to have been the aim of the clause concerning military service in the Gülhane Edict of 1839. The three principles of this new statement of Ottoman order were: (1) the guarantees promising subjects perfect security for life, honor and property; (2) a regular system of assessing taxes, and (3) an equally regular system for the conscription of requisite troops and the duration of the service, it being "the inescapable duty of all the people to provide soldiers for the defense of the fatherland [*vatan*]."[25] The Edict continued:

Although, as we have said, the defence of the country is a matter of importance, and ... it is the duty for all the inhabitants to supply soldiers for this purpose, it has become necessary to establish laws to regulate the contingents which each locality, according to the necessity of the moment, must provide, and to reduce to four or five years the period of military service. For to take, without regard to the respective population of different areas, from one more, and from another fewer,

---

[24] The *redif* and later developments are well described by Erik J. Zürcher, "The Ottoman Conscription System in Theory and Practice, 1844–1918," in Erik J. Zürcher (ed.), *Arming the State: Military Conscription in the Middle East and Central Asia, 1775–1918* (London: I. B. Tauris, 1999), pp. 80–9.

[25] J. C. Hurewitz, *The Middle East and North Africa in World Politics*, 2nd edn, 2 vols. (New Haven, CT: Yale University Press, 1975), vol. I.

men than they can supply, is simultaneously to do an injustice and strike a moral blow to agriculture and industry; in the same way to keep soldiers in the service for the whole of their lives is to reduce them to despair and contribute to the depopulation of the countryside.[26]

The expectation that subjects would provide soldiers for the defense of the homeland was not necessarily to achieve Napoleon's vaunted "citizens' army." The edict had a dual character, or more accurately a split personality. It promoted a universality of citizenship based on equity and the rule of law, which was grounded in the principle of a religious hierarchy: Muslims and the non-Muslim communities. The reformers needed to foster a new "Ottomanism" that would rally support for the empire; but, in fact, the ambiguities about universal equality alienated even many Muslims after the initial fervor.[27] An expression of constitutional reform and universality, in effect, inaugurated an age of sectarianism. For the Ottoman bureaucrats the next three decades were spent in working out what the new disciplinary regime actually meant concerning military service. In 1869–70 an elaborate conscription law attempted to cross the religious divide, with little success. Universal conscription was enacted in October 1909 by the Young Turks, the only time it was actually enforced across the diverse religious populations of the Ottoman territories.[28]

The social transformation described had the effect, intended or unintended, as Göçek has ably argued, of creating a bifurcated late Ottoman society, a "Turkic" military elite, and a non-Muslim entrepreneurial class.[29] The Ottoman society that emerged after 1839 did succeed in extending the rule of law in limited ways, though the transformation itself had been brutally imposed on unwilling and proudly independent warrior societies. The limits to the military transformation proposed here were those imposed by financial instability and global economic shifts, but also by dynastic rigidity and a cultural and spatial geography unique to the Middle East, which was reconfigured as the Ottoman world shrank, prefiguring Republican Turkey.

---

[26] M. S. Anderson (ed.), *The Great Powers and the Near East, 1774–1923* (London: Arnold, 1970), p. 61.
[27] Abu-Manneh has effectively refuted the notion that these principles contradict the shari'a, by pointing to their origins in Ottoman council debates of 1839 concerning their enactment via the shari'a, in "The Islamic Roots of the Gülhane Rescript," in his *Studies on Islam and the Ottoman Empire in the 19th Century* (Istanbul: Isis, 2001), pp. 73–97. This Tanzimat story is still best told in Niyazi Berkes, *The Development of Secularism in Turkey* (Montreal: McGill University Press, 1964). Selim Deringil has explored the evolving role of the sultan in his *The Well-Protected Domains: Ideology and the Legitimation of Power in the Ottoman Empire, 1876–1909* (London: I. B. Tauris, 1998).
[28] Zürcher, "Ottoman Conscription," p. 89.
[29] Fatma Müge Göçek, *Rise of Bourgeoisie, Demise of Empire: Ottoman Westernization and Social Change* (Oxford: Oxford University Press, 1995).

PART III

Evocations of sovereignty

6

Genre and myth in the Ottoman advice for kings literature

Douglas A. Howard

The advice for kings (*nasihatu'l-mülûk,* or *nasihatname*) is one of the best known of Ottoman literary genres of the sixteenth and seventeenth centuries. Dozens of works in the genre, and hundreds of manuscript copies of them, survive in libraries around the world. A *nasihatname* treatise was among the works published by Ibrahim Müteferrika on the first Ottoman printing press.[1] During the nineteenth and early twentieth centuries, several early *nasihatname*s were published in Istanbul, including those of Koçi Beg, Hasan Kâfî el-Akhisarî, Ayn Ali, Katib Çelebi, and Lutfi Pasha.[2] Many more works in the genre have since been edited and published, and in some cases republished, by scholars. These include two works by Koçi Beg,[3] a new publication of Akhisarî's work,[4] a facsimile republication of the 1864 book that included Ayn Ali's two works and that of Katib Çelebi,[5] and a new edition of Lutfi Pasha's work.[6] Besides these, other works became known. The first Ottoman *nasihatname* translated into English

[1] İbrahim Müteferrika, *Usûlü 'l-hikem fi nizâmi 'l-ümem* (Istanbul: İbrahim Müteferrika, 1732).
[2] *Risale-i Koçi Beg,* ed. Ahmed Vefik (Istanbul: n.p., 1860–1); Hasan Kâfî al-Akhisarî, *Usûl ül-hikem fi nizâm el-'alem* (Istanbul: n.p., 1861); Ayn Ali's two works, *Kavânîn-i Âl-i 'Osmân der hulâsa-ı mezâmin-i defter-i dîvân,* and *Risâle-i vazîfe-horân ve merâtib-i bendegân-ı Âl-i 'Osmân,* together with Katib Çelebi, *Düstûru 'l-'amel li ıslâhı 'l-halel,* in *Kavânîn Risâlesi* (Istanbul: Tasvir-Efvar, 1280/1863). Lutfi Pasha, *Âsafnâme,* ed. Ali Emiri (Istanbul: Matbaa-ı Amidi, 1326/1908). See also the references in M. Seyfettin Özege, *Eski Harflerle Basılmış Türkçe Eserler Kataloğu* (Istanbul: n.p., 1971–82).
[3] Ali Kemali Aksüt, *Koçi Bey Risalesi* (Istanbul: Vakit, 1939); modern Turkish translation by Zuhuri Danışman, *Koçi Bey Risalesi* (Istanbul: Devlet Kitapları 1972); Yılmaz Kurt (ed.), *Koçibey Risalesi* (Ankara: Burak, 1998). Koçi Bey's second treatise was the subject of a long scholarly debate about its authorship that was resolved by M. Çağatay Uluçay, "Koçi Bey'in Sultan İbrahim'e takdim ettiği Risale ve arzları," in *Zeki Velidi Togan Armağanı* (Istanbul: n.p., 1950–5), pp. 177–99.
[4] Mehmed İpşirli, "Hasan Kâfî el-Akhisarî ve devlet düzenine ait eseri Usûlü'l-hikem fi nizâmi'l-âlem," *Tarih Enstitüsü Dergisi* 10–11 (1979–80): 239–78.
[5] Ayn Ali, *Kavânîn-i Âl-i 'Osmân,* ed. Tayyib Gökbilgin (Istanbul: Enderun Kitabevi, 1979).
[6] Mübahat S. Kütükoğlu (ed.), "Lütfi Paşa Âsafnâmesi (Yeni Bir Metin Tesisi Denemesi)," in *Prof. Dr. Bekir Kütükoğlu'na Armağan* (Istanbul: Edebiyat Fakültesi Basımevi, 1991), pp. 49–99.

was that of Sarı Mehmed Pasha, done by the pioneering American Turkologist Walter Wright.[7] Hezarfenn Hüseyin was published twice, as well as the related Eyyubi Efendi;[8] Yaşar Yücel published an anonymous *nasihatname*;[9] Andreas Tietze published a model edition and English translation of Mustafa Ali's great work;[10] Rhoads Murphey published a previously unknown work by Aziz Efendi;[11] and I. A. Petrosian published a facsimile and Russian translation of the anonymous *Laws of the Janissaries.*[12]

Advice for kings was a very widespread premodern Eurasian genre that explored aspects of the practice of monarchical rule.[13] The antecedents of the Ottoman version of the genre lay in Persian and Turkic treatises written in the Islamic states of central Eurasia and Asia Minor during the eleventh to fifteenth centuries that incorporated strands from earlier Indo-Iranian examples. Especially important for the subsequent development of the *nasihatname* genre in Ottoman Turkish were three Persian-language works of the eleventh century, the *Kabusnama* of Kai Kabus ibn Iskandar,[14] the *Siyasatnama* of Nizam al-Mulk,[15] and the *Nasihat al-Muluk*

[7] Walter L. Wright (ed.), *Ottoman Statecraft; The Book of Counsel for Viziers and Governors* (Princeton, NJ: Princeton University Press, 1935).

[8] Robert Anhegger, "Hezarfenn Hüseyin Efendi'nin Osmanlı devlet teşkilâtına dair mülâhazaları," *Türkiyat Mecmuası* 10 (1953): 365–93; Hezarfen Hüseyin Efendi, *Telhisü'l-Beyân fî Kavânîn-i Âl-i 'Osmân*, ed. Sevim İlgürel (Ankara: Türk Tarih Kurumu Basımevi, 1998); Abdülkadir Özcan (ed.), *Eyyubî Efendi Kanunnamesi* (Istanbul: Eren, 1994).

[9] Yaşar Yücel (ed.), *Kitâb-ı Müstetâb* (Ankara: Ankara Universitesi Dil ve Tarih-Cografya Fakültesi, 1974).

[10] Andreas Tietze (ed.), *Mustafa 'Âli's Counsel for Sultans, 1581*, 2 pts. (Vienna: Österreichische Akademie der Wissenschaften, 1979–82).

[11] Rhoads Murphey (ed.), *Kanûn-nâme-i Sultânî Li 'Azîz Efendi: Aziz Efendi's Book of Sultanic Laws and Regulations; An Agenda for Reform by a Seventeenth-Century Ottoman Statesman* (Cambridge, MA: Harvard University Press, 1985).

[12] I. A. Petrosian (ed.), *Mebde-i Kanun-ı Yeniçeri Ocağı Tarihi* (Moscow: Nauka, 1987). On its generic features, see Pál Fodor, "Bir Nasihat-Name olarak Kavānīn-i Yeniçeriyan," in *Beşinci Milletler Arası Türkoloji Kongresi, Tebliğler* (Istanbul: Edebiyat Fakültesi Basımevi, 1986), vol. I, pp. 217–24.

[13] Aziz Al-Azmeh, *Muslim Kingship: Power and the Sacred in Muslim, Christian, and Pagan Polities* (London: I. B. Tauris, 1997). On the Arabic literature of the early Abbasid period, see Gustav Richter, *Studien zur Geschichte der älteren arabischen Fürstenspiegel* (Leipzig: J. C. Hinrichs, 1932). On European mirrors for princes see Walter Ullmann, *Law and Politics in the Middle Ages: An Introduction to the Sources of Medieval Political Ideas* (Ithaca, NY: Cornell University Press, 1975); and Wolfgang Weber, "What a Good Ruler Should Not Do: Theoretical Limits of Royal Power in European Theories of Absolutism, 1500–1700," *Sixteenth Century Journal* 26/4 (1995): 897–915. On the Chinese literature, see the chapter "Historical Writing during the Ming," by Wolfgang Franke, in *The Cambridge History of China*, vol. VII (Cambridge: Cambridge University Press, 1988), esp. pp. 766–9.

[14] Trans. Reuben Levy, *A Mirror for Princes; The Qabus Nama by Ka'us ibn Iskandar Prince of Gurgan* (New York: E. P. Dutton, 1951).

[15] Trans. Hubert Darke, *The Book of Government, or Rules for Kings; the 'Siyasat-nama' or 'Siyar al-muluk' of Nizam ul-Mulk* (London: Routledge and Kegan Paul, 1960).

of al-Ghazali,[16] which were available in Ottoman Turkish translations by the end of the fifteenth century.[17] Beginning in the late fifteenth century, the rapid development of literary Ottoman Turkish in the full range of recognized genres justified Ottoman leadership in the Islamic world. To the extent that this was taken on as a dynastic project, the Ottoman state competed with the Safavid dynasty of Persia and with the Mughal dynasty of India.[18] The advice for kings genre flourished in all three empires.[19] Language was a metonym of the dynasty: as Ottoman Turkish stood as the equal of Arabic and Persian, as it artfully synthesized these three great Islamic languages, so did the Ottoman dynasty stand as the equal of the great Islamic dynasties of the past and present, and so was Ottoman civilization the summation of all of Islamic history and Islamic civilization.[20] Adoption of the *nasihatname* among other literary genres wrote the house of Osman into the literary history of the Islamic world and, by tropes such as the Circle of Equity and tales of the Sassanian King Anushirwan, even into universal literary history. Parallel efforts can be observed in historiography[21] and in poetry.[22]

---

[16] *Ghazali's Book of Counsel for Kings*, trans. F. R. C. Bagley (New York: Oxford University Press, 1964).

[17] For references to manuscripts of Turkish translations of Nizam al-Mulk and Ghazali, see Agâh Sırrı Levend, "Ümmet Çağında Ahlâk Kitaplarımız," *Türk Dili Araştırmaları Yıllığı Belleten* (1963): 89–115, and "Siyaset-nameler," *Türk Dili Araştırmaları Yıllığı Belleten* (1962): 167–94. On the Turkish translation of *Kâbûsnâme*, see the facsimile edition and study of the earliest manuscript by Eleazar Birnbaum, *The Book of Advice by King Kay Ka'us ibn Iskander; The Earliest Old Ottoman Turkish Version of his Kabusname* (Cambridge, MA: MIT Press, 1981); and Eleazar Birnbaum, "A Lifemanship Manual, the Earliest Turkish Version of the Kabusname?" *Journal of Turkish Studies* 1 (1977): 3–64.

[18] Victoria Rowe Holbrook, *The Unreadable Shores of Love: Turkish Modernity and Mystic Romance* (Austin: University of Texas Press, 1994), pp. 77–8; see also Walter Feldman, "Imitatio in Ottoman Poetry: Three Ghazals of the Mid-Seventeenth Century," *Turkish Studies Association Bulletin* 21/2 (Fall 1997): 31–48.

[19] On the Safavid literature, see Ann K. S. Lambton, "Quis Custodiet Custodes: Some Reflections on the Persian Theory of Government," *Studia Islamica* 5 (1956): 125–48 and 6 (1956): 125–46. On the Mughal literature, see Sajida Sultana Alvi, *Advice on the Art of Governance: Mau'izah-i Jahangiri of Muhammad Baqir Najm-i Sani, An Indo-Islamic Mirror for Princes* (Albany, NY: SUNY Press, 1989).

[20] Cornell H. Fleischer, *Bureaucrat and Intellectual in the Ottoman Empire; The Historian Mustafa Ali (1541–1600)* (Princeton, NJ: Princeton University Press, 1986), p. 241; and Christine Woodhead, "Ottoman İnşa and the Art of Letter-Writing: Influences upon the Career of the Nişancı and Prose Stylist Okçuzade (d. 1630)," *Journal of Ottoman Studies* 7–8 (1988): 143–59, esp. 143–4.

[21] For the debate about early Ottoman historiography, see Colin Imber, *The Ottoman Empire 1300–1481* (Istanbul: Isis, 1990), pp. 1–13; and Cemal Kafadar, *Between Two Worlds: The Construction of the Ottoman State* (Berkeley, CA: University of California Press, 1995), esp. pp. 90–105.

[22] See the collection of papers on the *ghazal* form published in *Turkish Studies Association Bulletin* 21/2 (Fall 1997): 1–60.

The main thematic motif employed by the advice for kings was the polarity of order and disorder. In the Ottoman Empire the genre seems to have functioned to reconcile the post-1453 conception of Ottoman kingship with the Islamic cultural milieu, by collation with an ethic of personal justice that was demanded of the legitimate monarch. Reifying the ideal of the shepherd king whose commitment to justice guaranteed the well-being of his flock, Ottoman rhetoric of the sixteenth century sharpened the distinction between the monarch and his subjects, and between the ruling class of imperial administrators, the *askeri*, who carried out the monarch's orders and paid no taxes, and the *reaya*, the ordinary tax-paying subjects.[23] In Ottoman literature, as elsewhere, the advice for kings works were written largely by secretaries and administrators who served those monarchs.[24] Employing the formal tools and conventional fictions of the ideology of justice, the scribal class of the young Ottoman Empire strove to mediate and rationalize Ottoman rule, with its inevitable ambiguities and inequities, to a potentially alienated native financial and religious nobility. The genre worked to affirm the structures of bureaucratic monarchy and its values, including the rule of law, respect for tradition, and the primacy of merit.[25]

Historians of the Ottoman Empire have of course long recognized that the Ottoman *nasihatname*s comprise a literary genre, and that premodern literatures are characterized by greater attention to genre considerations than are modern literatures.[26] But historians have not adequately explored the substance of the Ottoman *nasihatname* genre. In two areas especially, a more detailed study of the generic attributes of these works might yield insights for Ottoman history. First, close study of the characteristics these works hold in common would enable a greater appreciation of their individual differences. Genres are not immutable, but exist in a perpetual state of development and are continually being redefined by new contributions. It is therefore necessary to study as many of these works as

[23] Al-Azmeh noted the metaphor of politics as the husbandry of humans, in *Muslim Kingship*, p. 118.
[24] On the literary output of the Ottoman scribal class, see Woodhead, "Ottoman İnşa and the Art of Letter-Writing"; see also Fleischer, *Bureaucrat and Intellectual*, passim.
[25] Al-Azmeh emphasized the role of advice for kings as literary enunciations of royal power in *Muslim Kingship*; see especially pp. 117–18. This was also a theme emphasized by Fleischer, *Bureaucrat and Intellectual*.
[26] See the insightful remarks of Marshall G. S. Hodgson, "Two Pre-Modern Muslim Historians: Pitfalls and Opportunities in Presenting them to Moderns," in John Nef (ed.), *Towards World Community* (The Hague: Dr. W. Junk N.V., 1968), pp. 53–68.

possible, since the Ottoman version of the genre differs in important ways from its antecedents, and if indeed we may identify an "Ottoman version" of the genre, within this Ottoman body of work individual authors introduced significant innovations that took it in new directions. Rhoads Murphey and Virginia Aksan have drawn attention to the interrelations of Ottoman advice for kings works and pushed forward awareness of little-known works in the genre.[27]

Second, historians of the Ottoman Empire who have used these works have paid scant attention to the nature of genres, their characteristic motifs, and relationships between theses and socially constructed meaning and myth, broadly defined.[28] In this regard, although it is by no means the most popular approach in literary criticism today,[29] myth criticism applied as a theoretical framework, together with insights from genre theory, may prove productive when looking at the Ottoman *nasihatname*s. Myth criticism, or archetypal criticism, permits analysis of links between literary language, forms, and motifs, and the structure and imagery of myth and ritual.[30] Certain genres may be seen to carry the freight for certain myths – that is, certain genres may articulate particular myths in characteristic configurations of language, form, and motif.

In this chapter my intention is to reconsider some issues of generic identification in the Ottoman *nasihatname*s and, since genres are closely associated with myth, contribute to a discussion about some of the foundational myths of Ottoman society. Finally, by looking at one Ottoman *nasihatname*, Ayn Ali Efendi's *Kavânîn-i Âl-i 'Osmân*, I hope to offer some observations about the Ottoman society in its premodern context.

---

[27] Murphey, *Kanûn-nâme-i Sultâni li 'Azîz Efendi*; Rhoads Murphey, "Solakzade's Treatise of 1652: A Glimpse at Operational Principles Guiding the Ottoman State during Times of Crisis," in *V. Milletlerarası Türkiye Sosyal ve İktisat Tarihi Kongresi; Tebliğler* (Ankara: Türk Tarih Kurumu, 1990), pp. 27–32. Virginia H. Aksan, "Ottoman Political Writing, 1768–1808," *International Journal of Middle East Studies* 25 (1993): 53–69.

[28] On genre theory, I have benefited from Tzvetan Todorov, *The Fantastic: A Structural Approach to a Literary Genre*, trans. Richard Howard (Ithaca, NY: Cornell University Press, 1975); Wesley A. Kort, *Narrative Elements and Religious Meaning* (Philadelphia, PA: Fortress, 1975); and Thomas Kent, *Interpretation and Genre: The Role of Generic Perception in the Study of Narrative Texts* (Lewisville, PA: Bucknell University Press, 1986).

[29] Note, for instance, the critical comments of Terry Eagleton, *Literary Theory: An Introduction*, 2nd edn (Minneapolis: University of Minnesota Press, 1996), esp. pp. 79–82.

[30] On myth criticism, or archetypal criticism, see Northrop Frye, *Anatomy of Criticism* (Princeton, NJ: Princeton University Press, 1957). A brief summary is reprinted in Northrop Frye, *Fables of Identity: Studies in Poetic Mythology* (New York: Harcourt, Brace and World, 1963), pp. 7–20; see also Northrop Frye, *The Stubborn Structure: Essays on Criticism and Society* (Ithaca, NY: Cornell University Press, 1970), esp. pp. 90–105.

THE *NASIHATNAMES* AND HISTORIOGRAPHY

The nineteenth-century Ottoman interest in this earlier *nasihatname* literature seems to have fitted a late imperial context in which the roots of Ottoman institutions, and the legal foundations of institutional reform, were the subjects of wide discussion. Several of the works mentioned above were published during the decade of the 1860s, a decade which, not coincidentally, also saw the beginning of the publication of the new Ottoman civil code (*mecelle*).[31]

Interest in the *nasihatname* literature among non-Ottoman Europeans dates from as early as the seventeenth century. Paul Rycaut used the work of Ayn Ali and probably that of Koçi Beg as sources for his *The Present State of the Ottoman Empire* (1668).[32] François Pétis de la Croix, who like his father of the same name served as Turkish and Arabic interpreter at the French court, published Koçi Beg in a French translation in 1725.[33] Two manuscript copies of Ayn Ali's work with French translations done at Constantinople in the 1730s survive in the Bibliothèque nationale.[34] The influential scholarly studies of Ottoman institutions written by the Swedish ambassador Ignatius Mouradgea D'Ohsson (1740–1807)[35] and by the Austrian diplomat Josef von Hammer-Purgstall (1774–1856)[36] made heavy use of this literature. Published translations of Ottoman advice for kings treatises into European languages appeared shortly after their

[31] Niyazi Berkes, *The Development of Secularism in Turkey* (Montreal: McGill University Press, 1964; repr. New York: Routledge, 1998), pp. 160–9.
[32] Reprinted Westmead: Gregg International, 1972. Rycaut has attracted recent scholarly attention. Consult Sonia P. Anderson, *An English Consul in Turkey: Paul Rycaut at Smyrna, 1667–1678* (Oxford: Clarendon Press, 1989); Colin J. Heywood, "Sir Paul Rycaut, A Seventeenth-Century Observer of the Ottoman State: Notes for a Study," in E. Kural Shaw and C. J. Heywood, *English and Continental Views of the Ottoman Empire, 1500–1800* (Los Angeles: William Andrews Clark Memorial Library, 1972), pp. 33–59. Linda T. Darling, "Ottoman Politics through British Eyes: Paul Rycaut's *The Present State of the Ottoman Empire*," *Journal of World History* 5 (1994): 71–97; and Zeki Arıkan, "Sir Paul Rycault Osmanlı İmparatorluğu ve İzmir," *Osmanlı Araştırmaları* 22 (2003): 219–55.
[33] See François Pétis de la Croix, *Canon de Sultan Suleiman II l'empire représenté à Sultan Mourad IV pour son instruction. Ou état politique et militaire, tiré des archives les plus secrètes des princes ottomans, & qui servent pour bien gouverner leur Empire* (Paris: n.p., 1725), pp. 163–218.
[34] *Supplément turc* nos. 883 and 885 in the catalogue of E. Blochet, *Catalogue des manuscrits turcs*, 2 vols. (Paris: Bibliothèque nationale, 1932–3).
[35] *Tableau général de L'empire othoman*, 3 vols. (Paris, 1786, 1787, 1820). On D'Ohsson, see the collection of papers edited by Sture Theolin, *Torch of the Empire* (Istanbul: Yapı Kredi Kültür Sanat Yayınları, 2002).
[36] *Des osmanischen Reichs Staatsverfassung und Staatsverwaltung, dargestellt aus den Quellen seiner Grundgesetze*, 2 vols. (Vienna: Camesinaschen Buchhandlung, 1815).

Ottoman publication in the cases of Koçi Beg,[37] Akhisarî,[38] Ayn Ali,[39] and Lutfi Pasha.[40]

Twentieth-century Anglo-American scholarly interest in the *nasihatname*, however, was due in no small measure to the role of these works in reinforcing an important modern historiographical metanarrative: the rise and fall of civilizations that culminated in the rise of western civilization. The cultural significance of this story in the twentieth century, communicated to millions of Americans through the university "Western Civ" course, can hardly be overstated.[41] In the metanarrative of rise and fall, the decline of Islamic civilization coincided with the rise of modern western civilization, and the decadent Islamic world became the main foil of the new and vigorous West and its nations. Traditional orientalist study of Islamic civilization buttressed the plot of rise and fall by describing the decay of the Islamic world, from its pure Arab origins, through its peak in a neo-Persian medieval renaissance, to its loss of creativity and vitality under Turkish domination. The work of three English historians of the mid twentieth century was especially significant in lending scholarly weight to this metanarrative: Sir Hamilton Gibb and Harold Bowen, and Bernard Lewis. Gibb and Bowen's *Islamic Society and the West* was the most detailed

---

[37] Koçi Beg's *Risâle*, published in Istanbul in 1860–1, appeared in a German translation by W. F. Behrnauer, "Koǵabegs Abhandlung über den Verfall des osmanischen Staatsgebändes seit Suleiman dem Großen," *Zeitschrift der Deutschen Morgenländischen Gesellschaft* 15 (1860): 272–332. It was translated into Hungarian by József Thúry in the *Török Történetírók* series, vol. II (1896); I have not seen this edition. A Russian translation appeared later, A. Tveritinova, "Vtoroi traktat Kochibeya," *Uchenyie Zapiski Instituta Vostokovedeniia* 6 (1953): 212–88.

[38] Akhisari was published in Istanbul three times between 1861–2 and 1870–1. A partial translation had already appeared in French, by Garcin de Tassy, "Principes de sagesse touchant l'art de gouverneur par Rizwan-ben-abd-oul-mennan Ac-hissari," *Journal Asiatique* 4 (1824): 213–26; full translations followed the Ottoman publication, into Hungarian by E. J. Karácsony, *Az egri török emlékirat a kornmányzás módjáról – Eger vár elfoglalása alkalmával az 1596 évben irja Molla Haszan Elkjáfi* (Budapest: n.p., 1909); and German, by Karácsony and Lajos Thallóczy, "Eine Denkschrift des bosnischen Mohammedaners Mollah Hassan elkjafi über die Art und Wese des Regierens," *Archiv für slavische Philologie* 32 (1911): 139–58.

[39] Published in Istanbul in 1863, Ayn Ali's *Kavânîn-i Âl-i 'Osmân* was translated into French by M. Belin, "Du régime des fiefs militaires dans l'islamisme, et principalement en Turquie," *Journal Asiatique* 15 (1870): 187–222; and into German by Paul Tischendorf, *Das Lehnswesen in den moslemischen Staaten insbesondere im osmanischen Reich mit dem Gesetzbuche der Lehen unter Sultan Ahmed I* (Leipzig: Giesecke und Devrient, 1872; repr. Berlin: Klaus Schwarz Verlag, 1982).

[40] Published in Istanbul by Matbaa-ı Amidi in 1908. Rudolf Tschudi prepared a critical edition encompassing four manuscripts for his doctoral dissertation at Erlangen, published as *Das Asafnâme des Lutfi Pasche* (Leipzig: W. Drugulin 1910; republished Berlin: Mayer und Müller, 1910).

[41] A systematic account of the role of Islamic civilization in the standard western civilization textbook and course is needed. On western civilization in American higher education, see Gilbert Allardyce, "The Rise and Fall of the Western Civilization Course," *American Historical Review* 87 (1982): 695–725; and Daniel A. Segal, "'Western Civ' and the Staging of History in American Higher Education," *American Historical Review* 105 (2000): 770–805.

study of Ottoman institutions at the time of its publication.[42] Lewis's *The Arabs in History* was used in countless university survey courses,[43] and his *Emergence of Modern Turkey* was a literary tour de force.[44] Both Gibb and Bowen's work and Lewis's *Emergence* outlined a narrative of Ottoman decline that relied on the Ottoman advice for kings literature. Meanwhile, Lewis also published an influential survey of the advice for kings genre called "Ottoman Observers of Ottoman Decline."[45]

Scholars chipped away at Gibb and Bowen's edifice in the 1960s and 1970s,[46] but Edward Said brought the criticism of their approach and that of Lewis into the public spotlight. In Said's formulation, orientalist discourse rationalized European imperialist control of much of the Islamic world in the nineteenth century.[47] Especially after 1978 in the United States academic historians, motivated partly by appeals to a standard of verisimilitude that required a corrective to the older historical metanarrative, increasingly became preoccupied with refuting the Ottoman decline as an untrue myth.[48] In America, moreover, the task was inseparable from revulsion toward the extremely negative representations of Islam and the history of the undifferentiated "Middle East" that overwhelmed consumers of popular culture and the journalistic media.[49] The Iranian revolution and the hostage crisis, happening simultaneously with the publication of Said's

[42] H. A. R. Gibb and Harold Bowen, *Islamic Society and the West: A Study of the Impact of Western Civilization on Moslem Culture in the Near East*, one volume in two parts (Oxford: Oxford University Press, 1950, 1957). Publication was delayed by the war.
[43] Bernard Lewis, *The Arabs in History* (Oxford: Oxford University Press, 1962).
[44] Bernard Lewis, *The Emergence of Modern Turkey* (Oxford: Oxford University Press, 1961).
[45] Bernard Lewis, "Ottoman Observers of Ottoman Decline," *Islamic Studies* 1 (1962): 71–87.
[46] Prominently, Norman Itzkowitz, "Eighteenth Century Ottoman Realities," *Studia Islamica* 16 (1962): 73–94; Roger Owen, "The Middle East in the Eighteenth Century – An 'Islamic' Society in Decline? A Critique of Gibb and Bowen's *Islamic Society and the West*," *Review of Middle East Studies* 1 (1975): 101–12; Roger Owen, "Introduction [to part two]," in Thomas Naff and Roger Owen (eds.), *Studies in Eighteenth Century Islamic History* (Carbondale and Edwardsville, IL: Southern Illinois University Press, 1977), pp. 133–51.
[47] Edward W. Said, "Arabs, Islam and the Dogmas of the West," *New York Times Book Review*, October 31, 1976; *Orientalism* (New York: Pantheon, 1978).
[48] The revisionist argument was deeply influenced by the approach of Itzkowitz, "Eighteenth Century Ottoman Realities." The methodological critique of the Ottoman decline can be traced to Roger Owen, "The Middle East in the Eighteenth Century." My own unpublished PhD dissertation, "The Ottoman Timar System and its Transformation, 1563–1656" (Indiana University, 1987), belongs to this approach. For recent examples, see Linda T. Darling, *Revenue-Raising and Legitimacy: Tax Collection and Finance Administration in the Ottoman Empire 1560–1660* (Leiden: E. J. Brill, 1996); Jonathan Grant, "Rethinking the Ottoman 'Decline': Military Technology Diffusion in the Ottoman Empire, Fifteenth to Eighteenth Centuries," *Journal of World History* 10 (1999): 179–201. See also the remarks of Cemal Kafadar, "The Question of Ottoman Decline," *Harvard Middle Eastern and Islamic Review* 4/1–2 (1997–8): 30–75.
[49] Perhaps as influential as *Orientalism* has been Edward Said's polemic *Covering Islam: How the Media and the Experts Determine how We See the Rest of the World* (New York: Vintage, 1981).

Orientalism, transformed the field of academic history of the Islamic world in the United States.

Yet, although the rise-and-fall metanarrative was weakened in the last quarter of the twentieth century as orientalist discourse came under sustained critique, the recent Sicker trilogy[50] and the popularity and political influence of Lewis's bestselling *What Went Wrong?*[51] since September 11, 2001, show that its explanatory power has not been completely exhausted in the Anglo-American world. This observation leads me to say that while I accept the basic point that in orientalism the decline of the Ottoman Empire provided a scholarly rationale for imperialism, yet it does not seem to fully explain the attraction of the story of declining empires itself.

The structural resemblance of the basic plot of a history of rise and fall to the lifecycle of birth, growth, degeneration and death suggests that, as in all literature, the appeal of the story of the decline of the Ottoman Empire lies in the common elements that connect it to stories of universal human significance.[52] In particular, the elements of plot and motif contain mythic qualities. In isolation, the plot of a decline story is tragic. But the decline motif seems to have developed in post-Renaissance western historiographical literature out of nostalgia for the golden age, taking over from the nostalgia for paradise.[53] In this way the plot of decline, as an aspect of the metanarrative of the rise and fall of empires, is transformed into a romance. In the orientalist construction, the vigorous western civilization rises from the ashes of the oriental civilizations. In the nationalist construction, by contrast, decline functions as what Hayden White called the inaugural motif in a nationalist historiography.[54] The nation is awakened by the western incursions and, throwing off the foreign occupation, comes to life from the moribund medieval Islamic state. The metanarrative of rise and fall provided important rhetorical justification for the national movements

---

[50] Martin Sicker, *The Pre-Islamic Middle East* (New York: Greenwood, 2000); *The Islamic World in Ascendancy: From the Arab Conquests to the Siege of Vienna* (New York: Greenwood, 2000); and *The Islamic World in Decline: From the Treaty of Karlowitz to the Disintegration of the Ottoman Empire* (New York: Greenwood, 2000).

[51] Bernard Lewis, *What Went Wrong?: Western Impact and Middle East Response* (Oxford: Oxford University Press, 2002).

[52] I have treated this theme in Douglas A. Howard, "With Gibbon in the Garden: Decline, Death and the Sick Man of Europe," *Fides et Historia* 26 (1994): 22–37.

[53] Harry Levin, *The Myth of the Golden Age in the Renaissance* (Bloomington, IN: Indiana University Press, 1969). On the nostalgia for paradise, see Mircea Eliade, *Myths, Dreams and Mysteries; The Encounter Between Contemporary Faiths and Archaic Realities*, trans. Philip Mairet (New York: Harvill, 1960; repr. Harper and Row, 1975), pp. 59–72.

[54] Hayden White, *Metahistory: The Historical Imagination in Nineteenth-Century Europe* (Baltimore, MD: Johns Hopkins University Press, 1973), pp. 5–7.

and new nation-states in the Balkans in the nineteenth and twentieth centuries, and in Greater Syria, Iraq, and Anatolia after World War I.[55] In each case, the decline motif seems to be a displacement onto the genre of historiography of the universal lifecycle myths of death and regeneration.[56]

Kemalist Turkish historiography, alone of the post-Ottoman nationalist historiographies, annexed the Ottoman past to its nationalist narrative, embracing it as its own classical era. İnalcık's *The Ottoman Empire; The Classical Age 1300–1600*, published in 1973 in English, was the brilliant culmination of the Kemalist reconciliation with the classical Ottoman past.[57] Beginning with a chapter on "The Origins of the Ottoman State" and closing with chapters on "The Triumph of Fanaticism" and on Islamic mysticism, the book gave its compellingly nostalgic realism a Burkhardtian shape through ironic allusions to the situation of the Republic of Turkey in the year of its golden anniversary. This strategy was not, of course, isolated from impulses common to most scientific historiography and reminiscent of New Criticism, in which Ottoman history is too complex to permit emplotment. That is, Ottoman history is the ironic historian's story without a story, the story that confounds and frustrates all stories save that of the individual sources.[58] Despite the irony, the book could not fully escape the nationalist stamp. Because the model for all sources tended to be government documents, the strategy can be seen to endorse the perspective of the centralizing state, Ottoman or Republican.[59]

---

[55] For the Balkans, see Fikret Adanır and Suraiya Faroqhi (eds.), *Ottomans and the Balkans: A Discussion of Historiography* (Leiden: E. J. Brill, 2002); and Evangelia Balta, "Ottoman Studies in Modern Greek Historiography," *Journal of Turkish Studies* 28/1 (2004): 9–16. For the Arab world, see Rifaʿat ʿAli Abou-El-Haj, "The Social Uses of the Past: Recent Arab Historiography of Ottoman Rule," *International Journal of Middle East Studies* 14 (1982): 185–201. By contrast, Albert Hourani's bestselling *History of the Arab Peoples* (Cambridge, MA: Harvard University Press, 1991) has a remarkable essay on the Ottoman period.

[56] On displacement in literature, see Frye, *Anatomy of Criticism*, pp. 136–7. See also Mircea Eliade, *Myth and Reality*, trans. Willard R. Trask (New York: Harper and Row, 1963), pp. 92–113.

[57] Halil İnalcık, *The Ottoman Empire; The Classical Age 1300–1600*, trans. Norman Itzkowitz and Colin Imber (London: Weidenfeld and Nicolson, 1973).

[58] Note the observation of Marc Manganaro that the New Criticism "clearly approximates the modern monograph," in *Myth, Rhetoric, and the Voice of Authority: A Critique of Frazer, Eliot, Frye and Campbell* (New Haven, CT: Yale University Press, 1992). On "document fetishism" in Ottoman historiography, see Halil Berktay, "The Search for the Peasant in Western and Turkish Historiography," Halil Berktay and Suraiya Faroqhi (eds.), *New Approaches to State and Peasant in Ottoman History* (London: Frank Cass, 1992), pp. 109–15, and Suraiya Faroqhi, *Approaching Ottoman History: An Introduction to the Sources* (Cambridge: Cambridge University Press, 1999), pp. 38–9; cf. Hayden White's discussion of irony in Burkhardt, in *Metahistory*, pp. 244–7.

[59] On the work of Ömer Lutfi Barkan in this regard, see the comments of Berktay, "The Search for the Peasant," esp. pp. 149–56.

Perhaps one way of understanding how the Ottoman advice for kings texts, whose genre is not historiography, got mixed up in narrative plots of this kind might be to see it as the result of a kind of genre confusion. The *nasihatname*s were alluring for historiography because they formed a thematic (non-narrative) genre in which the imagery of disorder that they typically employ is analogous to the imagery of disintegration that dominates decline aspects of narrative historiographical plots.[60] Both orientalist and nationalist historians tended to read the advice for kings works as they would have read government documents – as more or less transparent primary sources. Thus, for some historians the advice for kings treatises were confidential memoranda, or bold initiatives for reform offered by Ottoman statesmen in the give-and-take spirit of internal policy discussions, or they were courageous challenges to Ottoman absolutist monarchical rule.[61] These interpretations relied on the equation of the audience of the works with the Ottoman sultan: the "king," such readings of these sources assume, was literally the recipient of this "advice."

Some Ottoman authors of advice for kings did use the official government document as a form. Since many of the works were dedicated to Ottoman officials, or presented to the sultan, or by some means found their way into the palace library, it cannot be denied that the Ottoman sultans may have read them. And each work was produced under specific historical circumstances; often these were political, and at a certain level the works cannot be fully understood outside of their specific contexts. Yet, as we shall see, some of the authors imitated Ottoman documentary forms for their own purposes. Personal and literary circumstances also influenced the production of these works, and these cannot always be reconstructed, nor is it always important to do so. In my view, modern historians have misunderstood and underestimated the generic features of the Ottoman advice for kings literature, and have not recognized Ottoman authors' manipulation of readers' generic expectations toward literary and artistic ends.

SOME GENERIC FEATURES OF THE OTTOMAN *NASIHATNAMES*

Besides Edward Said's literary output and the Iranian revolution, two other events bear mentioning for their impact on academic history writing

---

[60] See the summary of mythic phases in Frye, *Fables of Identity*, pp. 15–16.
[61] For the standard statement, see Lewis, "Ottoman Observers." See also Stanford J. Shaw and Ezel Shaw, *History of the Ottoman Empire and Modern Turkey*, vol. I (Cambridge: Cambridge University Press, 1976), pp. 169–216; Murphey, *Kanûn-nâme-i Sultâni li 'Azîz Efendi*; Murphey, "Solakzade's Treatise of 1652."

concerning the Ottoman Empire. One was the Turkish military coup of September 12, 1980, and the other was the fall of the Berlin Wall, the breakup of the Soviet Union, and the accelerating privatization of the economies of the east-central and southeastern European states, including Turkey. In the wake of these changes, many academic Turkish historians and Ottoman historians in Europe and the United States moved away from the state-centered Ottoman exceptionalism of earlier Kemalist-oriented historiography.[62]

For a handful of scholars beginning in the late 1980s, the aim of writing and teaching a mature Ottoman history required not simply discarding the *nasihatname*s as untrue, but reading them more deeply for evidence of a different sort: for insight into Ottoman intellectual and cultural history. Rifa'at 'Ali Abou-El-Haj and Ulrich Haarman saw the *nasihatname* works as ideologically driven, and as a vehicle for the articulation of class interests.[63] Cornell Fleischer and Pál Fodor, in different ways, traced these interests to their social origins in the political relations of the Ottoman political and administrative hierarchy.[64] In a rich study, Aziz al-Azmeh analyzed the ways that advice for kings served as literary enunciations of royal power, though he did not treat the Ottoman version of the genre.[65] I would like to take these efforts a step farther, by focusing on the way Ottoman writers of advice for kings manipulated form, language, and motif.[66] Let us see some examples of standard tropes in the well-known Ottoman works.

---

[62] Oktay Özel and Gökhan Çetinsaya, "Türkiye'de Osmanlı tarihçiliğinin son çeyrek yüzyılı: Bir bilanço denemesi," *Toplum ve Bilim* 91 (Kış 2001/2): 8–38.

[63] R. A. Abou-El-Haj, *Formation of the Modern State: The Ottoman Empire Sixteenth to Eighteenth Centuries* (Albany, NY: SUNY Press, 1991); Abou-El-Haj, "Power and Social Order: The Uses of the Kanun," in Irene A. Bierman, Rifa'at A. Abou-El-Haj, and Donald Preziosi (eds.), *Urban Structure and Social Order: The Ottoman City and its Parts* (New Rochelle, NY: Aristide D. Caratzas, 1991), pp. 77–91; Abou-El-Haj, "Aspects of the Legitimation of Ottoman Rule as Reflected in the Preambles to Two Early Liva Kanunnameler (sic)," *Turcica* 21–3 (1991): 371–83; Abou-El-Haj, "The Expression of Ottoman Political Culture in the Literature of Advice to Princes (Nasihatnameler), Sixteenth to Twentieth Centuries," in R. K. Bhattacharya and Asok K. Ghosh (eds.), *Sociology in the Rubric of Social Science: Professor Ramkrishna Mukherjee Felicitation Volume* (New Delhi: Anthropological Survey of India, 1995), pp. 282–92; Ulrich Haarmann, "The Plight of the Self-Appointed Genius – Mustafa 'Ali," *Arabica* 38 (1991): 73–86.

[64] Fleischer, *Bureaucrat and Intellectual*; Cornell H. Fleischer, "From Şehzade Korkud to Mustafa Âli: Cultural Origins of the Ottoman *Nasihatname*," in Heath W. Lowry and Ralph S. Hattox (eds.), *IIIrd Congress on the Social and Economic History of Turkey* (Istanbul: Isis, 1990), pp. 67–77; Pál Fodor, "State and Society, Crisis and Reform, in 15th–17th Century Ottoman Mirror for Princes," *Acta Orientalia Academiae Scientiarum Hungaricae* 40 (1986): 217–40; Pál Fodor, "Sultan, Imperial Council, Grand Vizier: Changes in the Ottoman Ruling Elite and the Formation of the Grand Vizieral *Telhis*," *Acta Orientalia Academiae Scientiarum Hungaricae* 47 (1994): 67–85.

[65] Al-Azmeh, *Muslim Kingship*.

[66] For my earlier work on the genre, see Douglas A. Howard, "Ottoman Historiography and the Literature of 'Decline' of the Sixteenth and Seventeenth Centuries," *Journal of Asian History* 22 (1988): 52–77.

As in all advice for kings literature, Ottoman authors cast themselves in the role of the trusted advisor to the king. Lutfi Pasha raised this image explicitly in *Âsafnâme* (1543), a work that, judging from references in later works, had far-reaching influence on the development of the genre in Ottoman literature. Invocation of the exemplary loyalty and proverbial sagacity of Asaph, the advisor of the biblical King Solomon, permitted Lutfi Pasha to position his political apologia as an honest and uncompromising evaluation of the current state of affairs.[67] Mustafa Ali of Gallipoli presented his work as the fulfillment of the sovereign's need for "an upright servant ... to discuss with him the affairs of the world ... a man of rectitude that has nothing to fear from anybody. Ali began his *Nushatu 's-Selâtîn* (*Counsel for Sultans*) with a scathing denunciation of the behavior of viziers, writing that "His Royalty the World-Conqueror has no helper nor assistant in managing the affairs of state." The sultan remained isolated from awareness of the real state of his realm, wrote Ali, but "on the Day of Judgment he himself will be asked to answer for it and it will become evident that his excuse that the viziers had not told him will not be accepted."[68]

By invoking the Last Judgment, the writers assumed the prophetic voice.[69] It is hard not to see Mustafa Ali's *Counsel for Sultans* as the admonition that, he asserted, the viziers in the real world had failed to give. "This is why," he wrote, "at the end of time, during the last days, Imam Muhammad the Mahdi will appear and will fill the spacious expanse of the world with strictness and justice, so that the ignoble ones may not like straw and chaff float on top of the ocean-hearted perfect ones, and the just may not suffer in his era like dregs as if they were unworthy traitors."[70] Lutfi Pasha wrote in *Âsafnâme*, "May God, from Whom we seek aid, and in Whom we trust, secure the laws and foundations of the house of Osman from the fear and peril of fate and the evil eye of the foe."[71] Koçi Beg reminded his readers that what made the Ottoman order successful was its "firm grip on the strong cord of Muhammad's law," and its conviction that "the humble subjects are a deposit of the lord of the two worlds."[72] 'Aziz Efendi

---

[67] On the legend and folklore surrounding Asaph, see Jacob Lassner, *Demonizing the Queen of Sheba: Boundaries of Gender and Culture in Postbiblical Judaism and Medieval Islam* (Chicago: University of Chicago Press, 1993), pp. 106–9.

[68] Tietze, *Mustafa 'Ali's Counsel for Sultans of 1581*, vol. I, 19–20.

[69] Compare Al-Azmeh's comments, *Muslim Kingship*, p. 163.

[70] Tietze, *Mustafa 'Ali's Counsel*, vol. I, p. 18.

[71] Quoted by Lewis, "Ottoman Observers," p. 71; see also Howard, "With Gibbon in the Garden," pp. 25–6.

[72] Aksüt, *Koçi Bey Risalesi*, p. 19.

began with a warning should "all-powerful and mighty God look upon that
country with the eye of rage," and concluded with the hope "that until the
end of time [the Ottoman sultans] will be the stock of the eulogists and
until the day of judgment constantly cited by way of example on the
tongues of the reciters of brave deeds."[73] And Katib Çelebi quoted
Quran II:156, "We are of God and to Him again do we return."[74]

The Ottoman advice for kings works seem preoccupied with language.
Ottoman literary stylists of the sixteenth and seventeenth centuries sought
to demonstrate that Ottoman Turkish, a relative latecomer to Islamic
intellectual circles, offered a vehicle as suitable for literary elegance and
educated Islamic discourse as Arabic and Persian.[75] Works from classical
Arabic and Persian had first been translated into Turkish, and Turkish had
begun to be used as a literary language in thirteenth-century western
Anatolia, perhaps because the Turkish chieftains who established courts
there in the wake of the Mongol withdrawal did not know Persian and
Arabic.[76] The subsequent development of Ottoman Turkish as a literary
language constitutes a major development in the cultural history of the
Islamic world. In a sophisticated prose idiom known as *inşa*, writers
developed the Ottoman Turkish literary language using a Turkish syntac-
tical and morphological base to synthesize the rich grammatical and lexical
catalogue of the traditional Islamic languages.

The *telhis* is an example of these developments.[77] Ottoman writers were
not the first to allude to their affiliation with vizierial authority by using the
memorandum form in advice for kings,[78] but they developed it as an art
form. The Ottoman *telhis*, a formal memorandum written to the sultan by
the grand vizier, typically began with some variation of the phrase, "let it

---

[73] Aziz Efendi, *Kanûn*, pp. 3, 24.   [74] Katib Çelebi, *Dustur*, p. 129.
[75] Woodhead, "Ottoman Inşa and the Art of Letter-Writing"; Fleischer, *Bureaucrat and Intellectual*,
pp. 241–2; see also Walter Andrews, *Poetry's Voice, Society's Song: Ottoman Lyric Poetry* (Seattle:
University of Washington Press, 1985), pp. 4–5; and Andreas Tietze, "Mustafa ʿAli of Gallipoli's
Prose Style," *Archivum Ottomanicum* 5 (1973): 297–319.
[76] M. Fuad Köprülü, *Türk Edebiyatı Tarihi* (repr. Istanbul: Ötüken, 1986), pp. 250–2; see also Mecdut
Mansuroğlu, "The Rise and Development of Written Turkish in Anatolia," *Oriens* 7 (1954): 250–64.
[77] On the *telhis* form, see the study of Suraiya Faroqhi, "Das Großwesir-telhîs: eine aktenkundliche
Studie," *Der Islam* 45 (1969): 96–116. For examples see Cengiz Orhonlu, *Osmanlı Tarihine Âid
Belgeler; Telhîsler (1597–1607)* (Istanbul: Edebiyat Fakültesi Basımevi, 1970). Compare the use of the
form by Koçi Beg, Hüseyin Hezarfen, and the anonymous author of the Veliyüddin treatise. See also
Rhoads Murphey, "The Veliyüddin Telhis: Notes on the Sources and Interrelations between Koçi
Bey and Contemporary Writers of Advice to Kings," *Belleten* 43 (1979): 547–71.
[78] From the Mamluk sultanate, Paulina Lewicka, "What a King Should Care About. Two Memoranda
of the Mamluk Sultan on Running State Affairs," *Studia Arabistyczne i Islamistyczne* 6 (1998): 5–45;
from the Ilkhanate, M. Minovi and V. Minorsky, "Nasir al-Din Tusi on Finance," *Bulletin of the
School of Oriental and African Studies* 10 (1939–42): 755–89.

not be concealed (*hafi olmaya ki*)." The report of the circumstances of the matter followed, and after the solicitous address "the petition of this poor servant is as follows (*arz-ı hal-i bi-mikdar budur ki zikr olunur*)," the author presented the proposed solution and request for action. The document concluded with the formula "the decree is my sultan's (*ferman sultanumundur*)," that is, authority lay in the hands of the sovereign.[79] Koçi Beg's *Treatise*, perhaps the most widely known Ottoman *nasihatname*, comprises a collection of twenty-one *telhis* reports, each beginning and ending with an elaborate variation of this simple form, such as "Let it not be concealed from the vigilance of the luminous conscience of his excellency the prosperous and majestic emperor and defender of the faith" or "the eternal order and decree belongs to his excellency the prosperous and majestic, sublime and compassionate emperor of exalted rank."[80]

Used increasingly after the middle of the sixteenth century, the *telhis* was an artifact of the bureaucratized and detached relationship between the sultans and their grand viziers.[81] The gradual withdrawal of the sultans from the imperial council and their growing isolation in the palace resulted not in an increase but in a diminution of the authority of the grand viziers, who found their access to the sultans limited. New coalitions of political power emerged, centered on officials of the palace inner service, and figures such as the sultan's mother and the mufti gained influence.[82] The grand vizier, who became more preoccupied with financing military campaigns, and often leading those campaigns, communicated with the sultan through these written reports. The sultan responded in comments entered in the margins of the report. The Ottoman central bureaucracy – its numerical growth notwithstanding – suffered a loss of influence paralleling that of the grand vizier, its head. The advice for kings genre gained currency during this period of bureaucratic eclipse and decreasing relevance. Its primary audience was not the sultan but the educated group of scribes and bureaucrats who staffed the great Ottoman administrative offices and who identified themselves with an idealized sultanic absolutism whose actual force depended heavily on them.

[79] Like the more humble *arz*, or petition, which it resembled and on which it was probably modeled. See Faroqhi, "Das Großwesir-telhis." On the *arz* form, see Halil İnalcık, "Osmanlı Bürokrasisinde Aklâm ve Muâmelât," *Osmanlı Araştırmaları/Journal of Ottoman Studies* 1 (1980): 1–14.

[80] As in the first *telhis*, Aksüt, *Koçi Bey Risalesi*, pp. 20–3. See also the work of Murphey, "Veliyüddin Telhis." W. F. A. Behrnauer recognized the form but did not elaborate in the brief introduction to his German translation of the work, "Koğabeg's Abhandlung."

[81] Fodor, "Sultan, Imperial Council, Grand Vizier."

[82] Leslie Peirce, *The Imperial Harem: Women and Sovereignty in the Ottoman Empire* (New York: Oxford University Press, 1993), pp. 153–85.

There was an important personal dimension to this preoccupation with language. The beauty and complexity of the rhymed prose, involving a variety of devices such as alliteration, assonance, primary and secondary rhymes, the use of homonyms, and patterns of stress and rhythm, and a range of rhetorical elements including hyperbole, humor and satire, references to famous historical or legendary figures, well-known proverbs, and even the author's own poetry, contributed to an overall impression of learning and wit that became the individual writer's scholarly and literary reputation.[83] As Fleischer showed in his study of the career of Mustafa Ali, reputation, read as merit, might through links of patronage translate into respected administrative posts in the more prosperous provinces or, in time, in the capital city, where writers could become participants in the blossoming literary culture of the empire.[84]

AYN ALI'S *KAVÂNÎN-I ÂL-I 'OSMÂN*

Ayn Ali[85] was an Ottoman career administrator who wrote two works on aspects of the Ottoman bureaucracy in the early seventeenth century. One, called *Treatise on the Salaried Personnel and the Ranks of the Servants of the Ottoman Dynasty* (*Risâle-i vazife-horân ve merâtib-i bendegân-i al-i 'Osmân*), analyzed human resources and Ottoman finance. The other, called *Laws of the Ottoman Dynasty, Comprising a Summary of the Contents of the Registry of the Council* (*Kavânîn-i Âl-i 'Osmân der hulâsa-ı mezâmîn-i defter-i dîvân*), contains a description and analysis of the administration of the *timar* system, the provincially based Ottoman cavalry organization.[86]

According to a few biographical notes he supplied in his own works, Ayn Ali was a scribe of the imperial council (*Katib-i divan*) and former intendant of the Ottoman imperial registry (*Emin-i defter-i hakani*).[87]

---

[83] Woodhead, "Ottoman İnşa and the Art of Letter Writing"; Fleischer, *Bureaucrat and Intellectual*; Holbrook, *Unreadable Shores*, pp. 111–12. See also Tietze, "Mustafa 'Ali of Gallipoli's Prose Style"; and Edith Gülçin Ambros, "'O Asinine, Vile Cur of a Fool Called Zātī!': An Attempt to Show that Unabashed Language is Part and Parcel of an Ottoman 'Idiom of Satire,'" *Journal of Turkish Studies* 27/1 (2003): 109–17.

[84] Fleischer, *Bureaucrat and Intellectual*.

[85] Not 'Ayn-ı 'Ali, as often reported. For an explanation of his name, see Feridun M. Emecen, "'Ali'nin 'Ayn'ı: XVII. Yüzyıl Başlarında Osmanlı Bürokrasinde Kâtib Rumuzları," *Tarih Dergisi* 35 (1984–94): 131–49.

[86] For an introduction, see "Timar," in EI2, vol. X (1999), pp. 502–7 (Halil İnalcık); and Nicoară Beldiceanu, *Le timar dans l'État ottoman (début XIV – début XVI siècle)* (Wiesbaden: Otto Harrassowitz, 1980).

[87] On the registry, see Douglas A. Howard, "The Historical Development of the Ottoman Imperial Registry (Defter-i hakanî): Mid-Fifteenth to Mid-Seventeenth Centuries," *Archivum Ottomanicum* 11 (1986[1988]): 213–30.

When he wrote *Risâle-i vazîfe-horân*, he was serving in the auditing (*mukâbele*) bureau. The Ottoman scholar and bibliographer Katib Çelebi (1600–49) referred to Ayn Ali as *Müezzinzade*, son of a prayer caller.[88] He appears with this epithet in a list of scribes of the divan in the Esztergom campaign inspection register (*yoklama defteri*) of early 1605.[89] Through his "registry service, and exertion and persistence in the performance of stages of duty at the exalted threshold of the junction of Saturn, and long time as scribe of the council of the title of justice," Ayn Ali wrote, he had become "informed about the circumstances of the classes of soldiers and troops, the common flock, and the country and all its servants."[90]

A strong case could be made for considering Ayn Ali's two works, the *Ranks* and the *Laws*, as inseparable. They were usually copied together in manuscripts, and their subjects, the organization of the provincial cavalry and the structure of state finances, form the main issues taken up by most advice for kings authors. For the purposes of this brief study, however, my remarks will be confined to the *Laws of the Ottoman Dynasty*.

Ayn Ali dedicated the *Kavânîn-i Âl-i 'Osmân* to Sultan Ahmed I (1603–17) and Grand Vizier Kuyucu Murad Pasha, who served from December 1606 until his death in August 1611.[91] This work contains a brief introduction, seven chapters, and an epilogue.[92] In the first chapter, the author first defines the Ottoman provinces (*vilayets*) as falling into one of two categories, according to the nature of their fiscal relationship to the state. Either state revenues were collected and redistributed for state demands in the province through the *timar* system, or instead state demands were satisfied by payment of an annual tribute (*salyane*). He goes on to list the amount of revenue accruing from the *timar* estates of the governors of each of these provinces. In chapters 2 and 3, he records the districts (*sancaks*) of each province and the *timar* estate revenues of the military commanders and senior administrative staff overseeing the *timar* system in each district. In the fourth chapter, the author inventories the numbers of *timar*s in each district of each province in which the *timar*

---

[88] Katib Çelebi, *Kashf al-zunûn*, 2 vols. (Istanbul, 1942–3), vol. I, p. 1314.
[89] *Tîmâr-ı kâtib 'Alî 'Ayn*. See the publication by Vera P. Mutafcieva and Strashimir Dimitrov, *Sur l'état du système des timars des XVIIe–XVIIIe ss.* (Sofia: Académie bulgare des sciences, Institut d'études balkaniques, 1968), p. 178.
[90] *Risâle-i vazîfe-h orân*, p. 84.
[91] İsmail Hami Danişmend, *İzahlı Osmanlı Tarihi Kronolojisi*, 4 vols. (Istanbul: Türkiye Yayınevi, 1947–55), vol. III, pp. 248–57.
[92] Published in *Kavânîn Risâlesi*; republished with an introduction by Tayyib Gökbilgin (Istanbul: Enderun Kitabevi, 1979).

system functioned, and calculates the numbers of troops from that district that the state could expect to muster for imperial campaigns. Chapter 5 contains definitions of basic technical terms used in administering the *timar* system. In chapter 6, the author describes the administrative process followed by the Ottoman central government in *timar* bestowals. In chapter 7, he details the steps necessary to address disturbances in the functioning of the system. In the epilogue the author makes several policy recommendations.

It was this version of the work, of which more than forty manuscript copies have been identified, that was printed in Istanbul in the nineteenth century. A separate recension of the work survives in a single manuscript, however, which is organized quite differently.[93] It contains only an introduction, four chapters and an epilogue. The first three chapters generally match chapters of the 1864 printed edition, but the order of the chapters is different and they include sometimes lengthy passages that do not appear in the printed edition. The fourth chapter of this recension includes entirely different material, though the chapter heading is the same as one chapter of the printed edition. Most of the twenty-one marginal notes in the manuscript begin "*Şimdiki halde* (at present)," and some have been incorporated verbatim in the printed edition. Significantly, this recension of the work is missing the dedication to the sultan and the grand vizier. It is a clean copy, free of errors. It therefore seems likely that this manuscript represents an earlier version of the text, and that it was a copy prepared for the author, who revised and updated the work for later presentation.

One might also conclude from this that production of the work was essentially unrelated to the political circumstances of the reign of Sultan Ahmed I or the *celali* rebellions that were suppressed by Grand Vizier Kuyucu Murad Pasha. The work was not a response to any specific event or crisis at all, but rather a response to changes in the administration of the *timar* system, changes that, according to the author, had developed over the course of some three decades and that should be interpreted not necessarily in political terms, as "decline," but in cosmic terms, as disorder. Only after making substantial revisions to the text did Ayn Ali present it as dedicated to the sultan and grand vizier. It was likely the author's wish to update the text that prompted the revisions rather than political circumstances.

---

[93] Rhoads Murphey called attention to the differences in this manuscript (Fatih 3497) in "The Veliyüddin Telhis," p. 566, n. 23.

Rather than employing the *telhis* form, the *Kavânîn-i Âl-i 'Osmân* expanded the boundaries of the Ottoman advice for kings by the extensive use of lists, and by assimilating to the *nasihatname* two other distinctively Ottoman bureaucratic genres, the register (*defter*), and the law book (*kanunname*). In this way, the work of Ayn Ali illustrates the interweaving of thematic language, form, and motif in the advice for kings genre, and is useful for showing the linkages between such literary patterns and myth.

Unlike many other Ottoman authors in the genre, Ayn Ali wrote in a Turkish syntax with relatively restrained use of Arabic and Persian elements. Contemporary Ottoman readers, however, may not have valued straightforward clarity over ornamental prose as much as modern readers do.[94] The comparative simplicity of Ayn Ali's prose and the author's occasionally verbatim use of Ottoman *kanunname*s have probably contributed to the habit among modern scholars of using the work as if it provides an objective description of the Ottoman military organization. Even though Ayn Ali does provide a wealth of information about the *timar* system, some of it unavailable elsewhere in such concise form, the apparent clarity of the language contrasts both with the lengthy lists that make up the first half of the work, and also with the author's often dense analysis of administrative procedures that make up the other half. Thus, although the style of Ayn Ali's work differs from that of Ottoman *inşa* prose, it reveals a similar fascination with and manipulation of language, in this case the technical lexicon of the Ottoman scribal service. The Ottoman reader may not have interpreted the author's vocabulary and syntax along a continuum between simple and complex, but rather as an "indication of the rules of interpretation appropriate to the work."[95]

Lists

In the first half of Ayn Ali's treatise the author produces several lists. In the first chapter he lists the *vilayet*s of the empire according to whether they pay annual tribute or the *timar* system functions in them; then he lists the size of the estate revenues of each provincial governor-general (*beylerbeyi*) in the latter group. In chapter 2 he lists the *vilayet*s again, this time also

---

[94] On this issue, see Andrews, *Poetry's Voice*, pp. 19–35 and 56–61, and Holbrook, *Unreadable Shores*, pp. 13–31.
[95] This is the suggestion of Andrews, *Poetry's Voice*, p. 59.

sets of registers, the *mufassal*, the *icmal*, and the *ruznamçe* registers. The *mufassal*, or detailed, registers contained the tax and census data compiled in the cadastral surveys carried out periodically in the Ottoman provinces. The *icmal*, or summary, registers reconfigured this data into a list of the revenues accruing to each *timar* fief, and recorded the names of the *timar* holders. The third set of registers comprised the *ruznamçes* or daybooks. The first two of these sets of registers – the *mufassal* and *icmal* registers – are well known and have been used by scholars of Ottoman economic and social history for more than half a century. The third set, however, the *ruznamçes*, are comparatively little known. They contained a chronological record of *timar* bestowals and were the daily record of activity in the registry itself.[104] These three sets of registers were used to assess the taxes collected by provincial cavalrymen (the *sipahis*) and record changes in fief possession, even accompanying the Ottoman army on campaign. The registry also archived all past registers, including both old daybooks and the records of earlier cadastral surveys.

The most recent cadastral surveys at the time of Ayn Ali's writing had been conducted in most provinces during the period 1570–90. An earlier series of cadastral surveys had been carried out in most provinces of the empire in the years 1540–60. Ayn Ali probably compiled his lists of the revenue figures of the fiefs of military governors and other provincial officials using the *icmal* registers. In most cases he also used the latest registers available to him to arrive at his figures for the number of *timar*s in each province. At the end of many of the original manuscripts of the *icmal* registers recording surveys conducted between 1570 and 1590, there are briefly scribbled notes in a scribal hand that record the total number of *timar*s and *zeamet*s listed in the register, and the revenue accruing from them.[105] These are not the totals recorded for the scribe of the survey, they are aggregate figures, written in a hand different than that of the register itself. In most cases these figures match those in the published edition of Ayn Ali's work (taking into account normal copying errors) and may be the notes of Ayn Ali himself. The figures in the earlier recension of the work, however, are considerably different and are likely based on the earlier

[104] Douglas A. Howard, "The BBA *Ruznamçe Tasnifi*: A New Resource for the Study of the Ottoman *Timar* System," *Turkish Studies Association Bulletin* 10/1 (March, 1986): 11–19. See also Nejat Göyünç, "Timar Ruznamçe Defterlerinin Biyografik Kaynak Olarak Önemi," *Belleten* 60/227 (Nisan, 1996): 127–38.
[105] Now housed in the Tapu ve Kadastro Umum Müdürlüğü, Ankara. See, for example, TK 233: 114b, TK 334: 41a, TK 222: 108a; often these notes appear on unnumbered front folios, as in TK 319, TK 241, TK 215, and others.

set of cadastral records. Thus the figures in Ayn Ali's tables of *timar*s and *zeamet*s in the empire were based on data that were at least twenty years, and in some cases up to forty years old by the time he wrote.

The law books

The *kanunname*s, or "law books," on the other hand, were compilations of secular, or state, laws and regulations (*kanun*s). In other words they were, at least formally though not always in fact, sultanic decrees. So defined, *kanun* law and regulation played a crucial role in Ottoman society, providing the legal foundation for major Ottoman political, military, economic, and social institutions.[106]

The best-known Ottoman *kanunname*s are the collections of regional tax laws appended to the front of the late fifteenth- and the sixteenth-century *mufassal defter*s, the provincial cadastral survey registers. There was also a general Ottoman *kanunname*, applicable throughout the empire. It seems to have been first issued during the reign of Bayezid II, but its nucleus was a code concerning peasant obligations that goes back to the reign of Mehemmed the Conqueror. This general Ottoman *kanunname* was amended and reissued by subsequent Ottoman rulers, Selim I (1512–20) and Süleyman the Magnificent (1520–66). It remained in effect until the late seventeenth century. The largest number of Ottoman *kanunname*s, however, fit neither of these two categories. They are simply collections of regulations and decrees of the Ottoman sultans on a variety of topics.[107] These texts can be found in hundreds of private manuscript collections of miscellanea (*mecmua*). Miscellanea have attracted comparatively little attention among Ottoman literary historians, but they are of potentially great interest to genre theory.[108]

In *Kavânîn-i Âl-i 'Osmân*, Ayn Ali specifically analyzed the *kanunname*s covering the *timar* system. *Kanunname* compilations exist for the ulema,

---

[106] On Ottoman law in the Islamic tradition, see Colin Imber, *Ebu's-su'ud: The Islamic Legal Tradition* (Edinburgh: Edinburgh University Press, 1997). See also the introduction in Halil İnalcık's article "Kanunname," in EI2, vol. IV, pp. 563–6; and the same author's "Süleyman the Lawgiver and Ottoman Law," *Archivum Ottomanicum* 1 (1969): 105–13; and the work of Uriel Heyd, *Studies in Old Ottoman Criminal Law*, ed. V. L. Ménage (Oxford: Oxford University Press, 1969).

[107] I follow the classification scheme offered by Inalcık, *The Ottoman Empire*, p. 71. A more refined version with five categories is laid out in his article "Kanunname," in *Encyclopaedia of Islam*, new edition.

[108] Bekir Kütükoğlu, "Münşeat Mecmualarının Osmanlı Diplomatiği Bakımından Ehemmiyeti," in *Tarih Boyunca Paleografya ve Diplomatik Semineri* (Istanbul: Istanbul Üniversitesi Edebiyat Fakültesi, 1988), pp. 169–76; see also the references in Woodhead, "Ottoman Inşa and the Art of Letter Writing."

the janissaries, and others, in miscellanea collections. It appears that sometimes decrees on a particular topic underwent a process of selection and
codification and achieved an official status. This was the case also with decrees
concerning the *timar* system. In 1531 Sultan Süleyman the Magnificent
had synthesized regulations concerning the process of bestowing *timar*s.
Several decrees followed in subsequent years, and in 1568, during the reign
of Süleyman's son and successor Selim II, the *timar* laws were codified
under the direction of the intendant of the registry, Mehmed Çelebi
Efendi.[109] But Ayn Ali also seems to have used another kind of collection
of *timar* regulations, one with different or additional material. As noted
above, Ayn Ali's lists of the provinces of the empire were probably based on
an anonymous administrative manual, the so-called "Ali Çavuş." The
lawbook codified by Mehmed Çelebi Efendi contains no such lists. Ayn
Ali refers at one point to a "book of terminology (*kitab-ı istilah*)," and calls
his own work a condensation (*muhtasar*). This and other evidence – for
instance, references to "basket (*sepet*) timars" in the earlier recension of
the work that were edited out of the version presented to the sultan and
grand vizier – once again points to the same anonymous work as his likely
source.

These laws and regulations describe a system in which a traditional
provincial military class of *sipahi*s that had served the Ottoman sultans
for generations, and in some cases the predecessors of the Ottomans as well,
received agricultural tax revenues in return for loyal military service.
Although their *timar*s were not strictly inheritable, but reverted to the
Ottoman central state on their death, they passed on to their sons their
status as *sipahi*s and therefore their claim to a *timar*, so long as the sons
also performed military service. The *kanunname* on the *timar* system
detailed the regulations by which these estates were bestowed on sons of
*sipahi*s. The central concern of the *kanun*s, and of Ayn Ali's treatise on the
system, was the integrity of the *kılıç* – literally, "sword" – the core revenues
of each *timar* that were intended to be indivisible and not to be partitioned
to supplement the revenues of other *timar*s. To Ayn Ali, changes in
the system had reduced these core revenues. Drawing on the regulations
that governed the system a generation before his time, he argued for a
return to rational order and the rule of law. There is a hint of professional
indignation as well in his rebuke to his predecessors in the imperial registry.

[109] For an edition and translation of this text, see Douglas A. Howard, "Ottoman Administration and
the Timar System: Suret-i Kanunname-i 'Osmani Beray-ı Timar Daden," *Journal of Turkish Studies*
20 (1996): 46–124.

Attracted by the apparent "hard data" in Ayn Ali's lists, Ottoman historians have continued to use the work as if it gave evidence for the state of affairs at the time the author presented it to the sultan and the grand vizier. To assume the accuracy of the figures in any published version of Ayn Ali's text without further documentation seems to me not only to be naïve, it misses the point of the work. As a council scribe who had recently served as intendant of the registry, Ayn Ali must have been well informed about the state of the *timar* system in his own day. His thesis in the *Kavânîn* emphasized that keeping proper records of things like the campaign inspections and *timar* transfers, and adherence to the cadastral surveys and the regulations, offered the only hope of improving the disordered system.

ORDER AND DISORDER AS A THEMATIC MOTIF

Ottoman law books and registers have not often been analyzed as literary genres, but there may be advantages to seeing them in this way.[110] Ayn Ali did not merely use them as sources. He appropriated their generic conventions and assumptions, employing them as the frame for his central motif, the polarity of order and disorder.

Ayn Ali articulated his version of this theme clearly in the preface of *Kavânîn-i Âl-i 'Osmân*. In the preface of such a work, the author customarily wrote a brief passage in praise of God and to honor the memory of the Prophet Muhammad, and dedicated the work to a patron. These components of a preface were standard, but authors might give them a particular formulation in order to link them to his specific themes.[111]

In his preface, Ayn Ali invoked the technical lexicon of the Ottoman law books and registers to suggest that the Ottoman legal and administrative order reenacted the paradigmatic created order. God was "Scribe [*katib*] of the editions of tablet and reed [pen], manager of the world's

---

[110] Suraiya Faroqhi, *Approaching Ottoman History: An Introduction to the Sources* (Cambridge: Cambridge University Press, 1999), pp. 95–101; Klaus Kreiser, *Der osmanische Staat 1300–1922* (Munich: R. Oldenbourg, 2001), pp. 104–6; Heath Lowry, "The Ottoman *Tahrir Defterleri* as a Source for Social and Economic History: Pitfalls and Limitations," in H. Lowry, *Studies in Defterology: Ottoman Society in the Fifteenth and Sixteenth Centuries* (Istanbul: Isis, 1992), pp. 3–18.
[111] On the importance of prefaces in Ottoman literature, see Lewis V. Thomas, *A Study of Naima*, ed. Norman Itzkowitz (New York: New York University Press, 1972), pp. 65–89. See also the comments of Holbrook on their neglect in Ottoman scholarship, in *Unreadable Shores*, pp. 9, 53, 99–100. Abou-El-Haj recognized the importance of these sections in his work on the *kanunname*s; see "Aspects of the Legitimation of Ottoman Rule." See also the study of Sholeh A. Quinn, "The Historiography of Safavid Prefaces," in Charles Melville (ed.), *Safavid Persia: The History and Politics of an Islamic Society, Pembroke Papers* 4 (1996): 1–25.

provisions, magistrate of the council room of judgment and destiny, artist of the studio of good and evil." God endowed livelihoods (the term Ayn Ali used is *dirlik* – literally benefice or prebend) through the Ottoman *timar*. He did so in accordance with the ranks of life. He gave gifts of "prosperous yields" and wealth from the yield of limitless fields (*mezâri'* – another term derived directly from the administrative vocabulary of the Ottoman agrarian economy) of generosity. The Prophet Muhammad was "ordered" (by God – but here Ayn Ali used the term *buyruldu*, referring to the sultan's decree) to point out and clarify the truth of the custom and determine the regulation of the law (*kanun-ı şeriat*). Muhammmad is "head of the register of the pages of apostleship, the index [*fihrist*] of the journal of greatness, the writer of the registers [*defatir*, the plural of *defter*] of law and religion [*şeriat-u-din*]." Finally, the Prophet is the Intendant of the Registry – the *Emin-i defter* (the Ottoman administrative office that Ayn Ali himself had held) – of the "inspired word of his excellency the Lord of the Two Worlds." Ayn Ali's choice of descriptors expressed praise of God and honor towards the Prophet Muhammad in the idiom of the *kanunname*s and *defter*s, that is, the idiom of the Ottoman intellectual and scribal class, and in so doing provided the reader with a layered interpretive scheme for his work.[112] Employing the legal and administrative manual of *kanun* and the records of the Ottoman *timar* system preserved in the *defter*s, the Ottoman social and political order might be read for its true significance, as a metaphor of God's perfect order.

The *kanunname*s and *defter*s were distillations of the Ottoman system. The *kanunname*s, and the agrarian economic and military system that they regulated and that the *defter*s recorded, became central texts in the description of the Ottoman imperial ideology.[113] Through Ayn Ali's pen, the Ottoman *kanunname*s and *defter*s were not only documentary sources for a supposed Ottoman historical reality, nor were they only articulations of the *Weltanschauung* of the Ottoman scribal class. The lists gave a geographical survey of the boundaries of the created order: the *kanunname*s of the Ottoman dynasty formed its legal structure, and the *defter*s were its notebook, the database of God's just social order. The *defter*s even accompanied the Ottoman army on campaign, so that after the chaos of battle,

---

[112] I owe the point to Holbrook; see *Unreadable Shores*, pp. 147–9.
[113] Rifa'at Ali Abou-El-Haj has led the discussion of the use of *kanun* in Ottoman ideology. See "The Expression of Ottoman Political Culture," as well as his "Power and Social Order: The Uses of the *Kanun*," in Irene A. Bierman, Rifa'at A. Abou-El-Haj, and Donald Preziosi (eds.), *Urban Structure and Social Order: The Ottoman City and Its Parts* (New Rochelle, NY: Aristide D. Caratzas, 1991), pp. 77–91; "Aspects of the Legitimation of Ottoman Rule."

Ottoman scribes of the imperial registry could restore order once again by noting changes in the distribution and bestowal of *timars*.

It is in this motif that we can discern the link between Ayn Ali's work and the enduring myths of Ottoman society, because in the opposition of order and disorder we recognize a nearly universal metaphor of creation. We have an image that belongs not only to the writer Ayn Ali. As Northrop Frye wrote, "when so many poets use so many of the same images, surely there are much bigger critical problems involved than biographical ones."[114] Neither does the image belong only to the Ottoman *nasihatname*s or even to the advice for kings more generally. All literature and even human consciousness itself imprints this image of societal order and disorder. In southwestern Eurasia the metaphor was older even than the Judeo-Christian-Islamic monotheistic tradition, going back at least as far as the *Enuma Elish*, the Babylonian creation myth, in which Marduk created the ordered world from the primeval chaos through a violent battle.[115] In the same southwest Eurasian tradition, at least since Hammurabi, the social order is inherent to the world order and guarded by the law, whose true author is God.[116] As Aziz al-Azmeh noted, just as chaos was the precondition of the created order, the state of nature was the precondition of the social order.[117] In the laws of Hammurabi, Marduk was the author of a rhetorically constructed system of perfectly retributive justice, in which punishment of evildoers and defense of the weak against the strong was analogous to the gods' care of the creation.[118]

In the monotheistic tradition, God's law, revealed through Moses, gives structure and content to the social order.[119] But the last sentence of the Book of Judges, "In those days there was no king in Israel: every man did that which was right in his own eyes," predicted the need for a social order that rationalized monarchy. The greatest danger for the community was to forsake God and lapse into polytheism, whose political counterpart was decentralization. In Islam, God's law was renewed through the Prophet

---

[114] Frye, *Fables of Identity*, p. 12.
[115] Stephanie Dalley (trans.), *Myths from Mesopotamia: Creation, the Flood, Gilgamesh, and Others* (Oxford: Oxford University Press, 1989), pp. 228–77.
[116] See the translation by M. E. J. Richardson, *Hammurabi's Laws* (Sheffield: Sheffield Academic Press, 2000).
[117] al-Azmeh, *Muslim Kingship*, p. 118.
[118] Jean Bottéro, *Mesopotamia: Writing, Reasoning and the Gods*, trans. Zainab Bahrani and Marc Van de Mieroop (Chicago: University of Chicago Press, 1992), pp. 156–84.
[119] al-Azmeh notes that Byzantine coronation ceremonies referred to the delivery of the tablets of the law to Moses; see *Muslim Kingship*, p. 44.

Muhammad. At Medina the establishment of the umma, God's covenant community, spelled the doom of the *jahiliyya* era – the era of ignorance, of unbelief, of primeval human chaos.[120] Thus, the constellation of images of law and order, disorder and rebellion are associated in Islamic literature with the genesis of the Muslim community at Medina.[121]

The stages by which the Ottomans appropriated this paradigm are far from clear. We can say, however, that on the one hand we are dealing with a universal fund of images and tropes of kingship that were reformulated in Islamic settings, as al-Azmeh has noted.[122] On the other hand, these writings excavate the deepest strata of common human stories, stories of God and the order of this world, beneath the terrain of literatures.[123] These common human stories are bound to be mythic – that is, religious – in the broadest sense.[124] Even as they present themselves in standard plots and sets of images,[125] the literary tropes reference pre-literary images and conceptions that are also captured in art, architecture, ritual, ceremonial, administrative structures, and the like.[126] In the mythic realm of potencies and potentialities, every kingdom is the kingdom of God; every king stands in the place of God's prophet, lawgiver and judge; every law is comparable to the law of God; and the original time is the model for all time. Literary archetypes, as fragments of myths, are the literary equivalents of rituals, the repetitions of the cosmogonic acts. The presence of these literary signs in a particular piece of literature awakens the reader to the universal aspects of the story being told.

---

[120] al-Azmeh, *Muslim Kingship*, p. 117.

[121] al-Azmeh noted the connection in monotheism between the dominion of the one God in the heavens and absolutist monarchy on earth, and the identification in monotheistic polities between God's law and the monarch, its physical embodiment. See *Muslim Kingship*, pp. 28–34.

[122] al-Azmeh, *Muslim Kingship*, passim.

[123] Mircea Eliade, *Images and Symbols: Studies in Religious Symbolism*, trans. Philip Mairet (Mission, KS: Sheed Andrews and McMeel, 1961); Frye, *Fables of Identity*, pp. 7–20.

[124] See Kort's discussion of the religious character of the four elements of narrative, in Kort, *Narrative Elements and Religious Meaning*, pp. 109–15.

[125] Frye, *Anatomy of Criticism*, passim. My thinking on this has also been shaped by the application of Frye to historiography in Hayden White, *Metahistory*, and by the phenomenology of Mircea Eliade. See especially *Myths, Dreams and Mysteries*, and *The Myth of the Eternal Return or, Cosmos and History*, trans. Willard R. Trask (Princeton, NJ: Princeton University Press, 1954).

[126] Gülru Necipoğlu, *Architecture, Ceremonial, and Power: The Topkapı Palace in the Fifteenth and Sixteenth Centuries* (Cambridge, MA: MIT Press, 1991), pp. 3–30; al-Azmeh, *Muslim Kingship*, passim. al-Azmeh referred to a study of Byzantine imperial art that compared "the imperial image to a chancery document, in which subtlety and realism gave way to clarity of essential and repeated outline." See *Muslim Kingship*, p. 11.

AYN ALI'S WORK AND THE PREMODERN WORLD

I have argued here that Ayn Ali's *Kavânîn-i Âl-i 'Osmân* should be seen in its fuller intellectual context. It is a work about the state organization of an agrarian society. The existence of strikingly similar works in other societies of the age draws our vision away from the particular Ottoman circumstances in which it was written, toward more generalized conditions of the premodern age. Despite continuous development and sharp differences between them, the Ottoman Empire was not completely unlike other agrarian states going back to antiquity. This impression is strengthened when comparison is made to the radically different organization of societies in the industrial age.[127] Differences, of course, exist. Long experience with writing, to take one relevant example, had by the sixteenth century largely eroded the specifically sacral aura and authority of scribes that is evident in the ancient river valley societies of the Nile, the Tigris–Euphrates, and the Yellow River and perhaps others.[128] Yet certain continuities are apparent. In the agrarian states of the sixteenth and seventeenth centuries literacy was still limited to a large degree to a scribal elite whose training was religious by and large. A scribe was *Ehl-i kalem ü sahib-i rakam*, literally "lord of the pen and master of figures." Skill with the pen was also associated with abilities in other areas, including the sciences, philosophy, theology, esoterica, and the occult: i.e. scribes were masters of more than merely state revenues and records. And these continuities seem the more significant when compared with the modern habit that sees primarily the functionality of communication and has mostly lost the sense of metaphoric symbolization that accompanied ancient views of literacy – except in the case of dyslexics and others with learning disabilities, for whom awareness of the evident magic of the written word is perhaps closer.

Similarly, the work of Ayn Ali helps us see that the Ottoman Empire should be placed alongside states like Safavid Iran, Mughal India, and Ming and Ch'ing China that exhibit similar political, economic, and intellectual concerns. These states represent the most advanced stage of efficiency in organizing and controlling the economic surplus of societies in that long agrarian age that dawned with the Neolithic revolution and waned with the gradual arrival of the constellation of forces that brought

---

[127] Hodgson, "Two Pre-Modern Muslim Historians," pp. 60–8.
[128] John A. Wilson, "Egypt: The Nature of the Universe," in *The Intellectual Adventure of Ancient Man: An Essay on Speculative Thought in the Ancient Near East* (Chicago, IL: University of Chicago Press, 1946), pp. 55–61; Bottéro, *Mesopotamia: Writing, Reasoning, and the Gods*; Mark Edward Lewis, *Writing and Authority in Early China* (Albany, NY: SUNY Press, 1999), pp. 18–28.

the modern age upon us. These include especially the printing press, the Protestant Reformation, the beginnings of European investment in long-distance trade, and the rise of an accompanying widespread and secularized literacy; the scientific method, the beginnings of industrialization, and the emergence of an accompanying functionalist and mechanistic set of values and modes of thought; and the English, French and American revolutions, and the sudden appearance of accompanying narrative fictions, in novels and histories, that simultaneously held out the teleological expectation of progress towards a secularized paradise, while encouraging romantic anticipation of redemption from the past in the rise of the West and its nations. With these notions Ayn Ali and other writers of advice for kings shared little in common.

7

The politics of early modern Ottoman historiography*

Baki Tezcan

"While the common starting point of many of [the] developments [leading to the spread of modernity to most of the world] was indeed the cultural program of modernity as it developed in Europe, its creative appropriation by those that followed inaugurated multiple modernities."[1] This is the framework within which the editors of a recent special issue of *Daedalus*, the journal of the American Academy of Arts and Sciences, situate their quest for multiple early modernities. Despite its revisionist stance, this approach does not give a genuine chance of imagining multiple cultural programs of modernity arising in different parts of the world. In the final analysis, what is accorded to the rest of the world is limited to a "creative appropriation" of the "real thing" that developed in Europe. This is not very different from the canonical treatment of Ottoman modernization, which starts either with the invasion of Egypt by the French led by Bonaparte in 1798, the British demands related to the British-Ottoman Trade Agreement of 1838, or some other event connected with Europe that put pressure on the Ottomans to modernize. A growing body of scholars have criticized this approach and instead have argued for the importance of internal dynamics that were transforming Ottoman society long before the nineteenth century as opposed to privileging external dynamics emanating

* The present chapter is very much shaped by the comments that Daniel Goffman and Virginia Aksan made after reading the earlier versions of my contribution to this volume. I am grateful to both of them. I must also thank Brett de Bary, director of the Society for the Humanities at Cornell University, for providing me with the most pleasant work environment in 2005–6, and the other fellows at the Society who shared their work in a series of seminar discussions on the theme of "Culture and Conflict," and who inspired me to completely rewrite this chapter. The research on which this study is based was made possible by an American Research Institute in Turkey postdoctoral grant funded by the National Endowment for the Humanities in 2001–2. Junior faculty research grants provided by the University of California, Davis, have enabled me to continue my research in Istanbul on and off since 2002.
[1] Shmuel N. Eisenstadt and Wolfgang Schluchter, "Introduction: Paths to Early Modernities – A Comparative View," *Daedalus* 127/3 (1998): 1–18, at 5.

from Europe.[2] As Aksan and Goffman state in their introduction, searching for "indications of a movement toward the "modern" in various aspects
of the Ottoman Empire" is a concern shared by several contributors to the
present volume. Although this chapter was not researched with a view to
finding a movement toward the "modern" in Ottoman historiography, its
findings lend themselves to construct such a movement in two areas: the
development of a state apparatus that is differentiated from the person of
the ruler and the limited expansion of the ruling class.

There is no single definition of modernity. Yet there are a number of
cultural, economic, intellectual, political, and social features the specific
combination of which distinguishes the modern period from its predecessors in history. The development of a state apparatus that is differentiated
from the person of the ruler is one of these features. A closely related feature
of modernity is the limited expansion of the ruling class. The medieval
period in Europe and around the Mediterranean was marked by a ruling
class that consisted of narrowly defined nobilities whose political power was
based on their control of agricultural surplus extraction which they secured
by means of military might. Whether or not these nobilities consisted of
inherited titles or slave origins did not change the basic fact of their exclusive
nature.[3] The only other social group these nobilities had to compete with
consisted of men who claimed to represent the divine will on earth. The late
Middle Ages and the early modern periods witnessed the growth of monetary economies and the selective opening of the exclusive nobilities to new
elements from economically powerful yet politically unprivileged classes,
such as merchants, professionals, and rentiers. It was this limited expansion
of the ruling class that eventually brought about the gradual development of
a collective identity that united the rulers and the ruled more directly and
became the basis of the modern nation-state in which the ruling classes
successfully mediate their domination of the political arena to the general
public thanks to their seeming openness. The theoretical possibility of
joining the ruling class strengthens the fiction that everyone in the polity
is of the same stock and shares the same ideals – we are all middle class in
America and, in theory, anyone could be the next president.

---

[2] See, for instance, Peter Gran, *Islamic Roots of Capitalism: Egypt, 1760–1840*, 2nd edn (Syracuse, NY:
Syracuse University Press, 1998); Rifa'at Ali Abou-El-Haj, *Formation of the Modern State: The
Ottoman Empire, Sixteenth to Eighteenth Centuries*, 2nd edn (Syracuse, NY: Syracuse University
Press, 2005); and Nelly Hanna, *In Praise of Books: A Cultural History of Cairo's Middle Class, Sixteenth
to the Eighteenth Century* (Syracuse, NY: Syracuse University Press, 2003).
[3] See Fred M. Donner, "Review of *Slaves on Horses: The Evolution of the Islamic Polity* by Patricia
Crone," *Journal of the American Oriental Society* 102 (1982): 367–71, at 370.

Obviously, the growth of an impersonal institution of rule and the selective expansion of the ruling classes are closely related to each other. As the politically unprivileged classes force their way into the ruling class, they pressure the ruler to concede some of his royal prerogatives to an impersonally constructed institution, that of the state. Although the state may ultimately be represented by the person of the ruler in the early modern period, its control is shared by a relatively larger – yet at the same time still very limited – segment of society. This relatively larger social base of the modern state makes it a stronger institution than medieval dynasties. The modern state thus represents the powerful groups of society in a much more unified and consolidated fashion than the medieval dynasty ever could – simply compare the English constitutional monarchy after the "Glorious Revolution" of 1688 with the royal absolutism of James I (1603–25). Thanks to this consolidation, the ruling institution becomes much more powerful in, among other things, projecting its own version of the truth, be it historical, religious, or scientific, as the ultimate one. It is with historical truth that this chapter is concerned.

This chapter provides a political history of Ottoman historiography produced at the imperial center in the period of 1550–1800. I argue that in the second half of the sixteenth century, the Ottoman dynasty made an attempt to directly control the development of historiographical expression that ultimately failed. In contrast with the failure of this attempt, in the eighteenth century the Ottoman state actually managed to establish a remarkable degree of control over Ottoman historiography. This marked difference between the outcomes of the two attempts requires an explanation. I argue that the eighteenth-century Ottoman state, with its expanded ruling class and impersonalized nature, was more able to project its version of historical truth than the sixteenth-century Ottoman sultanate. I also demonstrate that this new version of historical truth was much more secular in its understanding of historical time and almost positivist in its representation of the state. It is in this movement toward the eighteenth-century Ottoman state and the particular understanding of history produced by it that I suggest we may detect the "modern."

In the first part of the chapter, I focus on one of the works of Seyyid Lokman, the court historiographer of Murad III (1574–95), entitled the *Quintessence of Histories*. I argue that the publication of this work, which reflects a royalist approach to the Ottoman dynasty and its place in world history, has to be interpreted within the context of Murad III's absolutist politics that created strong reactions from the legalists who were concerned with placing certain limits on the political authority of the Ottoman sultan.

The available evidence suggests that the circulation of this work remained very limited despite the royal backing of the sultan himself.[4] I connect the failure of the work in terms of its circulation to the absolutist agenda it displays. Thus I suggest that the intellectual elite of the empire, most of whom seem to have been in the legalist camp in the late sixteenth century, resisted what they saw as a royal intrusion into their midst and ignored the *Quintessence of Histories* as they had ignored earlier projects of court historiography. In short, I suggest that the fate of the works produced by court historiographers should be interpreted as signs of a royal failure to dictate a certain understanding of Ottoman history to the intellectual elite, who developed in this period their own approach to Ottoman history and its place in world history that carried a legalist agenda.

In the second part of the chapter I make an attempt to look for some very general trends in the production and readership of historical works in the imperial center up to the early nineteenth century. Using the inventories of certain public libraries in Istanbul as they are represented in a manuscript catalog of history works, I argue that the official chronicles produced by the state historiographers in the eighteenth century seem to have established a monopoly over the articulation of Ottoman history in that period. I support this claim by looking at the bibliography of a major early nineteenth-century compilation of Ottoman history which reflects the same state monopoly on the interpretation of eighteenth-century history in its primary sources. Thus I establish that whereas the Ottoman court in the second half of the sixteenth century was not strong enough to propagate a certain take on Ottoman history, the eighteenth-century Ottoman state managed to do so with remarkable success.

The third and final part of the chapter is devoted to an attempt to explain how official eighteenth-century historiography may have been more successful than the court historiography of the sixteenth century in reaching the reading public at the imperial center. In this part I show that the understanding of historical time and the role of the Ottoman dynasty in history as reflected in these chronicles construct the fiction of an autonomous Ottoman state that does not need anything for its legitimation but

---

[4] The dynasty may have intended to limit the circulation of commissioned historiographies in general; see Gülru Necipoğlu, "Word and Image: The Serial Portraits of Ottoman Sultans in Comparative Perspective," in Selmin Kangal and Priscilla Mary Işın (eds.), *The Sultan's Portrait: Picturing the House of Osman* (Istanbul: İşbank, 2000), pp. 22–61, at pp. 43–4. While the royal manuscripts of these works were definitely produced for a limited audience, I believe that the texts they contained were not meant to remain within the confines of the palace. A detailed discussion of this important question has to await another occasion.

its very existence: "the eighteenth-century Ottoman state exists, therefore it *is*," implying a relatively secular and almost positivist understanding of the state. I relate this understanding of history and the construction of the state produced by it to the historical events of the long seventeenth century and their representation in the larger trends of historiography. I argue that the reduction of the dynasty to political insignificance, the disempowerment of the judicial elite who were the most powerful members of the intellectual elite, and the rise to power of new social groups around the vizier households, all of which are reflected in the historiographical output of the seventeenth and eighteenth centuries, created a new consensus which became the basis of the relatively impersonal Ottoman state in the eighteenth century.

COURT HISTORIOGRAPHY IN THE SECOND HALF OF THE SIXTEENTH CENTURY

This section explores the fate of Ottoman court historiography commissioned by Ottoman sultans in the second half of the sixteenth century and the reception it enjoyed among the members of the intellectual elite. In particular, the following analysis suggests that the historical assertions of the sixteenth-century Ottoman sultanate to establish a self-referential claim for political legitimacy were not accepted by the intellectual elite who successfully contested the attempt of the court to establish an ideological hegemony over the interpretation of Ottoman history. The intellectual elite, among whom the legalists seem to have been the strongest voice, insisted on their own role in defining and limiting the boundaries of royal authority.

From the 1550s until the early 1600s Ottoman sultans commissioned a series of historical works, most of which are either lost or extant in a single copy only. These works were produced by specifically appointed court historiographers, the *şehnâmecis*. Despite its limited circulation, this historiographical corpus has been relatively well studied as it has attracted the attention of both art historians and historians of Ottoman historiography.[5]

---

[5] Christine Woodhead, "An Experiment in Official Historiography: The Post of Şehnāmeci in the Ottoman Empire, c. 1555–1605," *Wiener Zeitschrift für die Kunde des Morgenlandes* 75 (1983): 157–82, provides an introduction to the subject. A number of articles in Kangal and Işın, *The Sultan's Portrait*, present art historical studies on some of the most important products of this historiographical corpus. The standard reference for biographical information on Ottoman historians is Franz Babinger's *Die Geschichtsschreiber der Osmanen und ihre Werke* (Leipzig: Otto Harrassowitz, 1927). This work is now being enlarged and updated by the "Historians of the Ottoman Empire," a project led by Cemal Kafadar, Hakan Karateke, and Cornell Fleischer; see http://www.ottomanhistorians.com.

Fleischer suggests evaluating the office of the court historiographer that was established around 1555 as an "attempt by the dynasty to assert direct control of the literary expression of historical ideology and imperial image."[6] In what follows, I will focus on one of the works produced by Ottoman court historiography, the *Quintessence of Histories* by Seyyid Lokman, the court historiographer who produced a massive output during the reign of Murad III.[7] The commissioner, Murad III, is known to have entertained strong absolutist ambitions for which he was criticized heavily by his contemporaries, especially by the legalists who successfully deployed the notion of *kanun*, or binding legal precedence in constitutional and public law, in order to set limits on royal authority. I will argue that there is a strong connection between his absolutist projects and the works produced by Seyyid Lokman. In the 1580s Murad III and Seyyid Lokman seem to have engaged in an active attempt to disseminate the products of royal historiography by presenting them to some of the highest functionaries of the Ottoman government, as is the case with the *Quintessence of Histories*. This attempt, which comes as close to the idea of "publication" as one can get in the pre-print age, does not seem to have brought any results, suggesting that the intellectual elite, who were dominated by the legalists in this period, sensed the agenda behind the royal commission and chose not to show any interest. Finally, I will demonstrate the hostile reception enjoyed by Seyyid Lokman among his contemporaries and emphasize the radically different understanding of Ottoman history that some of Seyyid Lokman's legalist adversaries proposed, which eventually came to circulate much more widely than any of his works. Thus my analysis will suggest that the work of Seyyid Lokman represents a royal attempt to disseminate a particular understanding of Ottoman history that ultimately failed in the midst of the growth of an oppositional construction of Ottoman history by the legalist intellectual elite.

---

[6] Cornell H. Fleischer, "The Lawgiver as Messiah: The Making of the Imperial Image in the Reign of Süleymân," in Gilles Veinstein (ed.), *Soliman le Magnifique et son temps* (Paris: Documentation Française, 1992), p. 172.

[7] On Seyyid Lokman and his works, see Bekir Kütükoğlu, "Şehnâmeci Lokman," in *Prof. Dr. Bekir Kütükoğlu'na Armağan* (Istanbul: Istanbul Üniversitesi Edebiyat Fakültesi Tarih Araştırma Merkezi, 1991), (hereafter *Armağan*) pp. 39–48. Additional biographical information is found in some of his works and Ottoman archival records; see Zekeriya Eroğlu, "Şehnâmeci Lokmān'ın Hüner-nâme'si (2. cilt – 1–154. varak): İnceleme – metin – sözlük," MA thesis, Istanbul University, 1998, pp. 1–6; Hüsnü Bodur, "Seyyid Lokman," senior thesis, Istanbul University, 1966, pp. 6–14; and Erhan Afyoncu, "Osmanlı müverrihlerine dair tevcihat kayıtları – II," *Belgeler* 26/30 (2005): 85–193, at 87, 97–104.

While it may be more difficult to argue for a royal intention to disseminate a certain take on history in the case of several Seyyid Lokman
productions because most of them exist in single copies, the *Quintessence
of Histories* is a real publication as far as the Ottoman pre-print age (before
c. 1730) is concerned. I call it a "real publication" as it consists of reproduc-
ing the contents of a document that was clearly not meant to be read by
many in its original form. This document is a royal record of history kept
on the Imperial Scroll, the *Tomar-ı Hümayun*. The Imperial Scroll as we
have it today is arguably the longest piece of Ottoman history writing: it is
102 feet long and 2.6 feet wide. It took hours for me and my art historian
colleague Emine Fetvacı to unfold it and then to fold it back in order to
place it in its proper case, confirming that it was not meant to be read
frequently.[8] Its present version does not carry the name of an author but
includes a dedication to Süleyman, suggesting that its original copy was
started during his reign. It lacks a proper ending but it seems to have been
updated until 1596. What it includes is nothing short of a full-scale
cosmography and a world history in the shape of an annotated genealogy.

The format of the Imperial Scroll suggests that it aims to project the
Ottoman dynasty as the culmination of a series of incidents that started
with the divine creation of the cosmos. In its extant form the Imperial
Scroll starts with a preface followed by a section on the creation of the
heavens and the earth that is heavily based on Islamic cosmology. The
cosmological part of the scroll is followed by an annotated genealogy of
prophets and kings starting from Adam and Eve and running in a number
of lines that parallel each other throughout the scroll. The lines are dotted
with circles in which names are recorded, the assumption being the man in
the circle below is related to the one above. At any point there may be a
number of families whose genealogies are recorded in parallel lines, such as
the ancient Persian kings and the ancestors of Muhammad, or the legendary forefathers of the Ottomans and the Mongol khans. Yet once the
Ottomans enter the stage of history, all of the other dynastic lines disappear. The lines at the two edges of the scroll are devoted to the grand
viziers and governors of Egypt, creating the impression that the only other
persons of note left in the world are the servants of the Ottoman emperor.

This image of a final order that is supposed to govern all the world is
strengthened by the way the genealogy is annotated. The annotations are

[8] This scroll is kept at the Topkapı Palace Library under the call number A. 3599; Kütükoğlu,
"Şehnâmeci Lokman," pp. 45–6. I must express my gratitude to Emine Fetvacı who shared with
me the heavy responsibility of examining it in 2002 at the Topkapı Palace Library.

much more detailed up to Muhammad and the first four caliphs of Islamic history. Then they become rare and the many dynasties of Islamic history are simply mentioned as lists of names. Yet once the Ottomans enter the stage of history, the annotations come back, becoming very detailed with the start of the reign of Süleyman. Most of Islamic history between the age of the caliphs in the seventh century and that of the Ottomans starting from the fourteenth becomes a period of anticipation for the final order to arrive. Just as Muhammad is the seal of the prophets after whom God's direct communication with mankind comes to a halt, the producers of the Imperial Scroll would like the reader to think that the Ottoman dynasty is the seal of all dynasties.[9]

The publication of the Imperial Scroll in the form of codices in the early 1580s aimed at propagating the dynastic understanding of world history, which presented the Ottoman dynasty as the culmination of a divinely pre-ordained cosmic plan, to a larger audience. The Ottomans had written world histories before, albeit not very frequently.[10] Both the number of world histories in Turkish and also their limited coverage were to change, as the late sixteenth and early seventeenth centuries witnessed an explosion in Ottoman world historical writing.[11] Thus the Imperial Scroll was published at a critical juncture when the world histories produced by the educated elite in the empire were about to shape the place of the Ottoman dynasty in the world. During the reign of Murad III, the updated contents of the scroll were copied in four codices three of which were lavishly illustrated.[12] The first of these codices was presented to Murad III

[9] In this particular regard, the *Silsilenâme*s studied by Bağcı create a similar impression; see Serpil Bağcı, "From Adam to Mehmed III: Silsilenâme," in Kangal and Işın, *The Sultan's Portrait*, pp. 188–201, p. 198, n. 22; see also Necipoğlu, "Word and Image," pp. 44–9.

[10] There is no systematic study of world histories produced in the Ottoman Empire. For those written in or translated into Turkish, one may consult *İstanbul Kütüphaneleri Tarih-Coğrafya Yazmaları Katalogları* (Istanbul: Maarif Matbaası, 1943–62) (hereafter *IKTCYK*), pp. 1–101.

[11] For a short discussion of Ottoman world historical writing in the second half of the sixteenth century, see Cornell H. Fleischer, *Bureaucrat and Intellectual in the Ottoman Empire: The Historian Mustafa Âli (1541–1600)* (Princeton, NJ: Princeton University Press, 1986), pp. 240–5; for a detailed study of an Ottoman world history, see Jan Schmidt, *Pure Water for Thirsty Muslims: A Study of Mustafâ 'Âli of Gallipoli's* Künhü l'ahbâr (Leiden: Het Oosters Instituut, 1991); for another Ottoman world historian and his work from the late sixteenth century, see Mehmet Canatar, "Cenâbî Mustafa Efendi: Hayatı, Eseri ve Tarih Görüşü," *Akademik Araştırmalar Dergisi* 4–5 (2000): 259–89.

[12] The illustrations in these three codices have been studied in detail by Günsel Renda; see her "Topkapı Sarayı Müzesindeki H. 1321 No.lu Silsilename'nin Minyatürleri," *Sanat Tarihi Yıllığı* 5 (1972–3): 443–95, including an English summary, pp. 481–95; Günsel Renda, "New Light on the Painters of the 'Zubdet al-Tawarikh' in the Museum of Turkish and Islamic Arts in Istanbul," in *IVème Congrès International d'Art Turc*, Aix-en-Provence, September 10–15, 1971 (Aix-en-Provence: Éditions de l'Université de Provence, 1976), pp. 183–200; Günsel Renda, "İstanbul Türk ve İslâm Eserleri Müzesi'ndeki Zübdet-üt Tevarih'in Minyatürleri," *Sanat* 6 (1977): 58–67; Günsel Renda, "Chester Beatty Kitaplığındaki Zübdetü't-Tevarih ve Minyatürleri," in *Armağan*, pp. 485–506.

in late 1583. Apparently it was the sultan himself who had ordered the production of this exquisite codex. This book is known as the *Zübdetü't-Tevârîh*, or the *Quintessence of Histories*, which is the name given to the text of the Imperial Scroll by its original author in the preface.[13] Mehmed Agha, the chief black eunuch of the imperial palace, and the Grand Vizier Siyavuş Pasha also received illustrated copies of the *Quintessence of Histories*, while Sadeddin Efendi, the mentor of the emperor, was presented with a modified version of the work.[14] I interpret these presentations of the work to be a royal attempt to publish a world history in the pre-print age. The titles of the men chosen to receive copies of the Imperial Scroll in codices, agha, pasha, and efendi, suggest that multiple audiences were targeted. Mehmed Agha was in charge of the palace, Siyavuş Pasha supervised the administrative–military structure of the empire, and Sa'deddîn Efendi was connected with the intellectual elite. While the actual copies presented to these dignitaries were expensive productions with lavish illustrations that supported the textual project with appropriate images, the three dignitaries, and the literary circles they sponsored among their respective audiences, could facilitate the further distribution of the work through the production of cheaper non-illustrated copies.[15] As it happens, there is evidence suggesting that at least one of these copies changed hands and another one was reproduced in an affordable copy, demonstrating that these works circulated beyond their original owners.[16] However, they did not leave any mark on the larger historiographical scene of the period. One does not find a single reference to Seyyid Lokman's *Quintessence of Histories* in contemporary historical sources or later ones.

[13] Durmuş Kandıra, a PhD candidate at Istanbul University, is working on a critical edition of the *Quintessence of Histories*. I am grateful to him for sharing his ongoing work with me.

[14] Entitled the *Mücmelü't-tomar*, or the *Summary of the Scroll*, this text is slightly different from that of the *Quintessence of Histories* as it skips the cosmological part as well as most of the annotated genealogy, presenting instead a list of rulers of Egypt from the time of Adam to the most recent Ottoman governor. Yet when it comes to the Ottomans, the *Summary of the Scroll* is mostly in agreement with the *Quintessence of Histories*; see British Library, OR 1135, ff. 18b–28b; there is a lacuna between ff. 25–6.

[15] For the artistic patronage of Mehmed Agha, see Emine Fatma Fetvacı, "Viziers to Eunuchs: Transitions in Ottoman Manuscript Patronage, 1566–1617," PhD dissertation, Harvard University, 2005, pp. 202–56.

[16] The Siyavuş Pasha copy seems to have returned to the Topkapı Palace Library, where it is held today (H. 1321), probably at some point after he died in 1601. The Mehmed Agha copy, which is held at the Chester Beatty Library in Dublin (no. 414), has an insert at the beginning that is written by someone who presents the work as a unique history. Despite his appreciation of the work, this unidentified presenter is so ignorant of Lokman that he places his work and Mehmed Agha in the reign of Süleyman (d. 1566). This insert suggests that the work must have changed hands after the death of Mehmed Agha in 1591. It was probably sold a few times before it reached its final destination in Dublin. The only codex that was copied elsewhere seems to have been the Sadeddin copy.

Why, then, did the *Quintessence of Histories* fail to attract any attention? Comparable works of world history, such as Mustafa Ali's *Künhü'l-ahbâr*, or the *Essence of History*, which Ali started writing some ten years after the *Quintessence* and kept working on until his death in 1600, survived in ninety manuscript copies.[17] Is it simply the supposedly poor literary qualities of Lokman's work that made him such an unwanted man among the Ottoman men of letters? Ali's critique of Lokman's literary abilities in his *Essence of History* is very harsh. Yet that he was not impartial must have been obvious to his readers because in the same work Âli quotes with approval another work by Lokman, the *Book of Features* which did not have such grandiose ambitions as the *Quintessence of Histories*.[18] The real question, I would argue, is not Lokman's literary qualities but rather what he and his work stand for with respect to the contemporary intellectual elite who seem to have been dominated by the legalists.

A comparison of the work of Ali and that of Seyyid Lokman suggests that the latter was pushing for a certain historical take on the Ottoman dynasty that would legitimize the absolutist politics of Murad III which Âli, the most prolific legalist writer of the period, was very critical of. On the one hand, the Imperial Scroll and the *Quintessence of Histories* codices that derive from it represent the Ottoman emperors as the final and divinely pre-ordained arbiters of the age with no rivals in the world. Âli, on the other hand, is not only a critic of Lokman's literary style, but also of his patron, Murad III. Ali was very critical of Murad III's absolutist policies, and his approach to Ottoman history was closely related to his critique of royal absolutism. Although not found in most of the manuscripts of the *Essence*, the preface Ali authored for the section of his work that deals with Ottoman history starts with counting the other major dynasties of the Islamic world, such as the Safavids in Persia, the Mughals in India, and the Uzbeks in Central Asia.[19] This presentation is entirely antithetical to the one found in the *Quintessence of Histories* and has a limiting effect on the political ambitions of the Ottoman dynasty by destabilizing its claim to absolute power. Another of his works, the *Season of Sovereignty*, is devoted mainly to past dynasties that had disappeared from the face of the earth. In the words of Fleischer, "the moral of this arrangement of material is clear: the Ottoman state, placed in a

---

[17] Schmidt, *Pure Water*, pp. 364–402, presents a list of these ninety manuscripts in great detail.
[18] Fleischer, *Bureaucrat and Intellectual*, pp. 105, 249. For the *Book of Features*, see Necipoğlu, "Word and Image," pp. 31–42.
[19] Jan Schmidt, *Mustafa Ali's Künhü'l-ahbar and its Preface According to the Leiden Manuscript* (Leiden: Nederlands Instituut voor het Nabije Oosten, 1987), pp. 50–1.

comparative historical context, was subject to the same historical cycles as other states, and could fall apart as quickly as it had risen."[20]

I would argue that Ali's critical line brought him his popularity whereas the conformist approach of Lokman buried him in oblivion because the absolutist politics of Murad III had created strong reactions among the contemporary intellectual elite who were drawn to the legalist line. Murad III wished to establish a more personal control of the imperial administration. His absolutist ambitions were well known and heavily criticized. According to Selânikî, who recorded a critical summary of Murad III's reign on the occasion of his death in January 1595, the sultan had not allowed any independence to his viziers and the high-ranking members of the judicial elite; he kept dismissing them and appointing new ones.[21] This charge by Selânikî is well taken. After the death of the Grand Vizier Semiz Ahmed Pasha in 1580, the sultan made a total of nine appointments to the grand vizierate within fifteen years, and only one of the appointees died in office.[22] While destabilizing the position of the grand vizier, the sultan found other means to create alternative foci of stable power that were centered within the court. One of these means was the creation of a new office at the palace, that of the chief black eunuch – the chief officer of the harem, which was the residential part of the palace. Mehmed Agha, who occupied this position until his death in 1591, built his own network of patronage that sought to provide the court with loyal supporters everywhere, including within the judicial elite whose membership was becoming a semi-monopoly in the hands of a number of prominent families. For instance, an African slave, whom Mehmed Agha took under his wing, was to become the senior justice (*kadıasker*) of the European provinces during the reign of Osman II in 1621.[23] Murad III was aiming to destabilize privileged groups, such as vizier households and the judicial elite, in

[20] Fleischer, *Bureaucrat and Intellectual*, p. 178.
[21] Selânikî Mustafa Efendi (d. after 1600), *Tarih-i Selânikî*, ed. Mehmed İpşirli, 2 vols. (Istanbul: Istanbul Üniversitesi Edebiyat Fakültesi Yayınları, 1989), vol. I, pp. 427–8, 431–2.
[22] The grand viziers appointed between 1580 and 1595 were: Sinan Paşa (1580–2, 1589–91, 1593–5, dismissed by Mehmed III), Siyavuş Paşa (1582–4, 1586–9, 1592–3), Özdemiroğlu Osman Paşa (1584–5, died in office), Hadım Mesih Paşa (1585–6), and Ferhad Paşa (1591–2).
[23] Mehmed Agha's office may well have existed before Murad III. However, historical sources do not mention it, suggesting that even if there were a chief officer of the harem before Mehmed Agha, his responsibilities were limited to the harem. On Mehmed Agha and his network see my "*Dispelling the Darkness*: The Politics of 'Race' in the Early Seventeenth Century Ottoman Empire in the Light of the Life and Work of Mullah Ali," in Baki Tezcan and Karl Barbir (eds.), *Identity and Identity Formation in the Ottoman World: A Volume of Essays in Honor of Norman Itzkowitz*, forthcoming from the University of Wisconsin Madison Center of Turkish Studies in 2007.

order to establish an empire tightly governed from his court by men like his chief black eunuch.

For the members of the privileged groups who remained outside the court circles, the court historiography of Murad III, which was disseminated through the highest dignitaries of the imperial administration who happened to be also very close to the sultan, was regarded as an agent of political absolutism. That is why Ottoman men of letters, most of whom stuck to the legalist position in order to save their privileges, did not warm to it and chose simply to ignore it. There is not a single contemporary biographical notice about Lokman, who, according to Ali, estimated his own literary production in verse at approximately 100,000 couplets. He had recited some of his earliest poetry in the presence of Süleyman the Magnificent.[24] Judging from the name of one of his sons – Aristo, that is Aristotle – and one of his brothers – Eflâtûn, that is Plato – Lokman, named after a Quranic figure who represents wisdom, must have come from a learned family. His epithet Seyyid suggests that his family descends – or claims to descend – from the Prophet. He was probably the only Ottoman historian who was able to describe astronomical instruments while composing Persian poetry. Besides writing, he was also responsible for overseeing the whole team of artists who painted the royal presentation copies of the many volumes he authored. According to Kütükoğlu, who studied the works of several official historians of the eighteenth century, his record of events is reminiscent of their style.[25] Yet the Ottoman intellectual elite of the late sixteenth century regarded him as an outsider and refused to accept him in their midst. Such a strong reaction begs for an explanation, which I find in his personification of Murad III's absolutism.[26]

The central thrust of my argument is that the relationship that a project like the *Quintessence of Histories* envisions between its author and its subject

---

[24] Mustafa Ali, *Gelibolulu Mustafa Âli ve Künhü'l-ahbâr'ında II. Selim, III. Murat ve III. Mehmet Devirleri*, ed. Faris Çerçi, 3 vols. (Kayseri: Erciyeş Üniversitesi Yayinlari, 2000), vol. III, p. 632; Eroğlu, "Şehnāmeci Lokmān'ın," pp. 1–6.

[25] See Bekir Kütükoğlu, "Lokmân b. Hüseyin," in *Türkiye Diyanet Vakfı İslâm Ansiklopedisi* (Istanbul: Türkiye Diyanet Vakfı, 1988–), vol. XXVII, pp. 208–9, at p. 208.

[26] Incidentally, this framework of interpretation may also be used for other projects of the court of Murad III, such as the Imperial Observatory, the destruction of which has traditionally been regarded as a triumph of religious fanaticism in Ottoman history. It may very well be the case that as a project of the court the Observatory was regarded with suspicion. It is interesting to note in this context that the next project for an astronomical observatory was to be developed by Feyzullah Efendi, the executed mentor of Mustafa II who was deposed in 1703 in response to his absolutist ambitions; see Aydın Sayılı, *The Observatory in Islam and its Place in the General History of the Observatory* (Ankara: Türk Tarih Kurumu, 1960), p. 305.

matter, the dynasty, was unacceptable to the Ottoman intellectual elite of the sixteenth century. The sultan had hired someone and placed him on his regular payroll to craft this project. While most members of the Ottoman literary establishment flourished thanks to the patronage of the dynasty, they did so with some form of agency, however limited that may be. They produced eulogies, epics, chronicles, and other types of literature that praised the dynasty, presented their work, and got rewards for their works that ultimately legitimized the dynasty. For the relationship to function in a credible manner in the eyes of the larger society, and for the intellectual elite to sustain their position in the long term, however, they had to have some autonomy. The dynasty had a monopoly over the source of the rewards to be distributed to the intellectual elite as the ultimate collector of surplus production in society. The relative position of power enjoyed by the elite came from their monopoly over literary articulations of political legitimacy which mediated the political authority of the dynasty to the reading public and beyond. If the dynasty found ways to articulate the legitimacy of its political actions in literary forms and disseminate them among the reading public, it would not need the mediation of the elites. The office of the court historiographer was the kind of position that had the potential to render the legitimizing and mediating functions of other voices unnecessary. Therefore Ottoman intellectuals were critical of court historiographers and their writings, belittling and ignoring them. They assumed the legalist position exemplified by Ali's work and became critics of royal absolutism.[27]

These critics were not only strong enough politically to resist the intrusion of court historiography into their readings but they also developed different conceptions of royal authority and articulated them in historical works, continuing the tradition of a pluralist historiography that Kafadar observes with regard to the earlier centuries of Ottoman history.[28] One of the better-known examples that represents the continuing historiographical pluralism is the way in which the regicide of Osman II in 1622 was narrated in early seventeenth-century Ottoman historiography. As argued by Piterberg, there were alternative narratives of this regicide that circulated. The one that became the hegemonic representation of the event in the later seventeenth and eighteenth centuries was the

---

[27] 'Âşık Çelebi, *Meşâ'ir üş-şu'arâ or Tezkere of 'Âşık Çelebi*, facsimile edn, ed. G. M. Meredith-Owens (London: E. J. W. Gibb Memorial, 1971), fol. 166a, engages in a defense of the literary merits of Ârifi, the first court historiographer commissioned by Süleyman.

[28] See Cemal Kafadar, *Between Two Worlds: The Construction of the Ottoman State* (Berkeley, CA: University of California Press, 1995).

one that was most critical of the absolutist policies of Osman II.[29] To sum
up, a historiographical tradition that was centered on the Ottoman court
and aimed at legitimizing royal absolutism failed to do so in the sixteenth
century. The seventeenth century witnessed the continuation of a pluralist
historiography, the prevalent tradition of which came to be critical of royal
absolutism. It was only in the eighteenth century that a monopoly established by the official chroniclers of the state replaced the pluralist historiography of the preceding centuries.

THE OFFICIAL CHRONICLES OF THE EIGHTEENTH CENTURY

Attempts to manipulate historiographical expression in the center of the
empire were undertaken once again with the establishment of the office of
the *vekâyi'-nüvis* (also known as *vak'a-nüvis*), or the "official chronicler."
Thomas and Kütükoğlu have explored this office, the chroniclers who
occupied it, and their writings in some detail.[30] The works of the official
chroniclers were widely circulated among the Ottoman reading public.
Around the mid-eighteenth century, the official chronicles actually came to
form a monopoly of historiographical expression in the center of the
empire. The present part of the chapter substantiates this claim and
introduces the question of how it is that the court historiography was
regarded as tainted propaganda in the sixteenth century, and yet the official
chroniclers of the Ottoman state became neutral and dependable bearers of
historical truth in the eighteenth century.

In order to measure the success of the works produced by the official
chroniclers in the eighteenth century, one needs to have an indicator of
relative circulations enjoyed by various historical works. It is, however,
difficult to establish the popularity of a book produced before the age of
print or even in the earlier part of that age. The task becomes even harder if
one is working on Ottoman books, definitive library catalogs of which
await publication in Turkey and elsewhere. Moreover, even if we had
catalogs of the Turkish holdings of every manuscript library, we would

[29] Gabriel Piterberg, *An Ottoman Tragedy: History and Historiography at Play* (Berkeley, CA:
University of California Press, 2003); see also Baki Tezcan, "The 1622 Military Rebellion in
Istanbul: A Historiographical Journey," *International Journal of Turkish Studies* 8 (2002): 25–43.
[30] Lewis V. Thomas, *A Study of Naima*, ed. Norman Itzkowitz (from the author's PhD dissertation of
1949) (New York: New York University Press, 1972); Bekir Kütükoğlu, "Vekayi'nüvis," in *İslâm
Ansiklopedisi*, vol. XIII, pp. 271–87; reprinted with revisions in Bekir Kütükoğlu, *Vekayi'nüvis:
Makaleler* (Istanbul: Istanbul Fetih Cemiyeti, 1994), pp. 103–38.

still have to collate them to produce an accurate inventory that would tell us the number of extant copies of each and every book, when and where they were copied, and so on. Even such a collation of public library holdings would not be accurate, as the private collections and lost books cannot be accounted for. One would also have to sort out the information found in the extant probate inventories. Most importantly, we would also have to consider the number of people who would read a book located in the library of the Topkapı palace, in a public library of Istanbul, in a library of, let us say, Damascus, and in a private collection. The task seems impossible to accomplish. However, we do need a yardstick to measure the circulation of a book if its intellectual impact is of any concern. Therefore I decided to use the catalog of Ottoman history works found in the public libraries of Istanbul and established a list of the "bestsellers" of Ottoman narrative history.[31]

Despite its apparent weaknesses, the "bestsellers" list of Ottoman narrative history, which is reproduced in the appendix to this chapter, discloses a general trend: a contrast between a period marked by historiographical pluralism followed by one in which a number of works seem to have established a monopoly on Ottoman historiography. None of the works covering the pre-eighteenth-century history of the empire that one finds in the "bestsellers" list is, strictly speaking, a product of the court historiography discussed in the first section of this chapter. While their authors had functions within the administration of the empire, they were not commissioned to produce contemporary chronicles, with the exception of Kemalpaşazâde.[32] Thus, in the period prior to the eighteenth century, Ottoman historiography seems to have developed a relatively independent voice in relation to the court that allowed the existence of multiple viewpoints. If one wished to read about the deposition of Osman II in 1622, for instance, there would be six books

---

[31] A committee of specialists that was first founded in 1927 only to be dismissed after six months was re-convened in 1935 and went through the records of several libraries in Istanbul. The result of their work was published between 1943 and 1962 in eleven fascicles that formed *IKTCYK* (see fn. 10 above), which remained incomplete. The first two of these fascicles catalog the Ottoman Turkish works of history that cover parts of the Ottoman period, either exclusively or as a component of a world history. It has to be noted that the representative set of Istanbul libraries covered in this catalog does not include the Topkapı Palace Libraries, the Library of the Turkish and Islamic Arts, and the Library of the Archaeological Museum; moreover its coverage of the Beyazıt Library and the Istanbul University Library is extremely sketchy. Despite these obvious weaknesses, it is only in this catalog that one finds an attempt to go through the inventory of several libraries which altogether constitute a representative set for those Istanbul libraries that would have been the most accessible to the educated classes of the imperial capital.

[32] It is important to note in his case, though, that his chronicle did not survive in its entirety and does not seem to have circulated widely in the sixteenth and seventeenth centuries if one were to take the copy dates of the extant manuscripts in the *IKTCYK* as a basis; see *IKTCYK*, pp. 120–4.

one could consult in this list. Yet the same list includes only one chronicle covering the deposition of Mehmed IV in 1687, that of Na'îmâ, which happens to be the first work regarded as an official chronicle.

The relatively monopolistic trend of the later period is also reflected in the bibliographies of general historical studies on this period. Moreover, both such studies and the "bestsellers" list in the appendix of this chapter suggest that this monopoly is formed by the works of official chroniclers. By far the most detailed narrative account of Ottoman history to be found in any language is arguably *Die Geschichte des osmanischen Reiches*, or the *History of the Ottoman Empire*, by Josef von Hammer-Purgstall (d. 1856). This Habsburg diplomat–orientalist noted his principal sources at the beginning of each volume he published as part of his Ottoman history. While he has diverse sources for all of his early volumes, on the eighteenth century what he relies on is a series of chronicles that cover the period in succession to each other, such as *Tarih-i Râşid* and *Tarih-i Âsım*, the historical narratives by Râşid and Âsım, respectively, both of which are official chronicles.[33] Actually all of the five chronicles in my "bestsellers" list that deal with the late seventeenth and eighteenth centuries – those of Na'îmâ, Şefîk, Râşid, Âsım, and Enverî – were produced by official chroniclers, the first one of whom, Na'îmâ, was appointed at the turn of the eighteenth century. As far as one can tell from the works of narrative history to be found in the public libraries of Istanbul and the bibliography of Hammer's work, official chronicles came to dominate the historiographical field from the early eighteenth century onwards, marginalizing alternative voices.[34]

One wonders whether the success of the official chronicles may be related to the backing most of them enjoyed from the Ottoman Imperial Press.[35] The role played by the printing press in the publication process of

---

[33] Compare the prefaces paginated in roman numerals, Josef v. Hammer-Purgstall, *Geschichte des osmanischen Reiches*, 10 vols. (Pest: C. A. Hartleben, 1827–35), vols. I–VII. For *Tarih-i Râşid* and *Tarih-i Âsım*, see the appendix.

[34] This is not to say that alternative voices did not exist. It is clear that this later period produced as many people interested in writing historical accounts as the earlier period. There are several contemporary chronicles on eighteenth-century Ottoman history which are not on my list. Although some of these missing chronicles may well be crucial to reconstruct the political history of the imperial center in the eighteenth century, the evidence of the Ottoman public libraries in Istanbul, as well as the bibliography of Hammer, suggest that they were marginalized by the official accounts. Babinger, for instance, records seventy-five individuals who wrote historical works in addition to Şefîk, Râşid, and Âsım between Na'îmâ and Enverî; see Babinger, *Die Geschichtsschreiber*, pp. 245–320.

[35] Three of the four works covering the eighteenth century in this list were printed relatively soon after they were produced, as indicated in the relevant entries of the list in the appendix. Later on, the official history of the third quarter of the eighteenth century was printed by the Imperial Press during the lifetime of its author Ahmed Vâsıf (d. 1806), and the official account of the annihilation of the

the official chronicles is undeniable. Thanks to the work of Orlin Sabev, the probate inventory of Ibrahim Müteferrika, the founder and director of the first Ottoman Imperial Press, has recently been recovered. This inventory includes the number of copies of books that were not sold during the lifetime of Müteferrika.[36] Based on these figures, Sabev estimates that approximately 190 copies of the official chronicle of Mehmed Râşid must have been sold within the first six years of its publication. This is more than twice the number of the known manuscript copies of Ali's *Essence of History* produced in three centuries.[37] But the question is whether the Imperial Press could bear all of the responsibility for the wide dissemination of the official chronicles. This institutional backing definitely facilitated the formation of a historiographical hegemony. Yet, as the analysis of the court historiography in the first part of this chapter suggests, the Ottoman reading public had earlier shown that it was capable of opting out of reading histories imposed upon it. How, then, was the attitude of the reading public transformed?

Both eighteenth-century Ottoman readers and later orientalists seem to have viewed the official historiography as a neutral source in contrast to the sixteenth-century court historiography which was clearly regarded as the propagandist voice of the court. Hammer and others must have thought that the official chronicles were as close to primary sources as one could get since they were tantamount to state records. So why should one bother to look for anything else? A younger contemporary of Hammer's in Berlin, Leopold von Ranke, was theorizing this approach around the same time that Hammer started publishing his *Geschichte*. The aim of history,

janissaries was printed a year after the event; see Ahmed Vâsıf, *Mehâsinü'l-âsâr ve hakâyıkü'l-ahbâr* (Istanbul: Matba'a-ı 'Âmire, 1219/1804); and Mehmed Es'ad, *Üss-i Zafer* (Istanbul: Matbaa-i Süleyman Efendi, 1243/1827).

[36] Sabev found this document at the Archive of the Mufti of Istanbul, in the collection *Kısmet-i Askeriye Mahkemesi* (register 98, fols. 39a–40b). A transcription of the document in modern Turkish and a facsimile are appended to his monograph, recently published in Bulgarian: Сăбев, Орлин. Пăрвото османско пăтешествие в света на печатната книга (1726–1746). Нов поглед [First Ottoman Trip in the World of Printed Books (1726–1746). A Reassessment] (София: Авангард Прима, 2004), pp. 340–51. A Turkish translation of this book will soon be published in Istanbul. Sabev also presented his findings and their impact on the interpretation of the success of Müteferrika's press at a conference in Princeton recently, the proceedings of which are edited by Dana Sajdi to be published by I. B. Tauris. I am grateful to Sabev who shared his work with me before its publication.

[37] Although there may be more manuscripts of the *Essence of History* than those identified by Schmidt, *Pure Water*, pp. 364–402, and it may be possible to find more copies among the holdings of manuscript libraries in Anatolia, whose inventories have not yet been cataloged in an accessible fashion, I would strongly doubt whether the revised record would come close to 190 copies. According to Sabev's figures, the chronicle of Na'îmâ did even better than that of Râşid with approximately 390 copies sold. However, it had been printed earlier than Râşid's chronicle, and thus had stayed twice as long on the market by the time the probate inventory was held.

according to Ranke, was only to show what actually happened.[38] History
could perform this function by concentrating first and foremost on archival
primary sources of state institutions that are supposed to be the most
neutral. Apparently, the state had succeeded in projecting itself as a neutral
institution to such a degree that its records were now regarded as the most
neutral sources one could rely on to write histories. This approach to the
state, which was also shared by the Ottoman reading public in the eighteenth and nineteenth centuries, as suggested by the "bestsellers" list in the
appendix, is very different from the way in which the Ottoman intellectual
elite had treated the ruling apparatus of the Ottoman dynasty in the
sixteenth century. What seems to have changed from the sixteenth century
to the eighteenth, then, is not only the attitude of the reading public toward
historical works produced by the institution that ruled them but also the
way in which this ruling institution projected itself and was perceived by
others. We seem to be facing a different institution altogether.

OTTOMAN HISTORIOGRAPHY AND THE FORMATION OF
THE EARLY MODERN OTTOMAN STATE

İnalcık suggests in the context of the rise of Ottoman historiography in the
fifteenth and early sixteenth centuries that "[t]he attempt to correlate the
phases of Ottoman historiography with the development of Ottoman
history itself can shed new light upon various problems."[39] Indeed, the
domination of historiographical expression in the center of the empire by
the hegemonic voice of the state in the eighteenth century is closely related
to the historical developments of the immediately preceding period, which
may be summed up as the formation of the early modern Ottoman state
apparatus as an institution that was distinct from the Ottoman dynasty.
What made this state more powerful in disseminating its own version of
historical truth than the Ottoman court of the sixteenth century is that it
represented a larger segment of the ruling classes and was based on a
consensus of sorts which was achieved after a long period of political
contestation between the various groups in Ottoman society. I argue that
this consensus was achieved by the reduction of the Ottoman dynasty to

[38] Leopold von Ranke, *Fürsten und Völker: Geschichten der romanischen und germanischen Völker von
1494–1514 – Die Osmanen und die spanische Monarchie im 16. und 17. Jahrhundert*, 4th edn, ed. Willy
Andreas (Wiesbaden: Emil Vollmer Verlag, 1957), p. 4. The first edition of Ranke's work was
published in 1824, three years before the publication of Hammer's first volume.

[39] Halil İnalcık, "The Rise of Ottoman Historiography," in Bernard Lewis and P. M. Holt (eds.),
Historians of the Middle East (London: Oxford University Press, 1962), p. 152.

relative political insignificance, the disempowerment of the judicial elite who included the most powerful members of the intellectual elite of the sixteenth century, and the rise of new political groups that concentrated around the vizier households. Finally, I demonstrate that the historical truth that the eighteenth-century Ottoman state successfully disseminated was also much easier to digest as it did not include a cosmic scheme to legitimize the ruling institution. The self-referential legitimacy of the modern state was based on simply being there.

There is a clear correlation between the formation of the hegemonic voice of the official chroniclers and the relative political peace established by the eighteenth-century political consensus that followed a series of political crises during the long seventeenth century. Out of the ten reigns of the nine sultans who occupied the Ottoman throne between 1617 and 1730, seven ended with dethronements. The next seventy-seven years passed without a single deposition. It was during this period that the official chronicles came to establish a hegemony over historiographical expression at the center of the empire that was facilitated by the establishment of the Imperial Press around 1730. Thus the success of the historiographical hegemony of the official chronicles is closely related to the political consensus of the eighteenth century. The first and arguably the most important component of this new political consensus was a weaker Ottoman dynasty.

The most obvious change in the new political structure of the empire in the eighteenth century was the destabilization and the resulting weakness of the position occupied by the Ottoman sultan as a result of the political crises of the long seventeenth century. The seven depositions that took place in 113 years (1617–1730) did not leave much that is sacred about the members of the Ottoman dynasty. These depositions demonstrated that the Ottoman emperor, who was supposed to be the Shadow of God on Earth, could easily be dispensed with and replaced. It is not a coincidence that starting from the late sixteenth century one finds in the historical sources occasional but serious articulations by the ruling elite of certain dynastic houses as viable alternatives to the Ottoman family.[40] Also, starting from the late sixteenth century, one witnesses a radical change in the Ottoman succession. With the eventual consolidation of the rule of

---

[40] Feridun M. Emecen, "Osmanlı Hanedanı'na alternatif arayışlar: İbrahimhanzâdeler örneği," in *XIII. Türk Tarih Kongresi, Ankara: 4–8 Ekim 1999: Kongreye Sunulan Bildiriler*, 5 vols. (Ankara: Türk Tarih Kurumu, 2002), vol. III, part 3, pp. 1877–86. For another example, see Baki Tezcan, "Searching for Osman: A Reassessment of the Deposition of the Ottoman Sultan Osman II (1618–1622)," PhD dissertation, Princeton University, 2001, p. 127.

seniority in the late seventeenth century, replacing the "succession of the fittest" formula of the earlier period,[41] the actual personality of the ruler became almost a non-issue. The Ottoman sultan came to occupy the throne by the sheer accident of being the oldest surviving male member of the dynasty.

The importance of the disempowerment of the dynasty as symbolized by the consolidation of the rule of seniority in understanding the eighteenth-century conception of the state cannot be overestimated. I would like to suggest that the eighteenth-century Ottoman state is a qualitatively differ-ent institution than the dynastic institution of rule in the sixteenth century, mainly because of this disempowerment that had an impact on the way in which the very notion of state was understood. Whereas the sixteenth-century Ottoman government was a personal enterprise in the final analysis, the eighteenth-century one was an impersonal institution in comparison with the former. While both of these institutions are desig-nated in the sources by the same term, *devlet*, the meaning of the term itself is caught in a process of change. The sixteenth-century usage of the term to refer to an institution of rule is very much intertwined with the primary meanings attached to the word in the Arabic language, such as turn, change, and fortune. It was Süleyman the Magnificent who composed the famous couplets:

> There is nothing as esteemed among the people as *devlet*
> yet there is no *devlet* in the world equal to one breath of health;
> That which they call sultanate is but a quarrel for the world
> there is no fortune and prosperity in this world to equal solitariness.[42]

Süleyman exploits the double meaning of the word *devlet* in the two parallels he establishes between the *devlet* of the first line and the "sulta-nate" of the third, on the one hand, and the *devlet* of the second line and the "fortune and prosperity" of the fourth, on the other. This close connection between *devlet* as fortune and the *devlet* as the sultanate, or more precisely, one's turn on the throne, renders the ruling institution very personal. It is Süleyman's personal *devlet*, his fortune, which granted him his *devlet*, his turn on the throne. He does not owe his position to anyone but God.

---

[41] For various issues related to Ottoman succession, see Leslie Peirce, *The Imperial Harem: Women and Sovereignty in the Ottoman Empire* (New York: Oxford University Press, 1993), pp. 79–86, 99–103. My term, the "succession of the fittest" corresponds to her "open succession."

[42] E. J. W. Gibb, *A History of Ottoman Poetry*, ed. Edward G. Browne, 6 vols. (London: E. J. W. Gibb Memorial, 1900–9; reprinted London: Luzac, 1967), vol. VI, p. 116; my translation.

Therefore he has grounds to claim that the ruling institution is his own personal device.

This particular understanding of the institution of government that projected it as a personal matter did not go unchallenged. For many other political groups in the empire, the control of the sultanate had to be shared and depersonalized. The sultan's turn on the throne, his *devlet*, had to be severed from a connection to divine fortune, also his *devlet*. The crises of the long seventeenth century succeeded in severing this connection. Whereas up to the sixteenth century the Ottoman princes had to "test their fortunes" (*devlet sınaşmak*) in the race of open succession where fratricide was a legitimate rule of the game, in the eighteenth century there had remained nothing to test. Upon the death of a sultan, the eldest male member of the Ottoman family was seated on the throne. It was not one's fortunes but certain rules that determined whose turn it was going to be on the throne. The *devlet* of a sultan, that is to say his turn on the throne, was now a much more impersonal affair. Not only was the sultan's fortune severed from his turn on the throne, but the physical center of governmental activity was also removed from the imperial palace. In the seventeenth century, one witnesses the physical separation of the office of the grand vizier from the confines of the palace, pushing the sultan further away from the center of administrative activity.[43]

The reduction of the Ottoman dynasty to relative political insignificance was not only experienced in the political developments of the seventeenth century and then simply narrated in historical works. The seventeenth century witnessed the gradual development of a new conception of historical time that came to maturity in the form the official chronicles took. One may call this development the desacralization of a regnal understanding of historical time. Ottoman men of letters who wrote chronicles before the seventeenth century conceived of Ottoman history in terms of the reigns of sultans. Although there were a number of short chronicles devoted to specific events such as military expeditions, comprehensive historical works that start from a random year in the calendar, or a significant event that defines an epoch, were not commonly known. The structural organization of historical works was determined by the beginning and end of the reign of a particular sultan. In world histories, the corresponding

---

[43] While the use of the term *Bâbıâli*, or Sublime Porte, denoting the office building of the grand vizier in reference to the Ottoman government is an eighteenth-century phenomenon, historical sources suggest that a permanent office building for the grand vizier already existed in the first part of the seventeenth century; see Semavi Eyice, "Bâbıâli – Mimari," in *Türkiye Diyanet Vakfı İslâm Ansiklopedisi*, vol. IV, pp. 386–9, at p. 386.

unit was a dynasty. In the seventeenth century, however, an alternative understanding of historical time came to be reflected in Ottoman historiography that was consolidated at the turn of the eighteenth century by Na'îmâ who is regarded as the first official chronicler. Although the beginning of this trend was related to the Muslim millennium, 1000 AH (1591–2 CE), why the Ottomans adopted the new perspective on history cannot be explained solely by the date.

Several seventeenth-century works demonstrate the emergence of this new perspective on historical time. The chronicle of Selânikî (d. after 1600), written by a secretary in the central administration, is one of the first historical works in which one finds evidence for the significance attached to the year 1000 AH.[44] The chronicle of Kadrî (d. after 1644), an officer in the artillery corps, seems to be the first Ottoman chronicle that starts narrating events from the year 1000 AH (1591–2 CE). Kadrî does not specify why he chose this year. Yet the introduction of his work suggests that he first thought of writing his chronicle soon after the year 1000 AH.[45] As noted by Fleischer, Ali started writing his *Essence of History* in 1000 AH as well.[46] Mehmed Rûmî of Edirne (d. 1640) wrote a biographical dictionary of Ottoman sultans, viziers, and higher-ranking judges and scholars who had held office since 1000 AH.[47]

The use of this new perspective on time cannot simply be explained by the experience of living through the millennium since subsequent authors also display this perspective on time. Selânikî, Ali, Rûmî, and Kadrî were alive around the year 1000 AH and may well have been influenced by the anxieties aroused by the coming of the Muslim millennium, which had been anticipated as a possible end of time. Thus one may argue that for them the millennium may have signified a new beginning worthy of celebrating by writing histories that began with it. Katib Çelebi started his Turkish chronicle from the same year. He, however, was born after the millennium. Moreover, he states plainly right at the beginning of his chronicle that the year 1000 AH was just another year in the calendar. His choice of the year 1000 AH as the starting point of his chronicle was supposed to do with the way he had organized a larger work of history

[44] Fleischer, *Bureaucrat and Intellectual*, p. 244; compare his reading with Selânikî, *Tarih-i Selânikî*, vol. I, p. 289.

[45] Abdülkadir (Kadrî) Efendi, *Topçular Kâtibi 'Abdülkâdir (Kadrî) Efendi Tarihi*, ed. Ziya Yılmazer, 2 vols. (Ankara: Türk Tarih Kurumu, 2003), vol. I, pp. xxxvi, 3–6.

[46] Fleischer, *Bureaucrat and Intellectual*, pp. 244–5.

[47] Mehmed bin Mehmed, *Ta'rîh*, Süleymaniye Kütüphanesi, MS Lala Ismail 300; recently edited by Abdurrahman Sığırlı, "Mehmed b. Mehmed er-Rûmî(Edirneli)'nin Nuhbetü't-Tevârih ve'l-ahbâr'ı ve Târîh-i Âl-i Osman'ı (Metinleri, Tahlilleri)," PhD dissertation, Istanbul University, 2000, part III.

he had authored in Arabic before he wrote his Turkish chronicle. He conceived of his chronicle in Turkish as an appendix to this earlier work. Since the earlier work covered history up to the end of the tenth century AH, the Turkish appendix starts with the year 1000 AH, the beginning of the eleventh century.[48]

I do not find Katib Çelebi's own explanation very convincing; his Arabic work, written *c.* 1641, is indeed divided into centuries, and includes the history of the Ottoman dynasty until the end of the reign of Murad IV (1623–40). The Turkish chronicle starting in 1000 AH, opens in an era of great political instability in Ottoman history. Katib Çelebi had witnessed four depositions during his lifetime, those of Mustafa I in 1618 and 1623, Osman II in 1622, and Ibrahim in 1648, the last two of which were followed by regicides. The eleventh century AH was not simply a new millennium in the way Muslims reckoned time but a new age for the Ottoman polity that had proven itself to be mature enough to survive the reduction of the dynasty to virtual impotency. Perhaps Katib Çelebi intended to convey the changed status of the Shadow of God, the Ottoman sultan, as part of his understanding of historical time.

Although it is possible to accept Katib Çelebi's own explanation for his use of 1000 AH as the starting point of his chronicle, the use of the same beginning by Na'îmâ is not accompanied by an explanation and suggests more clearly that the dating is associated with the emergence of the state. One could disagree with my reading and accept Katib Çelebi's own explanation for starting his work from the year 1000 AH, which reflects his principles of organizing an appendix to his earlier Arabic work of history. The first official chronicler Na'îmâ, however, had no specific reason to start his work with the same year. His first draft actually starts from the beginning of the reign of Murad III in 982/1574. Yet when he revised his work, he left out the period 982–1000/1574–91 and started with the year 1000 AH.[49] How he and his contemporaries perceived historical time is reflected in a petition he wrote to his patron, the Grand Vizier Hüseyin Pasha, in 1702. Na'îmâ wrote this petition soon after he finished the first edition of his work that covered the period

---

[48] Kâtib Çelebi, *Fezleke*, 2 vols. (Istanbul: Cerîde-i Havâdis, 1286–7), vol. I, p. 2; for Kâtib Çelebi's Arabic work of history, see Mükrimin Halil Yinanç, "Fezleket Ekvâl El-Ahyâr Hakkında," in *Kâtip Çelebi: Hayatı ve Eserleri Hakkında İncelemeler* (Ankara: Türk Tarih Kurumu, 1957), pp. 93–100; for *Fezleke*, his chronicle in Turkish, see Bekir Kütükoğlu, *Kâtib Çelebi 'Fezleke'sinin Kaynakları* (Istanbul: Istanbul Üniversitesi Edebiyat Fakültesi, 1974).

[49] M. Münir Aktepe, "Naîmâ Tarihi'nin Yazma Nüshaları Hakkında," *Tarih Dergisi* I/1 (September 1949): 35–52.

1000–65/1591–1654. In it he asks the grand vizier to commission to continue his work to cover the period 1066–1114/1655–1702. While he is making a case for the feasibility of this task, he presents his primary sources in the following manner:

> The *Appendix* of Aziz Efendi covers [the period] from İbşir Pasha until Köprülü Mehmed Pasha; Vecîhî [wrote] up to the first years of Köprülüzâde Ahmed Pasha; and the chronicle of İsâzâde of Skopje [narrates the period] from İbşir Pasha to the Pécs incident. [Moreover] from among the men of learning a certain secretary at the Treasury wrote [about the period] from the beginning of Köprülüzâde Fâzıl Ahmed Pasha's grand vizierate to his death in great detail.[50]

What is striking about this passage is that there is not a single mention of a sultan's name in this list of chronicles that cover the period from 1654, which is invoked by the name of İbşir Pasha who was appointed to the grand vizierate in this year, to 1692, which is the last year whose events are noted in the chronicle of İsâzâde.[51] In terms of reigns, this period covered the sultanates of Mehmed IV, Süleyman II, and Ahmed II. Yet neither Na'îmâ nor his sources seem to have thought of them when they wrote their chronicles.[52] Na'îmâ's choice of the year 1000 AH was closely related to this disassociation of historical time from regnal time and symbolizes the reduction of the dynasty to political insignificance that was the result of the depositions of the seventeenth century.

I would suggest that there is a correlation between the political disempowerment of the Ottoman dynasty implied in the new conception of historical time found in Na'îmâ's work and the construction of the Ottoman state. This new conception of historical time is in stark contrast with Ali's depiction of the past historians and their writings a century earlier, around 1600. Aşıkpaşazâde, Rûhî, Neşrî, and İsâ, according to Ali, had written the "events that occurred until the age of Sultan Bayezid Han

---

[50] Ibid., p. 51.
[51] Johann Strauß, *Die Chronik des 'İsazade: Ein Beitrag zur osmanischen Historiographie des 17. Jahrhunderts* (Berlin: Klaus Schwarz, 1991), p. xii.
[52] Vecîhî started writing in the year 1637, which is not a year in which a succession took place; see Buğra Atsız, *Das osmanische Reich um die Mitte des 17. Jahrhunderts nach den Chroniken des Vecihi (1637–1660) und des Mehmed Halifa (1663–1660)* (Munich: R. Trofenik, 1977). İsâzâde starts with the year 1654 during which Murad Pasha succeeded to the İbşir Pasha in the grand vizierate; see Strauß, *Die Chronik*, p. 1. "The *Appendix* of Aziz Efendi," which refers to the *Ravzatü'l-Ebrâr Zeyli* by Karaçelebizâde Abdülaziz Efendi, ed. Nevzat Kaya (Ankara: Türk Tarih Kurumu, 2003), starts with the beginning of the reign of Mehmed IV in 1648. However, one needs only to be reminded of the fact that the author himself was heavily involved in the deposition of Ibrahim and the enthronement of Mehmed IV in 1648 to realize that this starting point for the chronicle by no means suggests that the author believes in the central role of sultans in making history. See also Aktepe, "Naîmâ Tarihi'nin," pp. 39–40, n. 8, for a telling example of Na'îmâ's attitude to sultans.

and Sultan Mehmed Han."[53] Na'îmâ and the official chroniclers after him were supposed to record the events that took place between the point in time at which their predecessor had stopped writing and the one at which they were promoted to another post or dismissed.[54] In this way, by the end of the eighteenth century a historiographical canon had developed for Ottoman history that starts with the chronicle of Na'îmâ and ends with the *History of Vâsıf*, covering the period from the end of the sixteenth century up to the late eighteenth century in successive volumes of official chronicles, all of which were printed by the Imperial Press. Furthermore, the form this historiographical canon adopted obliterated the political significance of the specific members of the dynasty by collapsing different reigns together, or dividing them into chunks of periods that were covered by successive official chronicles. By reducing the dynasty to political insignificance, these works strengthened the construct of the state as they emphasized its continuity regardless of dynastic reigns.

Reducing the dynasty to insignificance relative to its place in the earlier period was a necessary condition for the success of the official historiography, yet it was not sufficient. Another significant political powerhouse that had a claim on historical ideology and historiographical production in the earlier period was the judicial elite, the most powerful segment of the intellectual elite whose resistance to the court historiography of the sixteenth century was formidable. Kemalpaşazâde, Sa'deddîn, Kudsî, and Karaçelebizâde, whose names are in the history "bestsellers" list in the appendix, are all members of this group. The judicial elite continued to supply historians in the form of official chroniclers in the eighteenth century as well. Râşid and Âsım, for instance, were both professors of Islamic law. Relative to the members of the state bureaucracy, however, the professors and judges of the empire had lost the power that they had enjoyed in the sixteenth century. Historically, the erosion of their power is demonstrated by the gradual shortening of their tenures in office that had started during the reign of Murad III. Historiographically, the loss of status

[53] Schmidt, *Mustafa Ali's Künhü'l-Ahbar*, p. 59.
[54] Thus Mehmed Râşid, official chronicler from 1715 to 1723, updated Na'îmâ's work by writing an account of the period 1660–1722. His successor İsmail Asım, official chronicler from 1723 to 1731, wrote the events of the period 1722–9. A later official chronicler, Mehmed Subhî, who occupied the position from 1739 to 1745, revised the work of his predecessors from 1731, and produced the account of the years 1730–43. His successor İzzî (official chronicler, 1745–55) updated Subhî, covering the years 1744–52. Although there were a number of chroniclers in the second half of the eighteenth century, the definitive chronicle of the third quarter of the century (1752–74) was produced by Ahmed Vâsıf (d. 1806) and printed by the Imperial Press in his lifetime; Kütükoğlu, "Vekayi'nüvis," in *Vekayi'nüvis: Makaleler*, pp. 111–23.

they suffered is symbolized in a different genre of historical writing, that of biographical dictionaries.

The gradual loss of significance attached to those biographical dictionaries devoted to the members of the judicial elite, which were the major expression of their hegemony, illustrates the consolidation of the state to the exclusion of this sector of the elite. Excluding hagiographies and biographical dictionaries of poets, the biographical writing in the sixteenth and seventeenth centuries was dominated by the judicial elite. It was produced exclusively and read mostly by the members of this elite group. The men whose lives were summarized in these dictionaries included not only the higher echelons of the hierarchy, such as the muftis of Istanbul, the senior justices (*kadıaskers*), the judges of the big cities, and the professors of the most prestigious law schools, but also more modest members of the judicial profession, such as judges of mid-size Anatolian and Balkan towns, professors of middle-ranking colleges, and preachers at major mosques. It was also the members of the judicial elite who constituted the reading public for such dictionaries, which were as widely read as the most popular chronicles. The exemplary biographical dictionary of the judicial elite by Atâyî from the first half of the seventeenth century would have been placed in the third rank of the history "bestsellers" list had I included biographical dictionaries in it.[55] From the eighteenth century onward, however, this genre gradually died out. Şeyhî's (d. 1731) biographical dictionary, the last representative of the genre from the first half of the eighteenth century, has many fewer copies in the libraries of Istanbul than Atâyî's.[56] A continuation of Şeyhî had to wait until the turn of the twentieth century and remains unfinished.[57] Reconstructing the lives of the members of the judicial elite who lived in the second half of the eighteenth century and thereafter is very difficult except for the most high-ranking, such as the muftis of the capital.[58] The sharply decreasing share of the judicial elite in the historiographical output in this period parallels the reduction of the

[55] *IKTCYK*, fascicle 8, pp. 617–753, covers biographical dictionaries. Atâyî's *Hadâ'iku'l-hakâ'ik fî tekmileti'ş-şakâ'ik*, reprint with indices in *Şakaik-ı Nu'maniye ve Zeyilleri*, ed. Abdülkadir Özcan, 5 vols. (Istanbul: Çağrı, 1989), vol. II, is the one with most manuscript copies in the Istanbul libraries covered in this catalog, see pp. 645–54.
[56] *IKTCYK*, pp. 743–7.
[57] Fındıklılı 'Ismet bin 'Osmân (d. 1904), *Tekmiletü'ş-Şakaik fî Hakk-ı ehli'l-hakaik*, in A. Özcan (ed.), *Şakaik-ı Nu'maniye ve Zeyilleri*, 5 vols. (Istanbul: Çagri Yayinları, 1989), vol. V.
[58] For the lives of the muftis of Istanbul, one may consult Süleyman Sa'deddîn Müstakîmzâde (d. 1202/1787–8), *Devhatü'l-meşâyîh*, and the appendices written for it, twice by the author himself, twice by Mehmed Münib 'Ayntâbî (d. 1238/1822–3), and once by Süleyman Fâ'ik (d. 1253/1837–8), see *IKTCYK*, pp. 725–38, 688–93, 721–3. Ahmet Rif'at Efendi (d. 1876) edited and updated the

dynasty to relative insignificance. The two most significant political bodies of Ottoman history in the sixteenth century were both weakened by the eighteenth century, the historiography of which witnessed the rise of a new genre, reflecting the ascendancy of a new group.

The replacement of biographical dictionaries of the judicial elite with biographies of ministers and secretaries displays the consolidation of the state institution through the political elite rather than the judicial elite. While the biographical dictionaries of the judicial elite start to disappear from the historiographical corpus in the eighteenth century, those of the viziers and high-ranking secretaries replace them. The rise of the status of viziers was anticipated by Rûmî's work mentioned above that included the lives of viziers as well as the higher echelons of the judicial elite. Şeyhî, too, included the grand viziers in his biographical dictionary of the judicial elite. A contemporary of Şeyhî, Ahmed Tâib Osmanzâde (d. 1136/1723–4) produced the first biographical work devoted exclusively to grand viziers. It is telling that one finds more copies of this work in the libraries of Istanbul than the biographical dictionary of Şeyhî.[59] The interest in the lives of the grand viziers was surpassing the attraction of the judicial elite. By the end of the eighteenth century, the bureaucrats from among whose ranks the viziers came to be recruited had also acquired historiographical significance. Ahmed Resmî's (d. 1783) biographical dictionary of high-ranking bureaucrats is a telling symbol of this development.[60]

The historiographical output of the eighteenth century, including the biographical works, suggests the relative decline of the political power of the dynasty and the judicial elite, on the one hand, and the relative rise of

biographies of Müstakîmzâde and his continuators; see *Devhatü'l-meşâyîh ma'a zeyl* (Istanbul [lithograph], no date [reprinted Çağrı, 1978]); see also Mehmet İpşirli, "Devhatü'l-meşâyih," in *Türkiye Diyanet Vakfı İslâm Ansiklopedisi*, vol. IX, pp. 229–30.

[59] It is quite significant to note that the biographical dictionary of Ottoman sultans by the same author has fewer copies listed; compare *IKTCYK*, pp. 633–6, 637–43. Ahmed Tâib Osmanzâde's work *Hadîkatü'l-vüzerâ* was also continued by later biographers, such as Dilâver-ağa-zâde Ömer Vahîd (d. 1172/1758–9), Ahmed Câvîd (d. 1218/1803–4), and ʿAbdülfettâh Şevket of Baghdad; see *IKTCYK*, pp. 717–21, Babinger, *Die Geschichtsschreiber*, pp. 313–15, 314, n. 1. The original work and its continuations were printed in Istanbul in 1271/1854–5; see its reprint *Hadîqat ül-vüzerâ (Der Garten der Wesire)* (Freiburg: D. Robischon, 1969).

[60] *IKTCYK*, pp. 625–8. Süleyman Fâ'ik (see above, n. 58) wrote a continuation of this work as well. The original with its continuation was published in lithograph form in the mid nineteenth century. For a recent reprint with additional material, see Ahmed Resmi, *Halifetü'r-Rüesa* (reprint of Mücteba İlgürel (ed.), *Halifetü'r-Rüesa*) (Istanbul: Enderun, 1992). For Ahmed Resmî, see Virginia H. Aksan, *An Ottoman Statesman in War and Peace: Ahmed Resmi Efendi, 1700–1783* (Leiden: E. J. Brill, 1995); for a discussion of the official chroniclers contemporary with Ahmed Resmî, see Aksan, *An Ottoman Statesman*, pp. 110–15.

the fortunes of viziers and bureaucrats, on the other.[61] This study proposes
that the historiographical consensus achieved in the narrative works of the
official chroniclers during the eighteenth century is closely related to the
shift of power observed in the biographical works of the same period. The
analysis of the place of the dynasty in the formal structure of the narrative
works of history, coupled with the preceding analysis of the biographical
dictionaries, point towards a balance of power between the constituents of
the Ottoman polity. The political space where this balance was struck was
the Ottoman state. The viziers, the bureaucrats, the judicial elite, and the
dynasty reached a fine equilibrium of power in the eighteenth-century
Ottoman state that made the production and consumption of official
chronicles possible. Rather than being regarded as the voice of one of the
segments of the political elite, the official chronicles of the eighteenth
century were perceived by the constituent groups of the Ottoman polity
as representatives of their shared interests.

Could one go beyond the balance struck in the political construct of the
state and find the rise of a new consensus in society of which the Ottoman
state is a product? Abou-El-Haj suggests that the period "beginning in the
late sixteenth century and proceeding through the seventeenth, saw the
erosion of one consensus within the ruling elite and the rise of another."[62]
The new ruling elite of the eighteenth century dominated by the viziers and
the bureaucrats emerged from within the social groups that had been
accumulating wealth in the last century and a half as a result of the ongoing
process of transformation of a land-based economy to a monetary one.
Thus while the rulers of the sixteenth century, the *devşirme*s, emerged from
the house of the ultimate landlord, the sultan himself, those of the eighteenth century started to come from among the wealthy members of society.

The shift from *devşirme* rule in the sixteenth century to rule by local
elites began in the seventeenth century and intensified in the eighteenth
century. Men who came from families with economic means and thus had
experience with managing money, such as Baki Pasha (d. 1625) who was the
son of a wealthy merchant from Aleppo, had already achieved the status of

---

[61] For the rising power of the viziers, see Rifa'at Abou-El-Haj, "The Ottoman Vizier and Paşa
Households 1683–1703: A Preliminary Report," *Journal of the American Oriental Society* 94 (1974):
438–47; Rifa'at Abou-El-Haj, *The 1703 Rebellion and the Structure of Ottoman Politics* (Leiden:
Nederlands Instituut voor het Nabije Oosten, 1984), pp. 94–114. For the concept of the "Efendi-
turned-Paşa" in the eighteenth century and the increasing number of bureaucrats reaching vizier
posts, see Norman Itzkowitz, "Eighteenth Century Ottoman Realities," *Studia Islamica* 16 (1962):
73–94.

[62] Rifa'at 'Ali Abou-El-Haj, *Formation of the Modern State: The Ottoman Empire, Sixteenth to
Eighteenth Centuries*, p. 59.

vizier in the early seventeenth century.[63] In the eighteenth century, however, one such man after another was heading the Ottoman government.
Grand viziers such as Mehmed Pasha (1717–18), Hâmid Hamza Pasha
(1763), Silahdâr Mâhir Hamza Pasha (1768), and Yağlıkçızâde Mehmed
Emin Pasha (1768–9), were unheard-of in the sixteenth century. The first
was the son of a Muslim merchant from a village in Kayseri; the second
one's father was a Muslim merchant in a town around Niğde; the third was
the son of a wealthy Muslim man from Karahisar; and the father of the last
one was a rich Muslim merchant from Istanbul who traded with India.[64]

The canon of the official chronicles by Na'îmâ, Râşid, Âsım, Subhî, İzzî,
and Vâsıf, which reflects the state hegemony of the historiographical
expression in the center of the empire, became possible as a result of the
eighteenth-century political consensus. The early sixteenth-century consensus consisted of the intellectual hegemony of the judicial elite and the
military power of the court. The chronicle of Kemalpaşazâde, which
the sultan commissioned to a member of the judicial elite, stands as the
historiographical symbol of this consensus. But the consensus was shattered later in the sixteenth century when the court started to develop closer
control of the judicial elite by shortening terms in office. Moreover new
power groups closely connected with the burgeoning financial elite were
emerging around the vizier households in the late seventeenth century.
These groups started laying a claim to the control of the ruling institution
dominated by the dynasty and the judicial elite. As the early sixteenth-
century consensus broke down, the court's historiographical commissions
failed to appeal to the world outside the confines of the palace. The
seventeenth century witnessed the continuous growth of the vizier households which came to supply an increasingly larger portion of the members
of the political elite. Men of economic means who had started to enter such
households in the late sixteenth century eventually came to establish their
own households. The political conflicts between the various ruling groups
in the long seventeenth century brought about seven depositions. These
conflicts came to a temporary resolution in the eighteenth century when a
new consensus was achieved between a weak but legitimate dynasty and a
disempowered judicial elite, on the one hand, and a new ruling group
which emerged from the vizier households that better represented the

---

[63] Mehmed bin Mehmed, *Ta'rîh*, ff. 61b–62b.
[64] See their biographies in Ahmed Tâib Osmanzâde, *Hadîqat ül-vüzerâ*, part II, pp. 27–9, part III,
pp. 8–10, 16–18, 18–19, respectively. See also Mücteba İlgürel, "Hamza Paşa, Silahdar," in *Türkiye
Diyanet Vakfı İslâm Ansiklopedisi*, vol. XV, pp. 515–16; Kemal Beydilli, "Mehmed Emin Paşa,
Yağlıkçızâde," in ibid., vol. XXVIII, pp. 464–5.

economic power holders in society, on the other. Their agreement on their common interests and the balance of power they established created the early modern Ottoman state as a relatively impersonal and autonomous ruling institution. Such an institution had to be run by professional bureaucrats who eventually came to advance as high as the grand vizierate. With the expansion of the state machinery, bureaucrats came to represent the largest educated class in the empire, which explains the ever widening circulation of the official historiography in the eighteenth and nineteenth centuries.

In conclusion, I would like to reiterate the novelty of the eighteenth-century Ottoman state. Although this state presents itself as the continuation of an institution of rule that had existed since the beginning of the Ottoman dynasty, it was actually a qualitatively different institution than the dynastic institution of rule that existed during the reign of Süleyman. The work of the court historiographers, the first of whom was commissioned by Süleyman, was practically forgotten within less than a century while the reign of Süleyman was being canonized as the golden age of everything Ottoman. There was indeed a wide gap between Süleyman's own conception of his royal authority reflected in his ambitious project of court historiography, which was taken over by his grandson Murad III, and the conception of royal authority limited by law entertained by the legalists who retrospectively constructed his reign as an Ottoman golden age. It is crucial to distinguish the eighteenth-century Ottoman state from the sixteenth-century Ottoman dynastic institution of rule in order to gain a more nuanced understanding of both periods. This distinction, which is very much inspired by the work of Abou-El-Haj and substantiated by historical developments, also enables a movement toward the "modern" in Ottoman history and historiography to be traced.

Finally, it is also important to point out the modern nature of eighteenth-century Ottoman historiography. For the professional bureaucrats who came to operate the Ottoman state in the eighteenth century, whether or not their institution was divinely pre-ordained was not a central question. What they cared for was the construction of their state as an autonomous, eternal, and impersonal institution. It would actually be best if their state did not need a legitimizing formula that would require an outside referent. It would be the absolutely perfect state if it simply *were*, justifying itself by simply being in a very positivist sense. That is exactly what the eighteenth-century historiographical canon constructed with its emphasis on continuity, its arbitrary division of historical time regardless of sultanic reigns, its representation of itself as a neutral expression of historical reality, and its ignorance of universal history as a larger scheme within which to legitimize the state. The modern state constructed in official historiography did not need an explanation. As of the year 1000 AH it simply *was*. Eighteenth-century Ottoman official historiography was very modern in this sense. Court historiography of the sixteenth century had been assigned the task of giving a certain sense to universal history and the place of the Ottoman sultanate within it. The official historiography of the eighteenth century did not aspire to such lofty functions. Its aim was merely to show how the Ottoman state had actually been there all along – and was going to continue to be there, which was all that the modern state needed to justify itself. It is not a coincidence that the founder of the modern discipline of history, Leopold von Ranke, was appointed royal historiographer of Prussia in 1841. His conception of history would also qualify him for the position of the Ottoman official chronicler:

History has had assigned to it the task of judging the past, of instructing the present for the benefit of the ages to come. To such lofty functions this work does not aspire. Its aim is merely to show how it has been [*wie es eigentlich gewesen*].[65]

APPENDIX

Based on the number of manuscript copies a history book is recorded to have in the *IKTCYK*, the bestsellers of Ottoman narrative history in the manuscript market of the period 1550–1850 would be as follows (prints after 1850 are not noted):[66]

Tarih-i Nişâncı Mehmed Paşa (34 copies) by Ramazanzâde Mehmed Pasha, known as Küçük Nişâncı (Seal-bearer [of the Sultan] the Younger, d. 1571): a brief world history up to the mid 1560s.

Tâcü't-tevârîh (31 copies) by Sa'deddîn (d. 1599): an Ottoman history from the beginnings of the dynasty up to the end of the reign of Selim I in 1520.

---

[65] Quoted by Stephen Davies, *Empiricism and History* (Houndmills: Palgrave, 2003) p. 28; my English rendering is slightly modified based on Ranke, *Fürsten und Völker*, p. 4.

[66] This list brings together books that were also available in print with those that were exclusively in manuscript. Also some of the works in the list are multi-volume sets, and not every copy counted in the *IKTCYK* represents a complete set. I have not included the *Takvîmü't-tevârîh* (27 copies and a print edition in 1733/4) by Kâtib Çelebi (d. 1657), which is a world historical chronology up to 1648, because it does not fall into the category of narrative history. A number of other genres that are historical in a certain sense are also excluded from this list, such as the biographical dictionaries. I have, however, incorporated some of their significant examples into the main body of the chapter.

Şefîknâme and related texts (25 copies) by Mehmed Şefîk (d. *c.* 1715): an
account of the deposition of Mustafa II and the enthronement of
Ahmed III in 1703.

Ravzatü'l-ebrâr (23 copies and a print edition in 1832) by Karaçelebizâde
Abdülaziz (d. 1658): a world history the appendix of which reaches the
year 1657.

Tarih-i Na'îmâ (21 copies and a print edition in 1734, an incomplete
print in 1843) by Mustafa Na'îmâ (d. 1716): an Ottoman history,
covering the period 1591–1660.

Tarih-i Râşid (20 copies and a print edition in 1741) by Mehmed Râşid
(d. 1735): an Ottoman history, covering the period 1660–1721.

Mir'at-i Kâ'inât (19 copies and a print edition in 1842) by Mehmed
Kudsî (d. 1621): a world history up to 1566.

Tarih-i Peçevî (15 copies) by Ibrahim Peçevî (of Pécs, Hungary, d.
c. 1649): an Ottoman history, covering the period 1520–1639/40.

Künhü'l-ahbâr (15 copies) by Âli (d. 1600): a world history up to the
late 1590s.

Tarih-i Âl-i Osman (14 copies) by Kemalpaşazâde (d. 1534): an incomplete Ottoman history from the beginnings of the dynasty to the early
years of the reign of Süleyman (1520–66).

Fezleke (11 copies) by Katib Çelebi (d. 1657): a history of the Ottoman
Empire, covering the period 1591–1654/5.

Tarih-i Selânikî (11 copies) by Mustafa Selânikî (d. after 1600): a history
of the Ottoman Empire, covering the period 1563–1600.

Tenkîhü't-tevârîh (10 copies) by Hezârfenn Hüseyin (d. after 1672): a
world history up to 1672.

Tuhfetü'l-kibâr ve esfârü'l-bihâr (9 copies and a print edition in 1729) by
Kâtib Çelebi (d. 1657): a history of Ottoman naval expeditions.

Tarih-i Enverî (8 copies and incorporation into the print copy of a later
chronicle in 1804) by Sa'dullâh Enverî (d. 1794/5): a fragmented
history of the Ottoman Empire in different periods of the eighteenth
century.

Âsım Tarihi (6 copies and a print edition in 1740) by Küçükçelebizâde
İsmail Âsım (d. 1760): a history of the Ottoman Empire, covering the
period 1722–8.

Hasanbeyzâde Tarihi (6 copies) by Hasanbeyzâde Ahmed (d. *c.* 1636): a
history of the Ottoman Empire up to 1635.

PART IV

Boundaries of belonging

8

Inside the Ottoman courthouse: territorial law at the intersection of state and religion

Najwa Al-Qattan

In an incident mentioned in Ken Cuno's study of Ottoman Egypt, a man is found dead a good distance away from a village in Lower Egypt. In their attempts to gauge the responsibility of the village for what appeared to be a murder, the authorities determine that the village's domain extends only as far as the reach of the muezzin's call to prayer.[1] In an abbreviated manner, this anecdote raises interesting questions about the conception of authority and the different imaginaries employed in its construction. In a similar vein this chapter, while focusing on the Ottoman shari'a court, raises questions about the kadi's authority, both political and religious/legal, in the period usually referred to by historians as the "premodern".

At the heart of this inquiry is the territorialization of shari'a law. This process, which pre-dated the nineteenth century, was complex, fluid, and incomplete. Unlike personal law which is a function of individual (say, religious) identity, and is as such transportable, territorial law privileges territorially based identities and subjects individuals as well as communities that may be otherwise diverse to one and the same law. In the Ottoman case, territorialization involved both the widening of the purview of shari'a law (in that it applied to Muslims as well as non-Muslims in the Ottoman domain) and its narrowing (insofar as it restricted its authority to the territorial boundaries of the state).

The territorialization of shari'a law was spawned in conjunction with (or perhaps as a function of) five historical developments: first, the state's co-optation and bureaucratization of the ulema into a centralized and hierarchical "ruling" institution which comprised kadis as well as other legal and religious functionaries – a novel practice in the Muslim context; second, the state's championing of the Hanafi legal tradition; third, imperial and religious claims to universal sovereignty and their intersection with

---

[1] Kenneth M. Cuno. *The Pasha's Peasants: Land, Society, and Economy in Lower Egypt, 1740–1858* (Cambridge: Cambridge University Press, 1992).

the necessities engendered by real geographical/political borders of empire whose territories mapped and limited the purview of universal law; and, finally, the development – unique in the Muslim context – of a specifically Ottoman innovation whereby the kadis became the archivists of the law.

Hence a number of structural as well as political developments brought into existence a specifically Ottoman kadi who, in the very practice of his profession, recast shari'a law in territorial terms. The territorialization of the law – significant in itself – also raises two other interrelated issues, the first involving the intersection of politics, law, and religion, and the second about the meaning of "territorialization" and related questions of sovereignty and space.

THE KADI AS STATE FUNCTIONARY

In the classical Ottoman system, the status of the shari'a court and the power vested in its functionaries were primarily subject to a centralized administrative system of checks and balances in which all authority flowed from the sultan alone. The system provided, at least in theory, for a division of labor whereby, broadly speaking, the *wali* (governor) was responsible for military and fiscal affairs, while the kadi was responsible for the administration of justice.[2]

The chief kadi, who presided over the judicial apparatus in the province, was appointed by direct sultanic *berat* (diploma) and dispatched directly from Istanbul. Called *al-hakim al-shar'i*, his office not only represented the highest judicial authority, but also exercised the prerogatives of political power. In this capacity, the kadi acted as the main provincial administrator and the purveyor of justice and order.[3] The status of the kadi and the range of his administrative responsibilities were in large part a function of the role his office played in the central bureaucracy. The position of the kadi combined civil, legal, and political authority. Attesting to this was the regularity with which political orders from Istanbul were announced in court and recorded in the *sicil* (court record).

Although the study of the records of the Ottoman Muslim court has become a virtual industry in the last two decades, the institution itself still awaits proper examination. Nonetheless, the combined efforts of Ottoman

[2] See Halil İnalcık, *Ottoman Empire: The Classical Age, 1300–1600*, ed. and trans. Norman Itzkowitz and Colin Imber (New York: Praeger, 1973; repr. New York: Aristide D. Caratzas, 1989), pp. 104–18.
[3] The title *al-hakim al-shar'i* encompasses both the political and legal attributes of its holder: *al-hakim* connotes both "ruler" and "judge" and *shar'i* refers both to the shari'a and, derivatively, to legitimacy.

historians and legal scholars have resulted in a growing appreciation of the court and its role in the Ottoman system of rule and government. The Muslim court exercised a variety of legal functions and enjoyed unrivaled official standing in the Ottoman system. In it, individuals registered the purchase, sale, and rental of residences and commercial establishments, formalized matters of marriage, divorce, and child support, established familial and charitable waqfs, sorted out inheritance disputes, and sought justice and compensation for civil and criminal infringements. In addition, the court appointed madrasa teachers, supervised market activities, and monitored individual behavior. Furthermore, although the court was a religious–legal institution, it also acted as public repository and register for all kinds of business. It thus supervised a wide range of transactions that, strictly speaking, were not of legal interest. In all these capacities, the court was accessible to the population at large, including zimmis (non-Muslim Ottoman subjects), who regularly sought its notarial services as well as its legal jurisdiction.[4]

THE HANAFI TRADITION AND THE OTTOMAN APPLICATION OF THE LAW

In his classic study of the legal status of non-Muslims, Fattal has noted the territorialization of shari'a law and has suggested that, by insisting on applying shari'a law to all who live in a Muslim domain, the Hanafi school of law understood the jurisdiction of the kadi over zimmi affairs as obligatory and the competence of the zimmi courts as discretionary. In consequence, they came close to regarding law in "territorial" terms – a territoriality that was born out of an understanding that (political) sovereignty necessarily involved juridical control.[5] Along similar lines, Jennings has noted that the shari'a "was religious law for Muslims in the multi-religious Ottoman Empire. Nevertheless . . . it was applied to zimmis in essentially the same way as to Muslims." The fact that the zimmis were subject to the law on much the same terms as Muslims eased their integration into the social and economic order of the city.[6]

---

[4] See, for example, Abraham Marcus, *The Middle East on the Eve of Modernity: Aleppo in the Eighteenth Century* (New York: Columbia University Press, 1989).
[5] Antoine Fattal, *Le status légal des non-musulmans en pays d'Islam* (Beirut: Imprimerie Catholique, 1958), pp. 357–8.
[6] Ronald Jennings, "Limitations on the Judicial Powers of the Kadis in 17th C. Ottoman kayseri," *Studia Islamica* 50 (1979): 151–84.

THE SHARI'A: UNIVERSAL REVEALED LAW AND THE
QUESTION OF POLITICAL SOVEREIGNTY

The territorialization of law is analytically and historically connected to the
existence of territorial boundaries of empire that geographically contained
the purview of shari'a law, on the one hand, and raised questions as to the
legal status and treatment of non-Muslims within the empire, on the other.
Politics, in other words, made for a world in which Muslims in non-
Muslim domains lived beyond the authority of Muslim law at the same
time as large non-Muslim communities inhabited Muslim (and in this
case, Ottoman) territory. In addition, politics and commerce also made for
a world, as Daniel Goffman insightfully notes for the early Ottoman
period, here and elsewhere, in which the distinction between *muste'min*
(here, foreign resident) and zimmi was fluid – a fluidity which came to be
contested by foreign resident communities who sought to safeguard the
extra-territorial rights to which they felt entitled.

In his analysis of the relationship between law, territory, and political
power, Johansen notes that all the discussions of the jurists on the relationship of Muslims and non-Muslims concerned religion and politics. What
was at stake here was the *application* of the law as predicated on political–
military power. According to Johansen, the jurists replaced religious conversion with political submission and the universality of revealed norms
with the territorialism of the norms of politico-military power.[7]

Territorialization, then, was not only predicated on zimmi status – itself
an expression of political power – it also circumscribed the application of
the shari'a, which, by definition (or self-definition), makes claims to
universality. At the same time, territorialization involved an opposite
process, because the Ottomans did not always clearly distinguish between
shari'a and *kanun* (sultan's law). The word *shar'an* (sanctioned by the
shari'a) often referred to that which was deemed "legal" in a general
way.[8] Thus territorialization involved the creation of a legal space wherein
the kadis applied religious law in a manner in which religious identity was
often inconsequential.

Nevertheless, territorialization was primarily the function of a historically
specific kind of court – a hybrid institutional innovation. The Ottoman

[7] Baber Johansen, "Entre révélation et tyrannie: le droit des non-musulmans d'après les juristes
musulmans," in *Contingency in a Sacred Law: Legal and Ethical Norms in the Muslim Fiqh* (Leiden:
Brill, 1999), p. 235.
[8] Uriel Heyd mentions this fuzziness in connection with Ottoman legal discourse in his *Studies in Old
Ottoman Criminal Law*, ed. V. L. Ménage (Oxford: Clarendon Press, 1973), p. 188.

state supported and assimilated an empire-wide network of centrally controlled courts in which kadis were significant political practitioners.[9] In this system, they became the interpreters, keepers, and archivists of the law. This last development, kadis as archivists, was a specifically Ottoman innovation and represents one of the main interests of this chapter.

THE KADIS

Jennings, one of the first Ottoman historians to research kadi records, has argued that the kadi, alone among officials in the "rational" Ottoman administrative system, derived authority from "divine" – that is, shari'a – sources.[10] As a consequence, he enjoyed a unique kind of legitimacy best captured by al-Mawardi's description of the kadis as "those who have limited authority of unlimited scope."[11] More recent scholarship on the kadi has appropriately focused on the duality of the court's authority, most evident in the duality of the law (*kanun* versus shari'a) and on the role of the kadi in this process. Gerber, for example, has argued that the kadi who "in his sources of legitimacy was not an Ottoman institution," was "allowed" a bureaucratic place and hence a share in power.[12]

The institution of this uniquely authorized kadi calls for further attention, particularly in order to steer it away from the Weberian critique according to which the kadi enjoys such discretion that his judgments are personal, arbitrary, and irrational. Much of the legal scholarship has responded to Weber by either elevating the mufti to center stage or by elaborating an anthropology of Islamic law that endows the actions of the kadi with a (rarely convincing) substantive consistency. Scholars such as Johansen, Messick, Gerber, and, most recently, Tucker have centered the

[9] See Khalid Ziyada, *Al-Sura al-taqlidiyya li'l-mujtama' al-madini: Qira'a manhajiyya fi sijillat mahkamat Trablus al-shar'iyya fi al-qarn al-sabi'-'ashar wa bidayat al-qarn al-thamin-'ashar* (Tripoli, Lebanon: Lebanese University, 1983). Ziyada insists that the *sijill*'s discourse is the discourse of state power, and more specifically of the urban elites associated with the state.

[10] Ronald Jennings, "Kadi, Court, and Legal Procedure," *Studia Islamica* 48 (1978): 133–72. See also Jennings, "Limitations of the Judicial Powers of the Kadi."

[11] 'Ali ibn Muhammad al-Mawardi, *al-Ahkam al-Sultaniyya, The Book of Islamic Governance* (London: Ta-Ha, 1996), p. 19.

[12] Haim Gerber, *State, Society and Law in Islam: Ottoman Law in Comparative Perspective* (New York: SUNY Press, 1994), p. 181. See, in this connection, Cornell Fleischer's textured analysis which complicates the significance of this duality and focuses on the slippery accommodation between "Ottoman regionalism" and religions' "universal" ideals in *Bureaucrat and Intellectual in the Ottoman Empire: The Historian Mustafa Ali (1541–1600)* (Princeton, NJ: Princeton University Press, 1986).

mufti's role in the interpretation and expansion of the law – at the expense
of the kadis. Others, such as Geertz and Rosen, have taken an anthropological turn that frames the understanding of law by cultural worlds of
signification. In other words, the role of the Muslim kadi has been either
diminished (by the first group of scholars) or ahistoricized (by the other).
Whereas the fatwa solution, in which the kadi simply carries out the orders
of the mufti, reduces the kadi to a mechanical role, the anthropological
solution turns the kadi and his court into a kind of cultural interface
outside time and place.[13]

THE OTTOMAN *DIWAN–SIJILL*

Hallaq has argued that the classic Muslim court was not so much a site as it
was an extension of and an assembly centered on the legal person of the
kadi: "the court structure was nothing but the extension of [the kadi's]
function and judicial personality."[14] Although this may, at first glance,
appear to represent a revisiting of the proverbial Muslim judge who sits (or
more fittingly perhaps reclines) under the proverbial palm tree, Hallaq's is
not the Weberian judge of *Kadijustiz*.[15] Indeed, Hallaq's aim is rather to
establish a theoretical as well as a historical formalization of the Ottoman
kadi's legal role.

Hallaq focuses on the kadi's records (*diwan*) – "the kadi's body of archival material" – that includes, but is not limited to, the *sijill*s (the registers

---

[13] For solutions focused on the mufti, see Baber Johansen, *The Islamic Law on Land Tax and Rent: The Peasants' Loss of Property Rights as Interpreted in the Hanafite Legal Literature of the Mamluk and Ottoman Periods* (London: Croom Helm, 1988); David S. Powers, "A Court Case from Fourteenth Century North Africa," *Journal of the American Oriental Society* 110 (1990): 231; Brinkley Messick, *The Calligraphic State: Textual Domination and History in a Muslim Society* (Berkeley, CA: University of California Press, 1993); Uriel Heyd, "Some Aspects of the Ottoman Fetva," *Bulletin of the School of Oriental and African Studies* 32 (1969): 36–56; and Judith Tucker, *In the House of the Law: Gender and Islamic Law in Ottoman Syria and Palestine* (Berkeley, CA: University of California Press, 1998). For works of legal anthropology, see Lawrence Rosen, *The Anthropology of Justice: Law as Culture in Islamic Society* (Cambridge: Cambridge University Press, 1989); Lawrence Rosen, "Islamic Case Law and the Logic of Consequence," in June Starr and Jane F. Collier (eds.), *History and Power in the Study of Law: New Directions in Legal Anthropology* (Ithaca, NY: Cornell University Press, 1989), pp. 302–19; Clifford Geertz, "Thick Description: Toward an Interpretive Theory of Culture," in *The Interpretation of Cultures: Selected Essays by Clifford Geertz* (New York: Basic Books, 1973), pp. 3–30; Clifford Geertz, "Found in Translation: On the Social History of the Moral Imagination," in *Local Knowledge: Further Essays in Interpretive Anthropology* (New York: Basic Books, 1983), pp. 36–54.

[14] Wael Hallaq, "The Kadi Diwan (Sijill) before the Ottomans," *Bulletin of the School of Oriental and African Studies* 61 (1998): 415–36.

[15] Lawrence Rosen attributes this visualization of Max Weber's *Kadijustiz* to Lord Justice Goddard of the English Court of Appeals, and, following him, to Justice Felix Frankfurter (*The Anthropology of Justice*, p. 58).

that historians of the Ottoman period have been busily mining for all types of socioeconomic and legal history). The keeping of the *diwan* (which comprised a large variety of legal documents such as witnessed statements, contracts, lists of witnesses, agents, guarantors and prisoners, registers of bequests and trusts, as well as correspondence) was a formal and systematic practice throughout Islamic lands. Written by the indispensable scribe (*katib*), the *diwan* was quintessentially "the successor [*khalifa*] of the kadi in terms of the local sociolegal continuity as the next appointed kadi is the representative of the institutional continuity." In light of this relationship, it is not surprising that the transference [*tasallum*] of the *diwan* from one kadi to another was regarded as a central and formalized responsibility incumbent upon both the old kadi and the new. In the Muslim legal imagination, the demands of sociolegal continuity and the need to ensure sociolegal justice and order necessitated the transference of authority and record.[16]

Hallaq insists that the institution of the *diwan* goes back to the early centuries of Islamic history (and notes that it may have its origins in one or another of the region's pre-Islamic empires). Because "the Islamic legal system never acknowledged a well-defined, legally instituted, physical space for courts of law," however, once the *diwan* was copied and transferred, the original became private property and of no legal or any other interest. As Hallaq further argues, "by all indications, this private ownership continued until such time when the state dictated that the *diwan*s should be deposited in a public domain, which the Ottomans seem to have done." The Ottomans, in other words, provided for and dictated a public space for storing the documents. Although the argument convincingly demonstrates that the Ottoman innovation lies in the institutionalization of the art of record-keeping rather than that of record-making itself, its author does not develop the conceptual significance of this Ottoman innovation, which according to him consisted of the carving out of a "public domain." This archiving of the public record, however, is of tremendous significance and requires a closer look.

---

[16] It is essential to keep in view the importance of the court in the ordering of socioeconomic life and the consequent preponderance of business and property transactions in the court records – in other words the economic expression of political power. For an interesting comparison, see T. Clanchy, *From Memory to Written Record: England 1066–1307* (Cambridge, MA: Harvard University Press, 1979).

THE KADI AND THE ARCHIVE

It was Aristotle who first recognized the act of record-making as a quin-
tessential political act. Among the offices necessary for "harmony and good
order" in the state, Aristotle included the office of the "Recorders."[17]
Aristotle was registering recognition of what Posner refers to as one of
the "constants" of political practice – the making of records in all their
wonderful ancient variety (Persian "royal skins" and Roman *commentarii*,
for example).[18] Posner, however, also points out that Aristotle's *archeion*
was not merely a depository of documents no longer in use or a place where
a variety of records originating elsewhere were kept. Archiving involved
much more than capturing in writing what the "memory man" had fixed in
his person. It authenticated the record through witnessing and entered it
into the public record. And it was, with the exceptions of the Roman
Tabularium and the Byzantine *skeuophylakion*, a rare practice in the ancient
world.[19]

In a rather convoluted essay, Derrida reminds us that the archive – *arche* –
"names at once the commencement and the commandment." Whereas it
is the former that sets him on a Freudian path of exploration, it is the latter
principle of commandment that is of interest here. Derrida means by
archive "the principle according to the law, *there* where men and god
command, there where authority, social order are exercised, in this place
from which order is given."[20]

Derrida's insight speaks of the exercising of authority and power. He
reminds us that the meaning of "archive" "comes from the Greek *archheion*:
initially a house, a domicile, an address, the residence of the superior
magistrate, the *archons*, those who commanded." And it is precisely in this

---

[17] Aristotle: *The Politics. The Basic Works of Aristotle*, ed. and intro. Richard McKeon (New York: Random House, 1970), p. 1274.
[18] Ernst Posner, *Archives in the Ancient World* (Cambridge, MA: Harvard University Press, 1972), pp. 3–4.
[19] Ibid., pp. 4–5; 93–5. Posner also notes the following – most interesting, though of tangential significance in this context: when the Greeks under Alexander the Great conquered Persia and seized its archives, they called them the "royal skins" (*diphtherai basilikai*). The term *diphtherai* was inherited by the Arabs and the Turks, and in the form *defter* (register) it designates a key series in Turkish archival terminology. With the Arabs the term went to Sicily, where *deftarii* indicate the financial records of the Norman *doana regia*. To close the circle, the term returned from Turkish into modern Greek as *tefteri*, which means notebook (*Archives*, p. 9).
[20] Jacques Derrida, *Archive Fever: A Freudian Impression*, trans. Eric Prenowitz (Chicago: University of Chicago Press, 1995), p. 1. This particular English-language edition was published as part of a series on religion and postmodernism.

"*domiciliation*, in this house arrest, that archives take place. The dwelling ... marks this institutional passage from the private to the public."[21]

Archiving is intrinsically political. It creates an institutionalized space in which to store a record of the exercise of political and legal power. Its documents testify tangibly to authority: they speak its name, bear its stamp, register its commands, and detail the extent of its imprint in everyday life. In the case of the Ottoman kadi who, as already mentioned, occupied a central place in the system of government, the institutionalization of the record-keeping process and its housing in a public space – a court – involved a further embodiment of authority. If in his person he already stood to implement a territorialized gloss of shari'a law, his court now also became the locus of the authenticated and sanctioned record.

THE LAW, THE ARCHIVE, THE STATE, AND RELIGION

This discussion invites several considerations. The assimilation of the religious/legal establishment into the hierarchical apparatus of the Ottoman state – an Ottoman innovation that was symptomatic of Ottoman consolidation – was marked not only by the appointment of kadis to a widespread network of urban courts, but also by the designation of courts as specific kinds of spaces for the practice and archiving of justice. This designation in turn suggests the need to view the court as both less and more than an institution dedicated to the dispensation of "Muslim" justice and the primacy of religious identity, and more as a political/legal space in which "law" partook of both sacred as well as political authority.

There is a tendency to attribute much of the corruption of the Ottoman kadi court system to the illegal and arbitrary intervention of the state. This is a wrong attribution. This is not to claim that justice never miscarried – corruption was as much a part of this court system as any other political institution – but it was not the consequence of arbitrary state intervention. Indeed, it was precisely this systematic, as opposed to arbitrary, intervention by the state in the functioning of the courts (or more accurately, their co-optation by the state) that bureaucratized and streamlined the practice of justice.

One notable consequence of this was the leveling of the legal playing field, as far as zimmis were concerned, for it fostered a more "secular" and territorial discourse of "Islamic" law. In other words, the court was not only an Islamic court – as opposed to a court for Muslims – whose law, which

[21] Ibid., pp. 2–3.

formalized distinctions of religion into differences of legal status (non-Muslim into zimmis), applied its justice to them as well as Muslims; it was also the court of the state, and the legal venue that transformed those zimmis into Ottoman subjects.

As a result of this, the kadi courts were the most important legal institutions in the everyday lives of Ottoman non-Muslims. Unlike the communal courts whose authority they always overrode, the kadi courts territorialized religious law. At times, Jews and Christians benefited, as in cases where Islamic law recognized economic rights denied to Jews or Christians by the *halakha* and canon law, respectively. In general, this territorialization denied them full juridical autonomy (in transgression of the so-called pact of Umar) and gave rise to arresting dissonances as in the cases of zimmis marrying and divorcing in accordance with shari'a law.[22]

This is not to say that the presence of zimmis in the "Muslim" court was not noted. On the contrary, the recorders of the court highlighted religious identity, and in the process testified to the significance of religious distinctions and their political weight. The court records contain consistent and pervasive forms of orthographic and linguistic distinctions that highlight zimmi identity and make it conspicuous. The scribes use specific zimmi transcriptions of shared names (such as Yusuf [*sad*] as opposed to the "correct" Yusuf [*sin*]) as well as a repertoire of subtle and not-too-subtle titles to designate religious identity (such as *khawaja* or *yahudi*). Often the effect is visually striking and difficult to ignore.[23]

But it is not only those scribal practices of "discrimination" that suggest the import of religious identity. More interesting is that the court registers the identity of zimmi men and women against consistently unmarked Muslim ones. In contrast to conspicuously flagged zimmi individuals, the great majority of Muslims inhabit the body of the text by virtue of almost total semantic omission and silence. In other words, the unmarked (Muslim) identity is posited as natural, a process that Pierre Bourdieu calls the projection of "naturalized arbitrariness," a discourse on power.[24] The scribes used religion as a marker of difference in documenting a territorial legal practice that was predicated on the suspension of religious distinction.

[22] Najwa Al-Qattan, "Dhimmis in the Muslim Court: Legal Autonomy and Religious Discrimination," *International Journal of Middle Eastern Studies* 31 (1999): 429–44.

[23] Najwa Al-Qattan, "Discriminating Texts: Orthographic Marking and Social Differentiation in the Court Records of Ottoman Damascus," in Yasir Suleiman (ed.), *Arabic Sociolinguistics: Issues and Perspectives* (London: Curzon Press, 1994): 57–77.

[24] Pierre Bourdieu, *Outline of a Theory of Practice* (Cambridge: Cambridge University Press, 1977), p. 164.

As such their practice recalls the logic of sartorial regulations, which were necessitated by the spatial integration of zimmis into Muslim society. To put it differently, it is the very territorialization of the law and the erasure or suspension of religion as a marker of legal discrimination that brought about – even perhaps necessitated – the highlighting of religious identity by the recorders of the court who simultaneously flagged and integrated zimmis in the registers.

The territorialization of shari'a law at the Ottoman court made available for the zimmi and Muslim inhabitants of Ottoman cities a shared and legally integrated space that had its parallel in the shared documentary space of the *sijill* record. Reflecting socioeconomic integration across religious communities as well as its limits, the court refracted religious identity though the prism of state authority, and in the process both highlighted and erased it.

CONCLUSIONS

Historians of the Ottoman Empire, including several authors in this volume, have explored the projection and performance of sovereignty in architecture, ceremonials, cartography, and diplomacy. The Ottoman Muslim court also makes possible the analysis of understandings of sovereignty and authority. The court in fact does so at several levels, as suggested in this chapter. First, as both a politico-religious institution and through the agency of the Istanbul-appointed kadi, its practice of shari'a law was inflected with accents of political exigency and empowered by the authority of the state; second, and as a result, it was a space that allowed for historically interesting (as well as historically variable) intersections of religion and politics. And it was also the site in which both legal judgments as well as state orders were archived and preserved. In purview, practice, and documentation, the law of the courts exhibited a marked territorialization of shari'a law, an innovating process that was pragmatic as well as creative.

But what did this territorialization mean exactly? As evident from the anecdote cited at the opening of this chapter, as well as in several articles in the present volume, particularly Palmira Brummetts, territoriality is itself an imaginary – and in the premodern period one that is distinctly different from the precisely delineated border-bound territoriality of the nation-state. It is also one that allows us to ask questions about the politics of religion in the pre-Tanzimat era.

Much has been and continues to be written about the role of Islam in politics. In Ottoman historiography, as in the historiography of Ottoman

successor states such as Lebanon and more recently Iraq, there now exists a
large number of profoundly insightful works dealing with historically
specific ways in which religion came to be politically inflected over the
course of the long nineteenth century.[25] Accounts such as these, which so
convincingly complicate the question of religion in the late Ottoman
period (albeit in different ways), invite us to complicate the role of religion
in earlier times as well. This is particularly urgent for several reasons: first,
the recent focus on the politicization of religion in the later Ottoman
period has tended to gloss over or minimize parallel but different earlier
understandings. Second, any attempt at injecting religion back into the
historical arena runs the risk of faltering on the double slippery slope of
Orientalist and primordialist readings of religion. And, finally, the question allows us yet again to revisit the issue of continuity and change and
hence of periodization in the Ottoman Empire.

To suggest historical continuities between premodern Ottoman notions
of politics and religion and later sectarian and Hamidian politics and
violence, for example, is not to argue that later developments were historically inevitable; neither is it to resort to primordial identities or to the
ubiquitous nature of inter-communal strife as historical and constant
causes. It does suggest, however, a measure of continuity attached not to
religious tension and violence but to the importance of religion in marking
relations of power.

---

[25] See, for example, Ussama Makdisi, *The Culture of Sectarianism: Community, History, and Violence in Ottoman Lebanon* (Berkeley, CA: University of California Press, 2000); Bruce Masters, "The 1850 Events in Aleppo: An Aftershock of Syria's Incorporation into the Capitalist World System," *IJMES* 22 (1990): 3–20; Selim Deringil, *The Well-Protected Domains: Ideology and the Legitimation of Power in the Ottoman Empire, 1876–1909* (London: I. B. Tauris, 1998).

9

The material world: ideologies and ordinary things

Leslie Peirce

It did not take much for people in premodern Ottoman times to view themselves as men or women of property. Even the poor took care in amassing, ordering, and protecting their possessions. For example, when the woman Sare passed away in the year 1540, she left an "estate" valued at 114 silver coins – not much when you consider that two silver coins was the standard daily allowance for the upkeep of an orphan child, a runaway slave in detention, or a stray animal waiting to be claimed by its owner.[1]

The possessions that Sare left behind consisted of things that a woman of modest means typically valued: a pair of ankle bracelets, a caftan, a chemise, and, finally, a mattress, a pillow, and a quilt. It may seem that Sare managed to leave only the bed she died on and the simple finery she wore on special occasions. Such basic items, however, had value beyond their practical functions. For one thing, they signaled one's social standing in the community. Sare's black caftan was worth only fifteen *akçes* (the *akçe* was the standard silver coin produced in Ottoman mints) and her ankle bracelets thirty, but the wealthy Lady Jansur – fellow resident of the city of Aintab, who registered her rich dower at the local court on the same day as Sare's estate was documented – owned a fancy red satin caftan and pieces of gold jewelry worth 2,000 *akçes* each.[2]

The Lady Jansur's expensive adornment communicated her elite status despite the practice among women, especially upper-class women, of not displaying their persons in public. It is true that, in the Ottoman world, protocols of gender segregation were most strictly observed among the upper classes (particularly – but not only – among Muslims). But women of high

---

[1] Yvonne Seng, "Standing at the Gates of Justice: Women in the Law Courts of Early Sixteenth-Century Üsküdar, Istanbul," in S. Hirsch and M. Lazarus-Black (eds.), *Contested States: Law, Hegemony and Resistance* (New York: Routledge, 1994), p. 204.
[2] Gaziantep Şeriye Sicili No. 161 (145a, b). The Gaziantep court records cited here and elsewhere are fully explored in Leslie Peirce, *Morality Tales: Law and Gender in the Ottoman Court of Aintab* (Berkeley, CA: University of California Press, 2003), p. 223.

social standing were far from invisible. Most obviously, they were visible to the half of the population that was female. Women visited and entertained one another, and major social events like weddings provided separate ceremonies for the sexes.[3] It was primarily in these female gatherings that women's adornment conveyed their own and their household's material status.

Female servants and domestic slaves were additional vehicles of information about their mistresses' possessions. One can imagine them on their errands outside the house discreetly advertising their mistress's wealth and refined taste, which of course reflected well upon them. Suppliers of cloth, tailors, jewelers, and house-to-house peddlars could also speak to the consumption habits of an elite household. And while Lady Jansur did not appear herself at court to register her dower, the personnel of the court gained an intimate if veiled glimpse of her person through the long and detailed list of her valuables. Gossip might go far since many ears were eager to be entertained by tales of the local rich. Lady Jansur, hailed in the court record as "pride of women," was no doubt a particular item of scrutiny since she was married to Kasım Beg, "pride of the notables," a slave of the sultan whose household perhaps introduced to provincial Aintab the latest in Istanbul fashions.

Looking at early modern Ottoman society through the lens of things possessed, consumed, and passed along to future generations – clothing, dwellings, professional equipment, money, as well as living wealth in the form of slaves, mounts, and farm animals – reveals striking gaps as well as commonalities in the material lives of the many peoples and regional cultures that made up the Ottoman Empire. Both the particularities and the universals in the empire's material geographies help to illuminate preferences and practices shaped by gender, social status, religious identity, and regional habits. Possessions were designed and deployed to communicate individual taste and personality as well as allegiance to family and social group. But while Ottoman society appreciated the usefulness of material goods for family and social well-being, at the same time it disapproved of undisciplined materialism. The vocabulary of the material world was ordered by an ideological grammar that insisted on giving as well as getting, concealing as well as displaying. The cardinal sins of materialism were the unseemly flaunting of one's wealth and the failure to honor the moral imperative of philanthropy. It would not be wrong to say that the material culture of early

---

[3] Fanny Davis, *The Ottoman Lady: A Social History from 1718 to 1918* (Westport, CN: Greenwood Press, 1986), chapters 8 and 9. While Davis treats a later period in Ottoman history, many of the activities she describes were characteristic of earlier centuries as well.

modern Ottomans was governed by a "rule of ethical proportion" that insisted on the circulation of wealth through charity and patronage as a counterweight to the accumulation of wealth and possessions. Fashions might come and go, but the belief in ethical proportion persisted, at least until it was challenged by social upheavals of the nineteenth century.

A WORLD OF THINGS

Clearly, women valued personal and domestic possessions, things that, if not carried on their person, were never far from the reach of their hand or the scope of their eye. For that reason, we find items such as substantial copper cooking pots and vessels as well as cash (gold or silver coins) among women's estates or the gifts they gave to kin. (When another Sare from Aintab hid her possessions in a neighbor's house upon her husband's jailing, a box containing eighty-four *akçes* was revealed when the unsuspecting neighbor discovered the hidden sacks.[4]) Jewelry, textiles (uncut or done up as dress), and one's own embroidery work – handkerchiefs, head scarves, pillow and quilt covers – could be investments to be sold in time of need or traded for desired items. Even the women of the imperial family were trained to embroider, and their work was sometimes included in gift presentations to other monarchs: to the king of Poland, Süleyman's favorite concubine, Hurrem, sent two sets of pyjamas, six handkerchiefs, and a handtowel (probably her own work). Menavino, a Genoese page in the royal palace, noted that ten teachers of embroidery came each day to instruct new slave recruits.[5] This skill proved helpful later in life to lesser women of the palace harem, who sold their handiwork in order to keep body and soul together.[6] In short, it is no overstatement to say that women in palaces and provinces alike created and maintained a specifically female economy of things and money.

The objects that were valued by women in different times and places reflected changing fashions as well as staple domestic and personal possessions. In the Galata district of eighteenth-century Istanbul, whose residents included many Christians and Jews as well as Muslims, women had the usual possessions (clothing, jewelry, bedding, cash), but they also owned furs (squirrel, rabbit, and ermine), implements for making coffee, and chairs

---

[4] Gaziantep Şeriye Sicili No. 2 (184a, b).
[5] Giovanantonio Menavino, *I cinque libri della legge: religione et vita de'Turchi della corte, & d'alcune guerre del Gran Turco* (Venice, 1548), p. 135.
[6] Robert Withers, "The Grand Signiors Seraglio" [translation of Ottaviano Bon, *Descrizione del seraglio del Gran Signore*], in S. Purchas, *His Pilgrimes*, 20 vols. (Glasgow: J. MacLehose and Sons, 1905), vol. IX, p. 390.

(a new fashion!). Religion did not seem to affect consumption preferences in
Galata, since Muslim and non-Muslim women owned the same sorts of
things. Nor did the general sociolegal hierarchy that privileged Muslims
necessarily correlate with wealth: the Galata woman leaving the largest estate
in a 1789 inventory – 154,520 *akçes* – was the Armenian Serpuhi.[7] We should
be cautious, however, in measuring the material wealth of the living by the
estates of the deceased. This may be particularly true of women, who gave
away much during their lifetimes, especially to their children.

If the ordinary family hearth was populated by women's possessions,
men were more likely to own the family dwelling, which they in turn
hoped to pass on to their sons. Male heads of household were also more
likely to own the income-producing property that was the source of the
family's livelihood. Such property varied with place of residence – city
quarter, town, or village – more than did the sorts of property owned by
women, which had a kind of domestic universality. City and town-dwellers
tended to own shops, workshops, and factories (small and large), while
peasant "estates" might consist of grain-producing fields, vineyards, and
orchards, the implements and animals to work them, and sometimes
money-making herds of goats or sheep.

The boundary between urban and rural life was not always sharp,
however. Town and city folk owned animals too. Donkeys, mules, and
horses were necessary for hauling and peddling goods. Urban residents also
kept animals for personal transport, the horse being preferred over the
donkey as a more honorable mount (in fact, forbidding non-Muslims to
ride horses was one of the measures periodically enforced by Muslim
authorities when they wanted to remind Christians and Jews of their legally
inferior status). Geography permitting, city folk also delighted in the
cultivated green spaces – vegetable gardens, vineyards, and orchards –
that they managed to sustain around their homes or at the edges of
urban settlements. Likewise, urban dwellers might own rural property
and hire local peasants to work it. Rural "estates" could be small: Lady Il
owned a single walnut tree as part of her dower, which she traded with a
relative for a walnut tree in another village. It is hard to know if she actually

---

[7] For this example (and others) from Galata, see Fatma Müge Göçek and Marc David Baer, "Social
Boundaries of Ottoman Women's Experience in Eighteenth-Century Galata Court Records," in
Madeline Zilfi (ed.), *Women in the Ottoman Empire: Middle Eastern Women in the Early Modern Era*
(Leiden: Brill, 1997), pp. 48–65. For a study of how communal relations "could be apprehended in
the daily exchange of goods, and in the concrete and symbolic uses to which goods were applied," see
Madeline C. Zilfi, "Goods in the *Mahalle*: Distributional Encounters in Eighteenth-Century
Istanbul," in Donald Quataert (ed.), *Consumption Studies and the History of the Ottoman Empire,
1550–1922* (Albany, NY: SUNY Press, 2000), pp. 289–311.

supervised the care of her tree, but the habit of visiting and even vacation-ing on one's rural "estate" is one of long standing. Today, people of the central Anatolian city of Kayseri sometimes own "vineyard houses" in their rural properties that are fancier than their regular homes in the city.

The mingling of urban and rural was not simply the result of one-way traffic. Although some Ottoman villages were isolated because of location or limited seasonal passability of roads, others were integrated into local market economies and commercial networks in a variety of ways. Close links between rural settlements and urban markets were especially characteristic of Egypt, where the narrow ribbon of cultivable land along the River Nile was closely tied to urban networks. Throughout the empire, wherever logistically possi-ble, peasants sold their agricultural produce and their wares in urban markets, shopped there, and sometimes found seasonal employment in the city. Indeed, many villagers in the Ottoman Empire were willy-nilly participants in a "global" monetary economy, or so the pickpocketing of a man from Anatolian Maraş suggests: while shopping at a local bazaar, the villager was relieved of three different denominations of coin – two gold florins (probably minted in Venice), a couple of *para* (a silver coin popular in the empire's eastern regions), and one "Ottoman *akçe*."[8]

City-dwellers and peasants were frequently linked through the local networks of borrowing and lending that were ubiquitous in Ottoman society. Ottoman cities and towns had professional moneylenders, but supplying credit seems largely to have been a local grassroots operation, with neighbors and even family members borrowing from one another and registering their transactions at the local court. Women participated in these homely enterprises just as keenly as men did, and religion was no barrier to lending among Muslims, Christians, and Jews. In early sixteenth-century Üsküdar, the bustling Istanbul quarter located on the Asian side of the Bosphorus, Hiristiniye borrowed a thousand *akçes* from Emir, a Muslim male, while Manula – like Hiristiniye a Greek Christian – sued the Muslim İskender for a debt he owed her (also a thousand *akçes*).[9] Likewise, joint commercial ventures in which profits were shared among the trader and the "silent partners" who provided capital sometimes linked surprising combinations of individuals. For example, the circle of investors in the enterprise of the Aintab cloth merchant Hoca Yusuf, who died owing his partners a total of 654 gold florins, included a villager from a

[8] Gaziantep Şeriye Sicili No. 161 (98d).
[9] Yvonne Seng, "Invisible Women: Residents of Early Sixteenth-Century Istanbul," in Gavin R. G. Hambly (ed.), *Women in the Medieval Islamic World* (New York: St. Martin's Press, 1998), pp. 257–8.

neighboring province, the woman Rahime, and that "pride of notables," Kasım Beg.[10] And in Üsküdar, one Captain İlyas, who was probably engaged in regional trade with the small ship he owned, died owing 8,200 *akçe*s to twelve residents of the quarter, three of them women.[11]

DWELLINGS REAL AND IDEAL

In Ottoman times, it did not take a lot to own a house or part of a shared family compound. Land was relatively cheap, and even the homes of the wealthy tended not to be large. Although renting a place to live was not uncommon, especially among transient populations, most people seem to have managed to own at least a share of a dwelling, if not a whole house.[12] Indeed, remarkable numbers of people – women and men, Muslims, Jews, and Christians alike – bought and sold odd fractions of houses known as *qirat*s (twenty-four *qirat*s made a whole). In eighteenth-century Damascus, the residential real-estate market yielded quick and sometimes substantial profit to an entrepreneur who could consolidate a property by buying up the shares of its various owners.[13]

In the typical dwelling of a moderately well-off family, the courtyard was a centripetal force. Around it were arranged the various functional parts of the house – kitchen, storerooms, toilet, perhaps a stable, and the "living rooms" that functioned as bedrooms by night. In larger multigenerational dwellings, the nuclear units of father and sons with their wives and children typically had separate "living rooms" but shared facilities such as the kitchen. Much of daily life, especially for women and children and especially in warmer climates, was lived in the courtyard, which might be adorned with fruit-bearing trees and other greenery. For today's wanderer in a traditional Middle Eastern neighborhood, with its high house walls and narrow shad-owed streets, there is nothing more tempting to the eye than an open doorway that might reveal a courtyard bright with life and color.

To be able to enjoy the privacy of one's own courtyard was no doubt everyone's ideal, for having to share a courtyard with families unrelated to

---

[10] Gaziantep Şer'iye Sicili No. 2 (30a, 30c, 31a, 43a, 48c).
[11] Seng, "Invisible Women," p. 256.
[12] Suraiya Faroqhi, *Men of Modest Substance: House Owners and House Property in Seventeeth-Century Ankara and Kayseri* (Cambridge: Cambridge University Press, 1987), p. 216; Abraham Marcus, *The Middle East on the Eve of Modernity: Aleppo in the Eighteenth Century* (New York: Columbia University Press, 1989), pp. 189–90.
[13] Najwa Al-Qattan, "Across the Courtyard: Residential Space and Sectarian Boundaries in Ottoman Damascus," in Molly Greene (ed.), *Minorities in the Ottoman Empire: A Reconsideration* (Princeton NJ: Marcus Wiener, 2005), pp. 13–45.

one's own was a sign of relative poverty. Even within families, the drive of married couples for domestic autonomy can be seen in the rush of male siblings to divide jointly inherited residential compounds into separate units. The popular stereotype of the extended patriarchal family of the Middle East is only partly valid, since joint residence could represent merely a stage in the lifecycle, where an important sign of a husband and wife's maturing status was getting their own place or at least marking their own domain within a shared residence.[14] Elsewhere, other traditions prevailed, for example the *zadruga*, a multi-family household wherein productive property was owned and regulated communally, with married males sharing decision-making authority. Mainly, but not exclusively a Christian phenomenon, and found in many parts of the Balkans, *zadruga*s might have as many as seventy members and hold together for a hundred years or more. Customs regarding women's position within the communal family seem to have differed region-ally, with females marrying exclusively outside the *zadruga* in some cases, in others inheriting shares in the land when male heirs were lacking.[15]

Unusual in the Ottoman Empire, the city of Cairo featured apartment buildings. These were typically to be found in the crowded commercial districts of the city and inhabited mainly by local Cairene artisans and small shopkeepers. Most apartment occupants were renters, though some owned their units, which tended to be cheaper than private houses. Although apartments sacrificed the ideal of the private courtyard, their duplex or triplex design featured some separation of domestic quarters from reception room and even an enclosed balcony.[16] (And they often enjoyed more square footage than this author's home in the San Francisco Bay area!) These apartment buildings were different from tenements that housed soldiers or (more usually) laborers, many of whom were transients, immigrants, or rural poor.[17] This sort of crude mass housing was common in several of the empire's cities, in part because of crowded living con-ditions in commercial districts, in part because of the strong prejudice

[14] Alan Duben, "Turkish Families and Households in Historical Perspective," *Journal of Family History* 10 (1985): 75–95; Marcus, *The Middle East on the Eve of Modernity*, pp. 197–8.
[15] On the *zadruga*, see the essays in R. F. Byrnes (ed.), *Communal Families in the Balkans: The Zadruga* (Notre Dame, IN: University of Notre Dame Press, 1976). I am grateful to Evdoxios Doxiadis for bringing both this social arrangement and this study to my attention.
[16] André Raymond, "The *Rab'*: A Type of Collective Housing in Cairo during the Ottoman Period," reprinted in *Arab Cities in the Ottoman Period: Cairo, Syria and the Maghreb* (Aldershot: Ashgate, 2002). Raymond characterizes the inhabitants of these buildings as lower middle class, "situated at equal distance from the 'proletariat' of Cairo (itinerant workers, craftsmen) and the upper middle class (mainly fabric merchants or care owners)" (p. 269).
[17] Marcus, *The Middle East on the Eve of Modernity*, p. 318.

against single men living in family neighborhoods. Such social isolation could breed discontent and even insubordination. When troops stationed in Istanbul staged an uprising in 1656 to protest irregularities in their stipends, a soldier described his plight to the young sultan Mehmed IV: "we languish in boarding houses hungry and impoverished," he lamented, "and our stipends aren't even enough to cover our debts to the landlords."[18]

There was, of course, one important segment of the population whose dwellings and other property did not figure in local housing markets or estate inventories. These were the nomads, present in much of Ottoman territory – Turkmen in Anatolia and northern Syria, Bedouin in Syria and Egypt, Kurds in eastern Anatolia, Vlachs and gypsies in the Balkans. While there was a good deal of fear and enmity between nomads and sedentary populations (nomads raided caravans and their animals trampled crops, sedentary authorities restricted nomad mobility and interfered with tribal autonomy), there was a striking economic symbiosis between them.[19] Nomads supplied meat, butter, cheese, wool, hides for leather goods, gut for bowstring, horses, and slaves, while urban markets supplied nomads with durable goods, grain, and various luxury items. The lack of records of nomads' possessions does not keep us from knowing about their material lives. If animals held pride of place in the nomad's world, domestic property could constitute a moveable art gallery: saddlebags, tent decorations, pillows, rugs, and clothing were woven or embroidered in a riot of color and design. Contrary to what one might expect, nomads did not necessarily own fewer possessions than settled people did. Rather, their possessions were crafted for portability.

The ideal in a male nomad's material world, at least in the fifteenth century, is revealed in a legendary account of Osman Ghazi's estate. In the historian Aşıkpaşazade's *History of the House of Osman*, this first Ottoman ruler is made out to be a well-to-do herdsman who owned "a saltcellar and spoon-holder, a robe and soft houseboots, several stables of good horses, several flocks of sheep, a few wild mares, several pairs of saddlepads, and flank armor."[20] Although this depiction of Osman as a herdsman may be nostalgia for simpler times (the famous Moroccan traveler Ibn Battuta, visiting the court of Osman's son Orhan, praised him as "the richest of the

---

[18] Mustafa Na'îmâ, *Tarih*, 6 vols. (Istanbul: n.p., 1280/1863–64), vol. VI, p. 141.
[19] Halil İnalcık, "The Ottoman State: Economy and Society, 1300–1600," in H. İnalcık and D. Quataert (eds.), *An Economic and Social History of the Ottoman Empire, 1300–1914* (Cambridge: Cambridge University Press, 1994), passim.
[20] Derviş Ahmed Aşıkpaşazâde, *Die altosmanischen anonymen Chroniken: Tevarih-i Al-i Osman*, ed. and trans. F. Giese, 2 vols. (Breslau: Selbstverlag, 1922), vol. I, chapters 12 and 13.

Turkmen"),[21] the story is useful in pointing to the cultural importance of maintaining and documenting one's worldly goods. After all, if Osman Ghazi cared about his houseboots, why should an ordinary nomad, or even a peasant or city-dweller, not take pride in his own footwear?

DISPLAYING/CONCEALING WEALTH

Inhabitants of the Ottoman world were highly sensitive to class differences and social hierarchies. Consumption and display were ubiquitous means by which people distinguished themselves from each another – through the clothes they wore, the food they ate, the animals they rode upon, the public charities they endowed, the number of slaves they owned. How one appeared in public counted for a lot, and individuals devoted careful calculation to where, when, and with what degree of ceremony they stepped outside their thresholds. Just as the Ottoman sultan never left the imperial palace without a retinue – and left only for such public duties as attending mosque prayers and embarking on military campaigns – so no man of status did his own business in the streets unaccompanied by underlings. The higher a man's social and professional standing, the more he could expect others to come to him – to petition or to call upon him in the reception hall of his residence. For business transactions that needed to take place elsewhere, such an individual dispatched an agent, perhaps a son or a slave. Even a slave communicated his owner's status since he was likely to be wearing one of his master's cast-off outfits.[22]

So it was with females. Upper-class women were even more careful than their husbands to guard their reputations by employing slaves and agents on matters of public business. Domestic seclusion was not a barrier to doing business: women of wealth were owners and managers of real estate, investors in tax farms and commercial ventures, and philanthropists. Stereotypes of Ottoman women forbidden by male family members to leave their homes, while not without basis in fact, are sometimes exaggerated. The point was less to confine oneself to the house than to avoid exposing oneself to strange men. Women of status might venture out so long as the excursion was socially approved – a wedding, for example – and so long as they were accompanied by servants who formed human walls

[21] Ibn Battuta, *The Travels of Ibn Battuta*, ed. and trans. H. A. R. Gibb, 2 vols. (Cambridge: Hakluyt Society, 1962), vol. II, p. 452.
[22] Yvonne Seng, "Fugitives and Factotums: Slaves in Early Sixteenth-Century Istanbul," *Journal of the Economic and Social History of the Orient* 39/2 (1996): 160–1.

enclosing a kind of portable privacy. Such at least was the opinion of the renowned sixteenth-century Muslim jurist Ebussuûd, who noted in one of his fatwas that non-Muslim women also sought to conform to these same measures of status.[23] Elite women in fact engaged in a lively round of calling upon each other, and in so doing confirmed each other's status. Female sociability provided the perfect occasion for the display of personal and family wealth. Visitors could expect their hostesses to provide elegant refreshment and, among the very rich, entertainment by trained female musicians and dancers. The letters of Lady Mary Wortley Montagu, wife of the English ambassador to Istanbul in 1718, narrate in sumptuous detail the costume of the ladies she called upon, the endless succession of dishes they pressed upon her, and the refined deportment of their slaves.[24]

In contrast to neighboring Europe, wealth and high social status among Ottoman subjects were broadcast less through domestic architecture than through the architecture of the person – one's dress, mount, retinue, and physical deportment. One reason for this importance of the person was the general cheapness of land compared to the high cost of luxury goods that could be displayed on or about one's body. In mid sixteenth-century Aintab, when a typical house cost 2,500 akçes (some could be had as cheaply as 300 akçes), a prominent textile merchant paid 10,750 akçes for less than a pound of lapis-blue dye.[25] But in late seventeenth-century Ankara, where the price of land in desirable neighborhoods was driven upward when urban prosperity attracted new residents, more elaborate dwellings began to be constructed and houses gained in height, some rising to three storeys.[26]

Ottoman analogs to the baronial mansions of European nobility and gentry certainly existed, but the residences of the urban wealthy were deliberately designed to escape the admiring (or perhaps resentful) gaze of the public. Rarely rising beyond two or three storeys, they were concealed behind walls, their grandeur to be inferred rather than observed. The point, in fact, was to escape the public gaze, to preserve the near-hallowed privacy of domestic life. Domestic structures were oriented inward, gardens were cultivated within walls, and the broad avenues that served in other societies to display the homes of the rich did not arrive in the Middle East until the late nineteenth century.

[23] M. E. Düzdağ, Şeyhülislam Ebussuûd Efendi Fetvaları Işığında 16. Asır Türk Hayatı (Istanbul: Enderun Kitabevi, 1983), 55.
[24] Lady Mary Wortley Montagu, Embassy to Constantinople, ed. C. Pick, intro. D. Murphy (New York: New Amsterdam, 1988), pp. 128–32.
[25] Gaziantep Şer'iye Sicili No. 2 (142b and passim).
[26] Faroqhi, Men of Modest Substance, pp. 212–13.

The ravages of fires and earthquakes have left few such mansions standing. In fact, the frequency of such urban disasters was a reason not to invest in palatial dwellings. But eighteenth-century residences such as that of the 'Azim family in Damascus or the Gübgüoğlu in Kayseri (both open to tourists today) are marvelous monuments of architectural refinement, with their multiple courtyards, gardens, fountains, and imposingly decorated reception rooms. But the conspicuously displayed luxuries of these homes were interior, visible only to select petitioners or guests who, once invited inside, were carefully escorted to either the men's or women's salons. Of course, another audience for the grandeur of these residences – an unsolicited one – was the bevy of domestic servants who circulated through these interior spaces and the suppliers who might catch a glimpse inside as they delivered goods to a mansion's gates. Once again, local gossip might conjure visions of what the eye could not directly behold.

The homes of the rich may have been shielded from the gaze of passers-by, but they were hardly isolated. Urban mansions were often located in the heart of the city, near the citadel or the grand bazaar, amidst the hubbub of city traffic. Urban mansions did not only belong to families whose fortunes derived from urban commerce and long-distance trade, since rural magnates also preferred to reside in the city and manage their country estates by employing stewards. The charisma of the city and the power of its politics to make or break the reputations of elite households was a legacy of ancient times – of the urban culture and the civic pride that were the hallmark of Mesopotamian city-states, the Greek *polis*, and the cities of the eastern Roman Empire. For the most part, the Ottoman world lacked imposing domestic structures in rural areas, with the notable exception of remote palaces such as those of Lebanese lords or Kurdish beys – one thinks of Beit al-Din, the Druze palace on Mount Lebanon, or the dramatic eyrie of İshak Pasha overlooking Mount Ararat. Even the newly prominent landed gentry of eighteenth-century Anatolia constructed their mansions in provincial urban centers.[27]

Toward the end of the nineteenth century, western European cultural and social practices had penetrated elite circles in the principal Ottoman cities. An emerging critique of westernizing life-styles harped on the pernicious

---

[27] Filiz Yenişehirlioğlu, "Architectural Patronage of *Ayan* Families in Anatolia," in A. Anastasopoulos (ed.), *Provincial Elites in the Ottoman Empire* (Rethymno: Crete University Press, 2005), pp. 321–39; Yenişehirlioğlu compares these gentry families to "Italian landlords who preferred to live in cities even though rural lands and cultivation provided most of their income" (p. 326).

effects of new suburbs where the wealthy flocked together.[28] The problem was that the upper classes were now isolated from the neighborhoods whose patrons they had been in earlier times. In other words, the local circulation of wealth – the effect of the purchasing power as well as the charitable largesse of the rich – was now constricted. The traditional location of urban mansions in the middle of the fray had made them local employment opportunities for servants, retainers, and suppliers. Like the religious foundations that punctuated the urban landscape – those conglomerates of mosque, college, soup kitchen, hospital, public bath, and children's Quran school – the residences of the wealthy functioned as nuclei of neighborhoods, vehicles of urban renewal, and durable resources in local economies.

MATERIALISM AND ETHICAL PROPORTION

Like many other societies, the early modern Ottoman world was beset by conflicting social ideologies. Chronic misgivings about the justice of class difference persisted alongside tenacious habits of honoring the wealthy and the prominent. In Muslim tradition, wealth was not seen as inherently corrupting, in contrast to the Christian view, nor was commerce frowned upon as it was in the Confucian view. Wealthy merchants who displayed civic-mindedness were *ayan*, "urban dignitaries," and it was not considered incongruous to pair the *ayan* with the *ashraf*, "religious dignitaries," as the two principal pillars of the community.

Hierarchy was everywhere in the Ottoman world, whether its organizing principle was ancestral lineage, learning, earned wealth, sectarian identity, or other forms of distinction such as military prowess. People were tolerant of the lavish consumption habits of the elites – indeed, they expected them. What *did* offend popular moral sentiment was the excessively ostentatious display of wealth. This criticism, directed less toward "having" than toward "showing off," was symptomatic of the general attitude that to break social and moral codes *publicly* was a greater sin than to do so within the walls of one's home. The measure of honor was, in the main, the quality of one's public conduct.

In the early eighteenth century, things got out of hand when the rich and prominent in Istanbul appeared to lose sight of the principle of ethical

---

[28] Şerif Mardin, "Super Westernization in Urban Life in the Ottoman Empire in the Last Quarter of the Nineteenth Century," in P. Benedict and E. Tümertekin (eds.), *Turkey: Geographical and Social Perspectives* (Leiden: Brill, 1974), pp. 409ff.

proportion in material possessions. The immediate problem was the mania for tulips and tulip gardens that seemed to set off a riot of decadent living.[29] Led by the sultan Ahmed III, his daughters, and his high officials, the elite of Istanbul spent fortunes on exotic varieties of tulips, pleasure palaces, and garden parties illuminated by candles fixed to the backs of turtles. The tulip craze was accompanied by an exaggerated consumerism and an appetite for foreign fashions and goods. In the eye of the resentful public, these ostentatious excesses went hand in hand with other moral disruptions, including the too public presence of women.[30]

The motives of the discontented who joined in a popular revolt in 1730 against Ahmed III and his circle were complex, but the ethics of conspicuous consumption loomed large. Normally, the public granted the sultan his entertainments, which had the virtue of advertising to the rest of the world (through the eyes of resident ambassadors) the refinement and prosperity of the empire's court. Moreover, Istanbul's economy benefited from supplying the needs of the city's elites. But it was hardly the appropriate time to indulge in such sustained and conspicuous partying, for the empire was currently waging an unsuccessful war with Iran. Old poetic tropes held that the enjoyment of forbidden pleasures such as wine-filled banquets (*bezm*) was the sultan's reward at the conclusion of battle (*rezm*). One of the principal grievances of the Istanbul rebels and their supporters in 1730 was the startling gap between the burden of wartime privation and extra taxation borne by ordinary people and the seeming "devil may care" behavior of the elite. When Ahmed III was forced to abdicate by the rebels, his successor not surprisingly attempted to turn around the capital's mood. He rescinded taxes, razed the royal palace called Sa'adabad – the "Abode of Happiness," modeled on Versailles – and organized a pilgrimage up the Golden Horn to the city's principal religious shrine.[31]

The 1730 revolt had a long genealogy of uprisings whose immediate causes differed but whose shared grievances included unjust burdens imposed on subjects by rulers, exacerbated by improper rewards bestowed on favorites who had not, in the public's judgment, earned the benefits they enjoyed. Earlier, such popular movements had been led by religious

---

[29] For a provocative reflection on the tulip in the imagination as well as the economy, see Ariel Salzmann, "The Age of Tulips: Confluence and Conflict in Early Modern Consumer Culture (1550–1730)," in İnalcık and Quataert, *Consumption Studies*, pp. 83–106. See also the perceptive remarks of Suraiya Faroqhi on representations of the sultans through festivity and ceremony (*An Economic and Social History of the Ottoman Empire*, pp. 616–19).
[30] Madeline Zilfi, "Women and Society in the Tulip Era," in A. Sonbol (ed.), *Women, the Family and Divorce Laws in Islamic History* (Syracuse, NY: Syracuse University Press, 1996), pp. 294–303.
[31] Salzmann, "The Age of Tulips," pp. 95–7.

figures: the 1241 revolt inspired by the charismatic Baba Rasul, the 1416 uprising of Sheikh Bedreddin, the huge revolt of Shah Kulu in 1511, and the Turkmen revolts that troubled the early years of Süleyman I's reign. Later, after the Ottoman regime consolidated its authority over provincial society, it was by its own rank-and-file soldiers and often in Istanbul that popular uprisings were spearheaded: the several janissary uprisings beginning in 1584 that protested pay irregularities, the regicide of Osman II in 1622, the 1656 uprising mentioned above, and finally the 1730 rebellion. Resistance might take on a radical dimension with regard to property. Bedreddin's Balkan revolt was accompanied by a dervish-led movement in western Anatolia that promised a utopia wherein all things would be held in common, except women.[32] Popular lore had its Robin Hood in Köroğlu, the legendary troubador and mountain bandit who was celebrated among Turks and Kurds as well as Armenians and Georgians for plundering caravans and distributing their wares among the dispossessed.[33]

THE MANDATE TO GIVE

What made the inevitable discrepancies in material well-being tolerable was the moral imperative to circulate wealth through charity and philanthropy. In premodern times, public assistance came more in the form of individual gifts and acts of charity than through state-supplied aid disbursed through bureaucratic agencies. Alms-giving, one of the five duties of a Muslim, had its roots in the belief that giving away a portion of one's income purified what remained (a belief that was widespread in late antiquity, when Islamic doctrine was taking form). Over time, however, Islamic *zakat* – the annual tithe on wealth – was not always regularly or systematically collected, and it was sometimes even resisted when governments imposed it as a tax.[34] By Ottoman times, voluntary giving – *sadaka* – was a much more powerful force in the everyday world in addressing imbalances in wealth and well-being. The habits of local giving – of giving where specific need was obvious – seem to have won out over state-managed redistribution, with its anonymity and also its potential for corruption.

---

[32] A good short account of this two-pronged movement can be found in Colin Imber, *The Ottoman Empire 1300–1481* (Istanbul: İsis Press, 1990), pp. 82–7.
[33] Köprülüzade Mehmet Fuat, *Türk Sazşairleri*, 4 vols. (Istanbul, 1930), vol. IV.
[34] Timur Kuran, "Islamic Redistribution through *Zakat*: Historical Record and Modern Realities," in M. Bonner, M. Ener, and A. Singer (eds.), *Poverty and Charity in Middle Eastern Contexts* (Albany, NY: SUNY Press, 2003), pp. 275–93.

Apart from recipients of charity, almost everyone gave, from the sultan on down to the peasant. In 1540, when Süleyman the Magnificent had just recently begun the repair and embellishment of Jerusalem's water supply, walls, and holy sites, the villager Köse Bayram was doing his part by donating a sizeable house (it had a stable and a full kitchen) to his local mosque as a residence for the village imam.[35] Köse Bayram was obviously a man of property, perhaps a leading figure in his village, but even people without much to share strove to do their part, although their charity was likely to escape public notice, let alone the annals of history.

For Muslims, charitable giving was a pious act whose contours were shaped by the Quran. The deserving were not only the poor and the indigent. The Quranic verse most explicit in naming those who merit alms (9:60) also lists debtors, those "in bondage" (slaves, war prisoners), converts to Islam, wayfarers, persons who administer alms, and those "in the cause of God."[36] In addition, Islam inherited from Jewish and Christian practice a concern for orphans and widows. In Ottoman towns, it was often the judge who was responsible for allocating public assistance to orphans and widows in distress. There was also the habit shared by some Muslim and Christian households of taking in poor orphans (especially girls) as something between servant and family member: although not paid a wage for their work, these girls were fed, clothed, and later provided with a dowry. This last concern – providing the poor with the material resources to get married – was widespread: the famous seventeenth-century queen mother Kösem sought out orphaned girls too poor to marry and provided them not only with a dowry but also with lodging and home furnishings. A formidable purveyor of charity, Kösem was also known for leaving the palace incognito to arrange for the release of imprisoned debtors.[37]

The form taken by much of Muslim giving was waqf, a practice so ubiquitous that it is worth dwelling on. Waqf was the endowment of an income source to an institution serving the public welfare (for example, a school or a mosque) or to direct charity (for example, the distribution of clothing or cooking supplies during the holy month of Ramadan). A person establishing a waqf specified, first, the source of income to be endowed (an agricultural tract, a rental shop, even a herd of sheep) and, second, the charitable use or institution to which the income was to be assigned. Or,

---

[35] Gaziantep Şer'iye Sicili No. 2 (120c, d).
[36] For a discussion of alms recipients, see Ingrid Mattson, "Status-based Definitions of Need in Early Islamic *Zakat* and Maintenance Laws," in Bonner et al., *Poverty and Charity*, pp. 31–51.
[37] Mustafa Na'imâ, *Tarih*, vol. V, p. 113.

like Köse Bayram, a person could simply make a gift of the income source (in this case, the house), which the institution (the local mosque) could then rent out. The very wealthy might first undertake to build a new institution – paying for land, labor, and costs of construction – and then create a waqf for its upkeep. Since the rules governing the establishment of a waqf were prescribed by the shari'a, making waqf was a religious act. However, the basic similarities between Muslim and non-Muslim charitable habits meant that a Christian monastery, with its sources of income, could be regulated under the Ottoman sultans as a waqf.[38]

Waqf shaped the geography of the Ottoman city. Mosques, madrasas, primary schools, hospitals and insane asylums, fountains, covered markets, khans (large commercial warehouses containing office space and rooms for traveling merchants), soup kitchens, sufi shrines and lodges, the tombs of sultans – all these were typically waqf-supported establishments that served subjects of the empire. As for the countryside, it had its own amenities financed by waqf: caravansaries (the highway version of the khan), bridges, reservoirs, acqueducts, and more shrines. The wealthiest patrons might establish a complex of buildings, typically anchored by a mosque. The greatest of these were, naturally, built and endowed by the sultans, primarily in the three Ottoman capitals of Bursa, Edirne, and Istanbul. The complex of Süleyman I, "the Magnificent," crowning one of Istanbul's highest hills, consisted of a mosque, four madrasas for the study of the religious sciences, one for the study of medicine, a school for the study of hadith, a soup kitchen, a hospital, a primary school, and the tombs of the sultan, his concubine-made-wife Hurrem, and Sinan, the famed architect of this and many other sixteenth-century complexes. A public bath and shops on the ground floor of two of the madrasas helped generate income for the waqf.

Royal women – the sisters, mothers, and concubines of the sultans – were also prominent patrons of major complexes who often located their projects in more distant centers of the empire. Hurrem, for example, endowed a large religious and charitable foundation in Jerusalem that included a hospice for religious pilgrims, a soup kitchen for the indigent, and an inn for travelers. It was surely no coincidence that Hurrem chose to locate her project on the alleged site of a pilgrim hospice built by Saint Helena. The mother of Constantine, the Byzantine emperor and founder

---

[38] For the Ottoman regime's attempts in the 1570s to reformulate the status of Christian monasteries in Ottoman-Islamic terms, see the discussion by Aleksandar Fotić, "The Official Explanations for the Confiscation and Sale of Monasteries (Churches) and their Estates at the Time of Selim II," *Turcica* 26 (1994): 33–54.

of Constantinople, Helena became a Christian before her son and mirac-
ulously discovered Christian sites and relics during her pilgrimage to the
holy city in the 330s. Hurrem thus honored her predecessor but also
signaled that Islamic patronage had replaced Christian patronage.

The local well-to-do did not lag far behind their rulers in making waqf.
"Noblesse oblige" – that universal social pressure on persons of means to use
their wealth for the betterment of society – was an important stimulus
motivating acts of charity and philanthropy in the hundreds of places that
were passed over by the dynastic family. Such places were dependent on their
own resources and initiative for the provision of urban amenities. In Iraqi
Mosul, for example, local notables built mosques in memory of a revered
family member or of a local saint.[39] "Citizen" waqfs proliferated because they
fused piety and generosity with urban (and sometimes family) pride. This is
the point of a legend from Aintab about a carpenter who built a mosque that
became the focal point of a city district that came to bear his name, Ali
Neccar ("Ali the carpenter"). As the story goes, Ali decides to test the money
he has painstakingly saved for the mosque he wants to build in order to be
sure that it is *helal* – that is, legitimately acquired. Concealing the gold in the
hollowed-out trunk of a tree, which he tosses into the River Sacur at a
moment when its waters are particularly turbulent, Ali then enters into a
period of pious resignation and waits to see if the log will be recovered (a sign
of the money's purity). When, months later, a peasant from one of the
villages on the shores of the Sacur brings the log into his shop with the
request that the carpenter repair his plow with a fragment from it, Ali gives
thanks to God and embarks on the construction of the mosque.[40] Such a
story, of course, was meant to inspire others to emulate this ordinary man.

Trends in charitable and philanthropic giving can tell us something
about cultural permanencies as well as cultural novelties and particularities.
The pairing of mosque and marketplace (income from the latter might
support the former) was so common as to become a hallmark of the
Ottoman city. And because so many founding patrons of these establishments belonged to the imperial elite, who shared an aesthetic canon
developed for their exclusive use,[41] Bosnian Sarajevo could be visually

[39] Dina Rizk Khoury, "Slippers at the Entrance or Behind Closed Doors: Domestic and Public Spaces for Mosuli Women," in Zilfi (ed.), *Women in the Ottoman Empire*, p. 111.
[40] Cemil Cahit Güzelbey, *Gaziantep Camileri Tarihi* (Gaziantep: Evkaf Matbaası, 1984, reprinted 1992), pp. 37–8. This story is taken from my *Morality Tales*, pp. 44–5.
[41] Gülru Necipoğlu, "A Kanun for the State, A Canon for the Arts: Conceptualizing the Classical Synthesis of Ottoman Art and Architecture," in Gilles Veinstein (ed.), *Soliman le Magnifique et son*

kin, at least in its city center, to cities in the Ottoman east. On the other hand, philanthropy was also flexible, and could respond to new forms of sociability. When enthusiasm for coffee, which became wildly popular in the seventeenth century, created a demand (by males) for coffeehouses, big waqf makers eagerly built them as a new way to generate income. Coffeehouses were typically associated with commercial establishments, and in fact that association continues today – a visitor to Istanbul's great covered bazaar can sip a cup of Turkish coffee right in the midst of shopper traffic. In particular locales, philanthropic choices by native elites could influence identity and political attachment. In eighteenth-century Mosul, for example, the powerful Jalili family promoted loyalties to the city as a whole and to itself, undermining the neighborhood as the locus of communal solidarity by building large commercial complexes that turned people's attention to new spaces and new social groupings (coffeehouses helped here too). Jalili women contributed to this reorientation of loyalties outward by building mosques in new districts.[42]

WAQF AND SELF-INTEREST

In obituary notices and in the biographical encyclopedias they habitually kept, the Ottomans routinely and scrupulously listed the *hayrat*, "good works" or "pious deeds," of notable members of the "giving classes." But it was difficult for charity and philanthropy to be selfless for the very reason that the acts of the wealthy and the prominent were both noticed and catalogued, just as their consumption habits and residential choices were commented upon. And no doubt many knowingly calculated the honor that their pious philanthropy would afford them. With ordinary people too, there was often a quid pro quo. Donations to churches and mosques were frequently made in return for the promise of prayers to be recited for the donor upon his or her death. People were certainly aware of the uncomfortable paradox that God's mandate to give could bring valuable returns. Particularly with aid delivered to the poor, ways were found to honor the belief that God was the ultimate giver and that the recipient should be spared the humiliation of accepting handouts. Anonymity was preserved by depositing food and cash in receptacles from which the needy

---

temps (Paris: Documentation Française, 1992), p. 207; see also Heghnar Zeitlian Watenpaugh, *The Image of an Ottoman City: Imperial Architecture and Urban Experience in Aleppo in the 16th and 17th Centuries* (Leiden: Brill, 2004), passim.
[42] Khoury, "Slippers at the Entrance," pp. 110–11.

could later retrieve them (in Anatolian Konya, for example, deep troughs were carved into the stone entrance portal of a mosque complex).[43]

Waqf was a complex and flexible practice, and the entrepreneurial classes of the Ottoman Empire were quick to make profitable use of the worldly benefit that could be derived from waqf-based charity. A sizable waqf was a vehicle for family employment because the waqf founder could specify who would act as the manager of the foundation and for what salary. Waqf managers could be women – for example, 'Atiyat al-Rahman, daughter of a Cairo merchant who chose the astute 'Atiyat over his two sons.[44] Waqfs were of course vulnerable to corruption: a dishonest manager might divert a waqf's capital from the purposes specified by the founder. Especially in times of weak government, even urban officials shamelessly exploited waqf institutions. In Damascus right before the Ottoman conquest (1517), the chief Hanafi judge was actually selling endowments, and another judge was allowing mosques and cemeteries to be dismantled so he could sell the material as scrap.[45]

Moreover, there was a "family" form of waqf in which the beneficiary was not a public institution but rather the waqf founder's own kin (to satisfy the religious nature of waqf, the founder had to name an existing religious foundation – often one of the venerable institutions in Mecca or Medina – as ultimate beneficiary should the family line die out). 'Atiyat's husband, the wealthy businessman Isma'il Abu Taqiyya, turned a khan he had just finished building into a family waqf when, in 1620, the Ottoman governor threatened merchants with confiscation of property (waqf was theoretically immune from seizure whereas private property was not).[46] Putting property into either family or charitable waqf could also be an inheritance dodge, since two-thirds of a person's estate went automatically to heirs dictated by Islamic law; waqf allowed its founder to choose who would benefit at his or her death. Gender interests were no doubt a factor in strategizing with waqf: males could disinherit female family members through waqf bequests, but women in turn could use waqf to the benefit of their children or other females. Indeed, people used the waqf deed as a kind of will, often leaving sums of money to non-kin dependants, including slaves. No wonder waqfs were so universal a feature of the Ottoman

---

[43] Ethel Sara Wolper, "Understanding the Public Face of Piety: Philanthropy and Architecture in Late Seljuk Anatolia," *Mesogeios* 25–6 (2005): 311–36.

[44] Nelly Hanna, *Making Big Money in 1600: The Life and Times of Isma'il Abu Taqiyya, Egyptian Merchant* (Syracuse, NY: Syracuse University Press, 1998), p. 150.

[45] Muhammad Adnan Bakhit, *The Ottoman Province of Damascus in the Sixteenth Century* (Beirut: Librairie du Liban, 1982), p. 5, notes 21 and 22.

[46] Hanna, *Making Big Money*, pp. 125–6.

landscape, since individuals could adapt them to their personal material goals, whether to accumulate or to give away.

***

Almost everyone in the Ottoman world, except perhaps for itinerant mystics, lived in an environment that was conditioned by material things, from jewelry to household and workshop implements to dwellings. Even the humble attended to their possessions, which had value not only as property but as an expression of who one was. The existence of women's carefully protected economy of objects serves to underline this point: this separate material world had to do with strategies of survival in a largely patriarchal society, but it also communicated female pride and identity. The interplay between consumption and high status was another social language spoken by material objects.

Yet for all that the display of possessions – whether on one's person, in one's reception room, or in a legal document – contributed to defining the self, the material world was underpinned by deeply held beliefs about the individual's relationship to family, to community, and to God. For Muslims, the fact that Islamic law prescribed how estates should be distributed among even distant degrees of relatives reminded people that ownership could not be separated, ultimately, from responsiblity for others. The universal concern for those who fell outside the safety net of family – widows and orphans – was another recognition that the family's collective material well-being was the best survival insurance.

The moral injunctions of religion were important in keeping people's attention focused on the larger picture, that is on the necessity for taking care of the needy who were not a part of one's kin, neighborhood, or workplace. We have, I think, to give the subjects of the premodern Ottoman Empire good marks on this score. It is customary to assume that the leaders of society – in this case, the sultan first of all, but also the notables of each city quarter, town, or village – set a model that more modest people then emulated. But this is a somewhat cynical view of causation that assumes that giving comes with social station. If charity and philanthropy were sometimes about looking good as well as doing good, that was far from the whole story. The legend about Ali the carpenter and his mosque reminds us that what is inevitably missed by the written historical record, but sometimes captured in oral lore, is the multitude of mundane actors who bore in mind the material and spiritual needs of others.

10

Urban voices from beyond: identity, status and social strategies in Ottoman Muslim funerary epitaphs of Istanbul (1700–1850)

Edhem Eldem

Much has been written about the strong relationship between cemeteries and the evolution of cities. In the past decades, western historiography has often dealt with this aspect of urban culture; a classic in the genre is Ariès' *Western Attitudes toward Death*, which, within the broader framework of analysis of the evolution of the perception of death from the Middle Ages to the present, devotes much attention to some crucial changes in funerary practices and in the use and design of burial grounds in western urban centers. Most remarkable in this respect are his observations concerning the emergence of medieval cemeteries as *charniers* (charnel houses) where corpses would be buried with little concern for individual graves.[1] These urban burial grounds were often contained within churchyards, and survived well into the eighteenth century, when they started to be replaced by "modern" cemeteries, lying outside the city walls, and reflecting a desire to assign a private and individualized tomb to the deceased.[2] This relative lack of interest for the individualization of sepulchers was to a certain extent compensated by a renewed concern for funerary inscriptions in the name of the deceased. The practice had been gradually abandoned from the fifth century on, but by the thirteenth century, anonymous gravestones gradually gave way to monuments for the illustrious and, more frequently, to modest plaques bearing a succinct inscription stating the identity of the departed.[3]

The development of Ottoman Muslim cemeteries and tombs seems to have followed a somewhat different path during the same period. Despite obvious similarities between the churchyard and the Ottoman *hazire*

---

[1] Philippe Ariès, *Western Attitudes toward Death: From the Middle Ages to the Present*, trans. Patricia M. Ranum (Baltimore, MD: Johns Hopkins University Press, 1975), pp. 18–22.

[2] Ibid., pp. 69–73; Hans-Peter Laqueur, "Cemeteries in Orient and Occident. The Historical Development," in J.-L. Bacqué-Grammont and A. Tibet (eds.), *Cimetières et traditions funéraires dans le monde islamique*, 2 vols. (Ankara: Türk Tarih Kurumu, 1996), vol. II, pp. 4–5.

[3] Ariès, *Western Attitudes*, pp. 46–9.

(enclosed graveyard, generally associated with a mosque), the Ottoman tradition appears to have preempted western burial practices on two crucial points. First, the principle of the sacredness and inviolability of the grave was applied with such severity as to render impossible the use of common graves or the reuse of individual sepulchral space.[4] This peculiarity was so strikingly different from western practices that, as late as the first half of the nineteenth century, Pardoe, observing Ottoman cemeteries, felt compelled to remark that "There is no burying and reburying on the same spot, as with us. The remains of the departed are sacred."[5] Second, from a very early date, Ottoman authorities had systematically promoted the development of *extra muros* or suburban burial grounds, much in the style of western cemeteries of the late eighteenth and nineteenth centuries. The large cemeteries surrounding Istanbul were a typical example of this practice, which could be traced back to the late fifteenth century when most of these lands were endowed for this purpose within the waqf of Sultan Bayezid II.[6] This phenomenon was so striking to early modern western visitors that practically no travel account failed to report on the remarkable nature of these "*champs des morts*,"[7] so different from anything in their homeland.[8] There is no doubt that these two basic aspects of Ottoman burial practices were linked: the inviolability of the tomb, rendering impossible the recycling of sepulchral space, required the designation of large stretches of land for the sole purpose of receiving the dead of a growing urban population.

One point where early modern western and Ottoman practices appear to have followed a rather similar path is the development of the epitaph. From

[4] Nicolas Vatin and Stéphane Yerasimos, *Les cimetières dans la ville. Statut, choix et organisation des lieux d'inhumation dans Istanbul intra-muros* (Paris: Institut français d'études anatoliennes Georges Dumézil, 2001), pp. 9–19.
[5] Julia Pardoe, *The City of the Sultan*, 4th edn (London: Routledge, 1854), p. 50.
[6] Vatin and Yerasimos, *Les cimetières dans la ville*, pp. 1–5.
[7] "Fields of the dead," a French expression often used to translate the Ottoman term of *kabristan* (cemetery) used to describe the large cemeteries surrounding the city, as opposed to the *hazire* (graveyard) within the city.
[8] Nicolas Vatin, "L'inhumation *intra-muros* à Istanbul à l'époque ottomane," in G. Veinstein (ed.), *Les Ottomans et la mort. Permanences et mutations* (Leiden: Brill, 1996), pp. 157–60. It appears that Ottoman cemeteries may even have played a role in inspiring western urban planners of the modern era, as the following passage from an article by a nineteenth-century British cemetery reformer would suggest: "The Turkish cemeteries are generally out of the city, on rising ground, planted with cedars, cypresses, and odoriferous shrubs, whose deep verdure and graceful forms bending in every breeze give a melancholy beauty to the place, and excite sentiments very congenial to its destination." John Claudius Loudon, "On the Laying Out, Planting, and Managing of Cemeteries and on the Improvement of Churchyards," *The Gardener's Magazine* (1843): 405; quoted in Brian Johnson, "Istanbul's Vanished City of the Dead: The Grand Champ des Morts," in Nezih Başgelen and Brian Johnson (eds.), *Myths to Modernity. Efsanelerden Günümüze, 1, Istanbul. Selected Themes. Seçme Yazılar* (Istanbul: Archaeology and Art Publications, 2002), p. 98.

the very start, the Ottomans had shown little sympathy for the most orthodox views in Islam that saw with great disgust (*ikrah*) even the most inconspicuous mound embellishing the grave.[9] Quite to the contrary, early Ottoman epitaphs, very much like other medieval Muslim epitaphs of Anatolia, made a point of stating precisely the name and date of death of each individual, adding to this biographical data an occasional passage from the Quran or from a hadith. Most of the surviving stones from this period display a very conscious desire to erect a durable and ornate tombstone in memory of the departed, often reaching truly monumental dimensions, as in the case of the tall and highly decorated structures of Ahlat, in eastern Anatolia.[10] True, the very small number of surviving gravestones from this early period suggests that, independently of the obvious destructive impact of time, the use of these monuments was to a large extent restricted to the elite, and that most probably commoners had to make do with much less durable stelae, or even with a grave left unmarked. Yet the phenomenon remains significant enough to assume that, their status and means permitting, early Ottomans had adopted the notion of associating an individual grave with the erection of a tombstone bearing an epitaph identifying the deceased, much as in contemporary western societies.[11]

A major turning point in Ottoman funerary art seems to have occurred around the sixteenth century, with the gradual emergence of a specifically Ottoman style. Three major changes constituted the basis of this transformation: first, the use of headgear to identify the deceased's status, the earliest examples of which can be traced back to the first half of the fifteenth century, with the adoption of a square section and stake-shaped stela topped by a turban imitating the headgear placed on the bier during

[9] Werner Diem and Marco Schöller, *The Living and the Dead in Islam. Studies in Arabic Epitaphs* (Wiesbaden: Harrassowitz, 2004), pp. 169–80.
[10] For examples of pre- and early-Ottoman Anatolian funerary epigraphy, see Beyhan Karamağaralı, *Ahlat Mezar Taşları* (Ankara: Kültür Bakanlığı, 1992); Demet Karaçağ, *Bursa'daki 14.–15. Yüzyıl Mezar Taşları* (Ankara: n.p., 1994); Karl Wulzinger, Paul Wittek and Friedrich Sarre, *Das islamische Milet* (Berlin: De Gruyter, 1935); Şerif Başkan, *Karamanoğulları Dönemi Konya Mezar Taşları* (Ankara: Kültür Bakanlığı, 1996); Assadullah S. Melikian-Chirvani, "Recherches sur les sources de l'art ottoman: les stèles funéraires d'Ayasoluk I," *Turcica* 4 (1972): 103–33; "Les stèles funéraires d'Ayasoluk II," *Turcica* 7 (1975): 105–21; "Les stèles funéraires d'Ayasoluk III. Deux colonnes funéraires de l'an 1439," *Turcica* 8/2 (1976): 83–90.
[11] "These plaques are relatively unknown because they have been neglected by art historians. They are, however, very interesting to the historian of mentalities, for they were the most common form of funeral monuments until the eighteenth century. Some were simple inscriptions in Latin or French: 'Here lies John Doe, who died on such and such a day,' and then his occupation" (Ariès, *Western Attitudes*, pp. 48–9).

funeral processions;[12] second, the passage from Arabic to Turkish in the inscription, a phenomenon that can be dated to the sixteenth century; and, third, the constitution of a standard model consisting of an invocation to God, followed by a description/identification of the deceased and a request for a prayer for his/her soul, and ending with a date.[13] There is no doubt that this basic model served a practical purpose, that of bringing greater clarity to the inscription and to the monument as a whole, by offering an easily recognizable representation of social standing through headgear, and a clear identification of the deceased through a direct and standardized epitaph written in the vernacular. By providing a perennial inscription to their dead, the Ottomans were, much like their western counterparts, displaying "a continuing effort to connect present and past, to attach the seemingly transient to the permanent, and also to assert individuality against the threat of personal annihilation."[14]

These inscriptions were laconic and would remain so until the end of the empire in a great number of cases, with a function limited to a very succinct identification of the departed.[15] Yet, starting with the eighteenth century,

---

[12] On the variety and typology of headgear, see Hans-Peter Laqueur, "Die Kopfbedeckungen im osmanischen Reich als soziales Erkennungszeichen, dargestellt anhand einiger Istanbuler Grabsteine des 18. und 19. Jahrhunderts," *Der Islam* 59/1 (1982): 80–92; Hans-Peter Laqueur, *Hüve'l-Baki. İstanbul'da Osmanlı Mezarlıkları ve Mezar Taşları* (Istanbul: Tarih Vakfı Yurt Yayınları, 1997), pp. 138–60. Many authors, including Laqueur, have tended to interpret the use of headgear as an indication of the survival of pre-Islamic Turkic traditions of human representation on gravestones (Laqueur, *Hüve'l-Baki*, pp. 3–6). While agreeing with the notion that Ottoman turbaned grave-stones *eventually* took on an anthropomorphic outlook, especially with the widening of the surface of the stela from the eighteenth century on, and that this phenomenon was widely internalized by the Ottoman Muslim population, I do not believe that the initial thrust in this direction ever went beyond a desire to use the headgear as a mere illustration of status, quite independently of a sculptural representation of the human body. If anything, early examples of stones displaying turbans remind one of hatstands rather than of any sort of humanoid sculpture. In fact, it seems that the main inspiration for this model was provided not by the human body, but by the practice of placing a turban at the head of the funeral bier during burial processions and on cenotaphs within mausolea. Edhem Eldem, *Death in Istanbul. Death and its Rituals in Ottoman-Islamic Culture* (Istanbul: Ottoman Bank Archives and Research Centre, 2005), pp. 49, 52, 86–7, 92–3, 172.

[13] For an analysis of the basic model for Ottoman funerary epitaphs, see Erich Prokosch, *Osmanische Grabinschriften. Leitfaden zu ihrer sprachlichen Erfassung* (Berlin: Klaus Schwarz, 1993); Laqueur, *Hüve'l-Baki*, pp. 80–95; Nicolas Vatin, "La notation du nom propre sur les stèles funéraires ottomanes," in A.-M. Christin (ed.), *L'écriture du nom propre* (Paris: Harmattan, 1998), pp. 135–48.

[14] Vanessa Harding, *The Dead and the Living in Paris and London, 1500–1670* (Cambridge: Cambridge University Press, 2002), p. 157.

[15] This was also the case with most western epitaphs: "Very many epitaphs celebrated private virtue as well as, or rather than, public careers . . . Far more numerous, however, were inscriptions which said nothing at all about the personal qualities of the deceased, but simply provided the basic facts of age at, and date of, death together with place of residence and names of closest relations," Ralph Houlbrooke, "The Age of Decency: 1660–1760," in Peter C. Jupp and Clare Gittings (eds.), *Death in England. An Illustrated History* (New Brunswick: Rutgers University Press, 2000), p. 196.

an ever-increasing number of epitaphs began to include a small narrative, more often than not taking the form of stock verses created and transmitted through an oral popular culture. Short distiches or quatrains would voice the laments of parents grieving after the untimely loss of their child, tell the story of a fresh rosebud mowed down by the autumn wind, request a prayer for the soul of the deceased with a promise of salvation in return, or simply remind the visitor of the transience of this world and of the permanence of the other.[16] This new literary format showed even more clearly what the ultimate purpose of tombstones was: to establish contact with an audience – the living – that would ensure the perpetuation of the memory of the dead, and the salvation of their souls through prayers.[17]

This long introduction brings us to the starting point of this study on the evolution of Ottoman epitaphs in Istanbul on the eve of modernity or, more precisely, between 1700 and 1850. The logic behind the selection of these dates is largely linked to the preceding observations on the evolution of the typical Ottoman epitaph. By the beginning of the eighteenth century, the standard epitaph described above had reached a level of maturation that set it as a model for practically all of the Ottoman territories, from Anatolia to Bosnia. The phenomenon was even more visible in Istanbul, from where the model and its variations had originated, and where the production and use of durable monuments, generally made of marble, had reached unprecedented levels. If one is to judge from the number of surviving stones today, it is clear that it is only from that time on

---

[16] Edhem Eldem, "L'écrit funéraire ottoman: création, reproduction, transmission," *Oral et écrit dans le monde turco-ottoman*, special issue of *Revue du Monde Musulman et de la Méditerranée*, 75/76 (1996): 65–78; Eldem, *Death in Istanbul*, pp. 130–4.

[17] Again, a rather universal concern, if one considers the similarities with western practice: "Medieval Londoners and Parisians seem to have shared the view that one of the principal aims of the monument, whatever form it took, was to create a link in the mind of the pious viewer between the name of the deceased and the responsibility of the Christian to pray for the salvation of others. Robert Garstang, grocer, of London ordered in 1460 that a new marble stone be placed over his body with the name and sign and the arms of his company, 'to have me in special memory'; William Turke, fishmonger, in 1480, asked his executors to provide 'a stone with a scripture thereon remembering my name and the names of my said wife and daughter Joan, to the intent of having our souls prayed for.'" Harding, *The Dead and the Living*, p. 158. The resemblance becomes all the more striking if one considers the parallelism between western and Ottoman epitaphs. Thus an epitaph dated 1433, found in the *charnier* of the Innocents, in Paris ("Quiconque passe par cette loye / je lui supplie quil me regarde / prie dieu pour moy et pense et voye / et a son etat preigne garde") could easily be translated by the very popular Ottoman epitaph of "Ziyaretden murad bir duadır / Bugün bana ise yarın sanadır" ("Visitor, say a prayer for me / As I lie today so tomorrow will be thee," or literally, "What is expected from a visit is a prayer / If today is my turn, tomorrow will be yours"). Ibid., p. 158; Eldem, *Death in Istanbul*, pp. 130–1.

that tombstones start to appear in significant numbers.[18] To what extent this disequilibrium may be related to the cumulative ravages of time is open to discussion, but there is little doubt that the phenomenon is closely linked to a number of factors of some relevance. For one, the synchronicity between the momentum gained by the exploitation of the marble quarries of the Isle of Marmara, conveniently located at a short shipping distance from the capital, and the apparent increase in the number of monuments points to a very probable "democratization" of funerary art as a result of the relative cheapening of marble,[19] as confirmed by the appearance of tombstones commemorating men and women from practically all walks of life. Nor can one discard the fact that the disparity between earlier monuments and tombstones of the eighteenth century cannot be reduced to a simple quantitative difference, but has to be sought in very concrete qualitative variations, such as a longer inscription, greater detail in the identification of the deceased, and a much more frequent use of poetry. This qualitative change is felt even more clearly in the overall outlook of the monuments. Their greater size and better finishing, the increased calligraphic quality of the inscriptions, and the growing use of architectonic and naturalist decorative elements all point in the direction of a major shift prefiguring the vast expanses covered with ornate tombstones that would fascinate western travelers of the nineteenth century. Once again, Ottoman tombstones appear to have embarked on a process of transformation very similar to that witnessed in contemporary western societies.[20]

If, then, one admits the existence of a turning point, arbitrary as it may be, located at around the beginning of the eighteenth century, a closer look at the century and a half that follows may reveal a number of aspects of the evolution of tombstones at the crucial juncture of the transition from a mature premodern environment to a modern or modernizing one. Setting 1850 as the end of this period is obviously also an arbitrary choice; yet it

[18] The sample we have used for this study (see n. 27 below) clearly shows the highly unbalanced distribution of tombstones in Istanbul. Only 2 percent of the sample consists of monuments erected before 1700; the proportion rises to 15 percent for the eighteenth century and the remaining 83 percent belong to the "long" nineteenth century, down to 1922.

[19] Nicolas Vatin, "Notes sur l'exploitation du marbre et l'île de Marmara Adası (Proconnèse) à l'époque ottomane," *Turcica* 32 (2000): 307–62.

[20] "It was during the later seventeenth century that more durable or substantial churchyard monuments first began to be erected in relatively large numbers. Social emulation in the middling ranks of society was probably an important reason for this development . . . The prosperous middling ranks of society were seeking during this period not only to protect the bodies of their relatives by means of more durable and substantial coffins but also to preserve their memories in stone. These were two manifestations of standards of politeness and decency which were shared by an increasing proportion of the population." Houlbrooke, "The Age of Decency," p. 197.

seems safe enough to assume that two decades after the movement of reform initiated by Sultan Mahmud II and one decade after the Tanzimat Decree should constitute a reasonable approximation for the appearance of the first signs of change induced by systematic modernization and its inevitable counterpart, westernization. The question remains, however, of knowing what exactly should be measured, and how. The aim being to qualify the nature of the evolution of Muslim epitaphs in Ottoman Istanbul at the end of the early modern period, one would have to find ways of determining some crucial elements of Ottoman funerary art that may be of some relevance in this respect and whose change can be measured against time. For purposes of simplification and in order to avoid a risk of dispersion induced by too many variables, this study will rely on one specific component of funerary monuments, the epitaph, and more particularly on that part of the epitaph devoted to the identification of the deceased. The contention behind this choice is that, as a result of the widening use of tombstones and of the growing complexity of the urban society of the capital of the empire, the traditional format used to describe an individual lost much of its efficiency and usefulness and had to be modified to adapt to the changing conditions of the time. In other words, the central argument is that, between 1700 and 1850, the way in which individuals were identified on their tombstones gained in sophistication, thus becoming a form of expression of the growing complexity of urban culture.

No doubt, a corollary of this way of looking at epitaphs is the assumption that tombstones functioned as social markers rather than as purely religious and sentimental mementos of the departed. Indeed, had the sole aim been to remember the deceased, and to erect some kind of a durable reminder in his memory, a simple mention of his name would have been quite sufficient. Yet most of the research conducted on Ottoman cemeteries and tombstones concurs to show that, especially in urban environments, a clear trend could be observed in the direction of a growing concern for a precise identification of the deceased in his social, professional, and familial setting. The simple fact that the spatial organization of Ottoman cemeteries was to a large extent determined by a desire to increase the visibility of the tombs is sufficient proof that the underlying aim, quite beyond "private" remembrance, was to reach an "audience" of visitors and viewers.[21] In other words, by presenting their temporal background and

---

[21] Nicolas Vatin, "Sur le rôle de la stèle funéraire et l'aménagement des cimetières musulmans d'Istanbul," in A. Temimi (ed.), *Mélanges Professeur Robert Mantran* (Zaghouan: Centre d'études et de recherches ottomanes, 1988), pp. 293–7.

status to the living, the dead were "going public" and were making use of
the secularized context of social positioning as their main tool of identification.[22] Ottoman cemeteries were an extension of the urban public
space, linking the dead to the living through a social discourse of status,
genealogy, and biography. Perhaps the most telling sign of the correlation
between tombstones and biographical data is the inevitable social and/or
prosopographical twist taken by most studies in the domain. This is true of
the majority of such works produced in the past few decades,[23] but even
more strikingly of late Ottoman biographical compilations: Mehmed
Süreyya Bey's *Sicill-i Osmanî*, a compilation of some 17,000 biographies
published in 1893, relied heavily on the author's frequent visits to the
cemeteries of the city, where he collected biographical data from the
tombstones of thousands of individuals whose lives would have otherwise
gone unrecorded.[24]

For rather obvious reasons, the nature of the present inquiry requires the
use of a quantitative – in fact, statistical – approach to apprehend the
evolution of funerary epitaphs.[25] This, in turn, entails the constitution of a
database large and diverse enough to constitute a significant and representative sample of epitaphs for the period and location under study. The

[22] Again, this combined effect of secularization and social consciousness can also be observed in early
modern western societies: "There seems, however, to have been an expansion of the genre, to include
more biographical detail, in both England and France, aiming to locate the deceased more fully in
his or her social and temporal setting. The epitaph seems to have become more secular, both in its
content and its purpose. Raunié's study of Paris epitaphs avers that in the sixteenth century the
primitive brevity of the medieval epitaph was succeeded by little pieces of eloquence, brief funeral
orations; these in turn fell into excess, pretension, mannerism, before returning in the seventeenth
century to their proper form as a simple and precise biographical document." Harding, *The Dead
and the Living*, p. 159.
[23] Hans-Peter Laqueur, "Grabsteine als Quelle zur osmanischen Geschichte. Möglichkeiten," *Osmanlı
Araştırmaları* 3 (1982): 31–44; Hans-Peter Laqueur, "Einige Anmerkungen zur Sozialgeschichte der
osmanischen Friedhöfe und Gräberfelder von Istanbul," *Istanbuler Mitteilungen* 39 (1989): 335–9;
Nicolas Vatin, "Les cimetières musulmans ottomans: une source d'histoire sociale," in D. Panzac
(ed.), *Les villes dans l'Empire ottoman: activités et sociétés* (Paris: CNRS, 1991), pp. 149–63.
[24] In his introduction to a recent edition of *Sicill-i Osmanî*, Nuri Akbayar notes that tombstones were
"the source that constituted the most original aspect" of the work, and reminds us that Mehmed
Süreyya Bey came to be known by the nickname of *Hırpanî* ("in tatters") because he would return to
his office all mud-spattered and filthy from his endless expeditions across the cemeteries of Istanbul.
Mehmed Süreyya, *Sicill-i Osmanî*, ed. Nuri Akbayar (Istanbul: Tarih Vakfı Yurt Yayınları, 1996),
vol. I, p. viii.
[25] "There is more useful work to be done on epitaphs and the use of verbal language in the dialogue
between living and dead, in the way that there has been on testamentary discourse and visual
language and symbolism. Sixteenth- and seventeenth-century historians of London and Paris noted
epitaphs as a significant source of information about the past and as a genre in themselves, but their
studies tend to report the exceptional, the fulsome, and to ignore the brief and commonplace, and
cannot safely be used to chart shifts in practice statistically." Harding, *The Dead and the Living*,
p. 159.

solution has been found in the exploitation of a large database already constituted as part of an ongoing project aiming at the systematic study of Ottoman epitaphs from the fourteenth century to the beginning of the twentieth.[26] This database consists of some 2,500 individual epitaphs, collected from a number of cemeteries throughout the Ottoman lands, most of which have been the object of previous publications. Of this documentation, a total of some 800 inscriptions have been singled out, corresponding to the subcategory of epitaphs from Istanbul between 1700 and 1850.[27] For purposes of verification and control, a second set of data, consisting of 700 epitaphs for the same period, but originating from a wide spectrum of Ottoman towns and villages are used to trace possible differences between trends in the capital and in the provinces.[28] As to the variables used in the analysis, they will be restricted to four basic aspects of the epitaph: the overall number of lines, the basic typology of the epitaph, the existence or not of an indication of the occupation of the deceased, and, finally, the nature of the familial or social links through which the deceased is identified.

[26] This project, undertaken in collaboration with Nicolas Vatin, has as its objective an exhaustive analysis of the evolution of funerary epitaphs as an indicator of changes in mentality. As such, it is more concerned with a textual analysis of the perceptions and feelings expressed in epitaphs than with the concrete biographical data used in the present study. The project, Edhem Eldem and Nicolas Vatin, *L'épitaphe ottomane musulmane (XVI–XX siècles). Contribution à une histoire de la culture ottomane*, is currently in press at Peeters of Leuven.

[27] The information for the following cemeteries is based on previous publications. Küçük Ayasofya: Jean-Louis Bacqué-Grammont, Hans-Peter Laqueur and Nicolas Vatin, "Stelae Turcicae I. Küçük Aya Sofya," *Istanbuler Mitteilungen* 34 (1984): 441–540; Sokollu Mehmed Pasha at Kadırga Limanı and Eyüp, and Bostancı Ali: J.-L. Bacqué-Grammont et al., *Stelae Turcicae II. Cimetières de la mosquée de Sokollu Mehmed Paşa à Kadırga Limanı, de Bostancı Ali et du türbe de Sokollu Mehmed Paşa à Eyüb, Istanbuler Mitteilungen*, Beiheft 36 (Tübingen: E. Wasmuth, 1990); Merdivenköy: J.-L. Bacqué-Grammont et al., "Le *tekke* bektachi de Merdivenköy," *Anatolia Moderna / Yeni Anadolu* 2 (1991): 29–135. To these one should add the epitaphs collected from three cemeteries by the author and some colleagues with a view to future research and publication: Rumelihisarı Şehitlik Dergâhı (in collaboration with Günay Kut, pending publication); Yahya Efendi Dergâhı, Nazperver Usta Sıbyan Mektebi, and Haşim Baba (in collaboration with Nicolas Vatin).

[28] Provincial epitaphs have been collected from the following cemeteries on the basis of earlier publications. Karacaköy: J.-L. Bacqué-Grammont et al. "Stelae Turcicae IV. Le cimetière de la bourgade thrace de Karacaköy," *Anatolia Moderna / Yeni Anadolu* 2 (1991): 7–27; Seyyid Bilal, Pervane Medresesi and Sinop Müzesi at Sinop: J.-L. Bacqué-Grammont and N. Vatin, "Stelae Turcicae VI. Stèles funéraires de Sinop," *Anatolia Moderna / Yeni Anadolu* 3 (1992): 105–207; Örcün: Ahmed Nezih Galitekin, *Osmanlı Dönemi Gölcük Mezar Taşları* (Gölcük: Gilcük Belediyesi, 2000); Diyarbakır: M. Mehdi İlhan, "Diyarbakır'ın türbe, yatır ve mezarlıkları," in Bacqué-Grammont and Tibet (eds), *Cimetières et traditions funéraires dans le monde islamique*, vol. I, pp. 179–221; Sarajevo, Mostar, and Travnik: Mehmed Mujezinovic, *Islamska Epigrafika u Bosni i Hercegovini*, 3 vols. (Sarajevo: Veselin Masksa, 1974–82); various cemeteries of the Aegean region: Gül Tunçel, *Batı Anadolu Bölgesi Cami Tasvirli Mezartaşları* (Ankara: Kültür Bakanlığı, 1989). The database also includes one unpublished source, namely the cemetery of Babakale, the epitaphs of which have been compiled by the author.

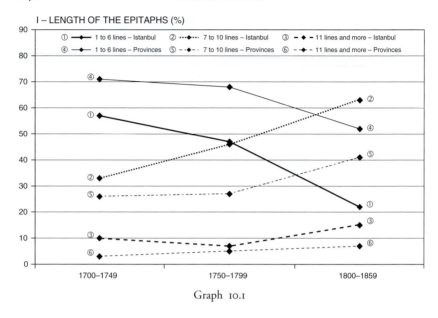

I – LENGTH OF THE EPITAPHS (%)

Graph 10.1

A first test conducted on the simplest of these variables, the number of lines, clearly confirms the initial assumption of a significant expansion of the epitaph throughout the period. If one distinguishes three major categories in this respect, namely epitaphs of six lines or less, of seven to ten lines, and of eleven lines or more, it appears that the proportional weight of each of these types shifts consistently in the direction of a lengthening of the epitaph. In concrete terms, the shortest epitaphs, representing about 57 percent of all epitaphs in 1700–50, drop to 47 percent in 1750–1800 and to a mere 22 percent in 1800–50. Inversely, the intermediate category of seven to ten lines moves from 33 percent in 1700–50 to 46 percent in 1750–1800, and finally culminates at 63 percent in 1800–50. Although they remain marginal throughout the period, the longest ones still show a rising trend, from around 10 percent in 1700–1800 to 15 percent in 1800–50 (graph 10.1). A calculation of the average number of lines for each of the fifty-year sub-periods allows for a more concrete visualization of the phenomenon: from 6.5 lines in 1700–50, the figure rises to 7 lines in 1750–1800 and to a little less than 8.5 in 1800–50 (graph 10.2). Knowing that the typical Ottoman epitaph had one line devoted to an invocation, another to the request for a prayer, and a third line to the date, the passage from 6.5 to 8.5 lines really meant an increase of the actual text from 3.5 to 5.5 lines, a major quantitative leap by any standard. In more concrete terms, while about three or

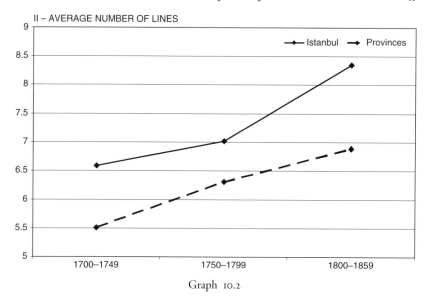

II – AVERAGE NUMBER OF LINES

Graph 10.2

four lines would allow for little more than a name, a profession, a patronym, and a very short comment on death, five or six lines would easily accommodate a detailed identification of the deceased, including complex affiliations, or a short identity combined with a stereotypical quatrain adapted to the circumstance.

Interestingly, epitaphs in Istanbul and in the provinces show significant and consistent differences in this particular respect. The trends are by and large identical in both cases, pointing to a comparable lengthening of the epitaph; yet, the drop of shorter epitaphs and the rise of longer epitaphs are decidedly more pronounced in the capital city, suggesting that the provinces followed the same trend as Istanbul, but with a significant time lag corresponding to an interval of about fifty years. The severe drop of short epitaphs in Istanbul from more than half the cases to a mere fifth is attenuated in the provinces as the same figure drops from a high 70 percent to a low 50. Similarly, while lengthier epitaphs in Istanbul almost double in frequency, representing two-thirds of the sample by the end of the period, the same phenomenon in the provinces represents a much more modest increase from around 25 to 40 percent (graph 10.1). Average figures confirm this trend: the provincial average also increases steadily, but from only 5.5 to a mere 7 lines (2.5 to 4 net), thus constantly remaining at least one line below the averages in the capital (graph 10.2). The fact that the gap between the capital and the provinces widens in time is meaningful: the need to squeeze in more text was felt throughout the empire, but it certainly reached a peak in the highly urbanized environment of Istanbul, where lack of a precise identification could well bring total anonymity.

Indeed, in a society evidently concerned with the preservation of the memory of the departed, what were the chances of thousands of Mustafa Aghas or Ayşe Kadıns – as they often appeared on their tombstones – to avoid being totally forgotten and unidentifiable after their death? The frequent use of the father's name brought no real remedy to this problem; how could one identify an Ahmed bin Mehmed and differentiate him from thousands of homonymic fathers and sons? The distinction between urban and rural areas makes particular sense in this context, for what really determined the relative efficiency of an inscription was the size and complexity of the community. In a small village, or for that matter in a modest and relatively isolated *mahalle* (neighborhood) of a city or town, the chances of confusion were certainly lower, and the capacity of the community to preserve a personalized memory of its late members was undoubtedly higher than in a complex urban setting.[29] The "intimacy" of such traditional settings, combined with the modesty of the material means available, certainly justified the use of laconic funerary inscriptions. When it came to the ever more complex environment of the city, however, the need arose to be more precise, and so did the occasions to do so. In the imperial capital there was more than one way to add a personal touch to an otherwise inconspicuous identity. A place of origin, a place of residence, or a nickname often did the trick, albeit at a very elementary level; much more efficient was the mention of an occupation, particularly if it could be shown to be of some prestige. More importantly, however, one could rely on familial relationships and patronage networks to link up the deceased to another individual – dead or alive – who provided him with an identity of some prestige. As many urban Ottomans soon discovered, two or three additional lines could open up totally new alleys of social positioning, or even social climbing.

One should not fail, however, to see that the most striking and revolutionary novelty in funerary art had to do with sentimental and esthetic

---

[29] A personal recollection will perfectly illustrate this point. While collecting epitaphs in the cemetery of the village of Babakale, an elderly villager approached me while I was deciphering the inscription on the tombstone of a certain Aziz Efendi, son of Hafız Ali Efendi, who had died in 1306/1889. After asking me to read the epitaph – which he himself could not do – he informed me that this young man had committed suicide with a rifle, adding that he held this information, completely absent from the epitaph, from his maternal uncle.

concerns reflected in the use of a poetic style based on the stock verses mentioned earlier. In the first half of the eighteenth century, such decorative verses appeared on a little more than one epitaph in twenty. By the second half of the century, this proportion had more than trebled, reaching over 20 percent. Between 1800 and 1850, 40 percent of Istanbul tombstones displayed some formulaic reference to lost youth, to parental grief, or to a naive but efficient philosophy of death. Clearly, in a century or so, what had started as a literary curiosity had developed into outright fashion. Interestingly, the same phenomenon was also observed in the provinces, but in an even more pronounced way: from a mere 5 percent in 1700–50, stock verses had become a standard feature of every other tombstone by the nineteenth century. The reason for this was quite simple: attractive as it may have seemed initially, the novelty had inevitably lost some of its appeal due to continuous repetition of the same formulas. It was only normal that this disenchantment should have been felt more strongly in the capital where the quest for new forms of expression – most notably "real" poetry – relegated the use of stock verses to the modest strata of the population. In the provinces, however, the phenomenon persisted much longer: what fit a modest Istanbulite was certainly good enough for the provincial elites.[30]

Even though the craze for popular poetry often denoted a rather remarkable move towards individualization by adding a sentimental and tragic dimension to death, recurrent metaphors of broken twigs and wilting roses did not bring much precision to the social context of the deceased. For those who wished to display their status and background, attention had to be given to the few lines at the end of the epitaph that surrounded the deceased's name. That was where a mention of the deceased's occupation could conveniently be placed: generally preceding his name, and possibly combined with other epithets defining him. A closer look at male epitaphs for the period – female occupations are too scarce to be included in such calculations[31] – shows that this element was already very significant at an early phase (one-third of the stones in 1700–50), and that it kept increasing steadily to include half the sample in 1800–50. Quite surprisingly, the trend is totally inverted in the provinces, the mention of an occupation dropping

[30] Statistics for the period 1850–1920 confirm this trend. While the use of stock verses in the provinces remained more or less stable at 45 percent, it was reduced to a mere third of the stones in the urban environment of the capital.

[31] In fact, Istanbul cemeteries do provide quite a number of "professional" women, but within a very restricted range of possible occupations. Apart from an occasional midwife here and there, most of these women were slaves, especially of the imperial harem. Given this very particular profile – concentrated in a few cemeteries of the capital – I have preferred to exclude them from any statistical estimate.

III – MALE EPITAPHS MENTIONING THE OCCUPATION OF THE DECEASED (%)

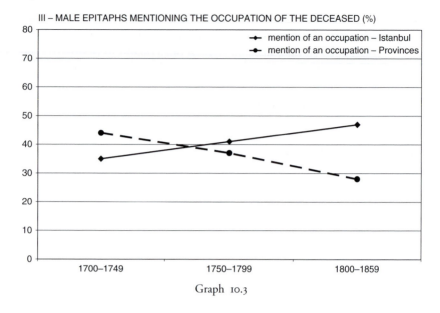

Graph 10.3

from an initial 45 percent in 1700–50 to less than 30 percent in 1800–50 (graph 10.3). One could tentatively explain this inversion by the relative scarcity of professions in provincial towns and villages and the fact that the few occupations that could be mentioned did not perform the same kind of role as the wide array of careers that could be displayed in the capital of the empire. The incentive for a provincial barber (*berber*) or butcher (*kasab*) to display his profession must have been much weaker than the urge for a palace servant to boast his identity in a cemetery of Istanbul. Indeed, the fact that almost four out of five provincial tombstones displaying a profession belonged to members of the military, bureaucratic, or religious establishment seems to indicate that "common" professions were most probably sacrificed to more efficient ways of praising the deceased.

This was to a certain extent true of Istanbul too. Artisans and shop owners were definitely much less represented than a middling and upper class of state employees, military officers, and individuals working in the service of the palace and of grandees. The difference lay in the fact that, in Istanbul, such positions and the prestigious titles that came with the offices were much more numerous. Moreover, in the capital city, many careers were so intimately linked to higher offices and patrons, that mentioning the occupation of the deceased automatically became an opportunity for name dropping. A similar phenomenon worked for those who lacked a professional identity, as was especially the case with women and younger children. One could then associate any individual to a relative whose occupation would be deemed worthy of being cited. On the average, some 15 percent of men were thus defined through the profession of some close relative. The proportion was highest for women, almost half of whom could display a profession by proxy, a phenomenon that was facilitated by the possibility of relying on both their own family and that of their in-laws. If one is to include such links, the proportions of individuals directly or indirectly defined by an occupation soar from a little less than half at the beginning of the period to almost two-thirds at the end.

What this suggests is that the way in which the deceased could be linked to other individuals, from the closest of relatives to more distant employers and patrons, was at least as important as his profession. Indeed, if he was lucky enough to have a profession of some prestige, he could afford to be buried under his name alone, or, in keeping with the tradition, with a reference to his father; but for those who, for one reason or another, had no occupational standing to boast of, linking up to other individuals could become a very useful tool of social promotion. It was, therefore, through the interplay of occupation, family links, and networking that status came to be defined on tombstones, each monument becoming the object of strategies aiming at an optimization of the deceased's public image.

A closer look at the evolution of the available options over time suggests significant changes in these strategies. During the first half of the eighteenth century, the "stand-alone" epitaph, where the deceased is defined without any reference to others but only through his own attributes, constitutes the dominant model, representing over half of the cases in the sample. By the second half of the century, the proportion drops to 43 percent, and finally to less than 30 percent in 1800–50 (graph 10.4). Not surprisingly, this is a dominantly male model, since the absence of any links suggests that, in most cases, the individual is defined through his occupation (50 to 75 percent, graph 10.6). "Stand-alone" women were, therefore, a rarity, representing a mere fifth of the sample at the beginning of the period, and only one-tenth at the end. Interestingly, if the proportion of epitaphs restricted to the identity of a single individual showed a drastic drop in time, their quality on the contrary increased sharply, as suggested by the increase in the average number of lines from 6.5 in 1700–50 to 8.5 in 1800–50 (graph 10.5). In other words, the "stand-alone" epitaph was not necessarily an economical model designed for modest individuals; quite to the contrary, if some individuals were left to their own devices to define themselves, it was because they *could* do so, thanks to a sufficiently high

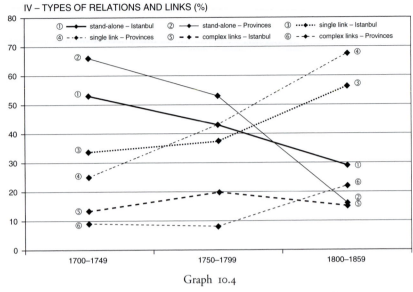

Graph 10.4

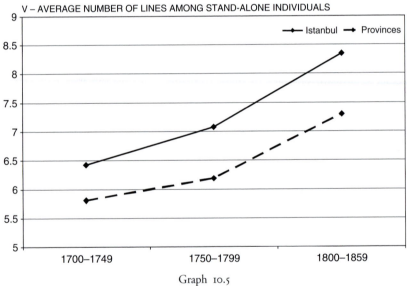

Graph 10.5

social status. The extra lines could then be put to better use by praising the deceased's virtues or displaying the poetic talent of a mercenary artist. Nor did the number of lines really matter in the most prestigious cases. For many a grandee, the *ne plus ultra* of distinction was sometimes to be found

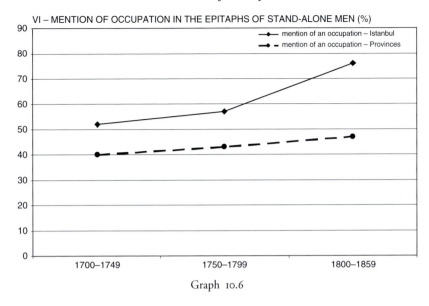

VI – MENTION OF OCCUPATION IN THE EPITAPHS OF STAND-ALONE MEN (%)

Graph 10.6

in the laconic nature of the inscription: were not the greatest men those who needed least to be described?

The sizeable drop in the use of the "stand-alone" epitaph meant that some alternative models were gaining ground. Among these, the most common one was certainly the "single-link" model, whereby the deceased was defined in terms of his relationship to one particular person. Representing about 35 percent until the nineteenth century, this model ended the period as the most common model, at nearly 60 percent (graph 10.4). Several factors could account for the popularity of this type of epitaph. This was, after all, one of the oldest and most spontaneous forms of identification – even among the living – especially in the case of the son defined by the father, very frequently used in the earliest periods, to the point of wondering if the "stand-alone" model itself had not risen to prominence only at a relatively later date.[32] Also influential in this respect was the relatively high proportion of the young among the sample,

[32] Among the fourteenth- and fifteenth-century tombstones of Bursa, only one-fifth define the individual alone, while practically all the rest use the deceased's father as a single reference (Karaçağ, *Bursa*). This may well suggest that the "stand-alone" epitaph really developed only later, possibly in relation to the emergence of a bureaucratic and military structure allowing for a better definition of status. The scarcity of pre-eighteenth-century stones, however, makes it practically impossible to test this hypothesis in any reliable way.

representing almost one-quarter of all epitaphs. Despite the difficulty of establishing a sound comparison with the preceding centuries, it seems that from the eighteenth century on, the number of monuments erected in memory of the young, especially of children, kept steadily increasing, as a result of the "democratization" of tombstones. Most probably, the cheapening of marble made it possible to commission a gravestone for young children who, in a time of very high infant mortality, would have until then benefited from a much less durable monument, or no monument at all. This, in turn, seems to have triggered a rise in father-and-child inscriptions, for youth was certainly the category that called most for a reference to the father, and made an epitaph concentrating on the deceased alone much less relevant.[33]

Not all of these single-link epitaphs were between father and child, however. In fact, a growing portion of these epitaphs had to do with another very basic link, that of marriage, through which the deceased was defined as the spouse of an individual. This proportion increased systematically, from 12 percent in 1700–50 to 23 percent in 1750–1800 and, finally, to 41 percent in 1800–50, almost doubling every half century. Not surprisingly, this was an exclusively female pattern, as men were simply *never* identified through their wives. Yet, even for women, the phenomenon seems to have been quite novel, as previously not a single case of a woman defined as a wife (*zevce* or *halile*) had made its way into the sample. Thus, in the case of early Ottoman tombs in Bursa, among the limited number of female epitaphs, all but one present the deceased as a daughter, the only exception being that of a woman presented as a mother.[34] Could this be due to a flaw in the sample? The possibility cannot be excluded, but nor can the fact that the proportion of surviving female tombstones is extremely low for the earlier periods and reaches a representative level only by the mid-eighteenth century.[35] Clearly such a bias cannot be explained as the result of a gender-based wearing and destruction of gravestones; it is more likely that, for a number of reasons, women had initially less of a chance to attain a durable monument. In a male-dominated society practicing polygyny – not to mention extensive domestic female slavery – and where women were often recruited into the household from a lower status, it

---

[33] For the period under study, only about 15 percent of epitaphs of the young fall into this category, against approximately double that for "adult" inscriptions. (The blurry distinction between the two categories is based on the presence or not of an explicit reference to youth.)

[34] Karaçağ, *Bursa.*

[35] Women represent 17 percent of the sample before 1700, 35 percent in 1700–50, 44 percent in 1750–1800, and 48 percent in the first half of the nineteenth century.

should not come as a surprise that they may have been denied some of the funerary honors bestowed on men. For those who were well-born, on the contrary, leaving aside those who would have died before wedlock, it was more likely that a way of preserving the paternal genealogy should have been devised, as their status as daughters was higher than their status as wives. The rapid rise in female representation from the eighteenth century on could thus be linked to a number of factors, from – as in the case of young children – the relative cheapening of marble to a greater visibility of the couple, perhaps even including a decrease in polygyny.

Whatever the causes may have been for the growing representation of women, the phenomenon was of crucial importance from the perspective of the evolution of epitaphs. Women lacked, generally speaking, access to the public sphere, and this handicap was all the more obvious in the case of the public-conscious epitaphs of the Ottoman tradition. Indeed, with no public function or occupation to display, their visibility in the public space constituted by the cemetery depended to a large extent on whatever attributes they could acquire from men. In this respect, marriage was a major advantage, as it provided them with not just one, but two lineages on which they could base their identity. Thus, among all the women, almost half were defined as daughters of their fathers, most probably because they died before marriage. For the rest, the great majority were presented as wives (almost 40 percent), and as mothers (8.5 percent); the remaining few were women presented as daughters *and* wives (6 percent). Marginal as it may have been, this last category can be subdivided into two groups: those who were defined as wives *then* daughters (2 percent) and those who were daughters *before* being wives (4 percent). The distinction was certainly not innocent, as the order of presentation between the two families doubtless referred to an unequal *rapport de force* between the two. On the male side of the picture, even though men were never presented as their wives' husbands, there nevertheless was a situation that implicitly put them in the position of a spouse. Rare as it may have been initially, towards the end of the period a growing number of stones presented some individuals as *damad*s (sons-in-law), which clearly indicated that the writer of the epitaph had made a strategic choice against the dominant trend of linking men to their fathers.[36]

---

[36] One striking example in that respect is that of a certain Mücteba Efendi, who died in 1282/1865, as the "son-in-law of Sabire Hanım, daughter of Konevî Osman Efendi." Although the deceased had a respectable position – he was a madrasa teacher, "müderrisin-i kiramdan" – and a family lineage of his own – he was descended from a mufti from Silistria, "Silistrevî Müftizade" – his epitaph nevertheless referred first and foremost to his "dominated" relationship to his mother-in-law.

These were only some examples of a more general trend that seems to
have characterized the period, namely the growing complexity of the links
and relations used to define the deceased. Throughout the period, the
proportion of such "complex" epitaphs remained more or less stable,
varying between 10 and 20 percent (graph 10.4). The notion of "complex"
epitaph as used here, however, is rather vague, as it includes any kind of
relationship involving more than one individual of reference. A closer and
more qualitative look may therefore be necessary to properly evaluate the
nature of these "complex" epitaphs. Complexity could take several forms,
one of which was a marked emphasis on the direct genealogy of the
deceased, through the mobilization of a number of ascendants named
one after the other. Such genealogical references could summon up to
four generations of names, with a marked preference for direct male
lineage.[37] A simple reference to the ancestral name of the family, when
there was one, could easily replace the list of names, which, once connected
to the deceased's father, would provide a useful shortcut to the same kind of
claim. Strategic considerations ruled most of these genealogical claims. For
a descendant of a prestigious lineage, the individual names and functions of
the ancestors were relatively less important than the naming of the dynasty;
but when one wanted to refer to a distant relative who drew his prestige
from his personal status, names would acquire more importance and the
links could become much more convoluted. Such was the case with a
certain Mehmed Âşir, who was defined as "the son of İbrahim Agha, son of
Teberdarzade Hacı Mustafa Agha, [himself] nephew of the late calligra-
pher Hasan Efendi."[38] Women benefited from the same advantages, *par
alliance*: a certain Ayşe Kadın was presented as "the wife of Hacı Ali Bey,
nephew of the late Rüşdî Mehmed Pasha."[39] For those with a familial
background matching that of their husband, both ancestries could easily be
displayed, as in the case of Zeliha Hanım, "daughter of Mustafa Efendi,

Evidently the whole point was to link him up to Konevî Osman Efendi, a former *kazasker* (military
judge); but in doing so, the only link being a woman, the epitaph had to "castrate" no less than two
men by putting them in the position of sons-in-law: Mücteba Efendi himself and, more drastically
even, his father-in-law, who was simply by-passed by the presence of his wife, Sabire Hanım
(Rumelihisarı Şehitlik Dergâhı Cemetery, NB A 24, 1282/1865).

[37] As in "Merhum Ömer Beğ ibni Ali Beğ ibni'l-merhum Ahmed Beğ ibni'l-merhum İbrahim Han
ibni'ş-Şehid Mehmed Paşa" (Cemetery of Sokollu Mehmed Pasha at Kadırga, SMK D 163, 1120/
1708).

[38] "Merhum Hattat Hasan Efendi'nin yeğeni merhum Teberdarzade el-Hac Mustafa Ağa'nın oğlu
İbrahim Ağa'nın oğlu e's-Seyyid Mehmed Âşir" (Cemetery of Bostancı Ali, BA 18, 1240/1824).

[39] "Müteveffa Rüşdî Mehmed Paşa yeğeni el-Hac Ali Beğ'in halilesi merhume ve mağfurün leha
el-muhtac ilâ rahmeti Rabbihi'l-gafur Âişe Kadın" (Cemetery of Sokollu Mehmed Pasha at Kadırga,
SMK C 144, 1252/1836).

son of the former *Kadiasker* (Chief Military Judge) of Rumelia Muhsinzade Ahmed Efendi, and venerable wife of Hacı Halil Beyefendi, descendant of the İbrahim Hanzades."[40] Perhaps the best illustration of this phenomenon is the series of four tombstones of women, all related to a certain Salih Efendi. His wife, Zeliha Hanım, his two daughters, Ayşe and Şerife Cemile Hanıms, and his slave, Şetaret Kadın, were all directly defined by Salih Efendi, husband, father or master according to circumstances. However, what is interesting is the standardized way in which the said Salih Efendi was himself defined. His identity consisted of two elements, which defined him in the following order: first, as the steward of the son-in-law of Çabraslı/Çaprazlı (*Çabraslı damadı* [*Hasan Efendi*] *kethüdası*); and, second, as an officer of the imperial divan (*hacegân-ı Divan-ı Hümayun'dan* [*ve Kethüda-yı Bâb-ı Vüzera-yı İzam*]). The result was a rather stereotypical rendition of Salih Efendi's titles and functions, slightly modified according to circumstances.[41] Yet, in terms of complexity, this was a perfect example of the lengths to which the Ottomans would go to provide the deceased with a proper epitaph. The definition of these women through Salih Efendi required no less than the mention of his occupation and a reference to his patron, who was himself defined through his dependent relationship with his father-in-law. The irony of this "system," when applied to women, was the inevitably high price to pay for public visibility: although devoted to the deceased, such tombstones ended up using almost all of the inscribable space to the glorification of "their" men.

Salih Efendi's case – or rather his women's case – showed clearly how flexible the system was in its response to social strategies. People were free to make use of whatever form of linkage was available, be it based on family ties, on service relationships or on patronage networks. Choices were essentially determined by a desire to maximize the social impact of the epitaph. In many cases family ties, once perceived as the core of an epitaph, could be entirely sacrificed to a more gratifying definition through service or patronage. This was all the more obvious in the case of servants and slaves whose tombstones were paid for and commissioned by the very people who defined them. What this resulted in displaying was more than a conscious strategy; it was a reflection of a social reality made of relations of dependency. Thus, Neşe Kadın, evidently a subaltern of a

---

[40] "Rumeli Kazaskeri esbak Muhsinzade Ahmed Efendizade Mustafa Efendi'nin kerimesi ve İbrahim Hanzade el-Hac Halil Beğefendi'nin ehl-i muhteremeleri merhume ve mağfurün leha Zeliha Hanım" (Cemetery of Sokollu Mehmed Pasha at Eyüb, SME B 18, 1228/1813).
[41] Cemetery of Küçük Ayasofya, KAS B 68, 1223/1808; Cemetery of Sokollu Mehmed Pasha at Kadırga, SMK B 85, D 164, D 173, 1227/1812.

powerful household, could be defined as "the emancipated slave of the former Grand Vizier Ragıb Pasha, and the daughter of his child nurse."[42] The epitaph thus constituted an accurate depiction of how the woman was viewed in the household, a vision that did not allow for any familial reference, except for a fleeting remark on the identity of her (anonymous) mother, who was also defined in terms of her service relationship with the former grand vizier. Yet, even in more "active" circumstances where the family may have had a say in the text of the inscription, conventional family ties could easily be stretched to incorporate a very different form of networking. A striking, if extreme, case is that of Emine Hanım, who was buried under a stone that presented her as "the sister of the son-in-law of the steward of the *Valide Sultan* (Queen Mother)."[43] The practical and strategic choices involved in the choice of this epitaph are rather obvious: by stretching the epitaph to include the most powerful and prestigious woman of the empire, not only was Emine Hanım pulled out of the obscurity of her doubtless mediocre life, but her brother, probably both instrument and actor in this daring promotional trick, enjoyed a moment of glory in the limelight of his father-in-law's exalted patron.

More was yet to come after the 1850s, when European influence and inspiration boosted even more the growing desire to individualize tomb-stones and epitaphs: the quest for monumental size and style, timid attempts at figurative sculpture, the introduction of romantic and natural-ist representations of death, the use of revivalist architectural elements, the emergence of a nationalist discourse gradually overshadowing religious references.[44] Yet these extreme cases of a somewhat "imported" modernity lay on a solid ground that had developed from the sixteenth century on, and more particularly during the century and a half that had preceded the first signs of westernization. By transforming an individual and religious marker into a social one, and by turning their epitaphs into extensions of the public image of the deceased and of their entourage, the Ottomans had created a funerary art of their own that reflected the evolution of their society. It would probably not be an exaggeration to qualify this evolution as a form of modernity "from within," triggered by the passage from a premodern society to one that displayed much higher degrees of hierarchy,

---

[42] "Sadr-ı esbak Ragıb Paşa hafidesi mutakesi ve dayezadesi merhume ve mağfurün leha Neşe Kadın", Cemetery of Küçük Ayasofya, KAS C 12, 1239/1824.
[43] Cemetery of Yahya Efendi, 1241/1825 (Eldem, *Death in Istanbul*, pp. 142–3).
[44] Eldem, *Death in Istanbul*, pp. 217–35; 238–45; 268–71; 276–89.

differentiation, and complexity. As if to belie the traditional Islamic precept of equality before death, Ottoman Muslims invested much of their efforts in ways of individualizing and, whenever possible, glorifying the memory of their dead. By the eighteenth century, what had initially been the privilege of a very narrow elite became available to a growing number of individuals from very different walks of life. What held them together and made them share this funerary practice was a common culture that viewed the cemetery as an extension of public space. In the face of this widening of the elite and of a gradual *embourgeoisement* of the middling classes, burial grounds became a parallel arena where identities, families, and networks competed, much as they did in the "real" world of the living.

II

Who is a true Muslim?
Exclusion and inclusion among polemicists of
reform in nineteenth-century Baghdad

Dina Rizk Khoury

In 1793, the judge of Medina, the second holiest city in Islam, wrote to the government in Istanbul warning it against the actions of one Muhammad ibn Abd al-Wahhab, who lived in Najd near Yamama, the land of Musaylima, the false prophet of early Islam. This Ibn Abd al-Wahhab had broken the Islamic law (shari'a), had pillaged and taken over cities, and had declared all those who did not renew their faith according to his teachings, as unbelievers (kuffar). The judge reminded the central government that he and the other signatories of this complaint, who included the jurisconsults of the four Islamic schools of law in Medina, as well as other Ottoman officials, had sent a number of epistles warning the government of the danger posed by this man. Because the government had chosen to ignore their warnings, Ibn Abd al-Wahhab had now acquired followers among the common people as well as the elite. The judge and his fellow signatories characterized Ibn Abd al-Wahhab alternatively as an atheist and a Qarmati.[1] For the judge the situation was as dangerous to the beliefs and legitimacy of the Ottoman state as it had been to the Abbasids in the tenth century, when the Qarmathians had taken over much of southern Iraq, parts of Syria and the Holy Cities of Mecca and Medina. They implored the central government to deal with Ibn abd al-Wahhab, as he was causing dissension in the Arabian peninsula.[2]

Nearly a quarter of a century later, Abu al-Fawz Muhammad Amin al-Suwaydi, scion of the scholarly family in Baghdad and son of Ali al-Suwaydi, one of the first sympathizers in Baghdad of some of the Wahhabi doctrines, wrote an epistle defending the religious reformer of sufism and the political activist Khalid al-Naqshbandi against accusations of

The research and writing for this chapter was made possible by funding from ACLS and ARIT/NEH.
[1] The Qaramatiyya (Qarmathians) was a movement led by a group of rebellious tribes in Arabia and southern Iraq that threatened the Abbasid state in the tenth century by establishing their independent ascetic state in Arabia after conquering Mecca and Medina.
[2] Başbakanlık Osmanlı Arşivi (BOA), Hatt-ı Humayun 3855-B.

unbelief (*kufr*) made by one of his enemies.[3] In this letter, he called for the careful consideration of the word *takfir*, that is, the act of declaring someone an unbeliever and excluding her or him from the Muslim community. As he defended and explicated the doctrines of his master, Khalid al-Naqshbandi, he expressed the opposition felt by many in the Baghdadi scholarly and political class against the increasing use of religious exclusion as a means to political ends.

These vignettes serve as windows into the political and religious debates – I shall call them, following Raymond Williams, "structures of feeling" – on what, in effect, was a redefinition of the place of a Muslim in the political order.[4] Williams uses the phrase "structures of feeling" to denote the *presence* (his italics) in social actors of a practical consciousness which draws meaning from formal belief systems and ideology grounded in the past but which ascribes meaning "over a range from formal assent with private dissent to the more nuanced interaction between selected and interpreted beliefs and acted justified experiences."[5] "Structures of feeling" in Williams' sense, are neither ideology (class or state determined) nor formal beliefs (supported by institutions), although they draw on both. Rather, they are a set of non-institutionalized mental outlooks and moods that often emerge in transitional periods of social and political conflict. Williams' concept helps explain what he, in the context of British history, calls the emergent new consciousness in conjunction with, and against, the dominant ideology and residual beliefs. It is an expression of new social interests, but is fluid and ill-defined, and cannot be reduced simply to ideology of class.[6]

In the case of the Ottoman Empire in general, and the Iraqi provinces in particular, debates on political and religious reform by elites and scholars, sufis and anti-sufis, in the transitional period between the 1790s and the 1820s, were not as yet fully articulated as an ideology of a class or state as they would be in the Tanzimat period, nor were they institutionalized into dominant culture as they were in the second half of the nineteenth century under the rubric of political *salafism*, but are best understood as a plethora of mental outlooks, often ill-defined and inclusive of a multiplicity of seemingly contradictory ideas. What differentiated them from earlier debates on reform, what marked them as a new style of political discourse,

---

[3] Abu al-Fawz al-Suwaydi, "Daf' al-zulm (al-dhulm) 'an al-wuqu' fi arz (ardh) hatha al-mazlum," Süleymaniye Kütüphanesi, MS Esad Efendi 1404.
[4] Raymond Williams, *Marxism and Literature*, "*Structures of Feeling*," (Oxford: Oxford University Press, 1977), pp. 128–35.
[5] Ibid., p. 132.   [6] Ibid., "Dominant, Residual, Emergent," pp. 121–7.

was a sort of nostalgia, or rather a politicized memory of the early Muslim community, deployed by the provincial proponents of reform as well as the central government in the face of European encroachments and the "corruption" of the ritual and legal practices.[7] Insofar as these debates involved discussions of reform, of correct Muslim practice, of definition of self (the Muslim orthodox community) and others (shi'is, infidels, non-conformist sects, and heterodox sufis), they did so not only in the language and venues of private discourse and limited circles of scholarly and bureaucratic elite, but also in the language of public discourse as well as in new forms of organization. Thus, as the Wahhabis threatened the Ottoman state, the propaganda mounted by the state generated a slew of public debates between Wahhabis and anti-Wahhabis, some of them sponsored by the state. The political language was polemical and public, less concerned with the niceties of dogma and more focused on the use of language to include and exclude the other. To be sure, the language of these debates drew on the ideology of exclusion and inclusion, the anti-Shi'ite literature and literature on sects (*firaq*) of the late medieval and early modern period.[8] The emergent idiom of these political and religious debates, however, was quite different. Here, from the beginning, a clear line was set between, on the one hand, public action and language or what could be called a public political language and, on the other, theology and religious dogma. While the latter continued to flourish as a language for the elites, it was now not the main venue for maintaining and regenerating a community. A language and a set of strategies more public in its orientation were beginning to take shape. Ibn Abd al-Wahhab, Khalid al-Naqshbandi, and the Ottoman government were acutely aware of this difference in the eighteenth and early nineteenth centuries, and helped create this political public language. This is not to say that an Ottoman public in the modern sense of

---

[7] Butrus Abu-Manneh, *Studies on Islam and the Ottoman Empire in the 19th Century (1826–1876)* (Istanbul: Isis Press, 2001), pp. 7–12, 41–57. Abu Manneh finds that under Selim III the spread and success of the Naqshbandi-Mujaddidi sufi order among the reforming elite played an important role in framing the agenda of reform in terms that called for the re-institution of shari'a at the center of Ottoman social and political practice. At the same time, the rhetoric of Islamic renewal, the example of the early Muslim community, was invoked to call Muslims to fight against infidels. Similarly, the Wahhabi movement, born as a result of developments internal to Arabia, and not as a reaction to western incursions, was intent on recreating the ideal Muslim community, based on the early community of the Prophet.

[8] On this literature see Sherman A. Jackson, *On the Boundaries of Theological Tolerance in Islam, Abu Hamid al-Ghazali's Faysal al-Tafriqa* (Oxford: Oxford University Press, 2002), pp. 2–32. See, for the earlier period of Islamic history, Yohanan Friedmann, *Tolerance and Coercion in Islam, Interfaith Relations in the Muslim Tradition* (Cambridge: Cambridge University Press, 2003), particularly pp. 54–86.

the word existed, or that the institutional structures to create such a public were in place. It is to say that the new mode of political discourse was struggling in a setting where institutions and social underpinning for such institutions were not as yet set. Yet the debates among reformers served as harbingers of an indigenous kind of political modernity.[9]

Among the most controversial of the issues resurrected by the political polemics was that of toleration, or inclusion in or exclusion from a Muslim community. The issue became particularly public with the Wahhabi movement's attempts to redraw the parameters of what constituted a truly Muslim community within Sunni Islam. I will focus on two aspects of these debates: the polemical and public nature of these debates and their difference from older medieval and early modern polemics, particularly as they pertain to the issue of who was a Muslim; and the complicated relationship among proponents and opponents of various reform agendas in the Iraq provinces to the politics of reform at the center.

Between the 1780s and 1820s, Ottoman Iraq became the battleground between two major reform movements: the Wahhabi and the Khalidiyya branch of the Mujaddidiyya/Naqshbandiyya mystical order. While the Wahhabi movement was from its inception a political movement, the Mujaddidiyya/Naqshbandiyya became politicized only after 1811, under the leadership of Mawlana Khalid. The two movements involved those sectors of Iraq's learned community (ulema) seeking a voice in the reform agendas of the Ottoman Empire. They were acutely aware of the sense of crisis that pervaded the Ottoman and Islamic worlds. The Russian defeat of the Ottomans in 1774, followed by Sultan Selim III's attempts at reform in the 1790s, reforms that were derailed by the conquest of Egypt by Napoleon in 1798, were followed by the Wahhabi conquests of Mecca and Medina in 1805. The deposition of Sultan Selim III in 1807 and the installation of young Mahmud II in 1808 by a provincial warlord made a structural change in the political system all the more imperative.

---

[9] I draw yet again for my discussion on the idea of a public political language on the work of Raymond Williams on political writing in England. See his *Writing and Society* (London: Verso, 1983), pp. 67–118. The question of audience is central in the context of language analysis. Despite the limited use of the printing press in the Ottoman Empire in this period, the language employed by all the protagonists involved in the debates on reforms assumed three kinds of audience: the educated but non-scholarly community, the scholarly community, and, depending on the point of view of the polemicist, the ignorant, the ordinary follower, the believer and preacher. See also Abu Manneh, *Studies on Islam*, pp. 7–12. Abu Manneh was among the first to argue that the roots of the defining Tanzimat document, the Gülhane Rescript of 1839, should be sought in an internal Islamic Sunni orthodox revival among the empire's elite. It was not a product of European models.

Mahmud II initiated a series of reforms aimed at centralizing political power and defeating local provincial magnates, but challenges to his rule by the Greek War of Independence in 1821, the continued occupation of the Holy Cities by the Wahhabi forces, and the expansionist policies of his Egyptian vassal Muhammad Ali in Syria and parts of Iraq hampered his projects. That the empire teetered on the edge of collapse became evident not only to European observers who constructed the diplomacy of the "Eastern Question," but also to the bulk of the political and scholarly class within the empire. This danger of the imminent demise of the *ancien régime* was one aspect of the context for the debates that took place in Iraq over what constitutes a good Muslim.

A second component of the context was occurring in Arabia. The Wahhabis spearheaded a puritanical religious/political movement inspired and led by Muhammad Ibn Abd al-Wahhab in mid eighteenth-century Najd. Its founder, influenced by a community of scholars centered in the Holy Cities of Arabia who stressed the primacy of a scripturalist and literal interpretation of the Quran, and a strict adherence to the example (*sunna*) of the Prophet and his early followers, called for the individual interpretation of the primary texts of Islam. He rejected the accretions of a great number of works produced by the scholarly legal establishment that were developed in the early centuries of Islam, and was adamantly opposed to all mystical practices that gave human beings the power to intercede between the individual and God.[10] In 1745, Ibn Abd al-Wahhab succeeded in forging an alliance with a tribal princely kin group, the house of Saud, and together they created a political imamate that threatened the legitimacy of the Ottoman state. Nevertheless, it was not until the first years of the nineteenth century, when the Saudi/Wahhabi forces sacked Karbala and Najaf, Shi'ite holy cities in Iraq, and laid siege to Mecca and Medina, that the Ottoman government became aware of the Wahhabi threat. A number of concerted efforts to counter the Wahhabi doctrine through

---

[10] The literature on the Wahhabis is voluminous. For a brief and succinct discussion on the connections of Ibn abd al-Wahhab to other reformist hadith scholars in Mecca and Medina, see John Voll, "Muhammad Hayya al-Sindi and Muhammad ibn abd al-Wahhab: An Analysis of an Intellectual Group in Eighteenth Century Medina," *Bulletin of the School of Oriental and African Studies* 38 (1975): 32–9. For an analysis of the social and political background of the Wahhabi movement in Najd and Iraq, see Hala Fattah, *The Politics of Regional Trade* (Albany, NY: SUNY Press, 1997). For an analysis of Ibn Abd al-Wahhab's views on scriptures and correct Muslim practice, see Natana Delong-Bas, *Wahhabi Islam, From Revival and Reform to Global Jihad* (New York: Oxford University Press, 2004), pp. 41–121. For an excellent analysis of Wahhabi/Saudi views on community, see Abdulaziz al-Fahad, "From Exclusivism to Accommodation: Doctrinal and Legal Evolution of Wahhabism," *New York University Law Review* 79/2 (2004): 485–519.

education and debates with the scholarly community of Istanbul, Baghdad, and Medina produced a wealth of information about the Wahhabis as well as Ottoman attitudes toward them.

The Wahhabi movement threatened the political and religious consensus of the dominant Sunni orthodoxy in the Ottoman Empire in general and in Iraq in particular. First and foremost was the idea of exclusion. Muhammad Ibn Abd al-Wahhab had declared that those who do not subscribe to his version of Islam were unbelievers, and he expected his followers not only to cast them out (*takfir*), but also to wage war against them.[11] This form of political/religious exclusion of fellow Sunnis within the community confused many Sunni scholars, as is evident in the complaint sent by the judge of Medina in 1793.[12] However, by 1802, the government was clearly branding Ibn Saud and the Wahhabis as propagators of a new sect (*madhhab/mezheb*) taking the matter to the *şeyhülislam* (grand mufti) and the *kadiaskers* (military judges) of Rumelia and Anatolia, and deputizing the kadi of Baghdad and other religious scholars to visit Dari'aya, the capital of the Wahhabi/Saudi state, engage the Wahhabi scholars and report to Istanbul. According to one order,

a note arrived from the part of the aforementioned Sherif (of Mecca) containing in its purport a detailed description of the … rebel's evil intention and aggression against the territory of Hejaz and Iraq … as well as statements that rebel made public that he – God the Highest Forbid – had the vain design of spreading and proselytizing his false religion and that he sent letters in order to call the aforementioned Sherif to his religion and make him enter under his rule.[13]

While earlier characterization by the Ottomans of the Wahhabis had seen them as misguided tribal rebels whose belief was incidental to their natural insubordination, by 1802 it became imperative for the government to put a label on these rebels that situated them within the theological discourse of exclusion and inclusion in the Sunni tradition. Their rebellion was no longer simply a matter of state imperatives covered under state law (*kanun*), but one that necessitated engagement with them at the level of religious/political polemics. The engagement was a reaction, as the particular order cited above demonstrates, to the Wahhabi insistence on

---

[11] Delong-Bas claims that Ibn Abd al-Wahhab never openly called for such extreme measures. However, her conclusions are debatable. What is clear from the sources is that the Wahhabi/Saudi forces did engage in such acts. The first mention of Ibn Abd al-Wahhab in the Ottoman archives is dated March 1764. An imperial order sent to the governors of Baghdad and Basra, it states that Ibn Abd al-Wahhab has commandeered a number of fortified places and had insisted that captured Muslims accept his "absurd sect" or be killed. BOA, Muhimme Defterleri, 164-206-2.

[12] See above.   [13] BOA, Hatt-ı Humayun, 3811 and for more information see Hatt-ı Humayun, 3766.

proselytizing their views of what constituted a true Muslim community in
a public manner. As a result, the Ottoman government, its official ulema,
and other anti-Wahhabi and pro-Wahhabi ulema in Iraq, resurrected the
debate on inclusion and exclusion in a highly politicized public manner
and in a language often divorced from the legalistic discourse of the
literature on sects (*firaq*) within Islam.[14] Thus the branding of the
Wahhabis as propagators of a new religion, or a new *madhhab*, became
the mantra of both official and unofficial discourse about them, often
without much analysis of their doctrines. Despite the efforts of Ibn Abd
al-Wahhab and his followers to disseminate their beliefs in a reasoned
discourse, through engaging with ulema in Iraq and Najd and through the
dissemination of blueprints on correct behavior and on debates with
opponents, what is most striking in the encounter between all parties is
the linguistic and intellectual shortcuts they took in their branding of the
other, depending which side they were on, as sectarian or unbeliever.[15] In
the melee of such confrontation, we see the birth of a new generalized
language on belief and disbelief in Sunni Islam. It is perhaps most evident
in the use of the term Khariji to brand the Wahhabis by the Ottomans and
the ulema who supported them.

The term Khariji denoted a cluster of specific ideas in the early nineteenth century. First, it referred to a group of dissenters in early Islam who
disagreed with all other views on the nature of legitimate political authority, and insisted that any "true" Muslim could become the leader of the
community. The problem, of course, was to define a true Muslim. The
debates on that issue generated excursuses on free will and predestina-
tion and furnished the basis for early Islamic speculative philosophy.[16] By
the early nineteenth century, Kharijism denoted a sectarian and exclusivist
view of what constituted a Muslim, one outside the mainstream of the
Muslim Sunni community. It also denoted in the Wahhabi context
an absolute commitment to works at the expense of faith in determining
inclusion in the community, the primacy of direct knowledge of the Quran
and the *sunna* of the Prophet as the only legitimate way to comprehend
and live as a true Muslim, the individual's own interpretation of this

---

[14] Jackson, *On the Boundaries of Theological Tolerance*, argues, for example, that the issue of tolerance in
the medieval period was a theological issue rather than a political one.

[15] Delong-Bas, *Wahhabi Islam*, pp. 41–91. Ibn Abd al-Wahhab wrote two kinds of tracts: commentaries
and fatwas, mostly well within the Hanbali tradition and scholarly in nature, and simple blueprints
on dogma and conversion. It was the latter that were intended for the public.

[16] The best discussion on these issues is to be found in Husayn Muruwah, *Al-Naza'at al-madiyya fi
al-falsafa al-'Arabiyah al-Islamiyya*, 2 vols. (Beirut: Dar al-Farabi, 1988).

knowledge without recourse to the reasoning of contemporary legal scholars, and a readiness to declare most Muslims as unbelievers.[17]

The Wahhabis' anti-mystical stance, their emphasis on outward demonstrations of belief (including political activism), and their hostility to any theological (*kalam*) and inherited traditions of legal reasoning (*fiqh*) threatened the monopoly that the interpreters of Islamic law had on determining rituals and defining what constituted Islamic behavior. In 1802 the state sent out an order to various cities in Syria and Iraq penned by its sponsored ulema justifying their comparison of the Wahhabis to Kharijis. The scholars pointed out that only with Islamic law could one determine a good Muslim. Furthermore, they asserted, the Wahhabis used the act of excluding and branding those who disagreed with them as unbelievers (*kuffar*) to justify killing those who did not adhere to their special brand of Islam. This exclusivity was contrary to the spirit of the community because it removed the process of communal inclusion and exclusion from the reasoned discourse of the ulema. Furthermore, if unbelief (*kufr*) is simply the result of a person's asking God and his Prophet for intercession, then the whole process of exclusion (*takfir*) becomes trivialized.[18] While these arguments certainly were based on the theology of tolerance within Sunni Islam to convince the learned community of the danger of espousing the Wahhabi version of Islam, the propaganda of the government, carried out by pro-government scholars, also stressed the hostility of the Wahhabis to the popular practice of visiting the tombs of saints and continuously alluded to Ibn Abd al-Wahhab as a false prophet, a Musaylima.[19]

The nineteenth-century resurrection of the Khariji debate over who was a believer developed into a discussion of who was a Muslim and what determines belief. This debate swirled around the idea of toleration, but toleration of a specific type. First and foremost, toleration in this context was distinctly different from Locke's liberal view, because it was not grounded in the concept of the natural right of the individual to practice his religion independent of the state's ideological preferences. The discussions that arose out of the Wahhabi challenge to Sunnism drew on the early

---

[17] These attitudes were discussed by a number of scholars in the nineteenth century. For a brief overview see Fattah, *The Politics of Regional Trade*. On the exclusivity of the Wahhabi movement and polity see Aziz al-Azmeh, *Islams and Modernities* (New York: Verso, 1993), pp. 104–21. The government's attitudes were evident in BOA, Hatt-ı Humayun, 3799-A and 3855-B. On the Ottoman government's reaction to the Wahhabis, see Zekeriya Kursun, *Necid ve Ahsa'da Osmanlı Hakimiyeti, Vehhabi Hareketi ve Suud Devleti'nin Ortaya Çıkışı* (Ankara: Türk Tarih Kurumu, 1998).
[18] BOA, Hatt-ı Humayun, 3799-A. [19] BOA, Hatt-ı Humayun, 3855-B.

community's concern over who were the majority (*ahl al-jama'a*), its determination to create a consensus (defined as one reached by those with knowledge), and the importance of maintaining the community intact in the face of dissension. Yet there was an essential newness to the Wahhabi challenge, at least to those who designated themselves as possessors of knowledge and legitimate power. What was noteworthy in the early nineteenth century was the alacrity with which the various sectors of Iraqi society incorporated a politicized, non-legalistic, and polemical vocabulary of exclusion (*takfir*) against fellow Sunni Muslims. In the sixteenth and seventeenth centuries, by contrast, such discrimination would have been unthinkable.

Certainly, the Ottoman government and various religious scholars had earlier produced treatises condemning Shi'i Islam and branding Shi'is as rejectionists (*rafada*) and unbelievers (*kuffar*). For example, an influential polemical tract of the sixteenth century, written by a resident of Mardin, Hüseyin ibn Abdallah al-Shirvani, attacked the Shi'i *kızılbaş* (followers of the Safavids) as unbelievers who deified their leader Shah Isma'il.[20] The treatise alternately branded them rejectionists (*rafada*), extremists (*ghulat*), and a host of other epithets. Unlike post-Wahhabi cases, the Ottoman sultans (in this case Süleyman the Magnificent) used such polemical tracts as political tools to justify war against Shi'ite Muslims. This and other such tracts pitted Sunni Islam against Shi'i Islam. They did not favor one sect within Sunni Islam over another.

Before the Wahhabis, definitions of unbelief within Sunni Islam had been quite legalistic and particularistic. They were designed to control and homogenize rituals and behaviors. For example, in *The Fortress of Islam* (*Hisnu al-Islam*), a widely circulated seventeenth-century tract printed several times by the Müteferikka Press in Istanbul and in nineteenth-century Egypt and Istanbul, Mullah Ghanim ıbn Muhammad al-Baghdadi (d. 1622), a resident of Baghdad, defined unbelief as a series of actions and beliefs, such as sleeping with your women at the prohibited time, belief in astronomy, speech that denigrates the Prophet and the companions, and a number of other specific transgressions that could be overcome with proper behavior (*adab*). Unbelief was not a generalized condition or an irremediable political act; it was an individual and reversible decision.[21] Unlike the Wahhabis, who branded all those who did not

---

[20] Husayn ibn 'Abdallah al-Shirvani, "Ahkâm diniyya," Süleymaniye Kütüphanesi, MS Hacı Mahmud Efendi, 1962.
[21] Mullah Ghanim ibn Muhammad al-Baghdadi, "Hisnu-al-Islam," Süleymaniye Kütüphanesi, MS Reşid Pasha, 858/25.

adhere to their political/religious doctrine as outside the community of Muslims, al-Baghdadi classified an individual transgression as an act of unbelief. The transgressor remained a Muslim as long as he or she acted to redress the lapse. Ibn Abd al-Wahhab himself tried to make a distinction between the lesser and greater polytheism (*shirk*), which for him led to unbelief (*kufr*), finding individualized infraction in private behavior as belonging to the former, and public displays of certain behaviors, such as the veneration of saints and failure to perform prayers, as belonging to the latter and hence punishable by death.[22] However, the line between the former and the latter in his work remained thin and his followers failed to make the distinction.

The politicization and generalization of vocabulary of inclusion and exclusion within the Sunni community in the late eighteenth and early nineteenth century dominated the polemics of the reforming scholars in Iraq.[23] It was particularly visible in the tracts of the other major reform movement in Sunni Islam in 1820s Baghdad, the Khalidiyya/Naqshbandiyya. Mawlana Khalid, a Kurdish scholar from Shahrizur in northern Iraq, drew on the Mujaddidiyya/Naqshbandiyya tradition of reformist Islam,[24] a movement that had its adherents in Iraq as early as the late seventeenth century; one of its Basrene proponents was a supporter of the reforms initiated under the Köprülü viziers.[25] Under the tutelage of a seventeenth-century Indian scholar, Sirhindi, the Mujaddidiyya/Naqshbandiyya pursued revitalization of a fourteenth-century sufi order. Born in reaction to the Mughal sultan Akbar's attempt to establish a syncretic new religion, Sirhindi's renewal of sufi practice called for adherence to a hadith-based interpretation of the Quran and reliance on the example (*sunna*) of the Prophet as a guide to believers in sufism. Wary of the intoxicating experiences and pantheistic implication of some popular practices and philosophical musings in mysticism, Sirhindi's emphasis was on the sober and critical examination through human reasoning (*ijtihad*) of the foundational texts of Islam, the Quran and hadith, and the experience of God's presence in transient mystical moments. More significant was

---

[22] Delong-Bas, *Wahhabi Islam*, pp. 61–78.
[23] Hala Fattah, "Wahhabi Influences, Salafi Responses: Shaikh Mahmud Shukri and the Iraqi Salafi Movement, 1745–1930," *Journal of Islamic Studies* 14/2 (2003): 127–48.
[24] Mawlana Khalid's name was Abu'l Baha' Dhia al-Din Khalid al-Shahrizuri. For a biography of Khalid, see Albert Hourani, "Shaykh Khalid and the Naqshbandi Order," in S. M. Stern, Albert Habib Hourani and Vivian Brown (eds.), *Islamic Philosophy and the Classical Tradition* (Oxford: Oxford University Press, 1972), pp. 89–103.
[25] Husayn al-Basri al-Mimi, "Nazm al-sumut al-zabajadiyya fi silsilat al-sadat al-Naqshabandiyya," Süleymaniye Kütüphanesi, MS Aşir Efendi, 176.

Sirhindi's call for an activist sufi practice that encouraged political and social life at the expense of older sufi practices of withdrawal from worldly affairs.[26]

Khalid was initiated into the Mujaddidiyya/Naqshbandiyya order by Shah Ghulam Ali (known to his Arab followers as Shaykh Abdullah al-Dihlawi) sometime in the year 1809–10. Shaykh Abdullah al-Dihlawi traced his spiritual chain back to Sirhindi and was one of the most respected religious figures in Delhi. Given the highest honor of being awarded full and absolute successorship (*khilafa tamma mutlaqa*), Khalid returned from India to Suleimaniyya in 1811, began preaching a distinctive version of Mujaddidiyya/Naqshbandiyya, and eventually converted followers to his particular brand of the order.[27]

Mawlana Khalid trained a large number of preachers (one estimate puts it at about 120) and became quite visible in the political and scholarly community of Iraq. In 1812, he incurred the wrath of the Barzinji family of Suleimaniyya, leaders of the Kadiriyya sufi order, and he was forced to flee Suleimaniyya. He took refuge in Baghdad where he acquired a number of followers, among them Abu al-Thana' al-Alusi and several scholars from the premier scholarly family of Baghdad, al-Suwaydis. In Baghdad, his enemies sought to discredit him with the governor. An investigation exonerated Mawlana Khalid, however, and he was able to stay in Baghdad for some time. The governor of Suleimaniyya eventually let him return, but he again was exiled to Baghdad in 1820. He stayed in Baghdad for two years, supported by its governor Dawud Pasha, but eventually left for Damascus where he spent the rest of his life.[28]

The Khalidiyya/Naqshbandiyya and the Wahhabi movements shared a number of ideas. Both were products of a reform movement within Islam that called for individual reasoning with emphasis on foundational texts; both were committed to activism in the practice of one's faith; both were involved in political reforms; and both harbored some antipathy toward the traditional and sacred hierarchy of their societies. Yet the two movements were also different in fundamental ways. On the one hand, Wahhabis chose to rebel and attempt to overturn the system by violence,

---

[26] Johan Ter Haar, "The Naqshbandi Traditions in the Eyes of Ahmad Sirhindi," in Marc Gaborieau, Alexandre Popovic, and Thiery Zarcone (eds.), *Naqshbandis, Historical Developments and Present Situation of a Muslim Mystical Order* (Istanbul: Isis, 1990), pp. 83–93.

[27] Hamid Algar, "The Naqshbandiyya Order: A Preliminary Survey of its History and Significance," *Studia Islamica* 44 (1976): 123–52; Hamid Algar, "A Brief History of the Naqshbandi Order," in Gaborieau et al., *Naqshbandis*, pp. 3–44, and Abu-Manneh, *Studies of Islam*, pp. 13–40.

[28] For his sojourn in Damascus, see Itzchak Weismann, *Taste of Modernity, Sufism, Salafiyya, and Arabism in Late Ottoman Damascus* (Leiden: Brill, 2001).

espoused an exclusivist stance, destroyed mausolea, were openly anti-clerical (calling all ulema who cooperated with corrupt power unbelievers), and undermined the basis for their legitimacy by stressing the importance of individual interpretation of hadith at the expense of law. On the other hand, the Khalidiyya/Naqshbandiyya's offered an urban reformed sufism that appealed to a powerful scholarly/mercantile elite in Baghdad interested in having a say in the reform agendas at the center. The response of the reformist Khalidiyya/Naqshbadiyya to the issue of exclusion and inclusion is particularly worthy of note, as is revealed in an epistle written by one of the followers of Mawlana Khalid, Abu al-Fawz al-Suwaydi, defending his master against accusations of unbelief. The letter was written sometime between 1820 and 1822, while Khalid was in Baghdad after being expelled for the second time from Suleimaniyya. Hourani speculates that Khalid had engaged in "a miracle-working contest with Shaikh Ma'ruf al-Barzinji (head of the Kadiriyya sufi order in the city), the setting of one *baraka* against another."[29] If this conjecture is accurate, this contest was between the leader of a venerable and established Kadiri sufi order (al-Barzinji) and an ambitious upstart (Khalid al-Naqshbandi) who was transforming an older order into an instrument for his particular vision for reform. Al-Suwaydi himself was the son of Ali al-Suwaydi, a prominent scholar whom the Ottoman state had recruited into its provincial administration, and whom state officials in Baghdad had accused at one time of harboring Wahhabi sympathies. Despite this charge, Ali was in fact a Naqshbandi and had initiated his son into the Mujaddidiyya/Naqshbandiyya order, thereby paving the way for his offspring to espouse the Khalidi version of that order.[30]

Al-Suwaydi's epistle was a response to accusations made by Uthman Beg bin Suleiman Beg al-Jalili against Mawlana Khalid.[31] Uthman accused Khalid of unbelief (*kufr*) and of subversion, and Abu al-Fawz took it upon himself to defend his mentor. Among the many accusations leveled against Khalid, three are of particular interest. First, Uthman accused Khalid of unbelief and of conspiring to destroy the Muslim order of things

[29] Hourani, "Shaykh Khalid," p. 98.
[30] Muhammad As'ad Sahibzadeh al-Uthmani al-Naqshbandi al-Khalidi, *Baghiyat al-wajid fi maktubat hadrat mawlana Khalid* (Damascus: Matb'at al-Tarraqi, 1334 AH), pp. 131–2; also see footnote (p. 132) on first meeting of Mawlana Khalid with Ali al-Suwaydi.
[31] Abu al-Fawz Muhammad Amin al-Suwaydi, "Daf' al-zulm 'an al-wuqu' fi 'ard al-mazlum," Süleymaniye Kütüphanesi, MS Esad Efendi, 1404. Uthman Beg al-Jalili was a scholar descended from an "aristocratic" Mosuli provincial household, which dominated the politics of Mosul until the 1820s. He was a literary annotator and was murdered when his son was overthrown as governor in a popular rebellion in 1826.

because he had brought innovations inspired by his contact with the English in India; second, he insisted that Khalid was attempting to create a new school of law (*madhhab*) through his use of reasoning (*ijtihad*); and, third, Uthman condemned him as a Kurdish saboteur appealing to those elements of society who were interested in the acquisition of wealth and land.

Uthman al-Jalili's attack, reproduced in Abu al-Fawz's text, began with a complaint. The world as we know it has been turned upside down, he proclaimed, since those with knowledge, the ulema, were no longer performing their functions properly and people were behaving in un-Islamic ways. Among the Rum (that is the Turks), he continued, a new European religion called Freemasonry had appeared, and it had picked up some followers for a while. But it had soon collapsed. Here in Iraq, meanwhile, a Kurd called Khalid distorted the Naqshbandi way, and went to India where the Christian English corrupted him. Abu al-Fawz immediately picked up the conflation of Freemasonry, the British, and the Naqshbandiyya. He rejected the links to European doctrines, marshaled the long history of the Naqshbandiyya, and listed Khalid's *silsila* (chain; line; pedigree). He also pointed out Khalid's many followers among the powerful in Istanbul and that he was in Sultan Mahmud II's good graces.[32] As for instituting a new *madhhab*, Abu al-Fawz insisted the four legal Sunni schools had been so distorted by explications, legal opinions, and other accretions that the original intent of the founders had been lost. In fact, the founders of these schools of law had prohibited people from imitating them blindly and encouraged them to use their reason.

Abu al-Fawz also dismissed the accusation leveled against Khalid as a saboteur and spokesman for a group of upwardly mobile individuals. He defended the acquisition of wealth if such wealth was used for the good of the community, and insisted that the political troubles of Khalid and his preachers in Suleimaniyya and Amadiyya stemmed from the fear of people like Barzinji of the power of his message and the threat implied by Khalid's popularity to their privileged position. As for the accusation of unbelief, Abu al-Fawz appealed to Uthman to use reasoned discourse in his discussion of difference, admonishing him for his loose use of the word *takfir*. No Muslims who believed in God and turned to the Ka'ba for prayers, he argued, should be excluded as unbelievers, even when legal scholars of the Ottoman state branded certain groups as apostates or unbelievers. Muslims should instead

---

[32] For Khalid al-Naqshbandi's connections in Istanbul during this period, see Abu Manneh, *Studies on Islam*, pp. 41–71.

follow the example of the companions of the Prophet, who refused to brand the Kharijites as unbelievers despite their rebelliousness, their killing of Muslims, and their appropriation of a personal vision of the Quran.

The discussions and accusations of unbelief that permeated both polemical literature and state orders took place in a period of extreme crisis that saw the emergence of new forms of political language. This language was marked by the generalized and public use of exclusion against enemies and by the deployment of a simpler literary style to communicate to a public (prospective believers, opponents and supporters). The debate on tolerance, particularly within the Sunni community, was no longer only in the purview of theology, but was firmly in the public realm, accessible to wider sectors of Ottoman society. At the same time, despite the hardening of lines on issues of inclusion and exclusion between different protagonists, it is difficult to pinpoint a clear correlation between one social group and a politico-religious affiliation. Rather the call for reform and for the rejuvenation of the Muslim community through the institution of correct Muslim practice was part of "structures of feeling," of an emergent consciousness among different sectors of Ottoman society, which permeated this period and was only associated with clearly articulated political ideologies in the later part of the nineteenth century.

Despite the difficulty in explaining these debates on exclusion as part of a clearly articulated ideology of specific and well-formed social groups in this period, they did have an important socio-political dimension. The 1790s to the 1830s marked a turning point for the Islamic empires and their relationship to European powers. On the economic and political level, Islamic empires experienced a period of severe ecological, fiscal, and military crisis starting in the 1770s that led to the emergence of what Bayly calls "Asian Mercantilism." The strengthening of regional economies dominated by monopolistic practices of a mercantile and bureaucratic elite, the emergence of tribal and military regional power holders, the assertion of regional identities, and the rise of reformist and regional (in the case of India, communal) movements of renewal characterized these crises. The centralizing reforms of the nineteenth century, whether carried out by foreign imperial powers or indigenous imperial elites, responded to developments in all of these spheres of human activity.[33] By the 1790s, the Napoleonic Wars and the ideological struggle in Europe between French

---

[33] C. A. Bayly, *Imperial Meridian: The British Empire and the World 1780–1830* (London: Longman, 1989).

Republican ideals and British ideals spilled over into the rest of the world. In practical terms, it meant the globalization of war and its imperatives. Both India and the Ottoman Empire were transformed in the European imagination from sources of economic power and resources to strategic spaces where the competing interests of various powers were played out. Thus the British Raj was born in India as a new imperial order, together with a new imperial ideology of race and difference.[34] In the Ottoman Empire, the strengthening of regional and provincial centers and their economic welfare that started in the 1760s, began, for various reasons, to dissipate by the 1820s. While the Napoleonic invasion of Egypt and the Greek War of Independence created the diplomacy of the "Eastern Question," for the inhabitants of southern and central Iraq the Napoleonic Wars and the Wahhabis defined their changing relationship with Europeans and Ottomans alike. By the 1790s, Baghdad had become the center of European intrigue as threats of Napoleon's expansion into Russia and Afghanistan, and the presence of French revolutionary troops in India, threatened British control of the Indian subcontinent and Persian Gulf trade.[35] Fattah has argued that the expansion of trade in southern Iraq and central Arabia in the eighteenth century gave rise to conditions that allowed for a centralizing political and religious movement such as the Wahhabi to emerge as a vehicle for state building.[36] And while she alludes to the polemics among the ulema that the Wahhabis generated, it is not clear what these debates were and what was particularly new about them. She does, however, situate them firmly in the regional cultural universe of southern Iraq and Najd. More recently, she has attempted to connect these debates to certain individuals in Baghdad and Basra. Yet, due to the paucity of material on links between Wahhabis and Iraqi ulema, it is not possible to establish a direct link between debates on reform and the politics of the Wahhabi movement.[37] What follows is an attempt to situate the debates on reform in the context of both provincial and imperial politics in Baghdad, keeping in mind that, until the second half of the nineteenth century, and

[34] For a fascinating analysis of this transformation, see C. A. Bayly, *Empire and Information, Intelligence Gathering and Social Communication in India, 1780–1870* (Cambridge: Cambridge University Press, 1999).
[35] M. E. Yapp, "The Establishment of the East India Company Residency in Baghdad, 1798–1806," *Bulletin of the School of Oriental and African Studies* 30 (1967): 323–36; and Edward Ingram, "From Trade to Empire in the Near East III: The Uses of the Residency in Baghdad, 1794–1804," *Middle Eastern Studies* 14 (1978): 278–306.
[36] Fattah, *The Politics of Regional Trade*, introduction.
[37] Fattah, "Wahhabi Influences, Salafi Responses."

despite the changed political language of these debates and their public nature, they remained the purview of a disparate number of individuals who sometimes espoused competing and contradictory views.

By 1801–2, Wahhabism had rattled enough skeletons in the closets of the Iraqi political and scholarly elite to involve them in one way or another with the factional politics of reform in Istanbul. Between 1801 and 1810, three of the most highly regarded religious scholars in the city – two of them from the Ottoman judicial establishment (Abu al-Thana' al-Alusi and Ali al-Suwaydi) – were accused of Wahhabi sympathies. It is worth recounting the incident in detail in order to demonstrate the complicated ways in which competing reform agendas between the provincial establishment and the central state became enmeshed in Baghdad. The Mamluk governor of Baghdad, Süleyman the Little (gv. 1808–10), had secured his governorship in the midst of the deposition of Selim III. According to a report issued three years later by an Ottoman official, the governorship was never really sanctioned by the Ottomans, who accepted it for lack of a viable alternative. Local histories describe Suleiman the Little as someone who tried to reform the administration of Baghdad and who curried favor with reforming ulema. Ali al-Suwaydi, one of the leading proponents of reform and an adherent of Mujaddidi/Naqshbandi sufism at that time, was one such scholar who advised the governor on abolishing non-shari'a-prescribed taxes. In 1810, the government sent Halet Efendi, a powerful emissary of the reforming Mahmud II, to Baghdad to reestablish control and get rid of the governor and his supporters.[38] Halet Efendi belonged to the Mujaddidi/Naqshbandi circle of advisors to Sultan Mahmud II, who were instrumental, until he was banished in 1822, in mapping out a reform agenda within the parameters of Sunni orthodoxy.[39] Instead of arbitrating what was quickly turning into a civil war between various factions in Baghdad, he proceeded to enter the fray by supporting anti-reform scholars against both those who had reformist sympathies and those he accused of being Wahhabi sympathizers. Despite the lack of any evidence of sympathy harbored by either Süleyman the Little or his advisors to the Wahhabis, Halet Efendi used the accusation of Wahhabism, as did his local supporters, to discredit the reforming party in Baghdad. The term had now become part of the public political lexicon of the Ottomans and locals for excluding their enemies.

In the Ottoman Empire of the early nineteenth century, the Wahhabi challenge might have meant a separatist regional identity to some, but for

[38] BOA, Hatt-ı Humayun 20896 and 20898, B/C/D.   [39] Abu Manneh, *Studies on Islam*, p. 44.

certain elements within the scholarly and commercial elite in Baghdad it was one way to insert themselves into the struggles to define and participate in reform. For sectors of the scholarly community as well as some political elites, the Wahhabi doctrine of political reform, its desire to standardize and simplify the taxation system to bring it in line with Islam, its stress on adherence to Islamic law, and its success in building a secure state in Arabia offered a clear alternative to Istanbul's rather ad hoc reforms. Such scholars, political leaders, and merchants appropriated Wahhabi views on the proper practice of religion and the proper role of Muslims in a new order, and expressed sympathy toward some aspects of Wahhabi doctrine even as they maintained allegiance to the Ottoman state. They rejected Wahhabi exclusivity, though. For them, creating a strong and virtuous Islamic order need not mean that anyone had to be excluded from that order. All that was needed was a scholarly and political elite devoted to recreating the politics of the early community.

It was here that the Khalidiyya-Naqshabandiyya played a role. Abu Manneh's pioneering work on Mujaddidiyya/Naqshbandiyya and Khalidiyya/Naqshbandiyya links to the reforming elites in the reign of Mahmud II establishes the political dimensions of that sufi order's doctrines.[40] As early as the seventeenth century, the Mujaddidiyya/Naqshbandiyya had acquired supporters from some of the upper ulema in Istanbul. When Mawlana Khalid started preaching his activist and sober version of Naqshbandiyya, however, he also found sympathizers among such reform-minded bureaucrats as Pertev Pasha. Even Mahmud II himself briefly thought that the Khalidiyya version of the order would be a good antidote to the Bektaşi order, which he outlawed when he abolished the janissary corps in 1826. Thus, the Khalidiyya/Naqshbandiyya quite early gave coherence to a reforming elite and, according to Abu Manneh, furnished the basis of the first general statement of reform in the nineteenth century, the Gülhane Rescript. For Abu Manneh, it is to the Khalidiyya/Naqshbandiyya, and not western models, that we should look in order to comprehend the reform edicts of the early nineteenth century.

In Iraq, Abu al-Fawz's defense of Mawlana Khalid coincided with three important social and political developments: (1) the rise of Dawud Pasha as

---

[40] Butrus Abu-Manneh, "The Naqshbandiyya-Mujaddidiyya in the Ottoman Lands in the Early 19th Century," *Die Welt des Islams* 22 (1982–4): 1–36, and "The Islamic Roots of the Gülhane Rescript," *Die Welt des Islams* 34 (1994): 173–204. In that connection, see also Carter Findley, *Ottoman Civil Officialdom: A Social History* (Princeton, NJ: Princeton University Press, 1988), pp. 70–2.

governor of Baghdad and his ambitious attempts to build a strong governorship based on cooperation with the high ulema and mercantile elite of the city, (2) the increasing power of the ulema and urban elites of tribal origin in the economic and social life of the city, and (3) the gradual subjugation of other localities and political centers of power in Iraq to Baghdad. Dawud Pasha was interested in reforming the military and tax structures of his province, and to that end drew upon the support of the Baghdadi elite against an entrenched provincial political leadership in other parts of Iraq. Mawlana Khalid had threatened the old landed elite and their supporters in Süleymaniyya and, it seems, also in other parts of Iraq. On one hand, Uthman al-Jalili, himself a representative of the provincial *ancien régime*, felt threatened by Khalid and his supporters. He had branded Khalid an unbeliever, one linked to all these reform ideas brought in through contact with the Christian world, a charlatan who created delusions among his supporters to build a personal fortune. On the other hand, al-Suwaydi belonged to a family of elite scholars who had consistently called for reform of religious learning and political power. In chaotic times, he viewed himself and his group as representatives and supporters of a reformed new order. He felt compelled to remind al-Jalili that the accusation of unbelief should be used judiciously and that Khalid was only building on a long tradition of reform within the world of Islam, a tradition that made it incumbent on Muslims to move away from the old ways (*taqlid*).

CONCLUSION

What do these discussions of a group of Baghdadi scholars about the nature of belief tell us about the political culture of the Ottoman Empire? First of all, the debates demonstrate that an important sector of the scholarly community (ulema) believed that political activism was a crucial element in being a good Muslim (even if those who monopolized knowledge and power considered such activism to be subversive). Nevertheless, these ulema did contest the manner of involvement in politics – should it be through rebellion or through working with the powerful? Although this point has a long history in Islamic political thought, what made it noteworthy in the early nineteenth century was the vehemence with which it resurrected the issue of inclusion and exclusion as an element in political activism. Such activism was linked to the formulation of indigenous reform agendas and helped map the contested terrain of Ottoman political modernity.

Second, it is clear that these Sunni debates over unbelief were different than they had been in earlier periods. They were less legalistic, less focused on the specifics of ritual, and more clearly political and categorical in their definitions of belief and unbelief. It seems evident that their proponents were debating the issue of toleration within an Islamic context. That is to say, rather than basing their concept of toleration on the concept of natural individual rights, they instead situated toleration firmly in the idea of communal consensus.

Finally, the Ottomans' reaction to the Wahhabis, the debates that ensued among supporters of detractors of the Wahhabis and the Khalidiyya/Naqshbandiyya sufi order marked the emergence of a new political language, one addressed to a public (potential converts, detractors, ulema) that was perceived to be essential to the definition of parameters of what constituted a strengthened Islamic community, whether it was defined within the territorial confines of the Ottoman or the Wahhabi community. What the Wahhabi movement and the Khalidi/Naqshbandi sufi order initiated was a battle for the hearts and minds of potential converts, a battle they waged through the use of the accessible word, through the simplification of theology to a set of clearly articulated formulas to certain correct practices, and the development of a network of active preachers who went out to get quick converts. In this sense, they were the harbingers of the kind of religious-political language that would permeate the Ottoman Empire in the second half of the nineteenth century, and get a strong boost from the spread of the printing press. They can be viewed as the first modern attempts in the Ottoman Empire at reconfiguring Muslim Sunni identity in the face of the challenges raised by a political crisis at the center of the empire. While Butrus Abu Manneh's work has stressed the links between the reforming Sunni orthodox elite and Ottoman policies at the center, the debates were part of an emerging trend in sensibilities across the Islamic world. What the Wahhabi movement did, perhaps more than it has been credited by traditional Ottoman historiography, was create an environment that made possible a redefinition of what it means to construct a viable Sunni community. While Wahhabism might not have had much influence in the long run beyond the lands of Najd, Syria, and Iraq, its legacy of what was to become a *salafi* trend in Muslim thought on renewal was enduring. In the case of Iraq, a large number of the polemical and sectarian texts produced in the eighteenth and early nineteenth centuries were printed and circulated after 1860.

PART V

Aesthetics of empire

Public spaces and the garden culture of Istanbul in the eighteenth century*

Shirine Hamadeh

And if you wish, oh spirit of life
That to you all manner of women be drawn
God be praised, [that] the Lord gifted you
With the attractive power of beauty
In the season of roses go for a pleasure trip
Especially around [the garden of] Kağıthane
Rub the scented oil of its shrubs on your brows
Cover your head with a Lahore shawl
. . .

Wear a coral-red vest, a gold embroidered robe
Let the dagger at your waist be choice
. . .

Drink one or two cups of wine
[So] that your eyes might look bloodshot
Toward whatever assembly women gather
Walk, oh! swaying cypress
Don't go stumbling along like an old man
Make your every stride like a lion's
. . .

Reveal a lock of hair from under the fez
Show them a build like Rüstem's
. . .

They are attracted to the most handsome
They'd sacrifice their heart for his sake
Here and there, tip that fez coyly
Scatter ambergris from your locks, my lovely

* Several colleagues have offered suggestions and comments on different versions of this piece. I would
like to express my deepest gratitude to all of them. Part of this research was done while I was a fellow
at Dumbarton Oaks, in 1999–2000. I extend special thanks to the Director of Landscape Studies,
Michel Conan, and to my colleague and friend, Linda Parshall, for their generosity in sharing their
ideas and insights. I am also grateful to Walter Andrews' wonderful suggestions for my translations of
the Ottoman poetry. A different version of this essay forms chapter 4 of my book, *The City's Pleasures:
Istanbul in the Eighteenth Century* (Seattle: University of Washington Press, 2007).

...

That one laughs from behind the veil
That one looks at the ground, blushing modestly
Those chuckles, that flirting, that glance
When she looks at you out of the corner of her eye, oh my!
One of them starts to sing a song
So they might work their arts on you
One hastens to entice you
[Her] mantle falls from her back
At times, a swing is set up in a cypress
Two of them sit in it, casually clad
One alluringly rocks the swing
The other recites lovely songs
As she swings her gown falls open
Showing every bit of her to you
To you she lets her trouser-tie be seen
To you, perhaps, her secret treasure.[1]

For painters and poets, chroniclers and travelers, the spectacle of urban life in eighteenth-century Istanbul was a source of perpetual fascination. Time and again, "Turks, Rayas, and Franks,"[2] "citizens of all ranks, of one and the other sex,"[3] men and women clad in an "infinite variety of Levantine habiliment,"[4] were sketched, painted, and described, as they strolled and sprawled, drank and smoked, sang and danced, feasted, flirted, and entertained in public squares and gardens around the city (figs. 12.1 and 12.2).

The rites and rituals of recreation of ordinary people anchored Ottoman and foreign representations of the city. Public gardens, in particular, stood out as the most vibrant venue of social and leisure life. There, a wide range of social classes, ranks, and ages appeared to share the same spaces of sociability and forms of entertainment. Women and children, seldom visible in earlier depictions of the mostly male recreational universe of taverns and coffeehouses, became a noticeable presence. All in all, the city seemed a far cry from the sober imperial capital of earlier European panoramic views, in which an aloof Topkapı Palace hid behind a veil of cypresses and stately domes and minarets punctuated the hilly

---

[1] Enderunlu Fazıl Bey, "Zikr-i mukaddime-i manzume" ("Preface in Rhyme"), in *Zenânnâme (Book of Women)*, İstanbul Üniversitesi Kütüphanesi MS Ty 5502, fols. 79–80.
[2] I.e. Turks, non-Muslims and Europeans; Thomas Allom and Robert Walsh, *Constantinople and the Scenery of the Seven Churches of Asia Minor*, 2 vols. (London: Fisher, Son and Co., 1838), vol. II, p. 34.
[3] Ignatius Mouradgea D'Ohsson, *Tableau général de l'empire othoman*, 4 vols. (Paris: Firmin Didot, 1788–1824), vol. IV, p. 185.
[4] James Dallaway, *Constantinople Ancient and Modern with Excursions to the Shores and Islands of the Archipelago* (London: T. Cadell and W. Davies, 1797), pp. 118–19.

Figure 12.1 From Thomas Allom and Robert Walsh, *Constantinople and the Scenery of the Seven Churches of Asia Minor*, vol. I (London, 1838). Scene of outdoor recreation at the garden of Kağıthane by Thomas Allom.

landscape. In eighteenth-century images and writings, public squares around monumental fountains, gardens with coffeehouse terraces, and promenades along the Bosphorus set against a magnificent backdrop of palaces and mansions emerged as the new landmarks of the growing Ottoman capital.

Of course, gardens and promenades were not new to the landscape of Istanbul; nor was appreciation of them as spaces of recreation limited to this period.[5] Nevertheless, they penetrated cultural expression in ways unseen before, and evoked a new intensity in the Ottoman public sphere. As in contemporary urban centers in France and England, gardens became a topos of the visual culture. Like the *fêtes champêtres* of Watteau

---

[5] In their accounts of the city in the latter half of the seventeenth century, Evliya Çelebi and Eremya Çelebi Kömürciyan mention several suburban gardens and describe the garden of Kağıthane as a popular holiday resort for the rich and the poor of the city. Eremya Çelebi Kömürciyan, *İstanbul Tarihi: XVII. Asırda İstanbul*, trans. from Armenian by Hrand D. Andreasyan, ed. Kevork Pamukciyan, 2nd edn (Istanbul: Eren, 1988), pp. 50–1, 54; Evliya Çelebi, *The Seyahatname of Evliya Çelebi. Book One: Istanbul* (fascimile of Topkapı Sarayı Bağdad 304), ed. Şinasi Tekin and Gönül Tekin (Cambridge, MA: Harvard University Press, 1993), fols. 18b–19a, 120a–146b passim, 171a, 188a.

Figure 12.2 From Enderunlu Fazıl, *Hûbânnâme ve Zenânnâme*, İstanbul Üniversitesi Kütüphanesi MS TY 5502, fol. 78 Garden Scene at Sa'dabad. Courtesy of İstanbul Üniversitesi Kütüphanesi.

and the English garden walks of Hogarth and Gainsborough, paintings and engravings of the gardens of Istanbul focused on the collective leisure of men, women, and children, capturing snapshots of their pleasures, activities, and experiences. They portrayed a wide sartorial spectrum that bespoke the social diversity of outdoor public life. In the stock of pictorial representations of Istanbul that were produced in the course of the eighteenth century, a remarkable portion depicted women leisurely lounging on the grass, smoking, eating, dancing, or engaged in musical gatherings; men walking, chatting, sipping their coffee, or napping in the shade of a tree; young boys and girls on swings and climbing trees (figs. 12.1 and 12.2). Strikingly full of movement, these images differed markedly from the composed garden scenes of the sixteenth century, which focused instead on courtly pleasures and conveyed a sense of staged and nearly codified entertainment ceremonial (fig. 12.3).

In poetry too, the garden as a social experience and public hangout predominated. Unlike the classical poetry of the sixteenth and seventeenth centuries that centered on the enclosed and exclusive garden and on the cultivation of private enjoyments through elite culture and sociability the new poetic discourse on gardens accommodated a broad social, professional, and cultural spectrum and a new range of sensibilities and expectations.[6] The nameless garden of classical poetry, with its standard euphemisms (the rose and the nightingale) and complex metaphors (sublimated love, power, and sovereignty) gave way to a panoply of genuine gardens that poets identified by name (Kandilli, Çubuklu), by location (mostly on the banks of the Bosphorus and the Golden Horn), and by the kinds of attractions they offered, or sometimes lacked:

> Göksu's weather is unpleasant now, Çubuklu is very crowded
> What if we had him row just us two as far as Saʿdabad, my love?[7]

From the songs of Nedim in the 1710s and the 1720s to the narrative poems of Enderunlu Fazıl at the turn of the nineteenth century, the gardens of Istanbul, the pastimes they afforded, and the sensory pleasures they

---

[6] For recent studies that examine the notion of garden in classical poetry, see especially Walter Andrews, *Poetry's Voice, Society's Song: Ottoman Lyric Poetry* (Seattle: University of Washington Press, 1985), pp. 143–74; Julie Meissami, "The Body as Garden: Nature and Sexuality in Persian Poetry," *Edebiyât* 6/2 (1995): 245–68; Julie Meissami, "The World's Pleasance; Hāfiz's Allegorical Gardens," in E. S. Shaffer (ed.), *Comparative Criticism* (Cambridge: Cambridge University Press, 1983), pp. 153–85; Shirine Hamadeh, "The City's Pleasures: Architectural Sensibility in Eighteenth-Century Istanbul," PhD dissertation, MIT, 1999, pp. 163–212.

[7] Ahmet Nedim, *Divan*, Halil Nihat Boztepe (Istanbul: İkdam Matbaası, 1920–22), p. 154; Ahmet Nedim, *Nedim Divanı*, ed. Abdülbâki Gölpınarlı (Istanbul: İnkılâp ve Aka Kitabevleri, 1972), p. 286.

Figure 12.3 From Ali Şir Neva'î, *Divan* MS, Topkapı Sarayı Müzesi Kütüphanesi H. 804.
Scene of a princely garden entertainment from the first half of the sixteenth century.
Courtesy of Topkapı Sarayı Müzesi Kütüphanesi.

provoked continued to infiltrate Ottoman poetic imagination. Like the contemporary poems of Hoogvielt and Huygens in Holland, Pope in England, and du Peyrat in France,[8] the poems of Nedim, Fazıl, Fenni, Nevres, or Süruri revealed a changing urban landscape in which gardens were becoming more numerous, more and more visible, more thriving, and more enmeshed in the life and the joys of the city.

The growing consciousness of public spaces in general, and of gardens in particular, reflected an urban fabric in the process of transformation. From the beginning of the eighteenth century, when the court returned to the capital after a long absence, Istanbul became the site of active and constant construction and renovation, infrastructure development, and extraordinary urban growth. Its center of gravity quickly moved away from the walled city toward the suburban waterfronts of the Bosphorus and the Golden Horn. There, the court and its entourage had dozens of palaces erected, often amid older, most modest residences; members of the ruling class as well as men and women across social classes endowed mosques, theological colleges, baths, shops, and fountains, many of which provided nuclei around which new towns emerged and older ones grew.[9] It was along these rapidly urbanizing shores on the outskirts of the old city that most of the gardens and squares mentioned, praised, sung about, and drawn in this period were located. These urban oases constituted a vital dimension of an elaborate and manifold process of urban development, and it was in this process that they became securely etched on the map of the city and in the minds of its inhabitants.

The new public gardens (and promenades and squares) were also a response to the new needs and desires of urban society. Their prominence in the new landscape of the capital and in the eyes of artists and poets was in itself an indication that noticeable changes had occurred in the way men and women went about their daily lives and conceived of their social and public life. These were not sudden changes, however. Gradual mobility among professional groups, emerging social and financial aspirations, increasing material wealth, and changing habits of consumption lay at the heart of these developments. They were the outward manifestations of more than a century of economic and social transformation as well as an

---

[8] See, for example, Erik de Jong, "Zijdebalen: A Late Seventeenth/Early Eighteenth-Century Dutch Estate and its Garden Poem," *Journal of Garden History* 5/1 (1985): 32–71; and Marcel Poëte, *Au jardin des Tuileries: l'art du jardin – la promenade publique* (Paris: A. Picard, 1924), pp. 164–71; 268–353.

[9] These developments are examined in detail in Tülay Artan, "Architecture as a Theatre of Life: Profile of the Eighteenth-Century Bosphorus," PhD dissertation, MIT, 1988, chs. 1 and 2; and in ch. 1 of Hamadeh, "The City's Pleasures."

eroding system of hierarchies that, for many, also meant the breakdown of order and stability.[10] These developments were more palpable, and visible, in eighteenth-century Istanbul than at other times and places, because of a particular juncture in the histories of the city and the empire during which the image of state sovereignty was being actively and thoroughly refashioned. This quest for a fresh image was not only an immediate response to the heavy military blow the empire had recently suffered at the hands of European powers; it also answered to the pressure of internal transformations. In Istanbul, much energy was directed towards affirming the renewed presence of the court. Shows of power and authority and displays of imperial magnificence went hand in hand. This context helps explain the construction and restoration frenzy that the court of Ahmed III's return from Edirne in 1703 precipitated, as well as the new and flamboyant visual vocabulary that continued, until late in the century, to stamp every corner of the city with reminders of imperial glory.[11] This context also clarifies the unusual scrutiny with which the authorities monitored changing social habits and practices and frequently enforced the sumptuary regulations

[10] For sixteenth- to eighteenth-century social transformations and revisionist interpretations of the paradigm of decline in Ottoman history, see Halil İnalcık, "Centralization and Decentralization in Ottoman Administration," in Thomas Naff and Roger Owen (eds.), *Studies in Eighteenth-Century Islamic History* (Carbondale, IL: Southern Illinois University Press, 1977), pp. 27–52; Halil İnalcık, "Military and Fiscal Transformation in the Ottoman Empire, 1600–1700," *Archivum Ottomanicum* 6 (1980): 283–337; Cemal Kafadar, "The Myth of the Golden Age: Ottoman Historical Consciousness in the Post-Süleymânic Era," in Halil İnalcık and Cemal Kafadar (eds.), *Süleymân the Second and his Time* (Istanbul: Isis, 1993), pp. 37–48; Cemal Kafadar, "The Ottomans and Europe," in T. Brady Jr., H. A. Oberman, and J. D. Tracy (eds.), *Handbook of European History 1400–1600: Late Middle Ages, Renaissance and Reformation*, 2 vols. (Leiden: Brill, 1994), pp. 613–15; Rifa'at Abou El-Haj, *The Formation of the Modern State: The Ottoman Empire, Sixteenth to Eighteenth Century* (Albany, NY: SUNY Press, 1991); Norman Itzkowitz, "Eighteenth-Century Ottoman Realities," *Studia Islamica* 16 (1962): 73–94; Norman Itzkowitz, "Men and Ideas in the Eighteenth-Century Ottoman Empire," in Naff and Owen, *Studies in Eighteenth-Century Islamic History*, pp. 15–26; Norman Itzkowitz, "Mehmed Raghib Pasha: The Making of an Ottoman Grand Vizier," PhD dissertation, Princeton University, 1959; Virginia Aksan, *An Ottoman Statesman in War and Peace: Ahmed Resmi Efendi 1700–1783* (Leiden: Brill, 1995); Virginia Aksan, "Ottoman Political Writing, 1768–1808," *International Journal of Middle East Studies* 25 (1993): 53–69; Madeline Zilfi, *The Politics of Piety: The Ottoman Ulema in the Postclassical Age (1600–1800)* (Minneapolis: Bibliotheca Islamica, 1988); Suraiya Faroqhi, "Crisis and Change, 1590–1699," in H. İnalcık and D. Quataert (eds.), *An Economic and Social History of the Ottoman Empire*, 1300–1914 (Cambridge: Cambridge University Press, 1994), pp. 413–636; Ariel Salzmann, *Tocqueville in the Ottoman Empire: Rival Paths to the Modern State* (Leiden: Brill, 2004); Ariel Salzmann, "An Ancien Régime Revisited: 'Privatization' and Political Economy in the Eighteenth-Century Ottoman Empire," *Politics and Society* 21/4 (1993): 393–424; Donald Quataert, *The Ottoman Empire, 1700–1922* (Cambridge: Cambridge University Press, 2000), pp. 37–53; Donald Quataert (ed.), *Consumption Studies and the History of the Ottoman Empire, 1550–1922* (Albany, NY: SUNY Press, 2000).

[11] I have addressed this subject in the context of the patronage of fountains in particular in "Splash and Spectacle: The Obsession with Fountains in Eighteenth-Century Istanbul," *Muqarnas* 19 (2002): 123–48.

that set and reset, doggedly and tirelessly, the parameters of acceptable behavior and demeanor in public spaces throughout the century.

"Public gardens," this social, cultural, and topographical phenomenon that has become in the context of western European cities so implicated in the rise of a middle class and in the march towards modernity,[12] represented an important dimension of change in eighteenth-century Istanbul, because there too they disturbed an established social and cultural order. They provided a major arena in which new and blossoming daily, social, and recreational practices were enacted; and these practices in turn partook of the process of reshaping the city's social and physical map. This chapter sets out to examine how these public gardens emerged as a distinctive feature of Istanbul's social and physical landscape. Pictorial images of gardens like Emirgan and Kağıthane (fig. 12.1), incessantly reproduced in books and postcards, and the carefree songs of Nedim, still remembered by many, leave us a sustained impression that these gardens really did exist; how they actually happened is a question that has rarely been discussed.[13] How these gardens became new foci of urban life and everyday venues in which new forms of distinction were tested, and how they upset our modern understanding of private and public, elite and popular, are other issues that I will address. At some level, one might argue that public gardens (and outdoor public spaces generally) were the "natural" extension of a burgeoning urban culture of coffeehouses, taverns, shadow theater, and story-telling street performances that had been in place since the latter half

---

[12] These relationships have been explored across the disciplines of cultural, landscape, art, and consumption history in and outside the context of Europe (though with a particular emphasis on early modern England), often by reexamining the Habermassian notion of public sphere and Veblen's theories of leisure and class. Thorstein Veblen, *The Theory of the Leisure Class* (New York: Modern Library, 2001 [1899]). See, in addition to the works cited below on public and royal gardens, David Solkin, *Painting for Money: The Visual Arts and the Public Sphere in Eighteenth-Century England* (New Haven, CT: Yale University Press, 1993), especially pp. 115–90; Tom Williamson, *Polite Landscapes: Gardens and Society in Eighteenth-Century England* (Baltimore, MD: Johns Hopkins University Press, 1995); Edward Harwood, "Personal Identity and the Eighteenth-Century English Landscape Garden," *Journal of Garden History* 13/1–2 (1993): 36–48; Craig Clunas, *Fruitful Sites: Garden Culture in Ming Dynasty China* (London: Reaktion Books, 1996).

[13] Maurizio Cerasi's *La città del Levante: civiltà urbana e architettura sotto gli Ottomani nei secoli XVIII–XIX* (Milan: Jaca Book, 1986); Maurizio Cerasi, "Il giardino ottomano attraverso l'immagine del Bosforo," in Attilio Petruccioli (ed.), *Il giardino islamico: architettura, natura, paesaggio* (Milan: Electa, 1994), pp. 217–36; and Maurizio Cerasi, "Open Space, Water and Trees in Ottoman Urban Culture in the XVIII–XIXth Centuries," *Environmental Design* 2 (1985): 36–49, are to my knowledge the only attempts at examining the development of public spaces in eighteenth-century Istanbul. These works, however, rely almost exclusively on western sources.

of the sixteenth century.[14] The difference, however, is that urban life was now resisted and propelled forward at one and the same time. In the eighteenth century, public gardens managed to negotiate new territory (physical, cultural, and mental) and become part of mainstream urban culture, in part because the state elite encouraged them to expand and proliferate. Their evolution, I contend, intersected with the building patronage of a ruling class searching for a fresh image, changing rituals of sociability and recreation among the middle classes, and concerns about public order. In other words, while the state elite sought to keep garden culture in check through constant law enforcement, this same elite, para-doxically, continuously nurtured the creation of new spaces in which it could prosper.

> So many attractive gardens and so many imperial promenades
> So many flourishing places left to us by our ancestors
> Sprung up during his noble age
> If I were to recount them the [other] poets would be shamed.[15]

The imperial court's long periods of absence from Istanbul in the late seventeenth century left their mark on the physical fabric of the city, and the task of rebuilding and restoration in the Ottoman capital must have been particularly daunting at the beginning of the following century. The state nonetheless addressed it shortly after the return of Ahmed III in the summer of 1703. Roads, bridges, and landing docks were repaired; in most imperial gardens (*hâss bahçeleri*) damage was surveyed and buildings restored.[16] Large restoration projects were launched. Between 1718 and

---

[14] See Andreas Tietze, *The Turkish Shadow Theater and the Puppet Collection of the L. A. Mayer Memorial Foundation* (Berlin: Mann, 1977), pp. 17–19; Cemal Kafadar, "Janissaries and Other Riffraff" (unpublished paper, 1991), pp. 10–13.
[15] Seyyid Vehbi, *Dîvân-ı Seyyid Vehbî*, Topkapı Sarayı Müzesi Kütüphanesi, MS E.H. 1640, fol 20.
[16] These included the gardens of Tersane, Karaağaç, Davudpaşa, Beşiktaş and the imperial palace of Topkapı. Repair and restoration activity in the years immediately following the return of Ahmed III to the capital is documented, for example, in BOA, Cevdet Saray nos. 6068 (1703–4), 5985 (1709), 5963 (1710), 3978 (1711), İbnülemin Saray Mesalihi nos. 3243 and 3245 (1705), Maliyeden Müdevver register no. 1655 (1708); İbnülemin Saray Mesalihi nos. 2886 and 2967 (1710). Repairs at the Topkapı are recorded in Cevdet Saray nos. 2184, 5486, for the years 1707, 1712, 1713, 1735 and 1740. Hundreds of other documents pertain to such activities in subsequent years and until the end of the century. See also Silâhdâr Fındıklılı Mehmed Agha, *Nusretnâme*, 2 vols. (Istanbul: Milli Eğitim Basımevi, 1962–9), vol. I, p. 732; Sarı Mehmed Pasha, *Zübde-i Veka'i'*, ed. A. Özcan 3 vols. (Istanbul: Tercüman Gazetesi, 1977), vol. I, p. 159; Râşid Efendi, *Tarih-i Râşid*, 5 vols. (Istanbul: Matbaa-i Âmire, 1865), vol. I, pp. 354–5; and Muzaffer Erdoğan, "Osmanlı Devrinde İstanbul Bahçeleri," *Vakıflar Dergisi* 4 (1958): 149–82. The earliest documentation on the repair of bridges, roads, and landing docks in this period dates back to 1707, Cevdet Belediye no. 4224 (1707); see also, for instance, nos. 4315 and 4583 (1774), no. 6609 (1783) and no. 5578 (1784) for later repairs. In this chapter, the term *hâss bahçe* refers strictly to imperial palace gardens.

1720, the grand vizier Damad Ibrahim ordered the revamping of the imperial gardens of Beşiktaş, Dolmabahçe, Kandilli, Tekfur Sarayı, Tersane, Karaağaç, and Davudpaşa, all of which had deteriorated "as a result of uninterrupted warfare and the usual negligence of state officials."[17] At different times throughout the century, these gardens and many others were repaired, renovated, and refurbished. Nevertheless, as newer and more lavish palatial gardens were erected along the suburban banks of the Bosphorus and the Golden Horn, older ones gradually lost their appeal as foci of court life. While efforts at renovation continued, some gardens were abandoned and others aged irretrievably. Many also turned into gardens for the wider public.

Such a turning point in the life of imperial palatial gardens was not unique. In early modern Europe too, royal gardens became more public once the court lost interest in them and stopped resorting to them. The state opened the Jardin du Luxembourg when Louis XIV began residing at Versailles and Marly. In England, the garden of St. James lost its exclusiveness when the court moved to Kensington Palace and Hampton Court. These gardens, in turn, became increasingly public when George III moved elsewhere in the 1760s. Even the celebrated Hyde Park, whose history as "a focus of fashionable life" had begun with Charles I in the early 1630s, was in fact left to the people only in 1737, after the death of Queen Caroline.[18] As in Paris and in England, in the case of Istanbul the exact details of this development remain relatively obscure. The fragments of evidence at our disposal do not always reveal the exact time and circumstances in which such conversions took place.

Contemporary accounts suggest, for example, that the state sometimes sought the opening or partial opening of an imperial garden to the public as a solution to repeated instances of public disorder. This was the case of the ill-fated garden of Kalender in Yeniköy, which, although fairly new (it was built by Damad Ibrahim in 1720) and well used through the 1720s (both as a court Âretreat and as a reception hall for foreign diplomats),

---

[17] Râşid Efendi, *Tarih-i Râşid*, vol. V, p. 160. See also Silâhdâr, *Nusretnâme*, vol. II, p. 246; İsmail Âsım Efendi, *Tarih-i İsmail Âsım Efendi* (Istanbul: Matbaa-i Âmire, 1865), pp. 253, 269–72; Erdoğan, "Osmanlı Devrinde İstanbul Bahçeleri," p. 177.

[18] Franck Debié, *Jardins des capitales: Une géographie des parcs et jardins publics de Paris, Londres, Vienne et Berlin* (Paris: CNRS, 1992), pp. 57–134; Susan Lasdun, *The English Park: Royal, Private and Public* (London: André Deutsch, 1991), pp. 41, 124, 128–9; Franco Panzini, *Per il piacere del popolo: l'evoluzione del giardino pubblico in Europa* (Bologna: Zanichelli, 1993), especially pp. 92–102; Poëte, *Au jardin des Tuileries*, pp. 100–266; David Coffin, "The 'Lex Hortorum' and Access to Gardens of Latium during the Renaissance," *Journal of Garden History* 2/3 (1982): 209–10.

Figure 12.4 From Allom and Walsh, *Constantinople and the Scenery of the Seven Churches of Asia Minor.*
View of the garden and fountain of Küçüksu (1809).

subsequently deteriorated rapidly. By the middle of the century, it had become a favored hangout for the city's riffraff. Eventually, in the 1760s (possibly in an effort to preempt further social disorder or to prevent more severe physical deterioration), Mustafa III ordered his chief gardener, Moldovalı Ali Agha (later grand vizier), to construct in the garden barracks for the gardener corps. By that time, the corps of gardeners, headed by the chief gardener (*bostancıbaşı*), had effectively become a police corps responsible for the upkeep of order in all public spaces located along the suburban shores of Istanbul. Soon after the barracks were built, a section of the imperial garden, adorned with a fountain, was turned into a promenade (*mesîre*) and opened to the general public.[19] A French *comtesse* traveling in the city around that time reports that "on Saturday it was at [the fountain of] *Kalinder*" that the people of Istanbul gathered, following an established ritual of sociability that took them to a different fountain on different days of the week, "as in France at the Tuileries and the Boulevard de Gand."[20]

A similar course of events occurred at the gardens of Küçüksu, on the Anatolian shore of the Bosphorus, shortly after Mahmud I had the gardens renovated and enlarged in 1749. There the monarch had a large wooden pavilion built and the landscape embellished with a pool, a fountain, and a stream brought down from the mountain.[21] The monarch also ordered new barracks erected and a battalion of gardeners stationed on the premises. The same year, the historian Şemdanizade described the place as a large and pleasurable promenade;[22] and two years later, Rasih glorified the promenade in this verse:

> Since its restoration by the august monarch Mahmud Khan
> Küçüksu became a vast pleasure ground, a mine of delight![23]

The pictorial images (fig. 12.4) of European artists were to confirm, some fifty years later, these two early testimonies.

The decision to refurbish an imperial garden often entailed its conversion into an imperial endowment (waqf). Typically, the monarch or a member of the ruling elite built a new mosque along with a complex of

---

[19] P. G. İnciciyan, *XVIII. Asırda İstanbul*, ed. and trans. from Armenian Hrand D. Andreasyan (Istanbul: Baha Matbaası, 1976), p. 119; see also Gönül A. Evyapan, *Eski Türk Bahçeleri ve Özellikle Eski İstanbul Bahçeleri* (Ankara: Orta Doğu Teknik Üniversitesi, 1972), p. 35.

[20] Comtesse de la Ferté-Meun, *Lettres sur le Bosphore* (Paris: Domère, 1821), pp. 100–1.

[21] Hüseyin Ayvansarayî, *Hadikat ül-Cevami*, 2 vols. (Istanbul: Matbaa-i Âmire, 1864), vol. I, p. 163.

[22] Şem'dânizâde Fındıklılı Süleyman Efendi, *Fındıklılı Süleyman Efendi Tarihi: Mür'i't-Tevârih*, ed. Münir Aktepe, 2 vols. (Istanbul: İstanbul Üniversitesi Edebiyat Fakültesi, 1976–81), vol. I, p. 162.

[23] Râsih, "Târîh" (AH 1165/1751–2), quoted in Ayvansarayî, *Hadikat*, p. 165; translation based on Howard Crane, *The Garden of the Mosques, Hafiz Hüseyin al-Ayvansarayi's Guide to the Muslim Monuments of Ottoman Istanbul* (Supplement to *Muqarnas*) (Leiden: Brill, 2000), p. 474.

commercial and recreational facilities that served as the mosque's endowment. The patron parceled and leased out part of the land, which eventually grew into a "village."[24] He or she also renovated extant palaces and
pavilions, and in certain cases opened the surrounding gardens to public
access. The imperial garden of Kandilli to the north of Küçüksu, which
dated back to the late sixteenth century, followed exactly this trajectory.[25]
Renovated in 1718, but neglected thereafter, it survived as a ruin until 1749.
In that year, Mahmud I annexed the land to the royal endowments, added
a mosque, a bath, a few shops, and leased out as much of the land as was
requested.[26] He restored the ruined pavilion of Ferahabad to its former
glory, turning the place, as the poet Nevres intimates, into a public show-
case of royal magnificence, a new sightseeing attraction for the leisured and
the curious among the people of Istanbul:

> The treacherous heavens had made such a ruin of it
> That even an architect could not imagine it restored
> . . .
>
> Now [Ferahabad] is a spectacle that the people go to see
> Well, take a look! Where is [this place] and where, [by comparison], is
> Saʿdabad.[27]

Not far from Kandilli, downstream on the Asian shore, the town of
İncirliköyü had developed, sometime in the latter part of the seventeenth
century, on plots of land located inland from the older imperial pavilion
and garden of İncirli Bahçesi and leased by the state to high-ranking
officials. As a courtier of Mustafa III, named Tahir Ağa, refurbished the
town in the 1760s, he also expanded it to the shore, reaching down to the
cape. The old garden, which had long disappeared from the imperial
garden registers,[28] was in all likelihood absorbed in this process, and part

---

[24] See, for instance, Şemʾdânizâde, *Mürʾiʾt-Tevârih*, vol. I, pp. 161–2; İzzi, *Tarih*, Istanbul, Daruttibaat
ul-Mamûre, 1784, fol. 273; İsmail Âsım, *Tarih*, p. 377, for the cases of Kandilli and Bebek.
[25] For the early history of these suburban imperial gardens, see Gülru Necipoğlu, "The Suburban
Landscape of Sixteenth-Century Istanbul as a Mirror of Classical Ottoman Garden Culture," in
Attilio Petruccioli (ed.), *Gardens in the Time of the Great Muslim Empires (Supplements to Muqarnas)*
(Leiden: Brill, 1997), pp. 32–71; Erdoğan, "Osmanlı Devrinde İstanbul Bahçeleri," pp. 149–82;
Evyapan, *Eski Türk Bahçeleri*; Orhan Şaik Gökyay, "Bağçeler," *Topkapı Sarayı Müzesi Yıllığı* 4
(1990): 7–20; and Muzaffer T. Gökbilgin, "Boğaziçi," in *İslâm Ansiklopedisi*, vol. II, pp. 666–92.
[26] Şemʾdânizâde, *Mürʾiʾt-Tevârih*, vol. I, p. 162; see also P. Luca Ingigi (P. G. İnciciyan), *Villeggiature
de' Bizantini sul Bosforo Tracio*, trans. from Armenian to Italian by P. C. Aznavour (Venice: Lazzaro,
1831), pp. 257–8; İnciciyan, *XVIII. Asırda İstanbul*, pp. 129–300; İzzi, *Tarih*, fols. 272–3; Râşid, *Tarih*,
vol. V, p. 160.
[27] Nevres, *Dîvân-ı Nevres*, İstanbul Üniversitesi Kütüphanesi, MS Ty 3414, fol. 38b.
[28] According to Erdoğan, the last royal garden register in which the garden appears is dated 1679;
Erdoğan, "Osmanlı Devrinde İstanbul Bahçeleri," p. 178.

of it opened to public access. Indeed, the town now boasted a public promenade whose name, Burun Bahçesi, or Cape Garden, suggests that it wrapped around the little cape on the waterfront, running along a segment of the former *hâss bahçe*. Considered a fashionable spot among the city's residents for some twenty years, it later became increasingly subjected to the chief gardener's harsh security measures, on account of repeated mischief and improper behavior among the garden's visitors. By the time İncicyan wrote his chronicle of the city at the end of the century, Burun Bahçesi had been abandoned and "its old joy was forgotten."²⁹

In another account of Istanbul, İncicyan described the imperial gardens of Sultaniye at Paşabahçe, south and uphill from İncirliköyü, as a "place of public recreation" ("luogo di pubblico divertimento").³⁰ By the late sixteenth century, this old suburban retreat, attributed to Bayezid II and celebrated as one of Süleyman's favorite spots, had been abandoned. In 1763–4, in an effort to revitalize the suburban town of Paşabahçe, Mustafa III endowed it with a mosque, a bath, a boys' school, an outdoor prayer place or *namâzgâh*, and a *meydan* fountain (a large, ornate cubical fountain of a type distinctive of the eighteenth century).³¹ Contemporary accounts are not specific about the exact location of the new imperial complex. But archeological evidence indicates that the project extended into the garden of Sultaniye. Indeed, Sedad Hakkı Eldem recorded traces of the lost imperial garden around the *meydan* fountain and the *namâzgâh*,³² the area which, one can surmise from numerous precedents in eighteenth-century Istanbul,³³ had become the very locus of public recreation described by İncicyan.

It is a commonplace of eighteenth-century writings and visual images that old imperial gardens are reincarnated as public gardens and squares. Such transformations must have occurred so routinely that they are usually reported in a very matter of fact way. We are often left without clues as to the time and circumstances in which the development from imperial to public occurred and uninformed about the fate of the imperial garden. What became, for instance, of the sixteenth-century garden of Karabâli at Kabataş – a rare example in Istanbul of the Persianate

---

²⁹ İnciciyan, *XVIII. Asırda İstanbul*, p. 127; P. G. İnciciyan, *Boğaziçi Sayfiyeleri*, trans. from Armenian by the priest of the Armenian Church of Kandilli and ed. Orhan Duru (Istanbul: Eren, 2000), pp. 171–2.
³⁰ İnciciyan, *Villegiatura*, p. 269.   ³¹ Ayvansarayî, *Hadikat*, vol. II, p. 155.
³² Sedad Hakkı Eldem, *Türk Bahçeleri* (Istanbul: Devlet Kitapları Müdürlügü, 1976), pp. 14–19; Gökbilgin, "Boğaziçi," p. 685; Gökyay, "Bağçeler," p. 8.
³³ See Hamadeh, "Splash and Spectacle," pp. 135–44.

Chaharbagh garden type – when in 1732 Hekimoğlu Ali Pasha (Mahmud I's grand vizier) erected a monumental *meydan* fountain by the Kabataş waterfront? All that is certain is that sometime in the early part of the eighteenth century, the imperial garden disappeared from the records of imperial estates and from accounts of contemporary observers; and by the 1730s a large public square had unfolded around the new fountain, reaching down to the landing docks of Kabataş and Karabâli, covering that very area in which the garden of Karabâli was supposed to have been located.[34] Despite the limitations imposed by our sources on the complex history and tenure of these gardens, however, a clear pattern emerges.[35] Considering the rapidity with which one dilapidated imperial garden after another was abandoned, and the zeal with which they were refurbished, it is likely that many gardens followed the same path as did Kalender, İncirli, Kandilli, and Sultaniye and were eventually opened to the public.[36]

Without a doubt, the history of public gardens in Istanbul long predated the construction of the first "modern" (western) municipal parks of Taksim and Büyük Çamlıca, during the reign of Abdülaziz.[37] As in Paris, London, Berlin, and Vienna (although for different reasons and in different circumstances) this history unfolded slowly, and not always in a progressive, linear fashion. In Europe, the first truly public parks emerged long after Hirschfeld proposed, in the last quarter of the eighteenth century,

---

[34] The garden was last mentioned in a firman from 1704, Gölbilgin, "Boğaziçi," pp. 673, 675; see also Erdoğan, "Osmanlı Devrinde İstanbul Bahçeleri," p. 170; Necipoğlu, "The Suburban Landscape," pp. 32–6. We also know, for example, that the sixteenth-century gardens of Süeleyman at Fenerbahçe had continued to be used by the court of Ahmed III until 1730, when they suffered considerable damage at the hands of the Patrona Halil rebels. The gardens were renovated in the 1740s and then again abandoned by the court, and by the second half of the eighteenth century they reemerge in accounts of the city as a public promenade; *Tarih-i Sami ve Şâkir ve Subhî* (Istanbul: Dârüttibaat il-Âmire 1783), vol. I, p. 106; Râşid, *Tarih*, vol. III, p. 105; İsmail Âsım, *Tarih*, p. 171; Şem'dânîzâde, *Mür'i't-Tevârih*, vol. II, p. 31; see also Reşat Ekrem Koçu, "Fenerbağçe, Fenerbağçesi – Kasrı ve Mescidi," in *İstanbul Ansiklopedesi*, pp. 5621–5; Münir Aktepe, "İstanbul Fenerbahçesi Hakkında Bâzı Bilgiler," *İstanbul Üniversitesi Edebiyat Fakültesi Tarih Dergisi* 32 (1979): 361–8 passim.
[35] A thorough exploration of *hâss bahçe* registers, imperial account documents of construction and renovation expenses, and endowment deeds should shed more light on this subject. This will be the subject of a separate project.
[36] One example that comes to mind is the fifteenth-century garden of Bebek which had deteriorated into a hideout for brigands until it was converted into an imperial waqf in 1725–6; İnciciyan, *XVIII. Asırda İstanbul*, p. 116.
[37] The Taksim public park, completed in 1869, was designed in collaboration with German and French urban planners, architects, and engineers and conceived along Beaux-arts guidelines; Zeynep Çelik, *The Remaking of Istanbul: Portrait of an Ottoman City in the Nineteenth Century* (Seattle: University of Washington Press, 1987), pp. 46, 64, 69–70; Evyapan, *Eski Türk Bahçeleri*, p. 72.

his idea of "people's gardens" (*Volksgärten*), in which "were embedded ideas of democracy and equality."[38] In the meantime, royal gardens were opened and shut to different publics at different times. St. James's Park and Hyde Park, in England, and the Tuileries and the Jardin du Luxembourg in France first opened their gates to a select public in the seventeenth century. Other gardens followed. By the 1760s and 1770s, Kensington Gardens in England, the Prater and Tiergarten in Berlin, Auergarten in Vienna, the Champs-Élysées, the Bois de Boulogne, and the Bois de Vincennes in France had all been renovated and opened, at least in part, to a restricted public.[39] Just as in the Ottoman capital, legal imperatives that determined some royal lands to be open or preserved for public use did not rule these developments.[40]

In Istanbul, the "handover" of imperial estates to the public domain illustrated a broader phenomenon, an important stage in the lifecycle not only of *hâss* property, but also of *mîrî*, or state land. The most celebrated, if little understood, example of state land being converted to the public domain was the formerly restricted forest of Belgrad, an extensive tract of state-owned land located in the southern outskirts of the capital and made famous by Lady Montagu in her letters to Alexander Pope in June 1717. Like several pictorial representations of the forest, her descriptions confirm that by the beginning of the eighteenth century Belgrad was a truly public forest and one of the most fashionable recreational spots in Istanbul:

The heats of Constantinople have driven me to this place, which perfectly answers the description of the Elysian fields. I am in the middle of a wood, consisting chiefly of fruit trees, watered by a vast number of fountains famous for the excellency of their water, and divided into many shady walks upon short grass, that seems to me artificial but I am assured is the pure work of nature, within view

---

[38] Linda Parshall, "C. C. L. Hirschfeld's Concept of the Garden in the German Enlightenment," *Journal of Garden History* 13/3 (1993): 127–55 especially. On Hirschfeld's garden theories, see C. C. L. Hirschfeld, *Theory of Garden Art*, ed. and trans. Linda Parshall (Philadelphia: University of Pennsylvania Press, 2001).

[39] After Le Nôtre's renovation of the Tuileries, for example, Louis XIV threatened to shut its gate to an already select entourage, but the garden was left open thanks to the intervention of Claude Perrault. Later in the seventeenth century, it became a favored spot among fashionable Parisians; Poëte, *Au jardin des Tuileries*, p. 266. For the somewhat tortuous history of public access in the royal gardens of Europe, see Lasdun, *The English Park*, pp. 41–62 passim, 124–9; Parshall, "C. C. L. Hirschfeld's Concept of the Garden," pp. 155–9 passim; Coffin, "The 'Lex Hortorum,'" pp. 209–14; Debié, *Jardins des capitales*, pp. 57–134; Panzini, *Per il piacere del popolo*, pp. 101–2.

[40] The notable exceptions were England's Land Acts of 1649 (the first year of the Commonwealth) and the Civil List Act and Revolution Settlement of 1689; E. P. Thompson, *Whigs and Hunters: The Origin of the Black Act* (New York: Pantheon Books, 1975), p. 241; Lasdun, *The English Park*, p. 46.

Figure 12.5 From Julia Pardoe, *The Beauties of the Bosphorus* (London, 1838), pl. 60.
The Garden of Emirgan, by W. H. Bartlett after an engraving by J. Cousen.

of the Black Sea, from whence we perpetually enjoy the refreshment of cool
breezes that makes us insensible of the heat of the summer.[41]

In the last quarter of the century, another hugely popular garden, located
at Emirgan (Mîrgûn) on the European side of the Bosphorus and immortalized in a nineteenth-century engraving by William Bartlett (fig. 12.5),
developed on a plot of *mîrî* (public property) land that Abdülhamid I had
reclaimed from a chief mufti, Mehmed Esad Efendi. Members of the
ruling class had long received leases of *mîrî* property. In this period,
though, the reclaiming of such property once their leaseholders fell from
imperial grace was severely enforced.[42] According to Ayvansarayî, author of
The Garden of the Mosques, the imperial endowments had absorbed the
property of Mehmed Esad Efendi in 1781, two years following the chief

---

[41] Lady Mary Wortley Montagu, *Turkish Embassy Letters*, ed. Malcolm Jack (London: W. Pickering,
1993), pp. 102–6. Montagu was often quoted on this subject by later visitors; see Baron de Tott,
Mémoires du Baron de Tott sur les turcs et les tartares, 2 vols. (Amsterdam: n.p., 1785), vol. I, p. 25;
Charles Pertusier, *Promenades pittoresques dans Constantinople et sur les rives du Bosphore*, 2 vols.
(Paris: H. Nicolle, 1815), vol. I, pp. 148–55; Julia Pardoe, *The Beauties of the Bosphorus* (London:
G. Virtue, 1838), pp. 96–7; Dallaway, *Constantinople*, p. 147.
[42] This routine also included the confiscation of the property of deceased wealthy individuals; Mehmet
Genç, "L'économie ottomane et la guerre au XVIIIe siècle," *Turcica* 27 (1995): 187; Yavuz Cezar,
Osmanlı Maliyesinde Bunalım ve Değişim Dönemi (Istanbul: Alan Yayıncılık, 1986), p. 135.

Figure 12.6 Photograph by the author. The *meydan* fountain of Abdülhamid
I at Emirgan (1782).

mufti's forced exile. On the same site and in the same year, the sultan
commissioned the construction of a mosque, a bath, and several shops; a
few months later he had a *meydan* fountain of white marble built across
from the mosque's courtyard (fig. 12.6).[43]

Like the fountain of Mustafa III at Paşabahçe and all the free-standing
meydan fountains built in this period in such suburban towns as Tophane,
Kabataş-Karabâli, and Beykoz, the fountain of Abdülhamid must have
provided, from the moment it was built, a communal focal point. By the
beginning of the nineteenth century, a vast public garden had spread
around the fountain of Emirgan. Julia Pardoe, who journeyed to the city
during the reign of Mahmud II, described the place:

A long street, terminating at the water's edge, stretches far into the distance, its
center being occupied by a Moorish fountain of white marble, overshadowed by
limes and acacias, beneath which are coffee terraces; constantly thronged with
Turks, sitting gravely in groups upon low stools not more than half a foot from the
ground, and occupied with their chibouks and mocha.[44]

43 Ayvansarayî, *Hadikat*, vol. II, pp. 137–8; see also Gökbilgin, "Boğaziçi," p. 679; Demirsar, "Emirgân
   Camii," in *Dünden Bugüne, İstanbul Ansiklopedisi*, vol. III, pp. 169–70.
44 Pardoe, *The Beauties of the Bosphorus*, p. 111; Julia Pardoe, *The City of the Sultan and Domestic
   Manners of the Turks in 1836*, 2 vols. (London: Henry Colburn, 1837), vol. II, p. 167.

Figure 12.7 From Antoine Ignace Melling, *Voyage pittoresque de Constantinople et des rives du Bosphore* (reprint of the 1819 edition, Istanbul, n.d.), pl. 22. The fountain of Mahmud I and the square of Tophane (1732).

Illustrating Pardoe's text, Bartlett's engraving portrays the fountain in the midst of a spacious garden that stretches to the shore. The garden is populated with groups of people walking, and others lounging on wooden platforms under the trees, sipping their coffee and smoking their water pipes (fig. 12.5). Although *The Garden of the Mosques* (which Ayvansarayî was completing the year construction of the imperial complex began) does not mention the coffeehouses of Emirgan, they were probably intended from the very start as part of the income-generating shops to which Ayvansarayî refers. Coffeehouses were becoming an integral feature of public spaces in the eighteenth century, and a commonplace of new waqf establishments, especially under Abdülhamid. In the first years of his reign, for example, the ruler had coffeehouses and "other shops" built across from the sixteenth-century Defterdar Mosque, located in the town of Eyüp, by the Defterdar landing dock on the Golden Horn, as income generators for the upkeep of the mosque. The new facilities were lined up on either side of the landing dock, neighboring the mosque, creating thus a new sense of enclosure out of which a public square emerged. The quarter soon took on the character of a marketplace.[45] It is likely that the coffeehouse terraces that still flourish on the Beylerbeyi, Bebek, and Ortaköy waterfronts, side by side with mosques, had also begun to take shape at that time.[46]

Like the new type of *meydan* fountains that proliferated all over the suburban shores of Istanbul, the integration of coffeehouses in gardens and squares in the eighteenth century testifies to the growing recreational demands of urban society. Much of the popularity of the Square of Tophane (*Tophane Meydanı*) no doubt derived from its amusements and services. Its large marble fountain (built in 1732 by Mahmud I) "singing welcoming greetings"[47] and its row of coffeehouses shaded by dense plane trees brought to the world of outdoor sociability the comfort and pleasures of shade, fresh water, coffee, and water pipes (fig. 12.7).[48]

Coffeehouse terraces, attendants serving water, ambulant "persons who vend refreshments," "bands of musicians," "sugar-candy and pastry vendors, itinerant coffee sellers and fruit juice vendors,"[49] became the sort of frills one expected to find at Tophane, Emirgan, and Kağıthane, and they

[45] Ayvansarayî, *Hadikat*, pp. 286–7; Crane, *The Garden of the Mosques*, p. 305, n. 2354.
[46] The roles of eighteenth-century imperial endowments in the making of public spaces at Bebek, Beylerbeyi, Emirgan, Üsküdar, and Ortaköy will be the subject of a separate study.
[47] Naîfî, *Tarih-i Çeşme-yi Tophane* (dated 1732–3); cited in Ayvansarayî, *Mecmuâ-i Tevârih*, ed. F. Derin and V. Çabuk (Istanbul: İstanbul Üniversitesi Edebiyat Fakütesi, 1985), p. 382.
[48] For descriptions of Tophane Square see, for instance, İnciciyan, *XVIII. Asırda İstanbul*, pp. 95, 112; Allom and Walsh, *Constantinople*, vol. I, pp. 8, 17, 21.
[49] Pertusier, *Promenades pittoresques*, vol. II, pp. 7, 328–31.

enhanced and enlivened an increasingly rich leisure ritual. The anticipation
of fun and pleasure extended even to places like the *namâzgâh*, which were
intended for the performance of more sober and sacred rituals. It had now
become necessary to appeal to a sensual rather than a spiritual cause, in
order to lure the congregation into performing its religious duties. Rather
than inviting his audience to turn towards the open-air *mihrab* (prayer
niche), this anonymous poet invoked instead the *mihrab*'s delightful
setting:

> Turn your face toward this beautiful recreation spot
> Come visitor, don't miss the time of prayer.[50]

Like fountains, coffeehouses, and *namâzgâh*s, waterfront mosques like
that endowed by Abdülhamid at Emirgan provided their own loci of
sociability within the larger public space. As contemporary observers
often noted, the courtyard of a mosque was a natural forum for men to
linger after prayer, meet with friends, and exchange news.[51] It is possible
that as the trend of building mosques right by the banks of the Bosphorus
developed among sultans and grand viziers, they may have developed new
mechanisms for financing public spaces through pious endowments. In
any case, such mosques as those at Emirgan, or at Beylerbeyi, Bebek, and
Ortaköy, must have contributed tremendously to the establishment of new
public spaces. The location of these mosques and (in some cases as in
Beylerbeyi) the relative transparency of their court enclosure must have
fostered the same kind of fluid relationship that could exist between the
sacred and the recreational in the space of a *namâzgâh* (or of a cemetery),
and encouraged an outward flow of male sociability to the less severely
gendered public arena along the water.

Whether or not the development of confiscated *mîrî* land and the
refurbishment of imperial gardens were merely steps toward the revitalization of the city's suburbs, they were undeniably essential to the emergence of new public spaces. Urban interventions from above initiated the
passage from courtly to urban and "private" to "public"; what happened
later around a new fountain, along the waterfront, or under the watchful
eye of the gardeners, was the result of how these interventions intersected
with social demands and public rituals.

---

[50] Anonymous (AH 1190/1776), quoted in Ayvansarayî, *Mecmuâ-i Tevârih*, p. 377.
[51] See, for example, Pertusier, *Promenades pittoresques*, vol. I, p. 189, vol. II, p. 107; Jean-Claude Flachat,
Observations sur le commerce et sur les arts, 2 vols. (Lyon: Jacquenod Père et Rusand, 1766), vol. I,
p. 401; Ayvansarayî, *Hadikat*, vol. II, pp. 171–81.

One question that emerges from contemporary accounts concerns the nature of the role of the state elite in the evolution of public spaces. Should we understand the active engagement of the court in the making of public spaces (whether directly or unwittingly) as a sign of its "endorsement" of a flourishing public sphere, at a time when fears of the breakdown of order seemed to have receded? I argue that we should not. Rather, the proliferation of public space constituted a precaution against the possible implications of changing social practices and it signaled, somewhat paradoxically, an attempt by the state to contain public life. The opening of *mîrî* and *hâss* property to the public provided new "official" and controllable venues of recreation that defined and delineated the physical sphere in which urban life could be lived. The construction of barracks for gardeners prior to the opening to the public of gardens like Kalender and Küçüksu testifies to intricate connections between public life and public order. The creation of new recreational venues encouraged the development of structured forms of public behavior and ritualized forms of leisure (to borrow a concept from Bourdieu), and these, in turn, helped preempt, subvert, counteract, or prevent other unmediated and unruly forms of recreation.[52] I am not suggesting that public life was, at any point, a site of confrontation between state and society. What I am saying is that in the eighteenth century issues of public life and concern for public order never ceased to overlap.

The two most telling aspects of this relationship were the transformation and administrative redefinition of the role of chief gardener (*bostancıbaşı*) and the unusually high frequency of enforcement of the sumptuary laws that dictated the scope, nature, and forms of public life. Already, by the second half of the seventeenth century, possibly as a response to a general climate of instability, the jurisdiction of the *bostancıbaşı* had spread beyond the boundaries of imperial gardens and into the public domain.[53] The role

---

[52] A similar pattern of "containment" of urban life is suggested in the development, from the beginning of the eighteenth century onward, of elaborate popular rituals to accompany the increasingly more numerous and extravagant imperial pageants; see Hamadeh, "City's Pleasures," pp. 197–200.

[53] It is likely that these changes were instituted during the periods of absence of the court from Istanbul in the seventeenth century, but it is difficult to determine, at this point, whether they occurred at one particular point in time or as the result of a series of gradual developments. Little has been written about gardeners and chief gardeners; see İ. Hakkı Uzunçarşılı, "Bostancı," in *İslam Ansiklopedisi*, vol. II, pp. 736–8 and "Bostancıbaşı," vol. II, pp. 338–9; Uzunçarşılı, "Bostandji," in EI2, vol. I, pp. 1277–8; and "Bostandji-Bashi," vol. I, p. 1279; Koçu, "Bostancıbaşı Defterleri," in *İstanbul Ansiklopedisi*, pp. 39–90; and Necdet Sakaoğlu, in "Bostancı Ocağı," vol. II, pp. 305–7; Robert Mantran, *Istanbul dans la seconde moitié du XVIIe siècle* (Paris: A. Maisonneuve, 1962), pp. 129, 149; Erdoğan, "Osmanlı Devrinde İstanbul Bahçeleri," pp. 149–82 passim; Evyapan, *Eski Türk Bahçeleri*, pp. 14–52, passim. The changing role of gardeners is reflected in the chronicles and travelogues of the seventeenth and the eighteenth century; see Henry Grenville, *Observations sur l'état actuel de l'Empire*

of the chief gardener, which was until then confined to the upkeep of the
gardens of the Topkapı Palace and of the imperial suburban retreats, now
extended to the maintenance of order in all the public gardens, promenades, meadows, and forests located along the shores of the Bosphorus, the
Golden Horn, the Sea of Marmara, the Black Sea, and the Princes' Islands.
Enforcement of building, hunting, and fishing regulations was also part of
the *bostancıbaşı*'s new responsibilities. By the beginning of the eighteenth
century, gardeners acted both as a police force and to enforce morality.
A gardener could, on his own authority, restrict access in a particular garden,
or grant it in another, depending sometimes on a suitable tip. He could
inflict immediate punishment on those who, in his judgment, infringed the
limits of normative public behavior, such as when "God forbid – [he] should
chance upon a [mixed] party of men and women singing on a boat. He
would sink the boat without further ado."[54] While these new prerogatives
revealed a growing preoccupation with the enforcement of public order, they
also countered questionable changes in the praxis of public life.

   As the sultan's representative in matters of public surveillance, it was to
the *bostancıbaşı*, among other police officials and legislative authorities
(notably, the Janissary Agha and the judge of the district concerned) that
imperial edicts that enforced sumptuary laws on matters of public outings
and behavior in the extra-muros city were usually addressed. Sumptuary
regulations encompassed broad domains of behavior and consumption,
and public recreation was chief among them. At the most basic level, these
laws were meant to ensure the upkeep of order and discipline in the city. As
was the case in early modern France, England, China, Italy, and Japan,
they were intended to maintain preexisting social (and, in the Ottoman
Empire, religious) structures and, perhaps even more importantly, to
preserve "stable status displays,"[55] or what Daniel Roche has termed "la

---

Ottoman, ed. Andrew Ehrenkreutz (Ann Arbor: University of Michigan Press, 1965), pp. 21–2;
Guillaume-Joseph Grelot, *Relation nouvelle d'un voyage de Constantinople* (Paris: Chez la veuve de
D. Foucault, 1630), pp. 84–5; Evliya, *Seyahatname*, fols. 33a–74a passim, 135a–140a passim, 171a–174b
passim; Mustafa Naima, *Tarih*, vol. IV, p. 386; Râşid, *Tarih*, vol. III, pp. 85, 89, 144; Silâhdâr,
Nusretnâme, vol. I, p. 223, vol. II, p. 347; Dallaway, *Constantinople*, p. 33; Tott, *Mémoires*,
pp. xxxiij–xxxiv, 26, 32–4, 61–2, 65; Joseph P. Tournefort, *Relation d'un voyage du Levant*, 3 vols.
(Paris: Frères Bruysat, 1727), vol. II, pp. 285–6; and Mouradgea d'Ohsson, who explains that the city
and its environs were policed, respectively, by the Janissary Agha and the chief gardener, *Tableau*,
vol. IV, pp. 349–50.
[54] Kömürciyan, *İstanbul Tarihi*, p. 51; see also İsmail Âsım, *Tarih*, p. 61.
[55] Craig Clunas, *Superfluous Things: Material Culture and Social Status in Early Modern China*
(Urbana, IL: University of Illinois Press, 1991), p. 147. Aside from this very insightful book see, on
the subject of sumptuary laws in the early modern world, James McClain and John M. Merriman,
"Edo and Paris: Cities and Power," in James McClain, John M. Merriman and Kaoru Ugawa (eds.),
Edo and Paris: Urban Life and the State in the Early Modern Era (Ithaca, NY: Cornell University

hiérarchie des apparences."⁵⁶ Insofar as these regulations controlled order in the city, they also defined the parameters of urban life, the normative sphere that is, within which public life was to be carried out. Sumptuary laws dated from at least the second half of the sixteenth century, and were rooted in shari'a law and ancient rules governing the public behavior of zimmi (non-Muslims). Promulgated in the form of imperial or grand vizierial edicts, they had often pertained to matters of public life and public places like baths, taverns, and coffeehouses.⁵⁷ Coffeehouses, in particular, became a major target from the moment they were introduced in the capital in 1551. In sixteenth- and seventeenth-century Istanbul, as much as in the London of Charles II, state authorities perceived coffeehouses as focal points of social unrest, rumors, indecent discourses, political gossip, and critique.⁵⁸ In Istanbul, the attack was often couched in a puritanical discourse that reacted both against coffee, as a nefarious innovation (*bid'a*), and against its public consumption. In the seventeenth century the state prohibited or shut down coffeehouses repeatedly, especially in periods of brewing discontent and mutiny.⁵⁹

Press, 1994), pp. 3–38; Daniel Roche, *La culture des apparences: une histoire du vêtement (XVIIe–XVIIIe siècle)* (Paris: Fayard, 1989); Arjun Appadurai (ed.), "Introduction: Commodities and the Politics of Value," in *The Social Life of Things: Commodities in Cultural Perspective* (Cambridge: Cambridge University Press, 1986), pp. 3–63; Peter Burke, "Conspicuous Consumption in Seventeenth-Century Italy," *Kwartalnik Historii Kultury Materialnej* (1982): 43–56.

⁵⁶ Roche, *La culture des apparences*, pp. 87–118.

⁵⁷ For examples of these edicts, see Ahmet Refik, *Hicrî On Birinci Asırda İstanbul Hayatı 1000–1100* (Istanbul: Devlet Matbaası, 1931), pp. 38–41, 141–2.

⁵⁸ This widespread perception was most explicitly articulated by Katib Çelebi, *The Balance of Truth*, trans. and annotated Geoffrey Lewis (London: Allen and Unwin, 1957), pp. 60–1; and Naima, *Tarih*, vol. III, pp. 170–2. On English coffeehouses as places of potential sedition see, for example, Graham John Barker-Benfield, *The Culture of Sensibility: Sex and Society in Eighteenth-Century Britain* (Chicago: University of Chicago Press, 1992), p. 52; and John Brewer, *The Pleasures of the Imagination: English Culture in the Eighteenth Century* (New York: Farrar, Straus, Giroux, 1997), pp. 34–7.

⁵⁹ This was particularly the case in the latter half of the seventeenth century under Murad IV, during the rise of the puritanical Kadızadelis. On coffeehouses and their controversial role in the social and political landscape of sixteenth- and seventeenth-century Istanbul see the articles by Hélène Desmet-Grégoire and Ayşe Saraçgil in Hélène Desmet-Grégoire and François Georgeon (eds.), *Cafés d'Orient revisités* (Paris: CNRS, 1997), pp. 13–38; Mantran, *Istanbul dans la seconde moitié du XVIIe siècle*, p. 106; Ralph S. Hattox, *Coffee and Coffeehouses: The Origins of a Social Beverage in the Medieval Near East* (Seattle: University of Washington Press, 1985), pp. 91, 102; Zilfi, *The Politics of Piety*, pp. 135–44; Madeline Zilfi, "The Kadızadelis: Discordant Revivalism in Seventeenth-Century Istanbul," *Journal of Near Eastern Studies* 45/4 (1986): 257; Derin Terzioğlu, "Sufi and Dissident in the Ottoman Empire: Niyāzī-i Mısrī (1618–94)," PhD dissertation, Harvard University, 1998, pp. 190–208; Kafadar, "'Janissaries and Other Riffraff,'" pp. 6, 12–13; and Cengiz Kırlı, "The Struggle over Space: Coffeehouses of Ottoman Istanbul, 1780–1845," PhD dissertation, Binghamton University, 2001. The significance of coffeehouses is revealed in several sources of the period, notably I. Peçevi, *Peçevi Tarihi*, ed. M. Uraz, 2 vols. (Istanbul: Neşriyat Yurdu, 1968–9), vol. I, pp. 23, 258, 364; Katib Çelebi, *The Balance of Truth*, pp. 60–1; Evliya, *Seyahatname*, fol. 63b; Na'imâ, *Tarih*, vol. I, p. 127, vol. III, pp. 170–2.

As the sphere of sociability expanded, its regulation intensified. In the eighteenth century, the state stepped up its enforcement of sumptuary rules to unprecedented levels. Strikingly, the locus of controversy expanded beyond the coffeehouse into the garden; that is to say beyond those places deemed to foster social and political unrest and into rival spaces of sociability where age, gender, social, and professional groups mixed relatively too freely and consequently could threaten established hierarchies. This is not to say that social heterogeneity was not often inherent to coffeehouse entertainment, but rather, that the state's discourse against them and the different methods adopted to punish, control, or monitor them centered chiefly on the perception of coffeehouses as dangerous sites of political rumor and critique, not on their social fluidity.[60] The nature of the controversy had thus changed. Sumptuary laws pointedly targeted public attire and garden recreation, displays in which signs of change and fluidity in the social structure were being publicly exhibited.

Repeatedly, throughout the century, authorities dictated and enforced the terms by which garden recreation could take place. Bans were occasionally imposed on specific types of activities like carriage rides and boat excursions. Other regulations barred certain groups from visiting specific gardens. A 1751 edict prohibited women's visits to a number of gardens in Üsküdar and Beykoz. During the festivities held in 1758 to celebrate the birth of Hibetullah Sultan, daughter of Mustafa III, women were again subjected to bans on visits to gardens, promenades, and marketplaces. Specific stipulations addressed the issue of gender segregation in gardens and mandated the allocation of specific areas, times of the day, or days of the week exclusively to women.[61] According to the French traveler Pertusier, "[Fridays], as well as Tuesdays, are allocated to women for their [social] visits, promenades, or visits to the bath, depending on their wishes."[62] Travelers continued to observe that "when parties proceed to

[60] Kırlı, "Struggle over Space," pp. 18–66.
[61] Ahmet Refik, *Hicrî On İkinci Asırda İstanbul Hayatı 1100–1200* (Istanbul: Enderun Kitabevi, 1988), pp. 131–2, 170, 174–5; see also Şem'dânizâde, *Mür'i't-Tevârih*, vol. I, p. 21; Raşid Efendi, *Münşeat*, Topkapı Sarayı, MS H. 1037, fols. 40–1; Seyyid Mehmed Hâkim, *Vekâyi'-nâme*, Topkapı Sarayı Müzesi Kütüphanesi, MS B 231, B 233, fols. 423, 482; Reşid Çeşmîzâde, *Çeşmî-zâde Tarihi*, ed. B. Kütükoğlu (Istanbul: Edebiyat Fakültesi Basımevi, 1993), p. 25; Mouradgea d'Ohsson, *Tableau*, vol. IV, pp. 79–81; Reşat Ekrem Koçu, *Türk Giyim Kuşam ve Süslenme Sözlüğü* (Istanbul: Sümerbank, 1969), p. 9; Filiz Çağman, "Family Life," in Günsel Renda (ed.), *Woman in Anatolia: 9000 Years of the Anatolian Woman*, exhibition catalogue, Topkapı Palace Museum, 29 November 1993 – 28 February 1994 (Istanbul: Ministry of Culture, 1993), pp. 203–4; Suha Umur, "Osmanlı Belgeleri Arasında: Kadınlara Buyruklar," *Tarih ve Toplum* 10/58 (Sept. 1988): 205–7.
[62] Pertusier, *Promenades pittoresques*, vol. II, p. 7.

those pic-nics, even the members of a family never mix together ... The women assemble on one side round the fountain, and the men on the other, under the trees."[63] Ottoman authorities actively worked to ensure that such segregation remained in place. In the closing lines of a wonderful *gazel* in which the garden of Kağıthane is equated to a lover's heart so big it could contain all the young lads of Istanbul, Süruri may have been applauding, or perhaps deferentially protesting against, those legal measures that prescribed the terms by which, and the time and space in which different forms of sociability could take place in a public garden:

> I fell in love with a handsome ink-seller; if he answers my prayers
> I'll write him a missive, an invitation to Kağıthane
> ...
>
> If all the boys of Istanbul gathered there, they would fit
> [For] Kağıthane is as spacious as a lover's heart
> Oh! Süruri, so what if it's forbidden to women?
> We will hold converse with young boys at Kağıthane.[64]

As the regulation of public recreation continued, matters of clothing in the specific context of fashionable gardens became a serious source of concern. The state began enforcing previously existing sartorial laws and repeatedly decreed new clothing regulations. Commenting on an edict issued in 1725, the court historian Küçük Çelebizade expressed his outrage at the level of impudence that women exhibited in both their outfits and demeanors, specifically at the gardens of Sa'dabad.[65] Sartorial impudence could lead to devastating consequences, as it did to the unfortunate daughter of one wicked Emine in 1730. She was drowned in the sea in broad daylight – a punishment that gave ample satisfaction to the conservative and virulent critic, Şem'dânizâde, for "not only did it reform women's dress, but it also mended their souls."[66]

From 1702 until 1748, and time and again under Osman III, Mustafa III, and Selim III, imperial edicts asserted the necessity and obligation of certain groups – notably women, and Jewish and Christian communities to abide by the Ottoman dresscode. Such edicts as well as those who commented on the changing sartorial landscape in the capital appealed not only to moral and financial considerations, but also invoked the need

[63] Allom and Walsh, *Constantinople*, vol. I, pp. 33–4.
[64] Süruri, *Dîvân-ı Süruri*, (n.d.), part 3: *Gazliyyât*, p. 45.
[65] İsmail Âsım, *Tarih*, pp. 375–6; see also Reşat Ekrem Koçu, *Tarihimizde Garip Vakalar* (Istanbul: Varlık Yayınevi, 1958), pp. 35–6.
[66] Şem'dânizâde, *Mür'i't-Tevârih*, vol. I, p. 26.

to maintain visible marks of distinctions, whether vis-à-vis other social or religious groups, or with respect to the residents of foreign countries. In 1758 a new sartorial law sought to check the growing inclination of non-Muslims to adopt the "Frankish style" of dressing and to wear yellow shoes, which were customarily reserved for Muslims. Two years earlier, an imperial edict condemned those "shameless [Muslim] women" who paraded about luxuriously adorned in innovative dresses that emulated the fashion of Christian women and those clad in provocative outfits that "stirred the nerve of desire."[67] Innovative fashion, be it in the color of a shoe, the style, cut, or design of a dress, or the length and width of a collar (all of which were sometimes mentioned and described with great precision in the edicts) blurred established boundaries between social, professional, ethnic, and religious groups.

Such preoccupations with clothing regulations certainly predated the eighteenth century.[68] In this period, though, the issue of innovative dress acquired a new significance. After two centuries of almost unaltered dress, noticeable changes were suddenly occurring in both women's and men's outdoor clothing. The writings of foreign merchants and travelers attest to a rising fashion consciousness among Istanbul's middle classes and describe

[67] Ahmet Refik, *İstanbul Hayatı, 1100–1200*, pp. 86–8, 182–3; Şem'dânizâde, *Mür'i't-Tevârih*, vol. I, p. 26, vol. II, p. 36; "Başbakanlık Arşivinde yeni bulunmuş olan ve Sadreddin Zâde Telhisî Mustafa Efendi tarafından tutulduğu anlaşılan H. 1123 (1711) – 1184 (1735) yıllarına ait bir Ceride (Jurnal) ve Eklentisi," excerpts edited by F. Işıközlü, in *VII. Türk Tarih Kongresi* (Ankara: Türk Tarih Kurumu, 1973), vol. II, pp. 521, 523; Pertusier, *Promenades pittoresques*, vol. II, p. 89; Koçu, *Garip Vakalar*, p. 63; Yücel Özkaya, *XVIII. Yüzyılda Osmanlı Kurumları ve Osmanlı Toplum Yaşantısı* (Ankara: Kültür ve Turizm Bakanlığı, 1985), pp. 145–57 passim; Umur, "Kadınlara Buyruklar," pp. 206–7; Çağman, "Women's Clothing," p. 258. Surprisingly, the literature on Ottoman sartorial laws is relatively poor; see Binswänger's chapter on discriminative measures against minorities in the Ottoman Empire in the sixteenth century: Karl Binswänger, *Untersuchungen zum Status der Nichtmuslime im Osmanischen Reich des 16. Jahrhunderts* (Munich: R. Trofenik, 1977), pp. 160–93; Donald Quataert, "Clothing Laws, State, and Society in the Ottoman Empire, 1720–1829," *International Journal of Middle East Studies* 29/3 (1997): 403–25, which focuses primarily on clothing laws as state disciplinary tools; see also his introduction to *Consumption Studies*, pp. 1–13; and Zilfi, "Goods in the *Mahalle*: Distributional Encounters in Eighteenth-Century Istanbul," pp. 289–311 in the same volume. Dress regulations were a central concern of sumptuary laws in early modern Europe, China, Japan and India as well. For examples of an immense literature on this subject see Hamadeh, "The City's Pleasures," ch. 3, note 98.

[68] See, for example, Ahmet Refik, *İstanbul Hayatı, 1000–1100*, pp. 51–2. See also Andreas Tietze, "Mustafa Ali on Luxury and the Status Symbols of Ottoman Gentlemen," in *Studia Turcologica Memoriae Alexii Bombaci Dicata* (Naples: n.p., 1982), pp. 580–1. Mustafa Ali's concern with the issue of dresscode within the ruling class indicates that it was not always maintained during his own time, at least not within this group. His and Koçi Bey's commentaries on the lack of enforcement of clothing regulations in the late sixteenth and seventeenth centuries are viewed by Rifaat Abou El-Haj as indications of increasing social mobility; Abou el-Haj, *The Formation of the Modern State*, p. 37.

new tastes in fabrics and colors.[69] Contemporary portraits by Levni and Buhari featured remarkable innovations in women's fashion such as their increasing *décolletage*, broad collars, transparent and loosely worn veils, extravagant head-dresses, and hair worn loose. Such innovations never failed to attract attention: "No woman covers her breast," wrote Mouradgea d'Ohsson, "especially in the summer, except with a blouse that is usually [made] of thin gauze."[70] If the state became more diligent about enforcing sartorial regulations, it was partly because changing consumption patterns had brought about new tastes, and partly because these tastes were being paraded in public more conspicuously than ever before. Such displays took the form of new styles, colors, hats, and hairdos that deviated considerably from traditional dresscodes. The persistent reiteration of these regulations suggests that dissolving social, professional, ethnic, and religious distinctions may have had far-reaching ramifications.

Of course, sumptuary regulations could not contain every dimension of urban life. Nor could they efficiently cover every fountain, *namâzgâh*, or cemetery, those "legitimate" points of convergence (for water supply, prayer, or visitation) that transformed spontaneously into unguarded and un-segregated forums for social encounters and, as the Baron de Tott put it, for many of women's "intrigues gallantes."[71] Eye-witness accounts of episodes of legal infractions and of illicit encounters between men and women in gardens and on river banks, contemporary critics' repeated concerns about the maintenance of law and order,[72] and the reiteration of regulations throughout the century all indicate that state measures could not prevent emerging social practices and new currents of public behavior. The reality revealed in Enderunlu Fazıl's "Preface" to his *Zenânnâme* (*Book*

---

[69] Flachat, *Observations sur le commerce et sur les arts*, vol. I, pp. 434–44; Mouradgea d'Ohsson, *Tableau*, vol. II, pp. 147–50, vol. IV, p. 152; Pertusier, *Promenades pittoresques*, vol. II, pp. 192–3. On women's changing fashion and tastes, see Çağman, "Women's Clothing," pp. 256–8 and pp. 260–87; Jennifer Scarce, "The Development of Women's Fashion in Ottoman Turkish Costume during the 18th and 19th Centuries," in *IVe Congrès International d'Art Turc*, Aix-en-Provence, 10–15 Sept. 1971 (Aix-en-Provence: Éditions de l'Université de Provence, 1976), pp. 199–219; Charlotte Jirousek, "The Transition to Mass Fashion System Dress in the Later Ottoman Empire," in Quataert *Consumption Studies*, pp. 201–41.

[70] Mouradgea d'Ohsson, *Tableau*, vol. IV, p. 152.

[71] Tott, *Mémoires*, vol. I, pp. xxxij–xxxiij; see also Flachat, *Observations sur le commerce et sur les arts*, vol. I, pp. 431–2; Pertusier, *Promenades pittoresques*, vol. I, pp. 370–3, 392; vol. II, pp. 434–5; Allom and Walsh, *Constantinople*, vol. I, pp. 23–5; Pardoe, *The City of the Sultan*, vol. I, p. 138; and Vasıf's *Muhammes*, published in E. J. W. Gibb, *A History of Ottoman Poetry*, 6 vols. (London: Luzac, 1967), vol. VI, pp. 323–31.

[72] See, for example, "Sadreddinzâde Telhîsî Mustafa Efendi," p. 523; Şem'dânizâde, *Mür'i't-Tevârih*, vol. I, p. 26; vol. II, pp. 36–8; Mehmed Hakim, *Vekâyi'nâme*, B 231, fols. 234b, 270a–b, 290a–291a; B.233, fols. 10b, 48a, 184a.

of Women), quoted in part in this chapter's epigraph, contradicts the
implications of contemporaneous imperial edicts, or the reflections of
some of his contemporaries. Although the poem does not claim to be
more than an imagined scenario, it is significant that Fazıl chooses a public
space for an encounter between young men and women, when a more
clandestine setting (in which such intercourse could be construed within
the realm of the private – a private garden, a concealed river bank, a house
of prostitution, all of which are integral to his poetic repertoire) would have
served his purpose equally well. But Fazıl's "Preface" is, in large part,
a counseling guide on the principles of seduction, as they pertain specifically to public gardens. It reads like a manual of public garden behavior in
which every detail of clothing, demeanor, social and courtship skill, and
faux pas is carefully outlined. It reveals a keen consciousness of clothing
fashion as a form of public expression through which new aspirations and
identities could be performed and displayed. It also captures the simplicity
with which a frivolous gaze or the location of a swing could trigger a
complete collapse of gender boundaries.

I have suggested that the rise of a garden culture and the development of
public spaces were linked to changing habits and practices among what I
called the "urban middle classes." I have deliberately used these terms
loosely in an attempt to bring together the wide and amorphous crowd
of grandees and commoners, merchants and artisans, rich and poor
women, children, Greeks, Jews, Armenians, Turks, "Rayas" and Franks,
people of "all classes," "every rank" and profession, the *halk* (populace) and
the ulema, the anonymous young men and women of the *Zenânnâme*,
Sürurî's handsome ink-seller, and "all the young boys of Istanbul" that
populated the paintings and writings of artists, poets, travelers, and chroniclers.[73] "Urban middle classes" as used in this chapter is therefore a
reference to the broad social constellation of eighteenth-century gardens
and to the blurred contours of the various groups it contained. It also
indicates the increasing difficulty in distinguishing between elite and
"popular" spheres of recreation.

In all evidence, the gardens we are talking about were venues in which a
non-courtly culture of sociability flourished. But this does not necessarily
mean that it flourished on the margins of a hermetically enclosed space of
elite recreation. On the contrary, the growth and vitality of both elite and

---

[73] Such references abound in the contemporary sources; see, for instance, Sürurî, *Dîvân*, part 3, p. 45;
Nevres, *Dîvân*, fols. 38b–39a ; Allom and Walsh, *Constantinople*, vol. II, p. 34; Mouradgea d'Ohsson,
Tableau, vol. IV, p. 185; Dallaway, *Constantinople*, pp. 118–19.

popular recreation depended upon their physical and visual proximity to each other. The popularity of the old public promenade of Kağıthane grew dramatically after 1721, when Ahmed III's grand vizier constructed the imperial garden of Sa'dabad right in the heart of it. Anyone strolling in the adjacent promenade was afforded the view of the magnificent palace, its landscape, and the glittering domes of the small garden pavilions that Mahmud I added some twenty years later. "It is one of the most pleasant promenades," d'Ohsson explained. "Little hills, plains, small pavilions with gilded domes, in sum, everything unites to offer [the viewer] the most picturesque and impressive sight."[74] The detailed engraving produced by l'Espinasse for d'Ohsson's *Tableau* intimates that people wandered in and out of the imperial garden enclosure as they pleased (fig. 12.8). Ferté-Meun also makes this point clear in her confident recommendation that in order to enjoy a "veritable pleasure, one must come and sit, on the first days of spring, in the pavilion [built by Mahmud I] that is situated right in the middle of the river," that is, at one end of the pool in the imperial garden. There, she continues, "the sound of this cascade at your feet, these groups of Turkish, Greek, Armenian and Jewish women whose mores, customs and outfits are so varied and who delight, undaunted, in all sorts of divertissements the countryside [*campagne*] [has to] offer, make of this promenade a ravishing spectacle."[75]

There are no indications that measures were imposed to limit access to Sa'dabad, as was the case in the royal gardens of Europe where entry was sometimes restricted to those with a letter of invitation, ticket-holders, or, more commonly, key-holders, and where strict rules of dress or small admission fees often deterred many (usually servants, workers, schoolboys, or soldiers) from entering the gardens.[76] In the nineteenth century, possibly after the palace was restored by Mahmud II, "the Valley of the Sweet Waters," as the Europeans called it, was "shut up with guards, and no stranger permitted to intrude" while the monarch or members of his

---

[74] Mouradgea d'Ohsson, *Tableau*, vol. IV, p. 185.
[75] Ferté-Meun, *Lettres sur le Bosphore*, p. 63.
[76] Laure Amar, *L'espace public en herbe* (Paris, 1986), p. 32; Lasdun, *The English Park*, pp. 41–2, 128–9; Debié, *Jardins des capitales*, pp. 65, 134–5, 199; Coffin, "The 'Lex Hortorum'", pp. 201, 209–11; Parshall, "C. C. L. Hirschfeld's Concept of the Garden," pp. 155–6. It is important to note here that although the term "public park" was used for the first time in 1661 (Lasdun, *The English Park*, p. 75), as Parshall remarks, "open to the public" was a very relative notion. In eighteenth-century France, the words public and public spaces were mainly used in police vocabulary and referred to people and places that required policing: Lisa Jane Graham, "Crimes of Opinion: Policing the Public in Eighteenth-Century France," in Christine Adams, Jack Cluser, and Lisa Jane Graham (eds.), *Visions and Revisions of Eighteenth-Century France* (University Park, PA: Pennsylvania State University Press, 1997), pp. 84–5.

Figure 12.8 From Mouradgea d'Ohsson, *Tableau général de l'empire othoman* (Paris, 1788–1814). View of the imperial palace of Saʿdabad and the garden of Kağıthane, by l'Espinasse.

household were visiting; "at other times, it is open to all classes, who come here to rusticate, particularly Greeks, on Sundays and festivals."[77] Sa'dabad may have been, since the years of Ahmed III, open to the broad public at particular times of the day or days of the week and otherwise restricted to the court household. Privacy and exclusivity at the imperial garden, however, must have been relative.

> Come quick, look this once! There is no ban on the eye
> Sa'dabad has now become garden upon hill, my love![78]

So exclaimed the poet Nedim, capturing beautifully the way in which people's desires and actual realities were negotiated.

In eighteenth-century consciousness, Sa'dabad and many imperial gardens such as those at Çubuklu, Bebek, and Feyzabad had become associated with the lives and diversions of ordinary people. Some hailed them as symbols of courtly splendor and architectural magnificence; others glorified them as icons of public pleasures. In these places, customarily regarded as imperial and exclusive, Nedim and his contemporaries saw wonderful arenas of urban life, leaving us uncertain about how eighteenth-century Istanbul conceptualized private and public and defined public space. These questions are implicated in large legal, social, and even linguistic issues. In this context, one can only speculate.[79] Did the word *hâss* (as used in "*hâss bahçe*") already carry the meaning of private in the eighteenth century or did it refer only to matters pertaining to the court or the elite (as used in "*hâss u 'âmm*")?[80] Were there any legal, or extra-legal, mechanisms that defined and negotiated the boundaries between private and public space? Did a binary opposition exist, in eighteenth-century minds, between

---

[77] Allom and Walsh, *Constantinople*, vol. I, p. 58. The Valley could be referring not only to the royal compound but to the whole area of Sa'dabad and Kağıthane. If this is the case, then Walsh's observation is all the more indication that no strict separation existed that divided the two gardens.
[78] Nedim, *Divan*, p. 193.
[79] A study of fatwa registers and tribunal records of the seventeenth and the eighteenth century might help elucidate how concepts of private and public were defined, and perhaps redefined, at different times.
[80] In Meninski's seventeenth-century multilingual thesaurus *hâss* is translated as (in Latin) *proprius, privates, peculiaris*; (in Italian) *proprio, privato, particolare*; and (in French) *propre, privé, particulier*. Franciscus à Mesgnien Meninski, *Thesaurus Linguarum Orientalium Turcicae – Arabicae – Persicae*, 6 vols., facsimile reprint, with an introduction by Mehmet Ölmez (Istanbul: Simurg, 2000). By the latter half of the nineteenth century "*hâss*" meant "special, particular"; "special to the state or sovereign," as well as "private, individual"; see J. W. Redhouse, *An English and Turkish Lexicon* (Constantinople, 1890); see also Cengiz Orhonlu's entry, "Khāss," in EI2, vol. IV, pp. 1094–1100; Pakalın, *Osmanlı Tarih Deyimleri ve Terimleri Sözlüğü*, 3 vols. (Istanbul: Milli Eğitim Basımevi, 1946), vol. I, pp. 750–2.

private and public space outside the legal shari'a sphere of harem and domestic space?[81]

The court historian Raşid's account of the building and restoration activities that took place in 1718–19 at the waterfront palace garden of Beşiktaş provides insights into these questions, for it points to a keen awareness of the concepts of privacy and public trespassing into the context of imperial gardens. Damad Ibrahim's restoration of the garden of Beşiktaş, Raşid tells us, had entailed its joining (*zamm u ilhâk*) to the neighboring, early seventeenth-century garden of Dolmabahçe. A public landing dock (*'Arab İskelesi*), which until then the residents of the district of Fındıklı had reached by walking between the two gardens, was now incorporated into the joint Beşiktaş–Dolmabahçe garden. From that moment onward, the authorities required residents of Fındıklı to hold a permit in order to gain access to the landing dock, through what came, in all evidence, to be perceived as the "private" imperial domain of Beşiktaş–Dolmabahçe.[82]

Despite this awareness of and concern for privacy, the preference of the eighteenth-century court to build palatial gardens, such as Beşiktaş, both in the midst of already populated neighborhoods and along the most public gateway of the city (the Bosphorus), in itself suggests how relative concepts of privacy and exclusiveness in these gardens remained. Their setting and architecture indicate that the court must have created these gardens in part for visual consumption by a broad public. The unusual openness, transparency, and lavishness of their palatial façades reflect an unusual tendency for exhibitionism, and constituted a remarkable change in Ottoman palatine tradition.[83] Moreover, contemporaries frequently mentioned the widespread routine of sightseeing, especially upon the completion or the restoration of an imperial garden, confirmation that these places were indeed intended for show. Court historians like Raşid emphasized "the restless desire of all the people of Istanbul to go out and marvel at"

---

[81] Countless neighbors' disputes recorded in the tribunal documents of the period over issues of physical proximity and/or visual intrusion into each other's living quarters reveal a keen sense of domestic privacy. This is further suggested by the legal definition of the concept of *hawala* (lit. vicinity, neighborhood) that comes across in the fatwas of 1674 to 1730, by which a householder was protected from "direct, intentional intrusion, either visual or actual, into the inner spheres and living quarters of his own household from vantage points in his neighbor's house." Rhoads Murphey, "Communal Living in Istanbul: Searching for the Foundations of an Urban Tradition," *Journal of Urban History* 16 (1990): 126. But what is very interesting here is that *hawala* legal protection did not extend to "portions of a property considered external," like gardens and courtyards.

[82] Râşid, *Tarih*, vol. V, pp. 165–6.

[83] On these topics and their relation to changing court ceremonial, see Hamadeh, "City's Pleasures," pp. 55–93, 109–13.

monuments of imperial magnificence like Hüsrevabad, Sa'dabad, or Ferahabad.[84] Şemdanizade's long and acerbic diatribes on the feasts and banquets that Damad Ibrahim frequently held in the imperial gardens of Sa'dabad, Çubuklu, Bebek, Dolmabahçe, Göksu, Beykoz, and Üsküdar show that these events were not limited to the court entourage and included the high and the low.[85] This participation of the plebeians in imperial festivities was unprecedented in the history of Ottoman court life.[86] While the embittered Şem'dânizâde was probably right in remarking that the state meant these events as uplifting distractions from the deteriorating affairs of the empire, surely it also intended such avuncular displays for the benefit of the court's public image as spectacles that confirmed to the people of Istanbul the empire's unwavering power and opulence.

None of this should imply, of course, the sudden disappearance of distinctions between court and city, or that the new imperial gardens of Sa'dabad, Çubuklu, Bebek, Dolmabahçe, and others were forums in which to cultivate ideals of social equality. There is no doubt, however, that in the minds of contemporaries at least, an intimate relationship existed between elite and urban cultural spaces that took on various forms at such gardens as Sa'dabad.

This relationship, and contemporary written and pictorial depictions of gardens, call into question the limits imposed (mostly implicitly) by modern historiography on the idea of pleasure in the eighteenth century: both historically, as confined to the somewhat arbitrary "Tulip Period" (1718–30), and socially and culturally, as a prerogative of the ruling elite handed down, or emulated, from top to bottom.[87] The ruling elite (particularly in the "Tulip Period" historiography) appears to be immersed in a world of recreational pleasures that gradually reached down and across all segments of society. Accordingly, the urban middle classes' culture of Bosphorus promenades and festive excursions in public gardens is but

---

[84] Râşid, *Tarih*, vol. V, pp. 305–6; see also, for example, İ. Erünsal (ed.), "Bir Osmanlı Efendisi'nin Günlüğü: Sadreddinzâde Telhisî Mustafa Efendi ve Cerîdesi," *Kaynaklar* 2 (Winter 1984): 242.

[85] Şem'dânizâde, *Mür'i't-Tevârih*, vol. I, pp. 3–4.

[86] Madeline Zilfi, "Women and Society in the Tulip Erẓ," in A. Sonbol (ed.), *Women, the Family and Divorce Laws in Family History* (Syracuse, NY: Syracuse University Press, 1986), pp. 297–8.

[87] This understanding of pleasure in the Ottoman context is strongly related to the silent acceptance, among scholars, of the very appealing but highly problematic modern notion of "Tulip Period" as a distinctive and self-contained historical period characterized by an atmosphere of peace and worldliness; see, for example, Ahmet Evin, "The Tulip Age and Definitions of 'Westernization,'" in H. İnalcık and O. Okyar (eds.), *Social and Economic History of Turkey (1071–1920) / Türkiye'nin Sosyal ve Ekonomik Tarihi* (Ankara: Meteksan, 1980), pp. 131–45; Artan, "Architecture as a Theatre of Life," pp. 4–5, 34, 120–1.

the ultimate consequence of this process. Contemporary sources show us, however, that we cannot really construe the development of public spaces as the expression of the trickling down of an elite culture of pleasures. If gardens had once been inextricably linked to the cultivation of elite pleasures in a relatively exclusive and enclosed sphere, in the eighteenth century they emerged as central venues of urban culture with a wholly different set of meanings and concerns. It is useful to recall here what Chartier described as "the processes of differentiated distribution, uses, and appropriation of ideas and material objects circulating within a given society" which are, in the end, "what distinguished cultural worlds."[88] In Istanbul in the eighteenth century ideas and forms traveled in every direction, and they were used, appropriated, and interpreted differently at every turn. In literature, Nedim canonized the oral, popular tradition of şarkı in the mainstream of court poetry. In architecture, the imperial court appropriated the urban tradition of wood construction, opening a new chapter in the history of Ottoman palatine architecture. Nevertheless, Nedim's şarkı was vastly different from the şarkı of the oral tradition, and the symbolism embodied in the new wooden imperial palaces owed little to their modest precedents. Similarly, the garden pleasures of urban society did far more than imitate an old courtly culture. As the prime avenue of a blossoming Ottoman public sphere, public gardens were forums that nurtured new forms and channels of sociability that, in turn, diminished social and cultural distances between different groups and between elite and popular spheres. They were also, as Nedim, Enderunlu Fazıl, and their contemporaries remind us, arenas in which people constantly negotiated the limits of the normative sphere of urban life and tested and reified new social habits, aspirations, and forms of distinction.

[88] Roger Chartier, "Culture as Appropriation: Popular Cultural Uses in Early Modern France," in Steven Kaplan, *Understanding Popular Culture: Europe from the Middle Ages to the Nineteenth Century* (New York: Mouton, 1984), pp. 229–53. Carlo Ginzburg's notions of circularity and "iconic circuits" reveal a comparable understanding of how cultural forms and knowledge were circulated, appropriated, and reinterpreted; see his second preface to *The Cheese and the Worms: The Cosmos of a Sixteenth-Century Miller*, trans. J. and A. C. Tedeschi (New York: Dorset, 1989); and, especially, his article, "Titian, Ovid, and Sixteenth-Century Codes for Erotic Illustration," in *Clues, Myths, and the Historical Method*, trans. J. and A. C. Tedeschi (Baltimore, MD: Johns Hopkins University Press, 1986), pp. 77–95.

Bibliography

PRIMARY SOURCES

ARCHIVES

Basbakanlık Osmanlı Arşivi (BOA), Cevdet Belediye no. 4224 (1707); see also, for instance, nos. 4315 and 4583 (1774), no. 6609 (1783), no. 5578 (1784).
BOA, Cevdet Saray nos. 2184, 5486, for the years 1707, 1712, 1713, 1735 and 1740. Nos. 6068 (1703–4), 5985 (1709), 5963 (1710), 3978 (1711).
BOA, Ecnebi Defteri 13/1, 14/2, 16/4.
BOA, Hatt-ı Humayun 3811, 3766, 3799-A, 3855-B, 20896, 20898, B/C/D.
BOA, İbnülemin Saray Mesalihi nos. 3243 and 3245 (1705), nos. 2886 and 2967 (1710).
BOA, Maliyeden Müdevver register no. 1655 (1708).
BOA, Mühimme Defterleri, various.
Gaziantep Şeriye Sicili no. 2, 120c, d, 142b and passim, 30a, 30c, 31a, 43a, 48c, 184a, b.
Gaziantep Şeriye Sicili no. 161, 98d, 145a, b.
Tapu ve Kadastro Umum Müdürlüğü, the *mufassal*, the *icmâl*, and the *rûznâmçe* registers TK 233: 114b, TK 334: 41a, TK 222: 108a; TK 319, TK 241, TK 215.

MANUSCRIPTS AND VARIANTS, AND PRINTED EDITIONS

Abdülkadir (Kadrî) Efendi, *Topçular Kâtibi 'Abdülkādir (Kadrî) Efendi Tarihi*, ed. Ziya Yılmazer, 2 vols. Ankara: Türk Tarih Kurumu, 2003.
Abu al-Fawz al-Suwaydi, "Daf' al-zulm 'an al-wuqu' fi arz hatha al-mazlum," Süleymaniye Kütüphanesi, Esad Efendi 1404.
Ahmed Cevdet, *Tarih*, 1st edn, 12 vols., Istanbul: n.p., 1858.
Ahmed Resmî, *Halifetü'r-Rüesa* (reprint of Mücteba Ilgürel (ed.), *Halifetü'r-Rüesa*,) Istanbul: Enderun, 1992.
Ahmed Tâib Osmanzâde, *Hadîkatü'l-vüzerâ*, continued by later biographers: Dilâver-ağa-zâde Ömer Vahîd, Ahmed Câvîd, and 'Abdülfettâh Şevket of Baghdad (editions: the original and the continuations were printed in

Istanbul in 1271/1854–5; reprint *Hadîqat ül-Vüzerâ* (*Der Garten der Wesire*), Freiburg: D. Robischon, 1969).

Ahmed Vâsıf, *Mehâsinü'l-âsâr ve hakâyıkü'l-ahbâr*, Istanbul: Matba'a-ı 'Âmire, 1804.

Akhisarî, Hasan Kâfî, *Usûl ül-hikem fi. nizâm el-'alem.* Istanbul: n.p., 1861. Translations: Garcin de Tassy, "Principes de sagesse touchant l'art de gouverneur par Rizwan-ben-abd-oul-mennan Ac-hissari," *Journal Asiatique* 4 (1824): 213–26; E. J. Karácsony, *Az egri török emlékirat a kornmányzás módjáról – Eger vár elfoglalása alkalmával az 1596 évben irja Molla Haszan Elkjáfi*, Budapest: n.p., 1909; and Karácsony and Lajos Thallóczy, "Eine Denkschrift des bosnischen Mohammedaners Mollah Hassan elkjafi über die Art und Wese des Regierens," *Archiv für slavische Philologie* 32 (1911): 139–58.

Allamî, Abul Fazl, *The Ain i Akbari by Abul Fazl 'Allami*, 3 vols., Calcutta: Asiatic Society of Bengal, 1873, 1891, 1894.

Allom, Thomas, and Robert Walsh, *Constantinople and the Scenery of the Seven Churches of Asia Minor*, 2 vols., London: Fisher, Son and Co., 1838.

Âşık Çelebi, *Meşâ'ir üş-şu'arâ or Tezkere of Âşık Çelebi*, facsimile edn, ed. G. M. Meredith-Owens, London: E. J. W. Gibb Memorial, 1971.

Aşıkpaşazâde, Derviş Ahmed, *Die Altosmanischen anonymen Chroniken: Tevarih-i Al-Osman*, ed. and trans. F. Giese, 2 vols., Breslau: Selbstverlag, 1922.

Atâyî, *Hadâ'iku'l-hakâ'ik fi tekmileti'ş-şakâ'ik*, reprint with indices in *Şakaik-ı Nu'maniye ve Zeyilleri*, ed. Abdülkadir Özcan, 5 vols., Istanbul: Çağrı, 1989, vol. II.

Ayn Ali, *Kavânîn-i Âl-i 'Osmân der hulâsa-ı mezâmin-i defter-i dîvân* in *Kavânîn Risâlesi*, Istanbul: Tasvir-Ekvar, 1863, with Katib Çelebi (below); ed. Tayyib Gökbilgin, republished Istanbul: Enderun Kitabevi, 1979. Editions, some erroneously ascribed to Ali Çavuş, a copyist: Hamid Hadžibegić, "Rasprava Ali Čauša iz Sofije o timarskoj organizaciji u XVII stoljeću," *Glasnik Zemajskog Muzeja u Sarajevo*, n.s. 2 (1947): 139–205; İsmail Hakkı Uzunçarşılı "Kanun-ı Osmanî mefhum-ı defter-i hâkanî," *Belleten* 15 (1951): 371–89; İlhan Şahin "Timar sistemi hakkında bir Risale," *Tarih Dergisi* 32 (1979): 905–35; Midhat Sertoğlu (ed.), *Sofyalı Ali Çavuş Kanunnâmesi*, Istanbul: Marmara University, 1992; Ahmed Akgündüz, *Osmanlı Kanunnâmeleri*, 9 vols., Istanbul, 1992–5, vol. IV, pp. 455–527. Translations: M. Belin, "Du régime des fiefs militaires dans l'islamisme, et principalement en Turquie," *Journal Asiatique* 15 (1870): 187–222; Paul Tischendorf, *Das Lehnswesen in den moslemischen Staaten insbesondere im osmanischen Reich mit dem Gesetzbuche der Lehen unter Sultan Ahmed I*, Leipzig: Giesecke und Devrient, 1872; repr. Berlin: Klaus Schwarz Verlag, 1982.
Risâle-i vazîfe-horân ve merâtib-i bendegân-ı Âl-i 'Osmân, in *Kavânîn Risâlesi*, Istanbul: Tasvir-Ekvar, 1863, with Katib Çelebi (below).

Ayvansarayî, Hüseyin, *Hadikat ül-Cevami*, 2 vols., Istanbul: Matbaa-i Âmire, 1864.
Mecmuâ-i Tevârih, ed. F. Derin and V. Çabuk, Istanbul: İstanbul Üniversitesi Edebiyat Fakültesi, 1985.

Aziz Efendi, *Kanûn-nâme-i Sultânî Li 'Azîz Efendi (Aziz Efendi's Book of Sultanic Laws and Regulations; An Agenda for Reform by a Seventeenth-Century Ottoman Statesman)*, ed. Rhoads Murphey, Cambridge, MA: Harvard University Press, 1985.

Çeşmîzâde, Reşid, *Çeşmî-zâde Tarihi*, ed. B. Kütükoğlu, Istanbul: Edebiyat Fakultesi Basımevi, 1993.

Dallaway, James, *Constantinople Ancient and Modern with Excursions to the Shores and Islands of the Archipelago*. London: T. Cadell and W. Davis, 1797.

Enderunlu Fazıl Bey, *Hûbânnâme ve Zenânnâme*, İstanbul Üniversitesi Kütüphanesi MS TY 5502.

Evliya Çelebi, *Evliya Çelebi in Albania and Adjacent Regions (Kosovo, Montenegro, Ohrid), The Relevant Sections of the Seyahatname*, ed. and trans. Robert Dankoff and Robert Elsie, Leiden: Brill, 2000.

The Seyahatname of Evliya Çelebi. Book One: Istanbul (fascimile of Topkapı Sarayı Bağdad 304), ed. Şinasi Tekin and Gönül Tekin, *Turkish Sources* IX, Cambridge, MA: Harvard University Press, 1993.

Eyyubi Efendi, *Eyyubi Efendi Kanunnamesi*, ed. Abdülkadir Özcan, Istanbul: Eren, 1994.

Ferté-Meun, comtesse de la, *Lettres sur le Bosphore*, Paris: Domère, 1821.

Fındıklılı 'İsmet bin 'Osmân (d. 1904), *Tekmiletü'ş-Şakaik fî Hakk-ı ehli'l-hakaik*, in Abdülkadir Özcan (ed.), *Şakaik-ı Nu'maniye ve Zeyilleri*, 5 vols., Istanbul: Çagri Yayınları, 1989.

Flachat, Jean-Claude, *Observations sur le commerce et sur les arts*, 2 vols., Lyon: Jacquenod Père et Rusand, 1766.

Grelot, Guillaume-Joseph, *Relation nouvelle d'un voyage de Constantinople*, Paris: Chez la veuve de D. Foucault, 1630.

Grenville, Henry, *Observations sur l'état actuel de l'Empire Ottoman*, ed. Andrew Ehrenkreutz, Ann Arbor: University of Michigan Press, 1965.

Hezarfen Hüseyin Efendi, *Telhisü'l-Beyân fî Kavânîn-i Âl-i 'Osmân*, ed. Sevim İlgürel, Ankara: Türk Tarih Kurumu Basımevi, 1998.

Hirschfeld, C. C. L., *Theory of Garden Art*, ed. and trans. Linda Parshall, Philadelphia: University of Pennsylvania Press, 2001.

Husayn al-Basri al-Mimi, "Nazm al-sumut al-zabajadiyya fi silsilat al-sadat al-Naqshbandiyya," Süleymaniye Kütüphanesi, MS Aşir Efendi 176.

Husayn ibn 'Abdallah al-Shirvani, "Ahkam diniyya," Süleymaniye Kütuphanesi, MS Hacı Mahmud 1962.

Ibn Battuta, *The Travels of Ibn Battuta*, ed. and trans. H. A. R. Gibb, 2 vols. Cambridge: Hakluyt Society, 1962.

İnciciyan, P. G., *Boğaziçi Sayfiyeleri*, trans. the priest of the Armenian Church of Kandilli and ed. Orhan Duru, Istanbul: Eren, 2000.

(Luca, Ingigi, P.) *Villeggiature de' Bizantini sul Bosforo Tracio*, trans. P. C. Aznavour, Venice: Lazzaro, 1831.

XVIII. Asırda İstanbul, ed. and trans. Hrand D. Andreasyan, Istanbul: Baha Matbaası, 1976.

İsmail Âsım Efendi, *Tarih-i İsmâil Âsım Efendi*, Istanbul: Matbaa-i Âmire, 1865.

İzzî Efendi, *Tarih*, Istanbul: Daruttibaat ul-Mamûre, 1784.

Kanunnâme-yi Asâkir-i Mansure-yi Muhammadiye, Istanbul: n.p., 1829.

Karaçelebizâde Abdülaziz Efendi, *Ravzatü'l-Ebrâr Zeyli*, ed. Nevzat Kaya, Ankara: Türk Tarih Kurumu, 2003.

Katib Çelebi, *The Balance of Truth*, trans. Geoffrey Lewis, London: Allen and Unwin, 1957.

Düstûru 'l-'amel li ıslâhı 'l-halel, in *Kavânîn Risâlesi*, Istanbul: Tasvir-Efvar, 1863, with 'Ayn 'Ali.

Fezleke, 2 vols., Istanbul: Cerîde-i Havâdis, 1286–7/1869–70. (Studies: Mükrimin Halil Yinanç, "Fezleket Ekvâl El-Ahyâr Hakkında," in *Kâtip Çelebi: Hayatı ve Eserleri Hakkında İncelemeler*, Ankara: Türk Tarih Kurumu, 1957, pp. 93–100; Bekir Kütükoğlu, *Kâtib Çelebi "Fezleke" sinin Kaynakları*, Istanbul: Istanbul Universitesi Edebiyat Fakültesi, 1974.)

Kashf al-Zunûn, 2 vols., Istanbul: n.p., 1942–3.

Kemalpaşazade, *Tevarih-i Al-i Osman, X. Defter*, ed. Şefaettin Severcan, Ankara: T. T. K. Basımevi, 1996.

Kitâb-ı Müstetâb, ed. Yaşar Yücel, Ankara: Ankara Universitesi Dil ve Tarih-Cografya Fakültesi, 1974.

Koçi Beg, *Risale-i Koçi Beg*, ed. Ahmed Vefik, Istanbul: n.p., 1860–1. Editions: Ali Kemali Aksüt, *Koçi Bey Risalesi*, Istanbul: Vakit, 1939; Zuhuri Danışman, *Koçi Bey Risalesi*, Istanbul: Devlet Kitapları 1972, Yılmaz Kurt (ed.), *Koçibey Risalesi*, Ankara: Burak, 1998. Translations: W. F. Behrnauer, "Koğabeg's Abhandlung über den Verfall des osmanischen Staatsgebändes seit Suleiman dem Großen," *Zeitschrift der Deutschen Morgenländischen Gesellschaft* 15 (1860): 272–332; in Hungarian József Thúry in the *Török Történetírók* series, 3 vols., Budapest: Magyar Tudományos Akadémia, 1892–1916, vol. II (1896), and A. Tveritinova, "Vtoroi traktat Kochibeya," *Uchenyie Zapiski Instituta Vostokovedeniia* 6 (1953): 212–88.

Kömürciyan, Eremya Çelebi, *İstanbul Tarihi: XVII. Asırda İstanbul*, trans. Hrand D. Andreasyan, ed. Kevork Pamukciyan, Istanbul: Eren Yayıncilik ve Kitapçilik, 1988.

Kritovoulos, *History of Mehmed the Conqueror*, trans. Charles T. Riggs, Westport, CT: Greenwood Press, 1970 reprint of 1954 edition.

Łaski, Hieronim, *Adparatus ad Historiam Hungariae, sive collectio Miscellanea* trans. by Mátyás Bél – Posonii, 1735; Eudoxiu de Hurmuzaki, *Documente privitóre la Istoria Românilor I/2, 1451–1575*, Bucharest: C. Göbl, 1891; and in Hungarian by Gábor Barta (ed.), *Két tárgyalás Sztambulban*, Budapest: Balassi, 1996.

Lutfi Pasha, *Âsafnâme*, ed. Ali Emiri, Istanbul: Matbaa-ı Amidi, 1908. Translation: Rudolf Tschudi, *Das Asafnâme des Lutfi Pasche*, Leipzig: W. Drugulin, 1910; republished Berlin: Mayer und Müller, 1910.

Matrakçı Nasuh, *Beyān-ı Menāzil-i Sefer-i 'Irākeyn*, ed. H. G. Yurdaydın, Ankara: Türk Tarih Kurumu Basımevi, 1976.

al-Mawardi, 'Ali ibn Muhammad, *al-Ahkam al-Sultaniyya, The Laws of Islamic Governance*, London: Ta-Ha, 1996.

Mehmed Es'ad, *Üss-i Zafer*, Istanbul: Matbaa-i Süleyman Efendi, 1827. Translation: *Précis historique de la destruction du corps des janissaries par le sultan Mahmud, en 1826*, trans. A. P. Caussin de Perceval, Paris: F. Didot, 1833.

Mehmed bin Mehmed, *Ta'rîh*, Süleymaniye Kütüphanesi, MS Lala Ismail 300. Edition: Abdurrahman Sığırlı, "Mehmed b. Mehmed er-Rûmî(Edirneli)'nin Nuhbetü't-Tevârih ve'l-ahbâr'ı ve Târîh-i Âl-i Osman'ı (Metinleri, Tahlilleri)," PhD dissertation, Istanbul University, 2000.

Mehmed Hâkim, *Vekâyi-nâme*, Topkapı Sarayı Müzesi Kütüphanesi MS B 231, B 233.

Mehmed Süreyya, *Sicill-i Osmanî*, ed. Nuri Akbayar, Istanbul: Tarih Vakfı Yurt Yayınları, 1996.

Minadoi, da Rovigo Giovanni Tommasso, *Historia della guerra fra Turchi et Persiani*, Venice: Andrea Muschio and Barezzo Barezzi, 1588.

Mouradgea D'Ohsson, Ignatius, *Tableau général de l'empire othoman*, 4 vols., Paris: Firmin Didot, 1788–1824.

Muhammad As'ad Sahibzadeh al-Uthmani al-Naqshbandi al-Khalidi, *Baghiyat al-wajid fi maktubat hadrat mawlana Khalid*, Damascus: Matb'at al-Tarraqi, 1334 AH.

Mullah Ghanim ibn Muhammad al-Baghdadi, "Hisnu-l Islam," Süleymaniye Kütüphanesi, MS Reşid Pasha, 858/25.

Mustafa Ali, *Gelibolulu Mustafa Âli ve Künhü'l-ahbâr'ında II. Selim, III. Murat ve III. Mehmet Devirleri*, ed. Faris Çerçi, 3 vols., Kayseri: Erciyeş Üniversitesi Yayınları, 2000.

Meva'idü'n-Nefa'is fi Kavâidi'l-Mecalis. Tables of Delicacies Concerning the Rules of Social Gatherings, trans. Douglas S. Brookes, Cambridge, MA: Harvard University Press, 2003.

Mustafa 'Âli's Counsel for Sultans, 1581, 2 vols., ed. Andreas Tietze, Vienna, Österreichische Akademie der Wissenschaften, 1979–82.

Mustafâ 'Âlî's Description of Cairo of 1599, trans. and ed. Andreas Tietze, Vienna: Österreichische Akademie der Wissenschaften, 1975.

Müteferrika, İbrahim, *Usûlü 'l-hikem fi nizâmi 'l-ümem*, Istanbul: İbrahim Müteferrika, 1732.

Na'îmâ, Mustafa, *Tarih*, 6 vols., Istanbul: n.p., 1280/1863–4.

Nedim, Ahmet, *Divan*, ed. Halil Nihat Boztepe, Istanbul, n.p., 1919–21.

Nedim Divanı, ed. Abdülbâki Gölpınarlı, Istanbul: İnkilâp va Aka Kitabevleri, 1972.

Nevres, *Dîvân-i Nevres*, İstanbul Üniversitesi Kütüphanesi MS TY 3414.

Nicolay, Nicholas de, *The Nauigations into Turkie: London 1585*, Amsterdam: Da Capo Press, 1968; reprint of London 1585 edition.

Pardoe, Julia, *The Beauties of the Bosphorus*, London: G. Virtue, 1838.

The City of the Sultan, 4th edn, London: Routledge, 1854.

The City of the Sultan; and Domestic Manners of the Turks, 2 vols., London: Neşriyat Yurdu, 1836–7.

The City of the Sultan and Domestic Manners of the Turks, 2 vols., London: Henry Colburn, 1837.

Peçevi, I., *Peçevi Tarihi*, ed. M. Uraz, 2 vols., Istanbul: Neşriyat Yurdu, 1968–9.

Pertusier, Charles, *Promenades pittoresques dans Constantinople et sur les rives du Bosphore*, 2 vols., Paris: H. Nicolle, 1815.

Râşid Efendi, *Münşeat*, Topkapı Sarayı, MS H. 1037.

Tarih-i Râşid, 5 vols., Istanbul: Matbaa-i Âmire, 1865.

Rycaut, Paul. *The Present State of the Ottoman Empire*, 1668; reprinted Westmead: Gregg International, 1972.

Sarı Mehmed Pasha, *Zübde-i vekayiat Olaylarin özü*, ed. A. Özcan, 3 vols., Istanbul: Tercüman Gazetesi, 1977.

Selâniki Mustafa, *Tarih-i Selâniki*, ed. Mehmed İpşirli, 2 vols., Istanbul: Istanbul Üniversitesi Edebiyat Fakültesi Yayınları, 1989.

Şem'danizade Fındıklılı Süleyman Efendi, *Fındıklılı Süleyman Efendi Tarihi: Mür'i't-Tevârih*, ed. Münir Aktepe, 2 vols. Istanbul: İstanbul Üniversitesi Edebiyat Fakültesi, 1976–81.

Seyyid Lokman, *Zübdetü't-Tevârîh (Quintessence of Histories)* Copies, summaries, variants: *Imperial Scroll*, the *Tomar-ı Hümayun*, Topkapı Palace Library A. 3599; *Mücmelü't-tomar*, or the *Summary of the Scroll*, British Library, Or. 1135; Türk ve İslâm Eserleri Müzesi (no. 1973) Murad III; Topkapı Palace Library (H. 1321) Siyavuş Pasha; Chester Beatty Library Dublin (no. 414) Mehmed Agha.

Seyyid Vehbi, *Dîvân-ı Seyyid Vehbî*, Topkapı Sarayı Müzesi Kütüphanesi, MS E.H. 1640.

Sidi Ali Reis, *Mir'at ül-Memalik*. Istanbul: İkdam Matbaası, 1313/1987.

Silâhdâr Fındıklılı Mehmed Agha, *Nusretnâme*, 2 vols., Istanbul: Milli Eğitim Basımevi, 1962–9.

Süleyman Sa'deddîn Müstakîmzâde, *Devhatü'l-meşâyîh*, and the appendices written for it, twice by the author himself, twice by Mehmed Münib 'Ayntâbî (d. 1238/1822–3), and once by Süleyman Fâ'ik (d. 1253/1837–8). Ahmet Rif'at Efendi (d. 1876) edited and updated the biographies of Müstakîmzâde and the continuations, see *Devhatü'l-meşâyîh ma'a zeyl* (Istanbul [lithograph], no date [reprinted Çağrı, 1978]).

Süruri, *Dîvân-ı Sürûrî*. n.d.

Tadhkirat Al-Muluk: A Manual of Safavid Administration, ed. V. Minorsky, London: E. J. W. Gibb Memorial Trust, 1943; reprint 1980.

Tarih-i Sâmî ve Şâkir ve Subhî, Istanbul, 1783.

Tott, François de, *Mémoires du Baron de Tott sur les turcs et les tartares*, 2 vols., Amsterdam: n.p. 1785.

Tournefort, Joseph P., *Relation d'un voyage du Levant*, 3 vols., Paris: Frères Bruysat, 1727.

Ungnad, David, *Ungnád Dávid konstantinápolyi utazásai*, Budapest: Szèpirodalmi Könyvkiadó, 1986 (partial translation of: *Stephan Gerlachs des aeltern Tage-Buch der von zween glorwürdigsten Römischen Käysern Maximiliano und Rudolpho beyderseits . . . und durch . . . David Ungnad . . . glücklichst-vollbrachter Gesandtschafft*, Frankfurt am Main, 1674).

Withers, Robert, "The Grand Signiors Seraglio" [translation of Ottaviano Bon, *Descrizione del seraglio del Gran Signore*], in S. Purchas, *His Pilgrimes*, 20 vols. Glasgow: J. MacLehose and Sons, 1905.

MAPS

Newberry Library, Chicago, Novacco 4F 374, Gastaldi, "Prima Parte dell'Asia," and Novacco 4F 377, Gastald, "Natolia," 1566, Novacco 4F 406 and 4F 385: Second Part of Asia, 1560.
Newberry Library, Novacco 2F 22. The Gulf of Artha or Ambracian Gulf, n.d.
Newberry Library, Novacco 2F 48. Antonio Lafreri, [Szigetvar], Rome, 1566.
Newberry Library, Novacco 4F 105. Paolo Forlani, "The Marvelous Order of the Grand Turkish Army," *c.* 1570.
Walker Collection, University of Melbourne Library Map Collection, Maps MX 410a 1511–1774, no. 130; Giacomo Cantelli (1643–95).
Walker Collection, Maps MX 410a 1511–1774, no. 54, Allain Manesson-Mallet (1630–?).
Walker Collection, Maps MX 410a 1511–1774, no. 104, Jacob Sandrart (1630–1708).
Walker Collection, Maps MX 410a 1511–1774, no. 12, Richard Blome (d. 1705).
Walker Collection, Maps MX 410a 1511–1774, no. 33, Pierre Duval (1619–82).
Walker Collection, Maps MX 410a 1511–1774, no. 4, Pieter van der Aa (1659–1733), *c.* 1729.

SECONDARY SOURCES

Abou-El-Haj, Rifa'at, "Aspects of the Legitimation of Ottoman Rule as Reflected in the Preambles to Two Early Liva Kanunnameler (sic)," *Turcica* 21–3 (1991): 371–83.
"The Expression of Ottoman Political Culture in the Literature of Advice to Princes (Nasihatnameler), Sixteenth to Twentieth Centuries," in R. K. Bhattacharya and Asok K. Ghosh (eds.), *Sociology in the Rubric of Social Science: Professor Ramkrishna Mukherjee Felicitation Volume*, New Delhi: Anthropological Survey of India, 1995, pp. 282–92.
Formation of the Modern State: The Ottoman Empire Sixteenth to Eighteenth Centuries, Albany, NY: SUNY Press, 1991; 2nd edn, Syracuse, NY: Syracuse University Press, 2005.
"The Ottoman Vizier and Paşa Households 1683–1703: A Preliminary Report," *Journal of the American Oriental Society* 94 (1974): 438–47.
"Power and Social Order: The Uses of the Kanun," in Irene A. Bierman, Rifa'at A. Abou-El-Haj, and Donald Preziosi (eds.), *Urban Structure and Social Order: The Ottoman City and its Parts*, New Rochelle, NY: Aristide D. Caratzas, 1991, pp. 77–91.
The 1703 Rebellion and the Structure of Ottoman Politics. Leiden: Nederlands Instituut voor het Nabije Oosten, 1984.

"The Social Uses of the Past: Recent Arab Historiography of Ottoman Rule," *International Journal of Middle East Studies* 14 (1982): 185–201.

Abu-Lughod, Janet, *Before European Hegemony: The World System A.D. 1250–1350*, Oxford: Oxford University Press, 1989.

Abu-Manneh, Butrus, "The Islamic Roots of the Gülhane Rescript," in B. Abu-Manneh, *Studies on Islam and the Ottoman Empire in the 19th Century*, Istanbul, Isis, 2001, pp. 73–97 (reprint of "The Islamic Roots of the Gülhane Rescript," *Die Welt des Islams* 34 (1994): 173–204).

"The Naqshbandiyya-Mujaddidiyya in the Ottoman Lands in the Early 19th Century," *Die Welt des Islams* 22 (1982): 1–36.

Studies on Islam and the Ottoman Empire in the 19th Century (1826–1876), Istanbul: Isis Press, 2001.

Abulafia, David, *The French Descent into Renaissance Italy, 1494–95: Antecedents and Effects*. Aldershot: Variorum, 1995.

Ács, Pál, "Tarjumans Mahmud and Murad: Austrian and Hungarian Renegades as Sultan's Interpreters," in Bodo Guthmüller and Wilhelm Kühlmann (eds.), *Europa und die Türken in der Renaissance*, Tübingen: Niemeyer, 2000, pp. 307–16.

Adanır, Fikret, and Suraiya Faroqhi (eds.), *Ottomans and the Balkans: A Discussion of Historiography*, Leiden: Brill, 2002.

Afyoncu, Erhan, "Osmanlı Müverrihlerine Dair Tevcihat Kayıtları – II," *Belgeler* 26/30 (2005): 85–193.

Ágoston, Gábor, "Birodalom és információ: Konstantinápoly, mint a koraújkori Európa információs központja," [Empire and Information: Constantinople as Center of Information Gathering in Early Modern Europe] in Gábor Hausner and László Veszprémi (eds.), *Perjés Géza Emlékkönyv*, Budapest: Argumentum, 2005, pp. 31–60.

"A Flexible Empire: Authority and its Limits on the Ottoman Frontiers," *International Journal of Turkish Studies* 9 (2003): 15–31.

Guns for the Sultan: Military Power and the Weapons Industry in the Ottoman Empire, Cambridge: Cambridge University Press, 2005.

"Ideologie, Propaganda und politischer Pragmatismus: Die Auseinandersetzung der osmanischen und habsburgischen Grossmächte und die mitteleuropäische Konfrontation," in Martina Fuchs, Teréz Oborni and Gábor Újvári (eds.), *Kaiser Ferdinand I. – Ein mitteleuropäischer Herrscher*, Münster: Aschendorff, 2005, pp. 207–33.

"Információszerzés és kémkedés az Oszmán Birodalomban a 15–17. században," [Information Gathering and Spying in the Ottoman Empire in the Fifteenth to Seventeenth Centuries] in Tivadar Petercsák and Mátyás Berecz (eds.), *Információáramlás a magyar és török végvári rendszerben*, Eger: Heves Megyei Múzeum, 1999, pp. 129–154.

"Ottoman Warfare, 1453–1826," in Jeremy Black (ed.), *European Warfare 1453–1815*, London: St. Martin's Press, 1999, pp. 118–44.

Akgündüz, Ahmed, *Osmanlı Kanunnameleri ve Hukuki Tahlilleri*, 9 vols., Istanbul: FEY Vakfı, 1990–6.

Aksan, Virginia, "Locating the Ottomans Among Early Modern Empires," *Journal of Early Modern History* 3 (1999): 103–34.

"Mutiny and the Eighteenth Century Ottoman Army," *Turkish Studies Association Bulletin* 22 (1998): 116–25.

"Ottoman Political Writing, 1768–1808," *International Journal of Middle East Studies* 25 (1993): 53–69.

An Ottoman Statesman in War and Peace: Ahmed Resmi Efendi 1700–1783, Leiden: Brill, 1995.

"Ottoman War and Warfare, 1453–1812," in Jeremy Black (ed.), *War in the Early Modern World*, London: UCL Press, 1999, pp. 147–75.

Aktepe, M. Münir, "İstanbul Fenerbahçesi Hakkında Bâzı Bilgiler," *İstanbul Üniversitesi Edebiyat Fakültesi Tarih Dergisi* 32 (1979): 361–8.

"Naîmâ Tarihi'nin Yazma Nüshaları Hakkında," *Tarih Dergisi* 1/1 (1949): 35–52.

Alberi, Eugenio (ed.), *Relazioni degli ambasciatori veneti al Senato*, series 3, vols. I–II, Florence: Tipografia all'Insegna di Clio, 1844.

Algar, Hamid, "A Brief History of the Naqshbandi Order," in Marc Gaborieau, Alexandre Popovic, and Thiery Zarcone (eds.), *Naqshbandis, Historical Developments and Present Situation of a Muslim Mystical Order*, Istanbul: Isis, 1990, pp. 3–44.

"The Naqshbandiyya Order: A Preliminary Survey of its History and Significance," *Studia Islamica* 44 (1976): 123–52.

Allardyce, Gilbert, "The Rise and Fall of the Western Civilization Course," *American Historical Review* 87 (1982): 695–725.

Alvi, Sajida Sultana, *Advice on the Art of Governance: Mau'izah-i Jahangiri of Muhammad Baqir Najm-i Sani, An Indo-Islamic Mirror for Princes*, Albany, NY: SUNY Press, 1989.

Amar, Laure, *L'espace public en herbe*, Paris, n.p., 1986.

Ambros, Edith Gülçin, "'O Asinine, Vile Cur of a Fool Called Zātī!': An Attempt to Show that Unabashed Language is Part and Parcel of an Ottoman 'Idiom of Satire,'" *Journal of Turkish Studies* 27/1 (2003): 109–17.

Anderson, M. S. (ed.), *The Great Powers and the Near East, 1774–1923*, London: Arnold, 1970.

The Rise of Modern Diplomacy, 1450–1919 (London: Longman, 1993).

Anderson, Sonya P., *An English Consul in Turkey: Paul Rycaut at Smyrna, 1667–1678*, Oxford: Clarendon Press, 1989.

Andrews, Walter, *Poetry's Voice, Society's Song: Ottoman Lyric Poetry*, Seattle: University of Washington Press, 1985.

Anhegger, Robert, "Ein angeblicher schweizerischer Agent an der Hohen Pforte im Jahre 1581," *Istanbuller Schriften* 11 (1943): 3–13.

"Hezarfenn Hüseyin Efendi'nin Osmanlı Devlet Teşkilâtına Dair Mülâhazaları," *Türkiyat Mecmuası* 10 (1953): 365–93.

Anscombe, Fred. *The Ottoman Gulf and the Creation of Kuwayt, Saudi Arabia and Qatar 1871–1914*, New York: Columbia University Press, 1997.

Appadurai, Arjun, "Introduction: Commodities and the Politics of Value," in A. Appadurai (ed.), *The Social Life of Things: Commodities in Cultural Perspective*, Cambridge: Cambridge University Press, 1986.

Arabian Nights Entertainments, ed. Robert Mack, Oxford: Oxford University Press, 1995.

Arbel, Benjamin, *Trading Nations: Jews and Venetians in the Early Modern Eastern Mediterranean*, Leiden: Brill, 1995.

"Venezia, gli ebrei e l'attività di Salomone Ashkenasi nella Guerra di Cipro," in Gaetano Cozzi (ed.), *Gli ebrei e Venezia secoli XIV–XVIII*, Milan: Edizione Comunità, 1987.

Archer, John Michael, *Old Worlds: Egypt, Southwest Asia, India, and Russia in Early Modern English Writing*, Stanford, CA: Stanford University Press, 2001.

Ariès, Philippe, *Western Attitudes Toward Death: From the Middle Ages to the Present*, trans. Patricia M. Ranum, Baltimore, MD: Johns Hopkins University Press, 1975.

Arıkan, Zeki, "Sir Paul Rycault [sic] Osmanlı İmparatorluğu ve İzmir," *Osmanlı Araştırmaları* 22 (2003): 219–55.

Aristotle, *The Politics. The Basic Works of Aristotle*, ed. and intro. Richard McKeon, New York: Random House, 1970.

Artan, Tülay, "Architecture as a Theatre of Life: Profile of the Eighteenth-Century Bosphorus," PhD dissertation, MIT, 1988.

Atsız, Buğra, *Das osmanische Reich um die Mitte des 17. Jahrhunderts nach den Chroniken des Vecihi (1637–1660) und des Mehmed Halifa (1663–1660)*, Munich: R. Trofenik, 1977.

Austro-Turcica 1541–1552: Diplomatische Akten des habsburgischen Gesandtschaftsverkehrs mit der Hohen Pforte im Zeitalter Süleymans des Prächtigen, ed. Srećko M. Džaja and Günter Weis, Munich: R. Oldenbourg, 1995.

al-Azmeh, Aziz, *Islams and Modernities*, New York: Verso, 1993.

Muslim Kingship: Power and the Sacred in Muslim, Christian, and Pagan Polities, London: I. B. Tauris, 1997.

Babinger, Franz, *Die Geschichtsschreiber der Osmanen und Ihre Werke*, Leipzig: Otto Harrassowitz, 1927.

Bacqué-Grammont, Jean-Louis, "Études turco-safavides, XV. Cinq lettres de Hüsrev Paşa, beylerbeyi du Diyar Bekir (1552–1532)," *Journal Asiatique* 279 (1991): 239–64.

Bacqué-Grammont, J.-L., and N. Vatin, "Stelae Turcicae VI. Stèles funéraires de Sinop," *Anatolia Moderna / Yeni Anadolu* 3 (1992): 105–207.

Bacqué-Grammont, Jean-Louis, Hans-Peter Laqueur and Nicolas Vatin, "Stelae Turcicae I. Küçük Aya Sofya," *Istanbuler Mitteilungen* 34 (1984): 441–540.

Stelae Turcicae II. Cimetières de la mosquée de Sokollu Mehmed Paşa à Kadırga Limanı, de Bostancı Ali et du türbe de Sokollu Mehmed Paşa à Eyüb, Istanbuler Mitteilungen, Beiheft 36, Tübingen: E. Wasmuth, 1990.

"Stelae Turcicae IV. Le cimetière de la bourgade thrace de Karacaköy," *Anatolia Moderna / Yeni Anadolu* 2 (1991): 7–27.

"Le *tekke* bektachi de Merdivenköy," *Anatolia Moderna / Yeni Anadolu* 2 (1991): 29–135.

Bağcı, Serpil, "From Adam to Mehmed III: Silsilenâme," in *The Sultan's Portrait: Picturing the House of Osman*, Istanbul: İşbank, 2000, pp. 188–201.

Bakhit, Muhammad Adnan, *The Ottoman Province of Damascus in the Sixteenth Century*, Beirut: Librairie du Liban, 1982.

Balakrishnan, Gopal (ed.), *Mapping the Nation*, London: Verso, 1996.

Balta, Evangelia, "Ottoman Studies in Modern Greek Historiography," *Journal of Turkish Studies* 28/1 (2004): 9–16.

Bárdossy, László, *Magyar politika Mohácsi vész után*, Budapest: Egyetemi Nyomda, 1943.

Barfield, Thomas, *The Perilous Frontier: Nomadic Empires and China*, Oxford: Blackwell, 1989.

Bariska, István (ed.), *Kőszeg ostromának emlékezete* [Remembering the Siege of Kőszeg Güns], Budapest: Európa Könyvkiadó, 1982.

Barker-Benfield, Graham John, *The Culture of Sensibility: Sex and Society in Eighteenth-Century Britain*, Chicago: University of Chicago Press, 1992.

Baron, Salo Wittmayer, *A Social and Religious History of the Jews. Late Middle Ages and Era of European Expansion 1200–1650*, vol. XVIII: *The Ottoman Empire, Persia, Ethiopia, India, and China*, 2nd edn, New York: Columbia University Press, 1983.

Barta, Gábor (ed.), *Két tárgyalás Sztambulban* [Two Audiences in Istanbul], Budapest: Európa Könyvkiadó 1996.

Başkan, Şerif, *Karamanoğulları Dönemi Konya Mezar Taşları*, Ankara: Kültür Bakanlığı, 1996.

Bayly, C. A., *Empire and Information, Intelligence Gathering and Social Communication in India, 1780–1870*, Cambridge: Cambridge University Press, 1999.

Imperial Meridian: The British Empire and the World 1780–1830, London: Longman, 1989.

Beldiceanu, Nicoară, *Le timar dans l'État ottoman (début XIV –début XVI siècle*, Wiesbaden: Otto Harrassowitz, 1980.

Benton, L., "Legal Spaces of Empire: Piracy and the Origins of Ocean Regionalism," *Comparative Studies of Society and History* 47 (2005): 700–24.

Berkes, Niyazi, *The Development of Secularism in Turkey*, Montreal: McGill University Press, 1964.

Berktay, Halil, "The Search for the Peasant in Western and Turkish History/ Historiography," in Halil Berktay and Suraiya Faroqhi (eds.), *New Approaches to State and Peasant in Ottoman History*, London: Frank Cass, 1992; reprinted from *Journal of Peasant Studies* 18 (1991): 109–84.

Beydilli, Kemal, "Mehmed Emin Paşa, Yağlıkçızâde," in *Türkiye Diyanet Vakfı İslâm Ansiklopedisi*, vol. XXVIII, pp. 464–5.

Biegman, Nicolas H., "Ragusan Spying for the Ottoman Empire. Some 16th-Century Documents from the State Archive at Dubrovnik," *Belleten* 27 (1963): 237–55.

The Turco-Ragusan Relationship. According to the Firmans of Murad III (1575–1595) Extant in the State Archives of Dubrovnik, The Hague: Mouton, 1968.

Binswänger, Karl, *Untersuchungen zum Status der Nichtmuslime im Osmanischen Reich des 16. Jahrhunderts: mit einer Neudefinition des Begriffes "Dimma,"* Munich: R. Trofenik, 1977.

Birchwood, Matthew and Matthew Dimmock (eds.), *Cultural Encounters Between East and West: 1453–1699,* Newcastle upon Tyne: Cambridge Scholars Press, 2005.

Birnbaum, Eleazar, *The Book of Advice by King Kay Ka'us ibn Iskander; The Earliest Old Ottoman Turkish Version of his Kabusname,* Cambridge, MA: Harvard University Press, 1981.

"A Lifemanship Manual, the Earliest Turkish Version of the Kabusname?" *Journal of Turkish Studies* 1 (1977): 3–64.

Birnbaum, Marianna D., *The Long Journey of Gracia Mendes,* Budapest and New York: Central European University Press, 2003.

Bisaha, Nancy, *Creating East and West: Renaissance Humanists and the Ottoman Turks,* Philadelphia: University of Pennsylvania Press, 2004.

Black, Jeremy, *Maps and Politics,* Chicago: University of Chicago Press, 1997.

Blochet, E., *Catalogue des manuscrits turcs,* 2 vols., Paris: Bibliothēque nationale, 1932–3.

Blockmans, Willm Pieter. *Emperor Charles V, 1500–1558,* London: Arnold, 2002.

Bodur, Hüsnü, "Seyyid Lokman," senior thesis, Istanbul University, 1966.

Bottéro, Jean, *Mesopotamia: Writing, Reasoning and the Gods,* trans. Zainab Bahrani and Marc Van de Mieroop, Chicago: University of Chicago Press, 1992.

Bourdieu, Pierre, *Outline of a Theory of Practice,* Cambridge: Cambridge University Press, 1977.

Braudel, Fernand, *The Mediterranean and the Mediterranean World in the Age of Philip,* 2 vols., New York: Harper and Row, 1972.

Brewer, John, *The Pleasures of the Imagination: English Culture in the Eighteenth Century,* New York: Farrar, Straus, Giroux, 1997.

Brotton, Jerry. *The Renaissance Bazaar: From the Silk Road to Michelangelo,* New York: Oxford University Press, 2002.

Trading Territories: Mapping the Early Modern World, London: Reaktion Books, 1997.

Brummett, Palmira, *Ottoman Seapower and Levantine Diplomacy in the Age of Discovery.* Albany, NY: SUNY Press, 1994.

Bucholtz, Franz Bernhard von, *Geschichte der Regierung Ferdinand des Ersten,* 9 vols., Vienna: Schaumburg und Compagnie, 1831–8.

Burke, Peter, "Conspicuous Consumption in Seventeenth-Century Italy," *Kwartalnik Historii Kultury Materialnej* (1982): 43–56.

"Presenting and Re-presenting Charles V," in Hugo Soly (ed.), *Charles V 1500–1558 and his Time,* Antwerp: Mercator Fonds, 1999, pp. 411–33.

Busbecq, Ogier Ghiselin de, *The Turkish Letters of Ogier Ghiselin de Busbecq: Imperial Ambassador at Constantinople 1554–1562,* trans. Edward Forster, Oxford: Clarendon Press, 1968.

Byrnes, R. F. (ed.), *Communal Families in the Balkans: The Zadruga*, Notre Dame: University of Notre Dame Press, 1976.

Çağman, Filiz, "Family Life," in Günsel Renda (ed.), *Woman in Anatolia: 9000 Years of the Anatolian Woman*, exhibition catalogue, Topkapı Palace, 29 November 1993 – 28 February 1994, Istanbul: Ministry of Culture, 1993.

Canatar, Mehmet, "Cenâbî Mustafa Efendi: Hayatı, Eseri ve Tarih Görüşü," *Akademik Araştırmalar Dergisi* 4–5 (2000): 259–89.

Çelik, Zeynep, *Displaying the Orient: The Architecture of Islam at Nineteenth-Century World Fairs*, Berkeley: University of California Press, 1992.

The Remaking of Istanbul: Portrait of an Ottoman City in the Nineteenth Century, Seattle: University of Washington Press, 1987.

Cerasi, Maurizio, *La città del Levante: civiltà urbana e architettura sotto gli Ottomani nei secoli XVIII–XIX*, Milan: Jaca Book, 1986.

"Il giardino ottomano attraverso l'immagine del Bosforo," in Attilio Petruccioli (ed.), *Il giardino islamico: Architettura, natura, paesaggio*, Milan: Electa, 1994, pp. 217–36.

"Open Space, Water and Trees in Ottoman Urban Culture in the XVIII–XIXth Centuries," *Environmental Design* 2 (1985): 36–49.

Cezar, Yavuz, *Osmanlı Maliyesinde Bunalım ve Değişim Dönemi*, Istanbul: Alan Yayıncılık, 1986.

Chartier, Roger, "Culture as Appropriation: Popular Cultural Uses in Early Modern France," in Steven Kaplan (ed.), *Understanding Popular Culture: Europe from the Middle Ages to the Nineteenth Century*, New York: Mouton, 1984, pp. 229–53.

Christensen, Stephen Turk, "'The Heathen Order of Battle,'" in S. T. Christensen (ed.), *Violence and the Absolutist State: Studies in European and Ottoman History*, Copenhagen: Copenhagen University, Humanistiske Forskningcenter, 1990, pp. 75–198.

Clanchy, T., *From Memory to Written Record: England 1066–1307*, Cambridge, MA: Harvard University Press, 1979.

Clunas, Craig, *Fruitful Sites: Garden Culture in Ming Dynasty China*, London: Reaktion Books, 1996.

Superfluous Things: Material Culture and Social Status in Early Modern China, Urbana, IL: University of Illinois Press, 1991.

Coffin, David, "The 'Lex Hortorum' and Access to Gardens of Latium during the Renaissance," *Journal of Garden History* 23 (1982): 209–10.

Cohn, Bernard, and William Sherman, "Stirrings and Searchings (1500–1720)," in Peter Hulme and Tim Youngs (eds.), *The Cambridge Companion to Travel Writing*, Cambridge: Cambridge University Press, 2002, pp. 17–36.

Crane, Howard, *The Garden of the Mosques, Hafiz Hüseyin al-Ayvansarayî's Guide to the Muslim Monuments of Ottoman Istanbul* (Supplement to *Muqarnas*) Leiden: Brill, 2000.

Cunningham, Allan, "Stratford Canning and the Treaty of Bucharest," in Edward Ingram (ed.), *Anglo-Ottoman Encounters in the Age of Revolution: Collected Essays*, vol. I, London: Frank Cass, 1993, pp. 144–87.

Cuno, Kenneth M., *The Pasha's Peasants: Land, Society, and Economy in Lower Egypt, 1740–1858*, Cambridge: Cambridge University Press, 1992.

Dalley, Stephanie (trans.), *Myths from Mesopotamia: Creation, the Flood, Gilgamesh, and Others*, Oxford: Oxford University Press, 1989.

Danişmend, İsmail Hami, *İzahlı Osmanlı Tarihi Kronolojisi*, 4 vols., Istanbul: Türkiye Yayınevi, 1947–55.

Darke, Hubert, *The Book of Government, or Rules for Kings; the 'Siyasat-nama' or 'Siyar al-muluk.'of Nizam ul-Mulk*, London: Routledge and Kegan Paul, 1960.

Darling, Linda, "Ottoman Politics through British Eyes: Paul Rycaut's *The Present State of the Ottoman Empire*," *Journal of World History* 5 (1994): 71–97.
 Revenue-Raising and Legitimacy: Tax Collection and Finance Administration in the Ottoman Empire 1560–1660, Leiden: Brill, 1996.

Dávid, Géza, "The Mühimme Defteri as a Source for Ottoman–Habsburg Rivalry in the Sixteenth Century," *Archivum Ottomanicum* 20 (2002): 167–209.

Dávid, Géza and Pál Fodor, "Ottoman Spy Reports from Hungary," in Ugo Marazzi (ed.), *Turcica et Islamica: Studi in memoria di Aldo Gallotta*, Naples: Università degli studi di Napoli L'Oriente, 2003, pp. 121–31.

Davies, Norman, *Europe: A History*, New York: Harper Collins, 1996.

Davies, Stephen. *Empiricism and History*, Houndmills: Palgrave, 2003.

Davis, Fanny, *The Ottoman Lady: A Social History from 1718 to 1918*, Westport, CT: Greenwood Press, 1986.

Debié, Franck, *Jardins des capitales: Une géographie des parcs et jardins publics de Paris, Londres, Vienne et Berlin*, Paris: CNRS, 1992.

De Jong, Erik, "Zijdebalen: A Late Seventeenth/Early Eighteenth-Century Dutch Estate and its Garden Poem," *Journal of Garden History* 5 (1985): 32–71.

Delong-Bas, Natana, *Wahhabi Islam, From Revival and Reform to Global Jihad*, New York: Oxford University Press, 2004.

Demirsar, Belgin, "Emirgân Camii," in *Dünden Bugüne İstanbul Ansiklopedisi*, vol. III, pp. 169–70.

Deringil, Selim, *The Well-Protected Domains: Ideology and the Legitimation of Power in the Ottoman Empire, 1876–1909*, London: I. B. Tauris, 1998.

Derrida, Jacques, *Archive Fever: A Freudian Impression*, trans. Eric Prenowitz, Chicago: University of Chicago Press, 1995.

Desmet-Grégoire, Hélène and François Georgeon (eds.), *Cafés d'Orient revisités*, Paris: CNRS, 1997.

Diem, Werner and Marco Schöller, *The Living and the Dead in Islam. Studies in Arabic Epitaphs*, Wiesbaden: Harrassowitz, 2004.

Dimmock, Matthew, *New Turkes: Dramatizing Islam and the Ottomans in Early Modern England*, Aldershot: Ashgate, 2005.

Donner, Fred M., "Review of *Slaves on Horses: The Evolution of the Islamic Polity* by Patricia Crone," *Journal of the American Oriental Society*, 102 (1982): 367–71.

Dressler, Markus, "Inventing Orthodoxy: Competing Claims for Authority and Legitimacy in the Ottoman-Safavid Conflict," in Hakan T. Karateke and

Maurus Reinkowski (eds.), *Legitimizing the Order: The Ottoman Rhetoric of State Power*, Leiden: Brill, 2005, pp. 151–73.

Duben, Alan, "Turkish Families and Households in Historical Perspective," *Journal of Family History* 10 (1985): 75–95.

Düzdağ, M. E., *Şeyhülislam Ebussuûd Efendi Fetvaları Işığında 16. Asır Türk Hayatı*, Istanbul: Enderun Kitabevi, 1983.

Eagleton, Terry, *Literary Theory: An Introduction*, 2nd edn, Minneapolis: University of Minnesota Press, 1996.

Eaton, Richard, *The Rise of Islam and the Bengal Frontier, 1204–1760*. Berkeley, CA: University of California Press, 1993.

Ebel, Kathryn, "City Views, Imperial Visions: Cartography and the Visual Culture of Urban Space in the Ottoman Empire, 1453–1603," PhD dissertation, University of Texas, 2002.

Eberhard, Elke, *Osmanische Polemik gegen die Safawiden im 16. Jahrhundert*, Freiburg: Schwarz, 1970.

Eisenstadt, Shmuel N. and Wolfgang Schluchter, "Introduction: Paths to Early Modernities – a Comparative View," *Daedalus* 127 (1998): 1–18.

Eldem, Edhem, *Death in Istanbul. Death and its Rituals in Ottoman-Islamic Culture*, Istanbul: Ottoman Bank Archives and Research Centre, 2005.

"L'écrit funéraire ottoman: création, reproduction, transmission," *Oral et écrit dans le monde turco-ottoman. Revue du Monde Musulman et de la Méditerranée*, 75/76 (1996): 65–78.

Eldem, Edhem, Daniel Goffman, and Bruce Masters, *The Ottoman City Between East and West: Aleppo, Izmir, and Istanbul*, Cambridge: Cambridge University Press, 1999.

Eldem, Sedad Hakkı, *Türk Bahçeleri*, Istanbul: Devlet Kitapları Müdürlüğü, 1976.

Eliade, Mircea, *Images and Symbols: Studies in Religious Symbolism*, trans. Philip Mairet, Mission, KS: Sheed Andrews and McMeel, 1961.

The Myth of the Eternal Return or, Cosmos and History, trans. Willard R. Trask, Princeton, NJ: Princeton University Press, 1954.

Myth and Reality, trans. Willard R. Trask, New York: Harper and Row, 1963.

Myths, Dreams and Mysteries; The Encounter Between Contemporary Faiths and Archaic Realities, trans. Philip Mairet, New York: Harvill, 1960; reprint Harper and Row, 1975.

Emecen, Feridun, "'Ali'nin 'Ayn'ı: XVII. Yüzyıl Başlarında Osmanlı Bürokrasisinde Kâtib Rumuzları," *Tarih Dergisi* 35 (1984–94): 131–49.

"Osmanlı Hanedanı'na Alternatif Arayışlar: İbrahimhanzâdeler Örneği," in *XIII. Türk Tarih Kongresi, Ankara: 4–8 Ekim 1999: Kongreye Sunulan Bildiriler*, 5 vols., Ankara: Türk Tarih Kurumu, 2002, vol. III, pt. 3, p. 187.

"Sefere Götürülen Defterlerin Defteri," in *Prof. Dr. Bekir Kütükoğlu'na Armağan*, Istanbul: Edebiyat Fakültesi Basımevi, 1991, pp. 241–68.

Erdem, Hakan, "Recruitment of 'Victorious Soldiers of Muhammad' in the Arab Provinces, 1826–1828," in Israel Gershoni, Hakan Erdem, and Ursula

Woköck (eds.), *Histories of the Modern Middle East: New Directions*, Boulder, CO: Lynne Rienner, 2002, pp. 189–204.

Erdoğan, Muzaffer, "Osmanlı Devrinde İstanbul Bahçeleri," *Vakıflar Dergisi* 4 (1958): 149–82.

Eroğlu, Zekeriya, "Şehnāmeci Lokmān'ın Hüner-nāme'si (2. cilt – 1-154. varak): İnceleme – metin – sözlük," MA thesis, Istanbul University, 1998.

Erünsal, I., "Bir Osmanlı Efendisi'nin Günlüğü: Sadreddinzâde Telhisî Mustafa Efendi ve Cerîdesi," *Kaynaklar* 2 (1984): 77–81.

Evyapan, Gönül A., *Eski Türk Bahçeleri ve Özellikle Eski İstanbul Bahçeleri*, Ankara: Orta Doğu Teknik Üniversitesi, 1972.

Evin, Ahmet, "The Tulip Age and Definitions of 'Westernization,'" in H. İnalcık and O. Okyar (eds.), *Social and Economic History of Turkey (1071–1920) / Türkiye'nin Sosyal ve Ekonomik Tarihi*, Ankara: Meteksan, 1980, pp. 131–45.

Eyice, Semavi, "Bâbıâli – Mimari," in *Türkiye Diyanet Vakfı İslâm Ansiklopedisi*, vol. IV, pp. 386–9.

al-Fahad, Abdulaziz, "From Exclusivism to Accommodation: Doctrinal and Legal Evolution of Wahhabism," *New York University Law Review*, 79 (2004): 485–519.

Faroqhi, Suraiya, *Approaching Ottoman History: An Introduction to the Sources*, Cambridge: Cambridge University Press, 1999.

"Crisis and Change, 1590–1699," in H. İnalcık and D. Quataert (eds.), *An Economic and Social History of the Ottoman Empire, 1300–1914*, 2 vols., Cambridge, Cambridge University Press, 1994, vol. II, pp. 413–636.

"Das Großwesir-telhîs: eine aktenkundliche Studie," *Der Islam* 45 (1969): 96–116.

Men of Modest Substance: House Owners and House Property in Seventeeth-Century Ankara and Kayseri. Cambridge: Cambridge University Press, 1987.

The Ottoman Empire and the World around it, London: I. B. Tauris, 2004.

Pilgrims and Sultans: The Hajj under the Ottomans, 1517–1683, London: I. B. Tauris, 1994.

Fattah, Hala, *The Politics of Regional Trade in Iraq, Arabia, and the Gulf, 1745–1900*, Albany, NY: SUNY Press, 1997.

"Wahhabi Influences, Salafi Responses: Shaikh Mahmud Shukri and the Iraqi Salafi Movement, 1745–1930," *Journal of Islamic Studies*, 14 (2003): 127–48.

Fattal, Antoine, *Le status légal des non-musulmans en pays d'Islam*, Beirut: Imprimerie Catholique, 1958.

Feldman, Walter, "Imitatio in Ottoman Poetry: Three Ghazals of the Mid-Seventeenth Century," *Turkish Studies Association Bulletin* 21/2 (Fall 1997): 31–48.

Fetvacı, Emine Fatma, "Viziers to Eunuchs: Transitions in Ottoman Manuscript Patronage, 1566–1617," PhD dissertation, Harvard University, 2005.

Findley, Carter, *Ottoman Civil Officialdom: A Social History*, Princeton, NJ: Princeton University Press, 1988.

"An Ottoman Occidentalist in Europe: Ahmed Midhat Meets Madame Gülnar," *American Historical Review* 103 (1998): 15–50.

Finkel, Caroline, *The Administration of Warfare: The Ottoman Military Campaigns in Hungary, 1593–1606*, Vienna: VWGÖ, 1988.

Osman's Dream: The History of the Ottoman Empire, New York: Basic Books, 2006.

Finlay, Robert, "Prophecy and Politics in Istanbul: Charles V, Sultan Süleyman, and the Habsburg Embassy of 1533–1534," *Journal of Early Modern History* 2 (1998): 1–31.

Fleet, Kate, "Turks, Italians and Intelligence in the Fourteenth and Fifteenth Centuries," in Çiğdem Balım-Harding and Colin Imber (eds.), *The Balance of Truth. Essays in Honour of Professor Geoffrey Lewis*, Istanbul: Isis, 2000, pp. 99–112.

Fleischer, Cornell, *Bureaucrat and Intellectual in the Ottoman Empire: The Historian Mustafa Ali (1541–1600)*, Princeton, NJ: Princeton University Press, 1986.

"From Şehzade Korkud to Mustafa Âli: Cultural Origins of the Ottoman *Nasihatname*," in Heath W. Lowry and Ralph S. Hattox (eds.), *IIIrd Congress on the Social and Economic History of Turkey*, Istanbul: Isis, 1990, pp. 67–77.

"The Lawgiver as Messiah: The Making of the Imperial Image in the Reign of Süleyman," in Gilles Veinstein (ed.), *Soliman le Magnifique et son temps*, Paris: Documentation Française, 1992, pp. 159–77.

"Royal Authority, Dynastic Cyclism, and 'Ibn Khaldunism' in Seventeenth-Century Ottoman Letters," *Journal of Asian and African Studies* 18 (1983): 198–220.

Flemming, Barbara, "Public Opinion under Sultan Süleyman," in Halil İnalcık and Cemal Kafadar (eds.), *Süleyman the Second and his Time*, Istanbul: Isis, 1993, pp. 49–56.

"Sahib-kıran und Mahdi: Türkische Endzeiterwartungen im ersten Jahrzehnt der Regierung Süleymans," in György Kara (ed.), *Between the Danube and the Caucasus*, Budapest: Akadémiai Kiadó, 1987, pp. 43–62.

Fodor, Pál, "A Bécsbe vezető út. Az oszmán nagyhatalom az 1520-as években" [The Road to Vienna: The Ottoman Empire in the 1520s] in P. Fodor, *A szultán és az aranyalma* [The Sultan and the Golden Apple], Budapest: Balassi, 2001, pp. 363–91.

"Bir Nasihat-Name olarak Kavānīn-i Yeniçeriyan," in *Beşinci Milletler Arası Türkoloji Kongresi, Tebliğler*, Istanbul: Edebiyat Fakültesi Basımevi, 1986, vol. I, pp. 217–24.

"Ottoman Policy towards Hungary, 1520–1541," *Acta Orientalia Academiae Scientiarum Hungaricae* 45 (1991): 271–345.

"State and Society, Crisis and Reform, in 15th–17th Century Ottoman Mirror for Princes," *Acta Orientalia Academiae Scientiarum Hungaricae* 40 (1986): 217–40.

"Sultan, Imperial Council, Grand Vizier: Changes in the Ottoman Ruling Elite and the Formation of the Grand Vizieral *Telhis*," *Acta Orientalia Academiae Scientiarum Hungaricae* 47 (1994): 67–85.

Fotič, Aleksandar, "The Official Explanations for the Confiscation and Sale of Monasteries (Churches) and their Estates at the Time of Selim II," *Turcica* 26 (1994): 33–54.

Frank, Andre Gunder, *ReOrient: Global Economy in the Asian Age*, Berkeley, CA: University of California Press, 1998.

Franke, Wolfgang, "Historical Writing during the Ming," in *The Cambridge History of China*, vol. VII, Cambridge: Cambridge University Press, 1988.

Friedmann, Yohanan, *Tolerance and Coercion in Islam, Interfaith Relations in the Muslim Tradition*, Cambridge: Cambridge University Press, 2003.

Frigo, Daniela (ed.), *Politics and Diplomacy in Early Modern Italy: The Structure of Diplomatic Practice, 1450–1800*, trans. Adrian Belton, Cambridge: Cambridge University Press, 2000.

Frye, Northrop, *Anatomy of Criticism*, Princeton, NJ: Princeton University Press, 1957.

Fables of Identity: Studies in Poetic Mythology, New York: Harcourt, Brace and World, 1963, pp. 7–20.

The Stubborn Structure: Essays on Criticism and Society, Ithaca, NY: Cornell University Press, 1970.

Galanti, Avram, *Türkler ve Yahudiler*, Istanbul: Gözlem Gazetecilik Basın ve Yayın, 1995.

Galitekin, Ahmed Nezih, *Osmanlı Dönemi Gölcük Mezar Taşları*, Gölcük: Gölcük Belediyesi, 2000.

Gallotta, Aldo, "Khayr al-Din Pasha, Barbarossa," in *EI2*, vol. IV, p. 1155.

Geertz, Clifford, "Found in Translation: On the Social History of the Moral Imagination," in *Local Knowledge: Further Essays in Interpretive Anthropology*, New York: Basic Books, 1983, pp. 36–54.

"Thick Description: Toward an Interpretive Theory of Culture," in *The Interpretation of Cultures: Selected Essays by Clifford Geertz*, New York: Basic Books, 1973, pp. 3–30.

Genç, Mehmet, "L'économie ottomane et la guerre au XVIIIe siècle," *Turcica* 27 (1995): 177–96.

Gerber, Haim, *State, Society and Law in Islam: Ottoman Law in Comparative Perspective*, New York: SUNY Press, 1994.

al-Ghazali, *Ghazali's Book of Counsel for Kings*, trans. F. R. C. Bagley, New York: Oxford University Press, 1964.

Gibb, E. J. W., *A History of Ottoman Poetry*, ed. Edward G. Browne, 6 vols., London: E. J. W. Gibb Memorial, 1900–9; reprinted London: Luzac, 1967.

Gibb, H. A. R. and Harold Bowen, *Islamic Society and the West: A Study of the Impact of Western Civilization on Moslem Culture in the Near East*, 1 vol. in 2 pts. Oxford: Oxford University Press, 1950, 1957.

Gills, Barry and Andre Gunder Frank, "World System Cycles, Crises, and Hegemonic Shifts, 1700 B.C. to 1700 A.D.," in B. Gills and A. Gunder Frank (eds.), *The World System*, London: Routledge, 1996, pp. 143–99.

Ginzburg, Carlo, *The Cheese and the Worms: The Cosmos of a Sixteenth-Century Miller*, trans. J. and A. C. Tedeschi, New York: Dorset, 1989.

"Titian, Ovid, and Sixteenth-Century Codes for Erotic Illustration," in J. and A. C. Tedeschi (trans.), *Clues, Myths, and the Historical Method*, Baltimore, MD: Johns Hopkins University Press, 1986, pp. 77–95.

Göçek, Fatma Müge, *Rise of Bourgeoisie, Demise of Empire: Ottoman Westernization and Social Change*, Oxford: Oxford University Press, 1995.

Göçek, Fatma Müge and Marc David Baer, "Social Boundaries of Ottoman Women's Experience in Eighteenth-Century Galata Court Records," in Madeline Zilfi (ed.), *Women in the Ottoman Empire:Middle Eastern Women in the Early Modern Era*, Leiden: Brill, 1997, pp. 48–65.

Goffman, Daniel, *The Ottoman Empire and Early Modern Europe*, Cambridge: Cambridge University Press, 2002.

Gökbilgin, M. Tayyib, *XV–XVI. Asırlarda Edirne ve Paşa Livası: Vakıflar, Mülkler, Mukataalar*, Istanbul: Üçler Basımevi, 1952.

"Boğaziçi," in *İslam Ansiklopedisi*, vol. II, pp. 666–92.

Gökyay, Orhan Şaik, "Bağçeler," *Topkapı Sarayı Müzesi Yıllığı* 4 (1990): 7–20.

Goldschmidt, Arthur, *A Concise History of the Middle East*, Boulder, CO: Westview, 2002.

Goodrich, Thomas D., *The Ottoman Turks and the New World: A Study of Tarih-i Hind-i Garbi and Sixteenth Century Ottoman Americana*, Wiesbaden: Otto Harrassowitz, 1990.

"Supplemental Maps in the Kitab-ı Bahriye of Piri Reis," *Archivum Ottomanicum* 13 (1993–4): 117–41.

Göyünç, Nejat, "Timar Ruznamçe Defterlerinin Biyografik Kaynak Olarak Önemi," *Belleten* 60 (1996): 127–38.

Gradeva, Rossitsa, "War and Peace along the Danube: Vidin at the End of the Seventeenth Century," in Kate Fleet (ed.), *The Ottomans and the Sea*, special issue of *Oriente Moderno* 20 (81), n.s. 1 (2001): 149–75.

Graham, Lisa Jane, "Crimes of Opinion: Policing the Public in Eighteenth-Century France," in Christine Adams, Jack Cluser, and Lisa Jane Graham (eds.), *Visions and Revisions of Eighteenth-Century France*, University Park, PA: Pennsylvania State University Press, 1997, pp. 84–5.

Gran, Peter, *Islamic Roots of Capitalism: Egypt, 1760–1840*, 2nd edn, Syracuse, NY: Syracuse University Press, 1998.

Grant, Jonathan, "Rethinking the Ottoman 'Decline': Military Technology Diffusion in the Ottoman Empire, Fifteenth to Eighteenth Centuries," *Journal of World History* 10 (1999): 179–201.

Greene, Molly, *A Shared World: Christians and Muslims in the Early Modern Mediterranean*, Princeton, NJ: Princeton University Press, 2000.

Guilmartin Jr., J. F., *Gunpowder and Galleys: Changing Technology and Mediterranean Warfare at Sea in the Sixteenth Century*, Cambridge: Cambridge University Press, 1974, rev. edn, London: Conway Marine, 2003.

Güzelbey, Cemil Cahit, *Gaziantep Camileri Tarihi*, Gaziantep: n.p., 1984, reprinted 1992.

Haarmann, Ulrich, "The Plight of the Self-Appointed Genius – Mustafa 'Ali," *Arabica* 38 (1991): 73–86.

Hagen, Gottfried, *Ein osmanischer Geograph bei der Arbeit, Entstehung und Gedankenwelt von Katib Celebis Gihannüma*, Studien zur Sprache, Geschichte und Kultur der Türkvölker, Berlin: Klaus Schwarz Verlag, 2003.
"Kātib Čelebis Darstellung der *Eyālets* und *Sanğaqs* des Osmanischen Reiches," *Archivum Ottomanicum* 16 (1998): 101–23.
"Some Considerations on the Study of Ottoman Geographical Writings," *Archivum Ottomanicum* 18 (2000): 183–93.
Halaçoğlu, Yusuf, *Osmanlılarda Ulaşım ve Haberleşme (Menziller)*, Ankara: Türk Tarih Kurumu, 2002.
Halasi-Kun, Tibor, "Ottoman Toponymic Data and Medieval Boundaries in Southeastern Hungary," in János Bak and Béla Király (eds.), *From Hunyadi to Rákoczi, War and Society in Late Medieval and Early Modern Hungary*, New York: Brooklyn College Press, 1982, pp. 243–50.
Hallaq, Wael, "The Kadi Diwan (Sijill) before the Ottomans," *Bulletin of the School of Oriental and African Studies* 61 (1998): 415–36.
Hamadeh, Shirine, "The City's Pleasures: Architectural Sensibility in Eighteenth-Century Istanbul," PhD dissertation, MIT, 1999.
"Splash and Spectacle: The Obsession with Fountains in Eighteenth-Century Istanbul," *Muqarnas* 19 (2002): 123–48.
Hammer-Purgstall, Josef von, *Des osmanischen Reichs Staatsverfassung und Staatsverwaltung, dargestellt aus den Quellen seiner Grundgesetze*, 2 vols., Vienna: Camesinaschen Buchhandlung, 1815.
Die Geschichte des osmanischen Reiches, 10 vols., Pest: C. A. Hartleben, 1827–35.
Hanna, Nelly, *In Praise of Books: A Cultural History of Cairo's Middle Class, Sixteenth to the Eighteenth Century*, Syracuse, NY: Syracuse University Press, 2003.
Making Big Money in 1600: The Life and Times of Isma'il Abu Taqiyya, Egyptian Merchant, Syracuse, NY: Syracuse University Press, 1998.
Harding, Vanessa, *The Dead and the Living in Paris and London, 1500–1670*, Cambridge: Cambridge University Press, 2002.
Harley, J. B., *The New Nature of Maps*, Baltimore, MD: Johns Hopkins University Press, 2001.
Harley, J. B. and David Woodward (eds.), *The History of Cartography*, vol. I: *Geography in Prehistoric, Ancient, and Medieval Europe and the Mediterranean*, and vol. II, book 1: *Geography in the Traditional Islamic and South Asian Societies*, Chicago: University of Chicago Press, 1987–92.
Harwood, Edward, "Personal Identity and the Eighteenth-Century English Landscape Garden," *Journal of Garden History* 13 (1993): 36–48.
Hattox, Ralph S., *Coffee and Coffeehouses: The Origins of a Social Beverage in the Medieval Near East*, Seattle: University of Washington Press, 1985.
Hazai, György (ed.), *Nagy Szülejmán udvari emberének magyar krónikája. A Tarih-i Ungurus és kritikája* [The Hungarian Chronicle of Süleyman the Magnificent's Courtier. The Tarih-i Ungurus and its Critique], Budapest: Akadémiai Kiadó, 1996.

Headley, John M., "Germany, the Empire and *Monarchia* in the Thought and Policy of Gattinara," in Heinrich Lutz (ed.), *Das römisch-deutsche Reich im politischen System Karls V,* Munich: Oldenbourg 1982, reprinted in J. M. Headley, *Church, Empire and World. The Quest for Universal Order,* Aldershot: Ashgate, 1997, article VI.

"The Habsburg World Empire and the Revival of Ghibellinism," *Medieval Renaissance Studies* 7 (1975): 93–127, reprinted in Headley, *Church, Empire and World,* article V.

Helmarth, Johannes, "The German Reichstage and the Crusade," in Norman Housley (ed.), *Crusading in the Fifteenth Century. Message and Impact,* Basingstoke: Macmillan, 2004, pp. 53–69.

Hess, Andrew, *The Forgotten Frontier,* Chicago: University of Chicago Press, 1978.

Heyd, Uriel, "Some Aspects of the Ottoman Fetva," *Bulletin of the School of Oriental and African Studies* 32 (1969): 36–56.

Studies in Old Ottoman Criminal Law, ed. V. L. Ménage, Oxford: Clarendon Press, 1973.

Heywood, Colin, "Between Historical Myth and Mythohistory: The Limits of Ottoman History," *Byzantine and Modern Greek Studies* 12 (1998): 315–45, reprinted in C. Heywood, *Writing Ottoman History: Documents and Interpretations,* Aldershot: Ashgate, 2002.

"The Ottoman Menzilhane and Ulak System in Rumeli in the Eighteenth Century," reprinted in Heywood, *Writing Ottoman History.*

"Sir Paul Rycaut, A Seventeenth-Century Observer of the Ottoman State: Notes for a Study," in E. Kural Shaw and C. J. Heywood, *English and Continental Views of the Ottoman Empire, 1500–1800,* Los Angeles: William Andrews Clark Memorial Library, 1972, pp. 33–59.

"Some Turkish Archival Sources for the History of the Menzilhane Network in Rumeli during the Eighteenth Century," reprinted in Heywood, *Writing Ottoman History.*

"The Via Egnatia in the Ottoman Period: The Menzilhanes of the Sol Kol in the Late 17th/Early 18th Century," reprinted in *Writing Ottoman History.*

Hinz, Walther, *Die Resālä-ye Falakiyyä des 'Abdollāh ibn Mohammad ibn Kiyā al-Māzandarānī,* Wiesbaden: Franz Steiner Verlag, 1952.

Hodgson, Marshall G. S., "Two Pre-Modern Muslim Historians: Pitfalls and Opportunities in Presenting them to Moderns," in John Nef (ed.), *Towards World Community,* The Hague: Dr. W. Junk N.V., 1968, pp. 53–68.

The Venture of Islam: Conscience and History in a World Civilization, 3 vols., Chicago: University of Chicago Press, 1974.

Holbrooke, Victoria Rowe, *The Unreadable Shores of Love: Turkish Modernity and Mystic Romance,* Austin: University of Texas Press, 1994.

Houlbrooke, Ralph, "The Age of Decency: 1660–1760," in Peter C. Jupp and Clare Gittings (eds.), *Death in England. An Illustrated History,* New Brunswick: Rutgers University Press, 2000.

Hourani, Albert, *History of the Arab Peoples*, Cambridge, MA: Harvard University Press, 1991.
"Shaykh Khalid and the Naqshbandi Order," in S. M. Stern, Albert Habib Hourani, and Vivian Brown (eds.), *Islamic Philosophy and the Classical Tradition*, essays presented by his friends and pupils to Richard Walzer on his seventieth birthday, Oxford: Oxford University Press, 1972, pp. 89–103.
Howard, Douglas A., "The BBA *Ruznamçe Tasnifi*: A New Resource for the Study of the Ottoman *Timar* System," *Turkish Studies Association Bulletin* 10 (1986): 11–19.
"The Historical Development of the Ottoman Imperial Registry (*Defter-i hakani*): Mid-Fifteenth to Mid-Seventeenth Centuries," *Archivum Ottomanicum* 11 (1986[1988]): 213–30.
"Ottoman Administration and the Timar System: Suret-i Kanunname-i 'Osmani Beray-ı Timar Daden," *Journal of Turkish Studies* 20 (1996): 46–124.
"Ottoman Historiography and the Literature of 'Decline' of the Sixteenth and Seventeenth Centuries," *Journal of Asian History* 22 (1988): 52–77.
"The Ottoman Timar System and its Transformation, 1563–1656," PhD dissertation, Indiana University, 1987.
"With Gibbon in the Garden: Decline, Death and the Sick Man of Europe," *Fides et Historia* 26 (1994): 22–37.
Hrushevsky, Mykhailo, *History of the Ukraine-Rus*, vol. VII: *The Cossack Age to 1625*, trans. Bohdan Struminski, Edmonton: Canadian Institute of Ukrainian Studies Press, 1999.
Huntington, Samuel, *The Clash of Civilizations and the Remaking of World Order*, New York: Simon and Schuster, 1997.
Hurewitz, J. C., *The Middle East and North Africa in World Politics*, 2nd edn, 2 vols., New Haven, CT: Yale University Press, 1975.
Ibarra, Miguel Ángel de Bunes, "Charles V and the Ottoman War from the Spanish Point of View," *Eurasian Studies*, 1 (2002): 161–82.
İhsanoğlu, Ekmeleddin, *Osmanlı Coğrafya Literatürü, History of Ottoman Geographical Literature During the Ottoman Period*, 2 vols., Istanbul: İslâm Tarih, Sanat, ve Kültür Araştırma Merkezi, 2000.
Ilardi, Vincent, "The First Permanent Embassy Outside Italy: The Milanese Embassy at the French Court, 1464–1494," in Malcolm R. Thorp and Arthur J. Slavin (eds.), *Politics, Religion and Diplomacy in Early Modern Europe. Essays in Honor of De Lamar Jensen*, special issue of *Sixteenth Century Journal* 27 (1994): 1–18.
İlgürel, Mücteba, "Hamza Paşa, Silahdar," in *Türkiye Diyanet Vakfı İslâm Ansiklopedisi*, vol. XV, pp. 515–16.
İlhan, M. Mehdi, "Diyarbakır'ın Türbe, Yatır ve Mezarlıkları," in J. L. Bacqué-Grammont and A. Tibet (eds.), *Cimetières et traditions funéraires dans le monde islamique*, Ankara: Türk Tarih Kurumu, 1996, vol. I, pp. 179–211.
Imber, Colin, *Ebu's-Su'ud: The Islamic Legal Tradition*, Stanford, CA: Stanford University Press, 1997.

"Ideals and Legitimation in Early Ottoman History," in Metin Kunt and Christine Woodhead (eds.), *Süleyman the Magnificent and his Age: The Ottoman Empire in the Early Modern World*, London: Longman, 1995, pp. 138–53.

The Ottoman Empire 1300–1481, Istanbul: İsis, 1990.

The Ottoman Empire 1300–1650: The Structure of Power, London: Palgrave, 2002.

"Süleyman as Caliph of the Muslims: Ebu's-Suùd's Formulation of Ottoman Dynastic Ideology," in Gilles Veinstein (ed.), *Soliman le Magnifique*, Paris: Documentation Française, 1992, pp. 179–84.

İnalcık, Halil, "Centralization and Decentralization in Ottoman Administration," in Thomas Naff and Roger Owen (eds.), *Studies in Eighteenth-Century Islamic History*, Carbondale, IL: Southern Illinois University Press, 1977, pp. 27–52.

"Gelibolu," in EI2, vol. II, p. 984.

"Imtiyazat," in EI2, vol. III, pp. 1178–89.

"Kanunname," in EI2, vol. IV, pp. 563–6.

"Military and Fiscal Transformation in the Ottoman Empire, 1600–1700," *Archivum Ottomanicum* 6 (1980): 283–337.

"Osmanlı Bürokrasisinde Aklâm ve Muâmelât," *Osmanlı Araştırmaları/Journal of Ottoman Studies* 1 (1980): 1–14.

The Ottoman Empire: The Classical Age 1300–1600, London: Weidenfeld and Nicolson, 1973; reprinted in New York, Aristide D. Caratzas, 1989; repr. 1995.

"Ottoman Galata, 1453–1553," in Edhem Eldem (ed.), *Première rencontre internationale sur l'empire ottoman et la Turquie moderne, Institut National des Langues et Civilisations Orientales: Maison des Sciences de l'Homme, 18–22 January 1985*, Istanbul: Isis, 1991, pp. 17–105.

"Ottoman Methods of Conquest," *Studia Islamica* 2 (1954): 104–29.

"The Ottoman State: Economy and Society, 1300–1600", in H. İnalcık and D. Quataert (eds.), *An Economic and Social History of the Ottoman Empire, 1300–1914*, 2 vols., Cambridge: Cambridge University Press, 1994, vol. I, pp. 9–379.

"The Rise of Ottoman Historiography," in Bernard Lewis and P. M. Holt (eds.), *Historians of the Middle East*, London: Oxford University Press, 1962.

"The Rise of the Turcoman Maritime Principalities in Anatolia, Byzantium and Crusades, *Byzantinische Forschungen* 9 (1985): 179–217.

"Selim I," in EI2, vol. IX, pp. 127–31.

"Süleyman the Lawgiver and Ottoman Law," *Archivum Ottomanicum* 1 (1969): 105–13.

"Timar," in EI2, vol. X (1999), pp. 502–7.

İnalcık, Halil and Cemal Kafadar (eds.), *Süleyman the Second and his Time*, Istanbul: Isis Press, 1993.

İnalcık, Halil and Donald Quataert (eds.), *An Economic and Social History of the Ottoman Empire 1300–1914*, 2 vols. Cambridge: Cambridge University Press, 1994.

İnalcık, Halil and Şevket Pamuk (eds.), *Osmanlı Devleti'nde Bilgi ve İstatistik/Data and Statistics in the Ottoman Empire*, Ankara: T. C. Başbakanlık Devlet İstatistik Enstitüsü, 2000.

Ingram, Edward, "From Trade to Empire in the Near East III: The Uses of the Residency in Baghdad, 1794–1804," *Middle Eastern Studies* 14 (1978): 278–306.

İpşirli, Mehmed, "Devhatü'l-meşâyih," in *Türkiye Diyanet Vakfı İslâm Ansiklopedisi*, vol. IX, pp. 229–30.

"Hasan Kâfî el-Akhisarî ve Devlet Düzenine Ait Eseri Usûlü'l-Hikem fî Nizâmi'l-Âlem," *Tarih Enstitüsü Dergisi* 10–11 (1979–80): 239–78.

Işıközlü, F. (ed.), "Başbakanlık Arşivinde Yeni Bulunmuş Olan ve Sadreddin Zâde Telhisî Mustafa Efendi Tarafından Tutulduğu Anlaşılan H. 1123 (1711) – 1184 (1735) Yıllarına Ait Bir Ceride (Jurnal) ve Eklentisi," in *VII. Türk Tarih Kongresi* II, Ankara: Türk Tarih Kurumu, 1973, pp. 508–34.

İstanbul Kütüphaneleri Tarih-Coğrafya Yazmaları Katalogları, Istanbul: Maarif Matbaası, 1943–62.

Itzkowitz, Norman, "Eighteenth-Century Ottoman Realities," *Studia Islamica* 16 (1962): 73–94.

"Mehmed Raghib Pasha: The Making of an Ottoman Grand Vezir," PhD dissertation, Princeton University, 1959.

"Men and Ideas in the Eighteenth-Century Ottoman Empire," in Thomas Naff and Roger Owen (eds.), *Studies in Eighteenth-Century Islamic History*, Carbondale and Edwardsville, IL: Southern Illinois University Press, 1977, pp. 15–26.

Itzkowitz, Norman and Max Mote (eds. and trans.), *Mubadele: An Ottoman-Russian Exchange of Ambassadors*, Chicago: University of Chicago Press, 1970.

Jackson, Sherman A., *On the Boundaries of Theological Tolerance in Islam, Abu Hamid al-Ghazali's Faysal al-Tafriqa*, Oxford: Oxford University Press, 2002.

Jenkins, Hester Donaldson, *Ibrahim Pasha: Grand Vizir of Suleiman the Magnificent*, New York: Columbia University Press, 1911.

Jennings, Ronald, "Kadi, Court, and Legal Procedure," *Studia Islamica* 48 (1978): 133–72.

"Limitations on the Judicial Powers of the Kadis in 17th C. Ottoman Kayseri," *Studia Islamica* 50 (1979): 151–84.

Jirousek, Charlotte, "The Transition to Mass Fashion System Dress in the Later Ottoman Empire," in Donald Quataert (ed.), *Consumption Studies and the History of the Ottoman Empire 1550–1922*, Albany, NY: SUNY Press, 2000, pp. 201–41.

Johansen, Baber. "Entre révélation et tyrannie: le droit des non-musulmans d'après les juristes musulmans," in his *Contingency in a Sacred Law: Legal and Ethical Norms in the Muslim Fiqh*, Leiden: Brill, 1999.

The Islamic Law on Land Tax and Rent: The Peasants' Loss of Property Rights as Interpreted in the Hanafite Legal Literature of the Mamluk and Ottoman Periods, London: Croom Helm, 1988.

Johnson, Brian, "Istanbul's Vanished City of the Dead: The Grand Champ des Morts," in Nezih Başgelen and Brian Johnson (eds.), *Myth to Modernity*.

Efsanelerden Günümüze 1, Istanbul. Selected Themes. Seçme Yazılar, Istanbul: Archaeology and Art Publications, 2002, pp. 93–104.

Juchereau de St. Denys, A., *Révolutions de Constantinople en 1807 et 1808: précédées d'observations générales sur l'état actuel de l'Empire Ottoman,* 2 vols. Paris: Brissot-Thivars, 1819.

Kafadar, Cemal, *Between Two Worlds: The Construction of the Ottoman State* Berkeley, CA: University of California Press, 1995.

"The Myth of the Golden Age: Ottoman Historical Consciousness in the Post-Süleymânic Era," in Halil İnalcık and Cemal Kafadar (eds.), *Süleymân the Second and his Time,* Istanbul: Isis Press, 1993, pp. 37–48.

"The Ottomans and Europe," in T. Brady Jr., H. A. Oberman and J. D. Tracy (eds.), *Handbook of European History 1400–1600: Late Middle Ages, Renaissance and Reformation – 1: Structures and Assertions,* Leiden: Brill, 1994, pp. 613–15.

"The Question of Ottoman Decline," *Harvard Middle Eastern and Islamic Review* 4 (1997–8): 30–75.

Káldy-Nagy, Gyula, "The Administration of the Sanjaq Registrations in Hungary," *Acta Orientalia Academiae Scientiarum Hungaricae* 21 (1968): 181–223.

Karaçağ, Demet, *Bursa'daki 14.–15. Yüzyıl Mezar Taşları,* Ankara: n.p., 1994.

Karal, Enver Ziya, *Selim III'ün Hattı Hümayunları, Nizam-ı Cedit 1789–1807,* Ankara: T. T. K. Basımeivi, 1946.

Karamağaralı, Beyhan, *Ahlat Mezar Taşları,* Ankara: Kültür Bakanlığı, 1992.

Karamustafa, Ahmet T., "Introduction to Ottoman Cartography," in J. B. Harley, and David Woodward (eds.), *The History of Cartography,* vol. II, book 1, Chicago: University of Chicago Press, 1987–92, pp. 206–8.

"Military, Administrative, and Scholarly Maps and Plans," in Harley and Woodward (eds.), *The History of Cartography,* vol. II, book 1, pp. 209–27.

Karateke, Hakan T., "Interpreting Monuments: Charitable Buildings, Monuments, and the Construction of Collective Memory in the Ottoman Empire," *Wiener Zeitschrift für die Kunde des Morgenlandes* 91 (2001): 183–99.

Karrow, Robert W., *Mapmakers of the Sixteenth Century and their Maps,* Chicago: Newberry Library, by Speculum Press, 1993.

Kent, Thomas, *Interpretation and Genre: The Role of Generic Perception in the Study of Narrative Texts,* Lewisville, PA: Bucknell University Press, 1986.

Kerslake, Celia J. "The Selim-name of Celal-zade Mustafa Çelebi as a Historical Source," *Turcica* 9/2–10 (1978): 39–51.

Khoury, Dina Rizk, "Slippers at the Entrance or Behind Closed Doors: Domestic and Public Spaces for Mosuli Women," in M. Zilfi (ed.), *Women in the Ottoman Empire,* Leiden: Brill, 1997, pp. 105–28.

Kırlı, Cengiz, "The Struggle over Space: Coffeehouses of Ottoman Istanbul, 1780–1845," PhD dissertation, Binghamton University, 2001.

Koçu, Reşat Ekrem, "Bostancıbaşı Defterleri," in *İstanbul Ansiklopedisi,* pp. 39–90.

"Fenerbağçe, Fenerbağçesi – Kasrı ve Mescidi," in *İstanbul Ansiklopedisi,* pp. 5621–5.

Tarihimizde Garip Vakalar, Istanbul: Varlık Yayınevi, 1958.

Türk Giyim Kuşam ve Süslenme Sözlüğü, Istanbul: Sümerbank, 1969.

Kohler, Alfred, *Karl V 1500–1558. Eine Biographie*, Munich: Beck, 1999.

Kołodziejczyk, Dariusz, *Ottoman-Polish Diplomatic Relations (15th–18th Century). An Annotated Edition of 'Ahdnames and Other Documents*, Leiden: Brill, 2000.

The Ottoman Survey Register of Podolia (ca. 1681): Defter-i Mufassal-i Eyalet-i Kamaniçe, Cambridge, MA: Harvard Ukrainian Research Institute, 2003.

Köprülü, M. Fuad, *Türk Edebiyatı Tarihi*, repr. Istanbul: Ötüken, 1986.

Köprülüzade, Mehmet Fuat, *Türk Sazşairleri*, 4 vols., Istanbul, 1930.

Kort, Wesley A., *Narrative Elements and Religious Meaning*, Philadelphia, PA: Fortress, 1975.

Kreiser, Klaus, *Der osmanische Staat 1300–1922*. Munich: R. Oldenbourg, 2001.

Kunt, Metin, *The Sultan's Servants: The Transformation of Ottoman Provincial Government, 1550–1650*, New York: Columbia University Press, 1983.

Kunt, Metin and Christine Woodhead (eds.), *Süleyman the Magnificent and his Age: The Ottoman Empire in the Early Modern World*, London: Longman, 1995.

Kuran, Timur. "Islamic Redistribution through *Zakat*: Historical Record and Modern Realities," in M. Bonner, M. Ener and A. Singer (eds.), *Poverty and Charity in Middle Eastern Contexts*, Albany, NY: SUNY Press, 2003, pp. 275–93.

Kursun, Zekeriya, *Necid ve Ahsa'da Osmanlı Hakimiyeti, Vehhabi Hareketi ve Suud Devleti'nin Ortaya Çıkışı*, Ankara: Türk Tarih Kurumu, 1998.

Kütükoğlu, Bekir, "Lokmân b. Hüseyin," in *Türkiye Diyanet Vakfı İslâm Ansiklopedisi*, vol. XXVII, pp. 208–9.

"Münşeat Mecmualarının Osmanlı Diplomatiği Bakımından Ehemmiyeti," in *Tarih Boyunca Paleografya ve Diplomatik Semineri*, Istanbul: Istanbul Üniversitesi Edebiyat Fakültesi, 1988, pp. 169–76.

"Şehnâmeci Lokman," in *Prof. Dr. Bekir Kütükoğlu'na Armağan*, Istanbul, Istanbul Üniversitesi Edebiyat Fakültesi Tarih Araştırma Merkezi, 1991, pp. 39–48.

"Vekayi'nüvis," in *Vekayi'nüvis: Makaleler*, Istanbul: Istanbul Fetih Cemiyeti, 1994, pp. 111–23.

Kütükoğlu, Mübahat S. (ed.), "Lütfi Paşa Âsafnâmesi (Yeni Bir Metin Tesisi Denemesi)," in *Prof. Dr. Bekir Kütükoğlu'na Armağan*, Istanbul: Edebiyat Fakültesi Basımevi, 1991, pp. 49–99.

Lambton, Ann K. S., "Quis Custodiet Custodes: Some Reflections on the Persian Theory of Government," *Studia Islamica* 5 (1956): 125–48 and 6 (1956), 125–46.

Laqueur, Hans-Peter, "Cemeteries in Orient and Occident. The Historical Development," in J.-L. Bacqué-Grammont and A. Tibet (eds.), *Cimetières et traditions funéraires dans le monde islamique*, 2 vols., Ankara: Türk Tarih Kurumu, 1996, vol. II, pp. 3–7.

"Einige Anmerkungen zur Sozialgeschichte der osmanischen Friedhöfe und Gräberfelder von Istanbul," *Istanbuler Mitteilungen* 39 (1989): pp. 335–9.

"Grabsteine als Quelle zur osmanischen Geschichte. Möglichkeiten," *Osmanlı Araştırmaları* 3 (1982): 31–44.

Hüve'l-Baki. İstanbul'da Osmanlı Mezarlıkları ve Mezar Taşları, Istanbul: Tarih Vakfı Yurt Yayınları, 1997, pp. 138–60.

"Die Kopfbedeckungen im osmanischen Reich als soziales Erkennungszeichen, dargestellt anhand einiger Istanbuler Grabsteine des 18. und 19. Jahrhunderts," *Der Islam*, 59/1 (1982): 80–92.

Lasdun, Susan, *The English Park: Royal, Private and Public,* London: André Deutsch, 1991.

Lassner, Jacob, *Demonizing the Queen of Sheba: Boundaries of Gender and Culture in Postbiblical Judaism and Medieval Islam,* Chicago: University of Chicago Press, 1993.

László, Bárdossy, *Magyar politika a mohácsi vész után* [Hungarian Politics after the Battle of Mohács], Budapest: Holnap Kiadó, 1992[1943].

LeDonne, John P., *The Grand Strategy of the Russian Empire, 1650–1831.* Oxford: Oxford University Press, 2004.

"Siyaset-nameler," *Türk Dili Araştırmaları Yıllığı Belleten* (1962): 167–94.

Levend, Agâh Sırrı, "Ümmet Çağında Ahlâk Kitaplarımız," *Türk Dili Araştırmaları Yıllığı Belleten* (1963): 89–115.

Levin, Harry, *The Myth of the Golden Age in the Renaissance,* Bloomington, IN: Indiana University Press, 1969.

Levy, Avigdor, "Military Policy of Sultan Mahmud II, 1808–1839," PhD dissertation, Harvard University, 1968.

Levy, Reuben, *A Mirror for Princes; The Qabus Nama by Ka'us ibn Iskandar, Prince of Gurgan,* New York: E. P. Dutton, 1951.

Lewicka, Paulina, "What a King Should Care About. Two Memoranda of the Mamluk Sultan on Running State Affairs," *Studia Arabistyczne i Islamistyczne* 6 (1998): 5–45.

Lewis, Bernard. *The Arabs in History,* Oxford: Oxford University Press, 1962.

"Dustūr," *Encyclopedia of Islam,* 1999 CD edition.

The Emergence of Modern Turkey, Oxford: Oxford University Press, 1961.

The Muslim Discovery of Europe, New York: Norton, 1982; reprint with a new introduction, 2001.

The Muslim Discovery of Europe, London: Phoenix, 1982; reprint 1994.

"Ottoman Observers of Ottoman Decline," *Islamic Studies* 1 (1962): 71–87.

What Went Wrong? The Clash between Islam and Modernity in the Middle East, New York: Oxford University Press, 2002.

Lewis, Mark Edward, *Writing and Authority in Early China,* Albany, NY: SUNY, 1999.

Lewis, Martin and Karen Wigen, *The Myth of Continents: A Critique of Metageography,* Berkeley, CA: University of California Press, 1997.

Lieven, Dominic, *Empire: The Russian Empire and its Rivals,* New Haven, CT: Yale University Press, 2002.

Lockman, Zachary, *Contending Visions of the Middle East: The History and Politics of Orientalism,* Cambridge: Cambridge University Press, 2004.

Lowry, Heath W., "The Ottoman Liva Kannunames contained in the Defter-i Hakani," in H. W. Lowry, *Studies in Defterology: Ottoman Society in the Fifteenth and Sixteenth Centuries,* Istanbul: Isis, 1992, pp. 19–46.

"The Ottoman *Tahrir Defterleri* as a Source for Social and Economic History: Pitfalls and Limitations," in H. W. Lowry, *Studies in Defterology*, pp. 3–18.

Luttwak, E. N., *The Grand Strategy of the Roman Empire from the First Century to the Third*, Baltimore, MD: Johns Hopkins University Press, 1976.

Macfarlane, Charles, *Constantinople in 1828: A Residence of Sixteen Months in the Turkish Capital and Provinces*, 2nd edn, London: Saunders and Otley, 1829.

Maclean, Gerald (ed.), *Re-Orienting the Renaissance: Cultural Exchanges with the East*, Houndmills: Palgrave Macmillan, 2005.

Makdisi, Ussama, *The Culture of Sectarianism: Community, History, and Violence in Ottoman Lebanon*, Berkeley, CA: University of California Press, 2000.

Mallia-Milanes, Victor, "From Valona to Crete: Veneto-Maltese Relations from the late 1630s to the Outbreak of the Cretan War," in Stanley Fiorini (ed.), *Malta: A Case Study in International Cross Currents* (Malta: Malta University Publishers, 1991, pp. 159–73.

Venice and Hospitaller Malta: Aspects of a Relationship 1530–1798, Marsa, Malta: Publishers Enterprises Group, 1992.

Manganaro, Marc, *Myth, Rhetoric, and the Voice of Authority: A Critique of Frazer, Eliot, Frye and Campbell*, New Haven, CT: Yale University Press, 1992.

Mansuroğlu, Mecdut, "The Rise and Development of Written Turkish in Anatolia," *Oriens* 7 (1954): 250–64.

Mantran, Robert, *Istanbul dans la seconde moitié du XVIIe siècle*, Paris: A. Maisonneuve, 1962.

XVI–XVII. Yüzyılda İstanbul'da Gündelik Hayat, Istanbul: n.p., 1991.

Marcus, Abraham, *The Middle East on the Eve of Modernity: Aleppo in the Eighteenth Century*, New York: Columbia University Press, 1989.

Mardin, Şerif, "Super Westernization in Urban Life in the Ottoman Empire in the Last Quarter of the Nineteenth Century," in P. Benedict and E. Tümertekin (eds.), *Turkey: Geographical and Social Perspectives*, Leiden: Brill, 1974, 409–46.

Masters, Bruce, "The 1850 Events in Aleppo: An Aftershock of Syria's Incorporation into the Capitalist World System," *International Journal of Middle Eastern Studies* 22 (1990): 3–20.

Mattingly, Garrett, *Renaissance Diplomacy*. Boston: Houghton Mifflin, 1955.

Mattson, Ingrid, "Status-based Definitions of Need in Early Islamic *Zakat* and Maintenance Laws," in M. Bonner, M. Ener, and A. Singer (eds.), *Poverty and Charity in Middle East Contexts*, Albany, NY: SUNY Press, 2003, 31–51.

Matuz, Josef, *Das Kanzleiwesen Süleyman des Prächtigen*, Wiesbaden: F. Steiner, 1974.

"Die Pfortendolmetscher zur Herrschaftszeit Süleyman des Prächtigen," *Südost-Forschungen* 34 (1975): 26–60.

McCarthy, Justin, *The Ottoman Turks*, London: Longman, 1997.

McClain, James, and John M. Merriman, "Edo and Paris: Cities and Power," in James McClain, John M. Merriman and Kaoru Ugawa (eds.), *Edo and Paris: Urban Life and the State in the Early Modern Era*, Ithaca, NY: Cornell University Press, 1994, pp. 3–38.

McNeill, William H., *A World History*, Oxford: Oxford University Press, 1999.

Mehmed Efendi, *Le paradis des infidèles: Un ambassadeur ottoman en France sous la Régence*, ed. Gilles Veinstein, Paris: Librairie François Maspero, 1981.

Meissami, Julie, "The Body as Garden: Nature and Sexuality in Persian Poetry," *Edebiyât* 6 (1995): 245–68.

"The World's Pleasance; Hāfiz's Allegorical Gardens," in E. S. Shaffer (ed.), *Comparative Criticism*, Cambridge: Cambridge University Press, 1983, pp. 153–85.

Melikian-Chirvani, Assadullah S., "Recherches sur les sources de l'art ottoman: les stèles funéraires d'Ayasoluk I," *Turcica* 4 (1972): 103–33.

"Les stèles funéraires d'Ayasoluk II," *Turcica* 7 (1975): 105–21.

"Les stèles funéraires d'Ayasoluk III. Deux colonnes funéraires de l'an 1439," *Turcica* 8/2 (1976): 83–90.

Ménage, V. L., "The Mission of an Ottoman Secret Agent in 1486," *Journal of the Royal Asiatic Society* (1965): 112–32.

Menavino, Giovanantonio, *I cinque libri della legge: religione et vita de' Turchi della corte, & d'alcune guerre del Gran Turco*, Venice, 1548.

Meninski, Franciscus à Mesgnien, *Thesaurus Linguarum Orientalium Turcicae – Arabicae – Persicae*, 6 vols., facsimile reprint, with an introduction by Mehmet Ölmez, Istanbul: Simurg, 2000.

Messick, Brinkley, *The Calligraphic State: Textual Domination and History in a Muslim Society*, Berkeley, CA: University of California Press, 1993.

Minovi, M. and V. Minorsky, "Nasir al-Din Tusi on Finance," *Bulletin of the School of Oriental and African Studies* 10 (1939–42): 755–89.

Mitchell, Timothy, *Colonising Egypt*, Cambridge: Cambridge University Press, 1988.

Montagu, Lady Mary Wortley, *Embassy to Constantinople*, ed. C. Pick, intro. D. Murphy, New York: New Amsterdam, 1988.

Turkish Embassy Letters, ed. Malcolm Jack, London: W. Pickering, 1993.

Morritt, John B. S., *The Letters of John B. S. Morritt of Rokeby, Descriptive of Journeys in Europe and Asia Minor in the Years 1794–1796*, ed. G. E. Marindin, London: John Murray, 1914.

Mujezinovic, Mehmed, *Islamska Epigrafika u Bosni i Hercegovini*, Sarajevo: Veselin Masksa, 1974–82.

Murphey, Rhoads, "Communal Living in Istanbul: Searching for the Foundations of an Urban Tradition," *Journal of Urban History* 16 (1990): 115–31.

Ottoman Warfare, 1500–1700, London: UCL Press, 1999.

"Solakzade's Treatise of 1652: A Glimpse at Operational Principles Guiding the Ottoman State during Times of Crisis," in *V. Milletlerarası Türkiye Sosyal ve İktisat Tarihi Kongresi; Tebliğler*, Ankara: Türk Tarih Kurumu, 1990, pp. 27–32.

"Süleyman I and the Conquest of Hungary: Ottoman Manifest Destiny or Delayed Reaction to Charles V's Universalist Vision," *Journal of Early Modern History* 5 (2001): 197–221.

"The Veliyüddin Telhis: Notes on the Sources and Interrelations between Koçi Bey and Contemporary Writers of Advice to Kings," *Belleten* 43 (1979): 547–71.

Muruwah, Husayn, *Al-Naza'at al-Maddiyah fi al-Falsafah al-'Arabiyah al-Islamiyah*, Beirut: Dar al-Farabi, 1988.

Mutafcieva, Vera P. and Strashimir Dimitrov, *Sur l'état du système des timars des XVIIe–XVIIIe ss.*, Sofia: Académie bulgare des sciences, Institut d'études balkaniques, 1968.

Necipoğlu, Gülru, *The Age of Sinan: Architectural Culture in the Ottoman Empire*, Princeton, NJ: Princeton University Press, 2005.

Architecture, Ceremonial, and Power: The Topkapı Palace in the Fifteenth and Sixteenth Centuries, Cambridge, MA: MIT Press, 1991.

"A Kanun for the State, A Canon for the Arts: Conceptualizing the Classical Synthesis of Ottoman Art and Architecture," in Gilles Veinstein (ed.), *Soliman le Magnifique et son temps*, Paris: Documentation Française, 1992, pp. 194–216.

"The Suburban Landscape of Sixteenth-Century Istanbul as a Mirror of Classical Ottoman Garden Culture," in Attilio Petruccioli (ed.), *Gardens in the Time of the Great Muslim Empires (Supplements to Muqarnas)*, Leiden: Brill, 1997, pp. 32–71.

"Süleyman the Magnificent and the Representation of Power in the Context of Ottoman-Habsburg-Papal Rivalry," in H. İnalcık and C.Kafadar (eds.), *Süleyman the Second and his Time*, Istanbul: Isis Press, 1993, pp. 163–91.

"Word and Image: The Serial Portraits of Ottoman Sultans in Comparative Perspective," in Selmin Kangal and Priscilla Mary Işın (eds.), *The Sultan's Portrait: Picturing the House of Osman*, Istanbul: İşbank, 2000, pp. 22–61.

Orhonlu, Cengiz, "Khāss," in EI2, vol. IV, pp. 1094–1100.

"Hint Kaptanlığı ve Pîrî Reis," *Belleten* 34 (1970): 234–54.

Osmanlı Tarihine Âid Belgeler; Telhîsler (1597–1607), Istanbul: Edebiyat Fakültesi Basımevi, 1970.

Ostapchuk, Victor, "The Human Landscape of the Ottoman Black Sea in the Face of the Cossack Naval Raids," in Kate Fleet (ed.), *The Ottomans and the Sea*, special issue of *Oriente Moderno*, n.s., anno 20/1 (2001): 23–95.

Owen, Roger, "Introduction [to part two]," in *Studies in Eighteenth Century Islamic History*, Carbondale and Edwardsville, IL: Southern Illinois University Press, 1977, pp. 133–51.

"The Middle East in the Eighteenth Century – An 'Islamic' Society in Decline? A Critique of Gibb and Bowen's *Islamic Society and the West*," *Review of Middle East Studies* 1 (1975): 101–12.

Özege, N. Seyfettin, *Eski Harflerle Basılmış Türkçe Eserler Kataloğu*, Istanbul: n.p., 1971–82.

Özel, Oktay, and Gökhan Çetinsaya, "Türkiye'de Osmanlı Tarihçiliğinin Son Çeyrek Yüzyılı: Bir Bilanço Denemesi," *Toplum ve Bilim* 91 (2001/2): 8–38.

Özkaya, Yücel, *XVIII. Yüzyılda Osmanlı Kurumları ve Osmanlı Toplum Yaşantısı*, Ankara: Kültür ve Turizm Bakanlığı, 1985.

Pakalın, Mehmed Zeki, *Osmanlı Tarih Deyimleri ve Terimleri Sözlüğü*, 3 vols. Istanbul: Milli Eğitim Basımevi, 1946.

Pálffy, Géza, *Európa védelmében* [In the Defense of Europe] Pápa: Jókai Mór Városi Könyvtár, 2000, pp. 1–162, Supplement I–VIII and facsimile map III.

Pamuk, Şevket, "Institutional Change and the Longevity of the Ottoman Empire, 1500–1800," *Journal of Interdisciplinary History* 35 (2004): 225–47.

A Monetary History of the Ottoman Empire, Cambridge: Cambridge University Press, 2000.

Panaite, Viorel, "The *Re'ayas* of the Tributary-Protected Principalities: The Sixteenth through the Eighteenth Centuries," *International Journal of Turkish Studies* 9 (2003): 79–104.

The Ottoman Law of War and Peace: The Ottoman Empire and Tribute Payers, Boulder, CO: East European Monographs, New York: Columbia University Press, 2000.

Panzac, Daniel, "L'Adriatique incertaine: capitaines autrichiens, corsaires barbaresques et sultans ottomans vers 1800," *Turcica* 29 (1997): 71–91.

La caravane maritime: marins européens et marchands ottomans en Meditérranée (1680–1830), Paris: CNRS Éditions, 2004.

Panzini, Franco, *Per il piacere del popolo: l'evoluzione del giardino pubblico in Europa*, Bologna: Zanichelli, 1993.

Parker, Geoffrey, *The Grand Strategy of Philip II*, New Haven, CT: Yale University Press, 1998.

Parshall, Linda, "C.C.L. Hirschfeld's Concept of the Garden in the German Enlightenment," *Journal of Garden History* 13 (1993): 127–55.

Pedani, Maria Pia, *Dalla frontiera al confine*, Quaderni di Studi Arabi, Studi e testi, vol. V, Rome: Herder, 2002.

In nome del gran signore: inviati ottomani a Venezia dalla caduta di Costantinopoli alla guerra di Candia, Venice: Deputazione Editrice, 1994.

Peers, Douglas, "Sepoys, Soldiers and the Lash: Race, Caste and Army Discipline in India, 1820–50," *Journal of Imperial and Commonwealth History* 23 (1995): 211–47.

Peirce, Leslie, *The Imperial Harem: Women and Sovereignty in the Ottoman Empire*, New York: Oxford University Press, 1993.

Morality Tales: Law and Gender in the Ottoman Court of Aintab, Berkeley, CA: University of California Press, 2003, p. 223.

Pétis de la Croix, François, *Canon de Sultan Suleiman II l'empire représenté à Sultan Mourad IV pour son instruction. Ou état politique et militaire, tiré des archives les plus secretes des princes ottomans, & qui servent pour bien gouverner leur Empire*, Paris: n.p., 1725.

Petritsch, Ernst Dieter, "Der habsburgisch-osmanische Friedensvertrag des Jahres 1547," *Mitteilungen des Österreichischen Staatsarchivs* 38 (1985): 60–66.

Petrosian, A. (ed.), *Mebde-i Kanun-ı Yeniçeri Ocağı Tarihi*, Moscow: Nauka, 1987.

Piterberg, Gabriel, *An Ottoman Tragedy: History and Historiography at Play*, Berkeley, CA: University of California Press, 2003.

Poëte, Marcel, *Au jardin des Tuileries: l'art du jardin – la promenade publique*, Paris: A. Picard, 1924.

Posner, Ernst, *Archives in the Ancient World*, Cambridge, MA: Harvard University Press, 1972.

Power, Daniel, "Frontiers: Terms, Concepts and the Historians of Medieval and Early Modern Europe," in Daniel Power and Naomi Standen (eds.), *Frontiers in Question: Eurasian Borderlands 700–1700*, New York: St. Martin's Press, 1999, pp. 1–12.

Powers, David S., "A Court Case from Fourteenth Century North Africa," *Journal of the American Oriental Society* 110 (1990): 229–54.

Preto, Paolo, "La guerra segreta: spionaggio, sabotaggio, attendati," in *Venezia e la difesa de Levante da Lepanto a Candia 1570–1670*, Venice: Arsenale, 1986.

I servizi segreti di Venezia, Milan: Il Saggiatore, 1994.

Prokosch, Erich, *Osmanische Grabinschriften. Leitfaden zu ihrer sprachlichen Erfassung*, Berlin: Klaus Schwarz, 1993.

Pullan, Brian, *The Jews of Europe and the Inquisition of Venice, 1550–1670*, 2nd edn. New York: I. B. Tauris, 1997.

al-Qattan, Najwa, "Across the Courtyard: Residential Space and Sectarian Boundaries in Ottoman Damascus," in Molly Greene (ed.), *Minorities in the Ottoman Empire: A Reconsideration*, Princeton, NJ: Marcus Wiener, 2005, pp. 13–45.

"Dhimmis in the Muslim Court: Legal Autonomy and Religious Discrimination," *International Journal of Middle Eastern Studies* 31 (August 1999): 429–44.

"Discriminating Texts: Orthographic Marking and Social Differentiation in the Court Records of Ottoman Damascus," in Yasir Suleiman (ed.), *Arabic Sociolinguistics: Issues and Perspectives*, London: Curzon Press, 1994, pp. 57–77.

Quataert, Donald, "Clothing Laws, State, and Society in the Ottoman Empire, 1720–1829," *International Journal of Middle East Studies* 29 (1997): 403–25.

(ed.), *Consumption Studies and the History of the Ottoman Empire, 1550–1922*, Albany, NY: SUNY Press, 2000.

The Ottoman Empire, 1700–1922, Cambridge: Cambridge University Press, 2000.

Quinn, Sholeh A., "The Historiography of Safavid Prefaces," in Charles Melville (ed.), *Safavid Persia: The History and Politics of an Islamic Society*, London: I. B. Tauris, 1996, pp. 1–25.

Ranke, Leopold von, *Fürsten und Völker: Geschichten der romanischen und germanischen Völker von 1494–1514 – Die Osmanen und die spanische Monarchie im 16. und 17. Jahrhundert*, ed. Willy Andreas, Wiesbaden: Emil Vollmer Verlag, 1957.

Raymond, André, "The *Rab'*: A Type of Collective Housing in Cairo during the Ottoman Period," reprinted in *Arab Cities in the Ottoman Period: Cairo, Syria and the Maghreb*, Aldershot, Hampshire: Ashgate, 2002 (original pagination), pp. 265–76.

Redhouse, J. W., *An English and Turkish Lexicon*, Constantinople, 1890.

Refik, Ahmet, *Hicrî On Birinci Asırda İstanbul Hayatı 1000–1100*, Istanbul: Devlet Matbaası, 1931.

Hicrî On İkinci Asırda İstanbul Hayatı 1100–1200, Istanbul: Enderun Kitabevi, 1988.

Reindl, Hedda, "Zu einigen Miniaturen und Karten aus Handschriften Matraqči Nasuh's," *Islamkundliche Abhandlungen, Beiträge zur Kenntnis Südosteuropas und des Nahen Orients* 16 (1974): 146–71.

Renda, Günsel, "Chester Beatty Kitaplığındaki Zübdetü't-Tevarih ve Minyatürleri," in *Prof. Dr. Bekir Kütükoğlu'na Armağan*, Istanbul: Istanbul Üniversitesi Edebiyat Fakültesi Tarih Araştırma Merkezi, 1991, pp. 485–506.

"İstanbul Türk ve İslâm Eserleri Müzesi'ndeki Zübdet-üt Tevarih'in Minyatürleri," *Sanat* 6 (1977): 58–67.

"New Light on the Painters of the 'Zubdet al-Tawarikh' in the Museum of Turkish and Islamic Arts in Istanbul," in *IVème Congrès International d'Art Turc*, Aix-en-Provence, September 10–15, 1971, Aix-en-Provence: Éditions de l'Université de Provence, 1976, pp. 183–200.

"Topkapı Sarayı Müzesindeki H. 1321 No.lu Silsilename'nin Minyatürleri," *Sanat Tarihi Yıllığı* 5 (1972–3): 443–95.

Richards, John F., "The Formulation of Imperial Authority under Akbar and Jahangir," in J. F. Richards (ed.), *Kingship and Authority in South Asia*, Madison, WI: University of Wisconsin Press, 1978, pp. 260–7.

Richardson, M. E. J., *Hammurabi's Laws*, Sheffield: Sheffield Academic Press, 2000.

Richter, Gustav, *Studien zur Geschichte der älteren arabischen Fürstenspiegel*, Leipzig: J. C. Hinrichs, 1932.

Roche, Daniel, *La culture des apparences: une histoire du vêtement (XVIIe–XVIIIe siècle*, Paris: Fayard, 1989.

Rodríguez-Salgado, M. J., *The Changing Face of Empire: Charles V, Philip II and Habsburg Authority, 1551–9*, Cambridge: Cambridge University Press, 1988.

Rogers, J. M., "Itineraries and Town Views in Ottoman Histories," in J. B. Harley and David Woodward (eds.), *The History of Cartography*, Chicago: University of Chicago Press, 1987–92, vol. II, book 1, pp. 228–55.

Röhrborn, Klaus, *Untersuchungen zur osmanischen Verwaltungsgeschichte*, Berlin: De Gruyter, 1974.

Rosen, Lawrence, *The Anthropology of Justice: Law as Culture in Islamic Society*. Cambridge: Cambridge University Press, 1989.

"Islamic Case Law and the Logic of Consequence," in June Starr and Jane Fisburne Collier (eds.), *History and Power in the Study of Law: New Directions in Legal Anthropology*, Ithaca, NY: Cornell University Press, 1989, pp. 302–19.

Rubiés, Joan-Pau, *Travel and Ethnology in the Renaissance: South India through European Eyes 1250–1625*, Cambridge: Cambridge University Press, 2000.

Sabev, Orlin, Събев, Орлин. Първото османско пътешествие в света на печатната книга (1726–1746). Нов поглед [First Ottoman Trip in the World of Printed Books (1726–1746). A Reassessment] София: Авангард Прима, 2004.

Sahillioğlu, Halil, "Dördüncü Muradın Bağdat Seferi Menzilnamesi," *Belgeler* 2/ 3–4 (1965): 1–36.

(ed.), *Topkapı Sarayı H.951–952 Tarihli ve E-12321 Numaralı Mühimme Defteri*, Istanbul: Islâm Tarih, Sanat ve Kültür Araştırma Merkezi, 2002.

Said, Edward W., "Arabs, Islam and the Dogmas of the West," *New York Times Book Review*, October 31, 1976.

Covering Islam: How the Media and the Experts Determine How We See the Rest of the World, New York: Vintage, 1981.

Orientalism, New York: Pantheon, 1978.

Sakaoğlu, Necdet, "Bostancı Ocağı," in *İslam Ansiklopedisi*, vol. II, pp. 305–7.

Salzmann, Ariel, "The Age of Tulips: Confluence and Conflict in Early Modern Consumer Culture (1550–1730)," in H. İnalcık and D. Quataert, (ed.), *Consumption Studies and the History of the Ottoman Empire, 1550–1922*, Albany, NY: SUNY Press, 2000, pp. 83–106.

"An Ancien Régime Revisited: 'Privatization' and Political Economy in the Eighteenth-Century Ottoman Empire," *Politics and Society* 21 (1993): 393–424.

Tocqueville in the Ottoman Empire: Rival Paths to the Modern State, Leiden: Brill, 2004.

Sarat, Austin, and Thomas R. Kearns (eds.), *Law in the Domains of Culture*, Ann Arbor, MI: The University of Michigan Press, 1998.

Sayılı, Aydın, *The Observatory in Islam and its Place in the General History of the Observatory*, Ankara: Türk Tarih Kurumu, 1960.

Scarce, Jennifer, "The Development of Women's Fashion in Ottoman Turkish Costume during the 18th and 19th Centuries," in *IVe Congrès International d'Art Turc*, Aix-en-Provence, 10–15 September 1971, Aix-en-Provence: Éditions de L'Université de Provence, 1976, pp. 199–219.

Schaendlinger, Anton C. and Claudia Römer, *Die Schreiben Süleymans des Prächtigen an Karl V., Ferdinand I. und Maximilian II. Transkriptionen und Übersetzungen*, Vienna: Verlag der Österreichischen Akademie der Wissenschaften, 1983.

Schmidt, Jan, *Mustafa Ali's Künhü'l-Ahbar and its Preface According to the Leiden Manuscript*, Leiden: Nederlands Instituut voor het Nabije Oosten, 1987.

Pure Water for Thirsty Muslims: A Study of Mustafâ 'Âli of Gallipoli's Künhü l'ahbâr, Leiden: Het Oosters Instituut, 1991.

Scholte, Jan Aart, "What is Globalization? The Definitional Issue – Again," Hamilton, Ontario: Institute on Globalization and the Human Condition Working Paper Series, 2003.

Scott, James C., *Seeing Like a State*, New Haven, CT: Yale University Press, 1998.

Segal, Daniel A., "'Western Civ' and the Staging of History in American Higher Education," *American Historical Review* 105 (2000): 770–805.

Seipel, Wilfried (ed.), *Der Kreiszug Kaiser Karls V. gegen Tunis Kartons und Tapisserien*, Vienna: Kunsthistorisches Museum, 2000.

Seng, Yvonne, "Fugitives and Factotums: Slaves in Early Sixteenth-Century Istanbul," *Journal of the Economic and Social History of the Orient* 39/2 (1996): 136–69.

"Invisible Women: Residents of Early Sixteenth-Century Istanbul," in Gavin R. G. Hambly (ed.), *Women in the Medieval Islamic World*, New York: St. Martin's Press, 1998, pp. 241–65.

"Standing at the Gates of Justice: Women in the Law Courts of Early Sixteenth-Century Üsküdar, Istanbul," in S. Hirsch and M. Lazarus-Black (eds.), *Contested States: Law, Hegemony and Resistance*, New York: Routledge, 1994, pp. 184–206.

Setton, Kenneth M., "Lutheranism and the Turkish Peril," *Balkan Studies* 3 (1962): 133–68.

The Papacy and the Levant (1204–1571), vol. III, Philadelphia: American Philosophical Society, 1984.

Venice, Austria and the Turks in the Seventeenth Century, Philadelphia: American Philosophical Society, 1991.

Shaw, Stanford J., *Between Old and New: The Ottoman Empire under Sultan Selim III 1789–1807*. Cambridge, MA: Harvard University Press, 1971.

Shaw, Stanford and Ezel Shaw, *History of the Ottoman Empire and Modern Turkey*, 2 vols., Cambridge: Cambridge University Press, 2000 and 1997, reprints of 1976 and 1977 editions.

Sicker, Martin, *The Islamic World in Ascendancy: From the Arab Conquests to the Siege of Vienna*, New York: Greenwood, 2000.

The Islamic World in Decline: From the Treaty of Karlowitz to the Disintegration of the Ottoman Empire, New York: Greenwood, 2000.

The Pre-Islamic Middle East, New York: Greenwood, 2000.

Solkin, David, *Painting for Money: The Visual Arts and the Public Sphere in Eighteenth-Century England*, New Haven, CT: Yale University Press, 1993.

Soucek, Svat, "Islamic Charting in the Mediterranean," in J. B. Harley and David Woodward, *The History of Cartography*, Chicago: University of Chicago Press, 1987–92, vol. II, book 1, pp. 265–79.

Piri Reis and Turkish Mapmaking after Columbus, 2 vols., London: Nour Foundation and Oxford University Press, 1996.

"The Rise of the Barbarossas in North Africa," *Archivum Ottomanicum* 3 (1972): 228–50.

Standen, Naomi, "Nine Case Studies of Premodern Frontiers," in Daniel Power and Naomi Standen (eds.), *Frontiers in Question: Eurasian Borderlands 700–1700*, New York: St. Martin's Press, 1999, pp. 13–31.

Stoye, John, *Marsigli's Europe 1680–1730: The Life and Times of Luigi Ferdinando Marsigli, Soldier and Virtuoso*, New Haven, CT: Yale University Press, 1994.

Strauss, Johann, *Die Chronik des 'Isazade: Ein Beitrag zur osmanischen Historiographie des 17. Jahrhunderts*, Berlin: Klaus Schwarz, 1991.

Strauss, Walter, *The German Single-Leaf Woodcut 1550–1600*, vol. I: *A–J*, New York: Abaris Books, 1975.

Subrahmanyan, Sanjay, "'A Tale of Three Empires,' Mughals, Ottomans, and Habsburgs in a Comparative Context," *Common Knowledge* 12 (2006): 66–92.

Szakály, Ferenc, *Lodovico Gritti in Hungary 1529–1534: A Historical Insight into the Beginnings of Turco-Habsburgian Rivalry*, Budapest: Akademiai Kiadó, 1995.

"Nándorfehérvár, 1521: The Beginning of the End of the Medieval Hungarian Kingdom," in Géza Dávid and Pál Fodor (eds.), *Hungarian-Ottoman Military and Diplomatic Relations in the Age of Süleyman the Magnificent*,

Budapest: Loránd Eötvös University/Hungarian Academy of Sciences, 1994, pp. 47–76.

Taeschner, Franz, "Ottoman Geographers," in "Djughrāfiyā," EI2, vol. II, pp. 587–90.

"A kalauzok és a kémek a török világban," in S. Takáts, *Rajzok a török világból*, 4 vols., Budapest: A Magyar Tudományos Akadémia Kiadasa, 1915–32, vol. II, pp. 133–212.

Takáts, Sándor, "A magyar és török íródeákok," in S. Takáts, *Művelődéstörténeti tanulmányok a 16–17. századból*, ed. Kálmán Benda, Budapest: Gondolat Kiadó, 1961, pp. 146–94.

Tansel, Selahattin, *Yavuz Sultan Selim*, Ankara: Milli Eğitim Basımevi, 1969.

Tekindağ, M. C. Şehabeddin, "Selimnameler," *İstanbul Üniversitesi Edebiyat Fakültesi Tarih Enstitüsü Dergisi* 1 (1970): 197–230.

Ter Haar, Johan, "The Naqshbandi Traditions in the Eyes of Ahmad Sirhindi," in Marc Gaborieau, Alexandre Popovic, and Thiery Zarcone (eds.), *Naqshbandis, Historical Developments and Present Situation of a Muslim Mystical Order*, Istanbul: Isis, 1990, pp. 83–93.

Terzioğlu, Derin, "Sufi and Dissident in the Ottoman Empire: Niyāzī-i Mısrī (1618–94)," PhD dissertation, Harvard University, 1998.

Tezcan, Baki, "Dispelling the Darkness: The Politics of 'Race' in the Early Seventeenth Century Ottoman Empire in the Light of the Life and Work of Mullah Ali," in Karl Barbir and Baki Tezcan (eds.), *Identity and Identity Formation in the Ottoman Middle East and the Balkans: A Volume of Essays in Honor of Norman Itzkowitz*, forthcoming from the University of Wisconsin Madison Center of Turkish Studies in 2007.

"The 1622 Military Rebellion in Istanbul: A Historiographical Journey," *International Journal of Turkish Studies* 8 (2002): 25–43.

"Searching for Osman: A Reassessment of the Deposition of the Ottoman Sultan Osman II (1618–1622)," PhD dissertation, Princeton University, 2001.

Theolin, Sture (ed.), *Torch of the Empire*, Istanbul: Yapı Kredi Kültür Sanat Yayınları, 2002.

Thomas, Lewis V., *A Study of Naima*, ed. Norman Itzkowitz, New York: New York University Press, 1972.

Thompson, E. P., *Whigs and Hunters: The Origin of the Black Act*, New York: Pantheon Books, 1975.

Tietze, Andreas, "Mustafa 'Ali of Gallipoli's Prose Style," *Archivum Ottomanicum* 5 (1973): 297–319.

"Mustafa Ali on Luxury and the Status Symbols of Ottoman Gentlemen," in *Studia Turcologica Memoriae Alexii Bombaci Dicata*, Naples: n.p., 1982, pp. 580–1.

The Turkish Shadow Theater and the Puppet Collection of the L.A. Mayer Memorial Foundation, Berlin: Mann, 1977.

Todorov, Tzvetan, *The Fantastic: A Structural Approach to a Literary Genre*, trans. Richard Howard, Ithaca, NY: Cornell University Press, 1975.

Tooley, R. V., *Maps and Map-Makers*, New York: Crown Publishers, 1982, reprint of 1970.

Török, Pál, *I. Ferdinand konstantinápolyi beketárgyalásai* [Ferdinand I's Peace Negotiations in Constantinople], Budapest: Magyar tudomanyós akadémia, 1930.

Tott, François de, *Mémoires du Baron de Tott sur les Turcs et les Tartares*, 2 vols., Amsterdam: n.p., 1785.

Tracy, James D., *Emperor Charles V, Impresario of War: Campaign Strategy, International Finance, and Domestic Politics*, Cambridge: Cambridge University Press, 2002.

Tucker, Judith, *In the House of the Law: Gender and Islamic Law in Ottoman Syria and Palestine*, Berkeley, CA: University of California Press, 1998.

Tunçel, Gül, *Batı Anadolu Bölgesi Cami Tasvirli Mezartaşları*, Ankara: Kültür Bakanlığı, 1989.

Uğur, Ahmet, *The Reign of Sultan Selim in the Light of the Selimname Literature*, Berlin: Schwarz, 1985.

Ullmann, Walter, *Law and Politics in the Middle Ages: An Introduction to the Sources of Medieval Political Ideas*, Ithaca, NY: Cornell University Press, 1975.

Uluçay, M. Çağatay, "Koçi Bey' in Sultan İbrahim'e Takdim Ettiği Risale ve Arzları," in *Zeki Velidi Togan Armağanı*, Istanbul: n.p., 1950–5, pp. 177–99.

Umur, Suha, "Osmanlı Belgeleri Arasında: Kadınlara Buyruklar," *Tarih ve Toplum* 10/58 (1988): 205–7.

Unat, Faik Reşit, *Osmanlı Sefirleri ve Sefaretnameleri*, Ankara: Türk Tarih Kurumu Basımevi, 1987.

Uzunçarşılı, İ. Hakkı, "Bostancı," in *İslam Ansiklopedisi*, vol. II, pp. 736–8.

"Bostancıbaşı," in *İslam Ansiklopedisi*, vol. II, pp. 338–9.

"Bostandji," in EI2, vol. I, pp. 1277–8.

"Bostandji-Bashi," in EI2, vol. I, p. 1279.

Osmanlı Devleti Teşkilatından Kapukulu Ocakları, 2 vols. Ankara: Türk Tarih Kurumu, 1944.

Valensi, Lucette, *The Birth of the Despot: Venice and the Sublime Porte*, trans. Arthur Denner, Ithaca, NY: Cornell University Press, 1993.

Vatin, Nicolas, "Les cimetières musulmans des Ottomans: une source d'histoire sociale," in D. Panzac (ed.), *Les villes dans l'Empire ottoman: activités et sociétés*, Paris: CNRS, 1991, pp. 149–63.

"L'inhumation *intra-muros* à Istanbul à l'époque ottomane," in G. Veinstein (ed.), *Les Ottomans et la mort. Permanences et mutations*, Leiden: Brill, 1996, pp. 157–64.

"Itinéraires d'agents de la Porte en Italie (1483–1495): Réflexions sur l'organisation des missions ottomanes et sur la transcription turque des noms de lieux italiens," *Turcica* 19 (1987): 29–50.

"La notation du nom propre sur les stèles funéraires ottomanes," in A.-M. Christin (ed.), *L'écriture du nom propre*, Paris: Harmattan, 1998, pp. 135–48.

"Notes sur l'exploitation du marbre et l'île de Marmara Adası (Proconnèse) à l'époque ottomane," *Turcica* 32 (2000): 307–62.

Sultan Jem. Un prince ottoman dans l'Europe du XVe siècle d'après deux sources contemporaines: Vaki'at-i Sultan Cem, Oeuvres de Guillaume Caoursin, Ankara: Türk Tarih Kurumu, 1997.

"Sur le rôle de la stèle funéraire et l'aménagement des cimetières musulmans d'Istanbul," in A. Temimi (ed.), *Mélanges Professeur Robert Mantran,* Zaghouan: Centre d'études et de recherches ottomanes, 1988, pp. 293–7.

Vatin, Nicolas, and Stéphane Yérasimos, *Les cimetières dans la ville. Statut, choix et organisation des lieux d'inhumation dans Istanbul intra-muros,* Istanbul: Institut français d'études anatoliennes Georges Dumézil; Paris: Diffusion, Librairie d'Amérique et d'Orient Adrien Maisonneuve, Jean Maisonneuve Successeur, 2001, pp. 9–19.

Veblen, Thorstein, *The Theory of the Leisure Class, 1899,* New York: Modern Library, 2001 [1899].

Veinstein, Gilles, "L'occupation ottomane d'Očakov et le problème de la frontière lituano-tartare 1538–1544," in *Passé turco-tatar, présent soviétique: études offertes à Alexandre Bennigsen,* Louvain: Éditions Peeters, 1986, pp. 123–55.

Voll, John, "Muhammad Hayya al-Sindi and Muhammad ibn abd al-Wahhab: An Analysis of an Intellectual Group in Eighteenth Century Medina," *Bulletin of the School of Oriental and African Studies* 38/1 (1975): 32–9.

Watenpaugh, Heghnar Zeitlian, *The Image of an Ottoman City: Imperial Architecture and Urban Experience in Aleppo in the 16th and 17th Centuries,* Leiden: Brill, 2004.

Weber, Wolfgang, "What a Good Ruler Should Not Do: Theoretical Limits of Royal Power in European Theories of Absolutism, 1500–1700," *Sixteenth Century Journal* 26 (1995): 897–915.

Weismann, Itzchak, *Taste of Modernity, Sufism, Salafiyya, and Arabism in Late Ottoman Damascus,* Leiden: Brill, 2001.

White, Hayden, *Metahistory: The Historical Imagination in Nineteenth-Century Europe,* Baltimore, MD: Johns Hopkins University Press, 1973.

Williams, Raymond, *Marxism and Literature, "Structures of Feeling",* Oxford: Oxford University Press, 1977.

Writing and Society, London: Verso, 1983, pp. 67–118.

Williamson, Tom, *Polite Landscapes: Gardens and Society in Eighteenth-Century England,* Baltimore, MD: Johns Hopkins University Press, 1995.

Wilson, Bronwen, *The World in Venice: Print, the City, and Early Modern Identity,* Toronto: University of Toronto Press, 2005.

Wilson, John A., "Egypt: The Nature of the Universe," in Henri Frankfort et al. (eds.), *The Intellectual Adventure of Ancient Man: An Essay on Speculative Thought in the Ancient Near East,* Chicago: University of Chicago Press, 1946, pp. 55–61.

Winichakul, Thongchai, *Siam Mapped: A History of the Geo-Body of a Nation,* Honolulu: University of Hawaii Press, 1994.

Wolper, Ethel Sara, "Understanding the Public Face of Piety: Philanthropy and Architecture in late Seljuk Anatolia," *Mesogeios* 25–6 (2005): 311–36.

Woodhead, Christine, "An Experiment in Official Historiography: The Post of Şehnāmeci in the Ottoman Empire, c. 1555–1605," *Wiener Zeitschrift für die Kunde des Morgenlandes* 75 (1983): 157–82.

"Ottoman Inşa and the Art of Letter-Writing: Influences upon the Career of the Nişancı and Prose Stylist Okçuzade (d. 1630)," *Journal of Ottoman Studies* 7–8 (1988): 143–59.

Woods, J. E., "Turco-Iranica I: An Ottoman Intelligence Report on late Fifteenth/ Ninth Century Iranian Foreign Relations," *Journal of Near Eastern Studies* 38 (1979): 1–9.

Woodward, David, *The Maps and Prints of Paolo Forlani: A Descriptive Bibliography*, Chicago: Newberry Library, 1990.

Wright, Diana Gilliland and John Melville-Jones, "Bartolomeo Minio: Dispacci 1479–1483 from Nauplion," dispatches of February 10, 1479 and August 14, 1480, pp. 4–14, "Stato da Mar," http://nauplion.net/statomar.html; forthcoming as, *The Greek Correspondence of Bartolomeo Minio*, vol. I: *Dispacci from Nauplion*.

Wright, Walter L. (ed.), *Ottoman Statecraft; The Book of Counsel for Viziers and Governors*, Princeton, NJ: Princeton University Press, 1935.

Wulzinger, Karl, Paul Wittek and Friedrich Sarre, *Das islamische Milet*, Berlin: De Gruyter, 1935.

Yapp, M. E., "The Establishment of the East India Company Residency in Baghdad, 1798–1806," *Bulletin of the School of Oriental and African Studies* 30 (1967): 323–36.

Yenişehirlioğlu, Filiz, "Architectural Patronage of *Ayan* Families in Anatolia," in A. Anastasopoulos (ed.), *Provincial Elites in the Ottoman Empire*, Rethymno: Crete University Press, 2005, pp. 321–39.

Yerasimos, Stéphane, *Les voyageurs dans l'Empire ottoman (XIVe–XVIe siècles): bibliographie, itinéraires et inventaire des lieux habités*, Ankara: Imprimerie de la Société Turque d'Histoire, 1991.

Yurdusev, A. Nuri (ed.), *Ottoman Diplomacy: Conventional or Unconventional*, Basingstoke: Macmillan, 2004.

Zachariadou, Elizabeth, "Monks and Sailors under the Ottoman Sultans," in Kate Fleet (ed.), *The Ottomans and the Sea*, special issue of *Oriente Moderno* n.s. anno 20/1 (2001): 139–47.

Ze'evi, Dror, "*Kul* and Getting Cooler: The Dissolution of Elite Collective Identity and the Formation of Official Nationalism in the Ottoman Empire," *Mediterranean Historical Review* 11 (1996): 177–95.

Zilfi, Madeline C., "Goods in the *Mahalle*: Distributional Encounters in Eighteenth-Century Istanbul," in Donald Quataert (ed.), *Consumption Studies and the History of the Ottoman Empire, 1550–1922*, Albany, NY: SUNY Press, 2000, pp. 289–311.

"The Kadızadelis: Discordant Revivalism in Seventeenth-Century Istanbul," *Journal of Near Eastern Studies* 45/4 (1986): 257.

The Politics of Piety: The Ottoman Ulema in the Postclassical Age (1600–1800), Minneapolis: Biblioteca Islamica, 1988.

"Women and Society in the Tulip Era," in A. Sonbol (ed.), *Women, the Family and Divorce Laws in Islamic History*, Syracuse, NY: Syracuse University Press, 1996, pp. 294–303.

Ziyada, Khalid, *al-Sura al-taqlidiyya li'l-mujtama`al-madini: Qira'a manhajiyya fi sijillat mahkamat Trablus al-shar`iyya fi al-qarn al-sabi`-`ashar wa bidayat al-qarn al-thamin-`ashar*, Tripoli, Lebanon: Lebanese University, 1983.

Zürcher, Erik J., "The Ottoman Conscription System in Theory and Practice, 1844–1918," in E. J. Zürcher (ed.), *Arming the State: Military Conscription in the Middle East and Central Asia, 1775–1918*, London: I. B. Tauris, 1999, pp. 80–9.

Index

353